GEO-BUSINESS: GIS IN THE DIGITAL ORGANIZATION

This book is dedicated with thanks to my wife Dr. Rosalyn Laudati and to the memory of my father-in-law Hector Laudati.

GEO-BUSINESS GIS IN THE DIGITAL ORGANIZATION

JAMES B. PICK
University of Redlands
Redlands, California

BICENTENNIAL
1807
WILEY
2007
BICENTENNIAL

JOHN WILEY & SONS, INC.

This book is printed on acid-free paper. ⊚

Copyright © 2008 by John Wiley & Sons, Inc. All rights reserved

Published by John Wiley & Sons, Inc., Hoboken, New Jersey
Published simultaneously in Canada

For general information about our other products and services please contact our Customer Care Department within the United States at (800) 762-2974, outside the United States at (317) 572-3993 or fax (317) 572-4002.

Wiley also publishes its books in a variety of electronic formats. Some content that appears in print may not be available in electronic books. For more information about Wiley products, visit our web site at www.wiley.com.

Library of Congress Cataloging-in-Publication Data:

Pick, James B.
   Geo-business GIS in the digital organization / James B. Pick.
     p. cm.
   "Published simultaneously in Canada."
   Includes index.
   ISBN 978-0-471-72998-3 (cloth)
   1. Management–Geographic information systems.   2. Business–Geographic information systems.   I. Title.   II. Title: Geo-business geographic information systems in the digital organization.
   HD30.213.P53 2007
   658′.05–dc22

                              2007013692

Printed in the United States of America

10 9 8 7 6 5 4 3 2 1

CONTENTS

12. GIS AND BUSINESS STRATEGY   **355**

PREFACE

Geographic Information Systems (GIS) support business decision-making by including a spatial component in the decision process. With GIS, businesses plan and make judgments based on more than the attributes of business entities, but on their spatial properties as well. Although GIS gained its early adoption mostly in government, today it is expanding rapidly in business. New corporate uses and applications are being discovered and developed.

The overall goal of the book is to provide a comprehensive coverage of GIS applied to and utilized by businesses and organizations. Unlike textbooks with a mainly geographical perspective, this book sets GIS in the context of the concepts and practices of information systems and other business sub-disciplines such as marketing, logistics, business ethics, management, and strategy. The real world is brought in through case studies, examples, explanations of technologies, and up-to-date references. For more advanced readers, the book adds to and updates their detailed knowledge of the latest trends and developments.

The book's mission is to thoroughly educate the reader on the principles and capabilities of GIS and to make managers and their businesses smarter, more efficient, productive, decisive, and ethically aware.

This book is written to fill in a gap in the knowledge of GIS and spatial technologies. Although business uses and applications have been included in books, they have not centered on well-organized frameworks of business, and information systems (IS).

When GIS is practically applied in the real world, it has a strong management component. Technical knowledge or geographic experience alone will not lead to successful GIS implementations. Failures have occurred most often because people and organizations did not communicate, leadership did not support or take interest in a spatial project, customers were not consulted, or the project was not scoped well and benefits assessed. These are not technical or geographic but management issues.

Likewise, GIS depends on information systems. The IS that underpins a GIS must meet the normal IS success criteria of user-responsiveness, usability, fit to the task, reliability, and maintainability, A GIS implementation needs to be conceptualized, designed, and built according to the best principles and practices from IS. Data need to be organized and well managed, which largely derives from IS. Controls for a GIS closely resemble those of information systems. As GIS expands to enterprise systems, the web, and mobile devices, much depends on the information technology.

Another perspective on the dependence on IS is reflected in the location of GIS units in organizational structures. For mid- and large-sized companies, the GIS unit is commonly in a separate small unit closely aligned and interacting with an older and larger IS unit. Sometimes GIS is brought right into the GIS unit. Either way, they are closely linked.

One of the challenges in the geobusiness area of study is paucity of academic research. For instance, in the decision-making literature, there were only a handful of research journal articles over the past decade on GIS decision-making (Huerta et al., 2005). Because the academic literature on GIS in business is scattered in a variety of types of journals, it takes some detective work to find it. One reason there is little literature relates to the proprietary nature of many spatial systems in business. If a major company is gaining competitive advantage from GIS, it might wish not to make it known and not open up that information to academic investigators.

Hence, the project needed to delve more into the recent professional and trade literature. Here, astute business observers and experts provided rich practical information about what is happening in geobusiness. Another source of such information were several annual conferences especially the Geospatial Information and Technology Association (GITA) Conference, the Location Intelligence Conference, the ESRI Business GeoSummit, and the Annual ESRI International User Conference.

The book has a total of 26 case studies. This includes twenty research case studies that were analyzed using rigorous case study methodology. Sometimes the term "research case" is used, which refers to a case in this group of 20. In addition, six cases were drawn from secondary references, which are included because they particularly reinforce points in the book. The cases and their chapter coverage are given in the table below.

For each research case, the corporate manager of GIS was interviewed for an average of two hours, following a protocol of questions. The interview protocol can be obtained from the author. Permission to record was largely granted and the interviews were transcribed. Other supporting documents were requested from the interviewees. The results were analyzed using standard case study methods (Yin, 1994). The findings are included in the book in several ways. Fourteen of the twenty research cases have narrative

Case Study Firms in GeoBusiness

Name or description	Chapter	Size of Firm
Research Case Studies (based on primary case study interviews)		
Global Integrated Oil (GIO)	1	large
Sperry Van Ness	1	medium
Bay State Health	2	medium
Large Corporate/Personal Bank (LCPB)	3	large
Large Insurance Co.(LIC)	3	large
Chico's	4	medium
Motion-Based Technologies	5	small
Engineering Systems	6	small
Sears Roebuck	7	large
Southern Company	9	large
Kaiser Permanente	10	large
Large Credit Bank (LCB)	10	large
Norwich Union	7, 12	large
Rand McNally	12	large
Arizona Republic	12 - summary	medium
Lamar Advertising Co.	12 - summary	medium
MapGistics	12 - summary	small
Prudential Preferred Realty	12 - summary	medium
URS Inc.	12 - summary	large
Western Exterminator	12 - summary	medium
Additional Textbook Case Studies (based on secondary sources)		
Pidpa	4	medium
Nesa	4	medium
DS Waters	5	small
Seaspan International Ltd	5	medium
Enmax	8	medium
Kyllo v United States	11	NA

NA = not applicable

case-study sections in the book. In Chapter 12, short profiles appear of all twenty research case firms, including the six that do not have separate chapter sections. All twenty or subsets of them are included in analyses and comparisons throughout the book.

For each research case, the firm was given the choice to remain anonymous, and four elected to do so. The firms allowing their names to be included are listed in the table, along with the four firms that elected anonymity, which were given the pseudo names of Large Credit Bank, Global Integrated Oil, Large Insurance Company, and Large Personal/Corporate Bank. In the table, their initials appear, which are sometimes used to refer to them. The information and knowledge flowing from the interviews was impressive and enriches the research cases throughout the book.

In addition to the primary research case studies, six other case studies are included in the book derived from secondary sources because they particularly illustrate chapter themes. They are Pidpa and Nesa, Belgian and Danish utility firms; DS Waters in Atlanta; and the Canadian firms Seaspan International Ltd and Enmax. Four of them are non-U.S. which gives more international flavor to the book overall, and reflects that spatial technologies are in use worldwide. Also a legal case study is included in Chapter 11 of Kyllo v. United States.

GIS and spatial technologies are currently moving towards the web. This reflects a broader trend of information systems generally towards the internet platform. Spatial capability is becoming prevalent in mobile devices, starting with GPS-enabled cell phones required in many countries. The data bank of spatial information is growing exponentially through collection by multiple types of sensors, satellites, RFID readers, and GPS-enabled devices. Data storage technologies and designs have advanced into spatial object-oriented and spatial database paradigms. Large-scale consumer web mapping appeared with Google Maps in 2005. The appearance of widespread RFID in supply chains in the U.S. was marked by Wal-Mart's mandate to its largest suppliers to make the shift in 2005. The book is fortunate to appear while these rapid changes are underway and can document and explain them.

In covering GIS for business, study of management and technology needs to be balanced with learning about the ethical, legal, and security dimensions. For instance, there are ethical and privacy issues related to the dissemination and use of sensor-based information. Chapter 11 examines what these issues are and how some of them are being resolved while other await future resolution. The treatment is not prescriptive, but rather informative—to expand awareness for the reader's benefit in viewing these issues and possibly having to formulate stances and make personal choices related to them.

The book is intended for several audiences. Managers in industry and organizations untutored in GIS and spatial technologies can benefit by understanding the business fundamentals of these phenomena and the potential to implement them in their companies. For skilled GIS managers, the book fills in gaps, provides some new ideas, and allows them to benchmark and compare with other companies. They can learn from seeing the successes and mistakes of others. The book stresses how well-established business and IS concepts can be applied to spatial problem-solving, and at the same time what is different and special about spatial systems. The book does not devote much space to geographical principles, which are well covered in many other textbooks. A business manager needs to be knowledgeable but not necessarily an expert in geography and GIS to be successful with spatial applications and projects, but he or she does need to be expert in management principles and practice in order to succeed. He/she can gain access to GIS technical expertise in-house or through external sourcing.

Another audience is academic. In teaching, the book is suitable for upper division and graduate courses in business, public administration, planning, environmental management, applied geography, and related disciplines. The book can contribute to improving the preparation of people entering a growing geospatial workforce (Marble, 2006).

The book is also intended for academic researchers in business, management, IS, planning, public administration, and applied geography disciplines who need an integrated and broader context in which to set their research. The book refers to many academic studies across a variety of subfields. The case study analysis in the book can be helpful to some on particular research.

It is the intent and hope that *GeoBusiness* will provide currency of ideas, new insights, practical benefits, and motivation to people already working in, or with interest in GIS and spatial applications in business.

REFERENCES

Huerta, Esperanza, Celene Navarrete, and Terry Ryan. 2005. "GIS and Decision-Making in Business: A Literature Review." In Pick, James B. (Ed.), *Geographic Systems in Business*, Hershey, PA: Idea Group Publishing, 20–35.

Marble, Duane F. 2006. "Who Are We: Defining the Geospatial Workforce." *Geospatial Solutions*, May, 14–21.

Yin, R.K. 1994. *Case Study Research: Design and Methods*, Second Edition. Thousand Oaks, CA: SAGE Publications.

ACKNOWLEDGMENTS

This project would not have been possible without the support, cooperation, and collaboration of many individuals.

Thanks to several people who provided early ideas at the inception and support: Julian Ray, formerly assistant professor at University of Redlands; John Stager, doctoral student at Claremont Graduate University; and Paul Gray, professor emeritus at Claremont Graduate University. Thanks also to Joe Francica, Peter Keenan, Xavier Lopez, and Bruce Ralston, who reviewed the proposed book content.

Thanks to chapter reviewers Rob Burke, Peter Keenan, Ray Papp, Monica Perry, Dave Petrie, Keith Roberts, Namchul Shin, Jeffery Smith, John Stager, Larry West, Vijay Sugumaran, and Nanda Viswanathan for their insightful critical comments, suggestions, and advice. Any errors that remain are the sole responsibility of the author.

Appreciation is expressed to Hindupur Ramakrisna for discussions on spatial decision support systems. The students in the fall 2006 MBA Connections-B course on GIS and faculty colleague Kimberly Cass were helpful in pre-testing several chapters of the draft manuscript. Their ideas and feedback on the material were helpful and most appreciated. Appreciation is expressed to the libraries of University of Redlands and University of California Irvine for the high quality and extent of their resources.

The School of Business at University of Redlands has been supportive in a number of ways. School research funding was helpful and is acknowledged for the final stages of the project. Faculty feedback is appreciated from several presentations related to the book in the school's research series. Thanks to the school's faculty support office of Joanie James, Shari Audelo, Susan Griffin, and Erin Ross, as well as undergraduate student assistants, who were consistently helpful. Special thanks to MBA student Matt Wick for his outstanding assistance, support, and ideas on organizing digital materials, obtaining permissions, and discussing book issues and to undergraduate student Matt Rogers for strong and energetic support at the end of the project.

Thanks to the GIS managers and leaders at twenty case study companies. Appreciation is expressed to Jill Boulton, Danny Childs, Amy Claar-Pressley, Joe DeVoy, Kurt Gunther, Steve Jones, Mike Lawton, Chris McKeever, Joel Minster, Jason Murray, Swapan Nag, Ken Pitts, Sheryl Poss, Tom Sanchez, Steve Schonhaut, Ric Skinner, Jay Visnansky, Clark Weber, as well as to individuals in the four companies that elected to remain anonymous. Special thanks to Swapan Nag, for some in-depth discussions subsequent to the interview and to Joe DeVoy who after the interview provided more ideas and made his office open to a field visit.

At ESRI Inc. thanks to Jack Dangermond for general support and ideas and to Steve Benner, Ann Bossard, Bill Davenaill, Roxanne Cox-Drake, Sean Fitzpatrick, Randy Frantz, Russ Johnson, Jim Herries, Lisa Horn, Bill Meehan, Alex Miller, Lew Nelson, Mike Phoenix, Simon Thompson, and Geoff Wade for their ideas and support.

The author had a sabbatical leave at University of California Irvine in summer and fall of 2005, which provided a quiet office and opportunities to discuss and present book ideas, moving the project forward significantly. Appreciation is given to Frank Bean in School of Social Sciences for arranging the sabbatical at UCI and encouragement and to Tony Soeller in Network and Academic Computing Services for helping to formulate some book ideas.

Thanks to Jim Harper of John Wiley and Sons for his insights on GIS and for editorial advice.

The author wishes to acknowledge all these people and many others not mentioned who provided assistance and backing.

Finally the author expresses special thanks to his wife, Dr. Rosalyn Laudati, for her great understanding, patience, and support during the many long hours of the project.

CHAPTER 1

GIS IN THE DIGITAL ECONOMY

BUSINESS IN THE DIGITAL ECONOMY

Spatial technologies and GIS are impacting the productivity of business and economies. As information technologies have become more pervasive, inter-active, mobile, internet-based, and diffused throughout the enterprise, likewise spatial technologies have done so. Information technologies became prevalent for mainframes in the late 1950s and early 1960s, while GIS only appeared commercially in the late 1960s and became widespread in government in the late 1970s. This lag means that information technologies became well established in organizations about fifteen years earlier than GIS. In the busi-ness world, the lag is greater because GIS was first adopted by governments, remained largely a public-sector feature for two decades, and only became widespread in businesses in the 1990s.

The reasons that GIS has not caught on until recently in the business sector include its high cost and lack of perceived benefits. Spatial datasets are larger than corresponding non-spatial ones. Often spatial data analysis requires more processing power than similar non-spatial analysis. Thus, computing capac-ity parameters took longer to provide enough speed and power to adequately support spatial analysis and its applications. Second, business people have had less overall knowledge of spatial principles and applications than their government counterparts. Until recently, exposure to spatial software in in-dustry was limited and fairly expensive. Training is sometimes difficult for the average business person to obtain. Software training is provided by GIS software vendor firms and many community colleges. An example is the GIS

Education at City College of San Franciso (CCSF, 2007). Universities have not until recently emphasized the business side of spatial technologies. GIS is a prevalent tool in schools of planning and public administration, but is only beginning to take hold in business schools (Pick, 2004). Generally, universities have not understood what is needed to educate and train the geospatial workforce (Marble, 2006). Third, business top management leadership in the 1990s infrequently recognized the importance of spatial dimensions. Today more business leaders do recognize it. As seen in cases in the book, some top leaders in companies that heavily utilize GIS/Spatial technologies do recognize its significance strategically, while others do not.

The Rise in the Internet Platform for GIS

Another set of trends that has stimulated spatial and GIS applications is the rise of the internet, web, and e-commerce applications. The following recap of the development of the internet, underscores how recently web-based GIS has been possible and how it serves as a driver for GIS.

Although the application of the internet started in 1969 at the U.S. Department of Defense Advanced Research Projects Agency (DARPA), the main protocol of TCP/IP was not developed until 1974 and only came into research and academic use at leading centers in the late 1970s. TCP/IP (transmission control protocol/internet protocol) is the protocol that controls internet communications between computers. The management of the internet shifted from Department of Defense (DOD) to the National Science Foundation in 1987 and to international commercial organizations in 1995. At that point, the backbone internet traffic was taken over by commercial telecommunications carriers worldwide such as MCI Inc., AT&T, Sprint, and Nippon Telephone Company. As seen in Table 1.1, the number of internet hosts worldwide increased steadily from the mid 1980s to 2005 (The Internet Society, 2006). An internet host is any computer system connected to the internet from a full- or part-time, direct or dial-up connection (more specifically, a host is any computer with an IP address). Since internet hosts only exceeded 100 million in 2000, this table underscores why widespread GIS and spatial applications on the internet are recent.

The World Wide Web (WWW) was originated in 1989 at the European Laboratory for Particle Physics by Tim Berners-Lee. It allowed a user to jump around the internet by links attached to text and imagery. The first browser, Mosaic, was invented in 1993 at the National Center for Supercomputing Applications at University of Illinois. This browser and others that followed such as Microsoft Explorer (1995) led to standard and user-friendly interfaces that made the web navigation much easier.

Businesses had been able to use the internet to conduct some business transactions in the 1980s through Electronic Data Interchange (EDI), but the control of the interchanges was not user-friendly, so it was mostly specialists in IT departments who developed, operated, and utilized EDI. With the advent of the WWW, a new form of business exchange became available,

TABLE 1.1   Number of Internet Hosts, 1984–2005

Year (January)	Number of Internet Hosts
1984	1,000
1991	376,000
1992	727,000
1993	1,300,000
1994	2,200,000
1995	5,000,000
1996	9,400,000
1997	16,000,000
1998	29,000,000
1999	43,000,000
2000	72,000,000
2001	109,000,000
2002	147,000,000
2003	171,000,000
2004	285,000,000
2005	318,000,000

Source: Internet Systems Consortium, Inc. (http://www.isc.org/).

electronic commerce. Electronic commerce is the conduct of commercial transactions on a widespread basis through internet-based exchanges, mostly WWW-based. It grew in the early to mid 1990s and today is estimated to underlie about 5 percent of the U.S. economy, a proportion that is growing. E-commerce can be business-to-consumer (B2C) or business-to-business (B2B). Business-to-consumer e-commerce consists of business transactions and exchanges between a customer and the business; for instance, if a consumer on the web purchases a laptop computer from Dell, or books from Amazon. Business-to-business involves transactions and exchanges between two or more businesses. An example is a B2B website for chemical companies to sell and purchase chemical products with other chemical firms. Often B2B applications provide the basis for market transactions.

The expansion of e-commerce in the United States has been rapid and continues. For instance, e-commerce as a percentage of U.S. retail sales grew steadily from 0.91 percent in 2000 to 2.37 percent for year 2005 (U.S. Census, 2006). E-commerce trends relate to GIS applications, since spatial interfaces are beginning to be involved. This can be through B2C user interfaces with spatial features, marketing of e-commerce, and delivery of goods. For instance, many Google Earth mash-ups, i.e. third party products based on Google code, allow customers to search for business products and services, and conduct online business transactions. The Sperry Van Ness case at the end of the chapter supports spatial features on the web so brokers and their customers can more quickly research, market, and close commercial real estate sales transactions.

Since spatial systems tend to lag information systems (IS) somewhat, web-based spatial applications have only appeared heavily since 2000. Today the shift in spatial applications is steadily towards the web and internet (Sonnen et al., 2004; Sonnen, 2006; Daratech, 2004). Users find the internet platform appealing, easy, and flexible between devices. However, the web protocols and the designs, servers, and software to support these spatial applications are still in development. For instance, the leading spatial web protocols such as GML (Geography Markup Language),WFS (Web Feature Services), and WMS (Web Map Service) are available through a leading standards body, the Open Geospatial Consortium (OGC), but are not yet fully accepted industry standards.

E-commerce applications with spatial components became evident in the Dot.Com boom of the late 1990s with the advent of real estate, transport routing, and other web-based services with map features. The e-commerce with spatial features is growing and particularly relates to B2C in such sectors as real estate, retail, tourism, transportation, and distribution. These spatial advances became evident in 2005 to larger audiences of hundreds of millions of internet users through the milestone advent of Google Earth, Google Map, Microsoft Virtual Earth, and Yahoo Map, and smaller "mash-up" applications. For example, a person ordering a pizza online compares pizza parlors based on their location and the web links describing them, and then ordering online at Pizza Hut (see Figure 1.1).

The breakthroughs in 2005 also swept through the GIS industry and influenced GIS software companies to undertake new strategies of web-based

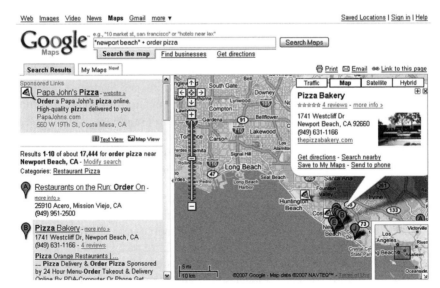

Figure 1.1 Spatial E-Commerce: Ordering a Pizza Online from Google Map Display. *Source:* Google Maps™ mapping service/NAVTEQ 2007

applications that are broadening and changing spatial applications for varied businesses, large and small, across many vertical sectors.

This trend towards the spatial-web is a recurring theme in this book, in the chapters that explain different aspects of GIS in business, and also in many case studies. The Sperry Van Ness case demonstrates how a medium-sized firm can make wise choices of internet platforms and software, not try to do too much, and be highly successful today in the spatial-web space.

Also in the 1990s, large-scale, enterprise-wide software applications became more prevalent (Gray, 2006). These include Enterprise Resources Planning systems (ERP), Customer Relationship Management (CRM), and Supply Chain Management (SCM). The difference from the functional systems available earlier is that these systems apply widely across all locations and many if not all divisions of a business. ERP supports integrated transaction processing systems across wide functional areas including accounting, finance, marketing, sales, production, human resources, and inventory. CRM systems support managing the long-term relationships with the company's customers, from initiation, through building and development and growing breadth of relationships, to transfer, termination, or upgrading of relationships (Gray, 2006). Supply Chain Management (SCM) monitors, manages, and projects companywide flow of raw materials, components, and finished products throughout the manufacturing, distribution, and delivery processes (Gray, 2006). It not only tracks physical items, but also the associated flows of information. If the materials, components, and products moving through the supply chain are geo-referenced at many points in the process, then the supply chain can be better understood, tightened up, optimized, and made more predictable than without geo-referencing.

Geo-referencing refers to adding X-Y (longitude-latitude) fields to an existing data record. Although less prevalent, this might be in 3-D, i.e. X-Y-Z (longitude-latitude-elevation). 3-D geo-referencing can be used for terrain elevation modeling and other applications. Roughly 80 percent of business data has the potential to be geo-referenced, i.e. have a spatial location attached to it (Bossler, 2002).

Because of its greater prevalence of web-based architecture, GIS is becoming more strategic in its applications, often extending across the enterprise. It is no longer restrained to traditional, 1990s departments that maintained compartmentalized datasets not accessible to the outside. Rather, following a long-term IT trend, spatial systems are beginning to be incorporated as a key part of enterprise-wide business applications such as ERP, CRM, and Supply Chain. The process of its movement into these domains has been inconsistent, bumpy, and sometimes resisted by management and users. Another constraint has been how to seamlessly bridge between the large enterprise business applications, which were originally developed without spatial modules, and the complex GIS software packages. However, vendors of both types of software, such as SAP and ESRI Inc., see the opportunity and are working on smoother and more efficient connecting interfaces. In medium and large firms, the enterprise applications were often implemented by IT specialist groups that were not grounded in spatial principles and often isolated from usually small GIS departments, creating other obstacles that have slowed the pace of development. Of the book's twenty research case studies, few yet have implemented GIS integrated with enterprise applications, and none fully.

Spatial Data

When spatial and GIS applications take place in business, whether traditional client-server systems or enterprise-web-based ones, they are based on business data. High quality spatial data (boundaries and attributes) are critical because they support any spatial application and serve as the foundation for analysis, modeling, and decision-making. Spatial data consists of two parts:

- the *digital map boundaries*, which constitute the map layer or map coverage
- data associated with the map layer, which are commonly alphanumeric but can also be video images, audio, and other forms. The non-spatial associated data are referred to as *attribute data*, and are considered more in Chapter 2.

The role of the two types of data can be seen in the simplified Generic Design of a GIS, shown in Figure 1.2. The digital boundary data on the bottom right are input from the internet, global positioning systems (GPS), satellites, and internal sources, and provide the digital boundaries for each map layer. The attribute data on the bottom left are input from other internal and external sources, and provide the non-spatial attributes associated with spatial features. For example, the diagram's middle boundary layer shows three roads. The non-spatial features of each road (width, materials, date of construction, date of most recent maintenance) are stored in an attribute table associated with the map layer (shown on the left). The model of GIS is explained in detail in Chapter 2, while spatial data are emphasized in Chapter 8. The Model also has analysis and modeling functions, which depend on the boundary and attribute data. This includes functions for statistics, simulation, forecasting, and spatial analysis. Finally the outputs at the top are the processing results of the GIS—maps, graphical displays, tables, and other information that is provided to the user for decision-making.

Important aspects of spatial data are its cost, ownership, security, privacy, data quality, and currency/updating. The need to assure all this makes data acquisition often costly and time-consuming for the following reasons:

- A well-known estimate is that 80 percent of the development costs of a GIS project are data expense (Bossler, 2002). The reasons are that spatial data are often voluminous, come from varied data sources, may have

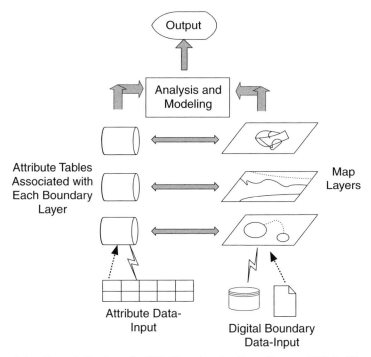

Figure 1.2   Generic Design of a GIS, Showing Attribute Data and Digital Boundary Data

quality issues, and they may not be compatible with each other or with the GIS software. The latter issue stems from the GIS industry's need to update and replace standards, as a consequence of business and technical change, a topic addressed in Chapter 5.

- Data quality is also a problem. Not only are there the usual problems with the attribute data, but in addition serious challenges exist with the accuracy of digital boundary files (Meeks and Dasgupta, 2005). Some of the digital boundary data were originally collected before GPS (Global Positionig Systems) and satellites provided precise locations. A prominent example of this are the base boundary files (TIGER) of the U.S. Census, which have been updated to GPS-accuracy for the 2010 Census. Even with GPS and satellites, errors can occur in the processing and management of the data, as well as in correctly identifying and labeling location. If the user needs exact locations, such as for pipelines or utility lines, then there is a need to do thorough checking for data accuracy. If necessary, accuracy assessments with GPS against physical features in the field may be necessary at extra time and expense to ensure the data quality. Accuracy is also needed to assure the precise connectivity of pipelines with each other.

- The data cleaning, checking, and modifications can exceed ordinary data quality assurances because both the attribute and spatial data need to be individually checked and often modified, but also they need to be compatible with each other and with the GIS software.
- A large proportion of business-generated data are *proprietary*. This means that they are either not released by a firm or only to trusted or partner firms and often at cost. The firm has legal ownership of the data, so in the event of disputes over ownership or data theft, threats or even lawsuits can occur.
- Coordinate systems in boundary layers may be mismatched. Modern software tools can help in achieving matching, but good technical understanding is often needed.

The scope of spatial and associated attribute data is vast and covers the range of business activities in multiple industries. Some of the lead industries that receive attention in this book are utilities, transportation, petroleum, insurance, banking, real estate, retail, environmental consulting, and health care. For just these, the scope of spatial data includes:

- *Utilities*. Attribute and boundary data on economic development, demographic patterns, vegetation, rates, loss evaluation, environmental contamination, maintenance, work-order status, weather, safety, crew and vehicle tracking, outages, transmission lines, land use, metering, labor, materials, customers, and accounting costs.
- *Transportation*. Attribute and boundary data on transport routing, congestion patterns, volume of traffic, vehicle types, loads, maintenance, fuel types, customers, and accounting costs.
- *Petroleum*. Data on geology, drilling, exploration, land use, pipelines, refineries, consumer markets, retail locations, customers, demographic patterns, political patterns, and assets.
- *Insurance*. Data on land use, property damage, vegetation, weather, premium pricing, environmental risks, tax jurisdictions, customers, competitors, natural catastrophe pricing, event loss estimation, population, injuries and deaths, homeless and missing persons, peril zones, and portfolio analysis.
- *Banking*. Data on branch and ATM locations, market areas, spatial diversification of investments, and individual and business customer profiles by location.
- *Real estate*. Data on property locations, layout of land and properties, pricing history, markets—buyers and sellers, taxes, mortgage rates, and customers.
- *Retail*. Data on inventory, supply chain, sales, store sites, customers, transportation networks, demographic profiles and trends, competitors, and purchase patterns.

- *Environmental consulting.* Data on environmental contamination, environmental treatments, management of clean-ups, and customer locations.
- *Health care.* Data on locations and attributes of doctors, other health-care workers, patients, diseases, treatments, facilities, service and regulatory boundaries, transportation, inventory, scheduling, and costs.

These and other data sources are considered in Chapters 9 and 10. Much of the vast reach of business spatial data has existed for many decades, pre-dating the advent of widespread business spatial uses in the 1990s. Since some of the data was not originally accurately geo-referenced, data collection procedures need to be modified so that old locations can now be brought up to the latest precision. For instance, a New York durable goods retailer with thousands of daily deliveries can record and check the X-Y locations of a customer by recording it from the GPS device on the delivery truck, during a home-delivery event. Geo-referenced records have both spatial and non-spatial uses. For example, some companies have geo-referenced their inventory. This can be done through older methods such as adding the location as items are received manually at facilities, or through automatic recording by RFID (radio frequency identification) devices. Knowing precisely where each item of inventory is located helps improve efficiency and timing. Geographically referenced inventory may or may not utilize the spatial referencing, depending on the business process. For example, a chain of grocery stores can calculate, by store, the monthly dollar value of its three current best-selling food items and map those values by store. The map utilizes the spatial location i.e. the point location of each store. Another analysis can do a line graph of the total corporate monthly sales for the three current best-selling items over the past ten years. This line graph is useful for corporate market planning but has no spatial-referencing. This point becomes important with enterprise business systems, which up to now have had minor spatial aspects. For example in the ERP for one large business, over 98 percent of analysis is non-spatial and only 2 percent is spatial. Hence, proportion of the non-spatial uses must be considered in recognizing the perceived importance of spatial data and the priorities given by managers and other stakeholders in utilizing it.

CASE STUDY: GLOBAL INTEGRATED OIL

Global Integrated Oil (GIO) is a world giant, with over 50,000 employees, more than $100 billion in revenues, and business conducted in 180 nations. Spatial technologies are applied enterprise-wide, including in exploration, leasing, transportation and storage, environmental, refining, pipelines, marketing, distribution, supply chain, and business planning. These areas can be better conceptualized with a picture of its Energy Value Chain, shown in Figure 1.3, from exploration to production through to distribution and marketing to customers.

These steps are supported by a mixture of technologies that includes information systems, e-commerce, mobile technologies, and GIS.

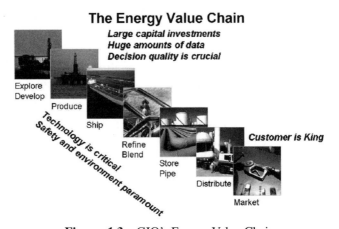

Figure 1.3   GIO's Energy Value Chain

Some notable examples of GIO's spatial activities are the following:

Upstream GIS uses are the heaviest. In *exploration and development*, geologists analyze the subsurface using 3-D modeling software, mostly purchased from outside vendors. This is a competitive aspect, since the global petroleum firms compete strongly on strategic knowledge of where petroleum reserves are located. In determining where to explore, the upstream GIS groups model the global petroleum basin formation from 500 million years ago to present. For instance, Figure 1.4 shows the location of subsurface oil and deposits,

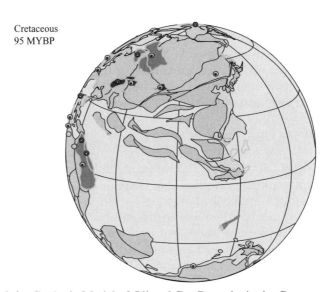

Figure 1.4   Geologic Model of Oil and Gas Deposits in the Cretaceous Period

as well as certain related fossil deposits in the Cretaceous Period that occurred earlier than 95 million years ago. The darker the shading, the larger the deposit.

Global discoveries by GIO over the past ten years of oil and natural gas are mapped, along with locations of dry holes and tar sands. This helps to strategically appraise the size and locations of exploration projects. The benefits are knowing not only where to explore, but also which zones to avoid. Once exploration has commenced, maps of seismic profiles can be produced and overlaid on exploration fields, to determine both the geologic properties and the risk of equipment damage from earthquakes once a production site is active. The exploration fields can be given in one map layer, shown on the left in Figure 1.5, that overlays another layer on the right which shows proposed locations of well sites and pipelines. The full GIS incorporates both terrestrial (topography, well sites, pipelines) and subsurface features (earthquake fault zones, oil deposits).

Another upstream application displays the leasing of exploration land areas held by GIO and its global competitors. It is crucial to know precisely the boundaries of what land is leased compared to competitors' leases and new blocks that might be bid on.

Once drilling starts, 3-D map images can show how the exploration field is laid out, both above and below the surface. These 3-D map images can be used to plan, monitor, and evaluate the construction, regulation, and environmental impacts of *pipelines*. Pipelines constitute GIO's second largest spatial use after geologic modeling.

 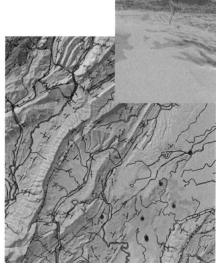

Figure 1.5 Map Overlay of Exploration Field Topography and Locations of Proposed Pipelines and Well Sites

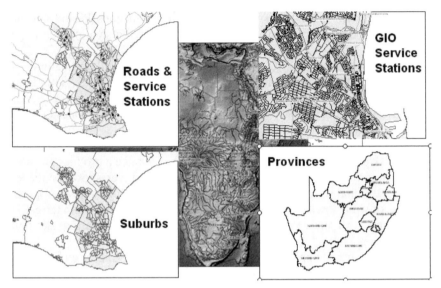

Figure 1.6 GIS in GIO's Retail Market Planning in Africa

For transportation and storage, multi-layered maps show routes, depots, and associated supply districts. For marketing, service station locations are analyzed relative to retail markets, price zones, urban and population areas from the census, and trade area maps.

An example of retail market planning is given in Figure 1.6 for a retail area in Africa. Map layers show major roads and service stations in a suburban area, suburban boundaries, service stations in a denser urban area, and provincial boundaries. Based on these, GIO managers can make improved decisions on locations of retail stations that take maximum advantage of traffic flows, and population proximities, and distribution of existing stations.

GIO has critical supply-chain models and information systems that support the planning and movement of items worldwide. The company has begun to add spatial analysis and mapping to its supply chain system. Figure 1.7 indicates routing pathways between plant and container locations for Europe, Africa, South Asia, and Australia. Questions can be answered such as what are the distances to ship items, how expensive are routes, and how can shipments be best timed and coordinated over space-time to create the most efficiency.

In the environmental realm, GIS is applied upstream and midstream to model layers of physical topography, hazards, and social impacts. Strategic planning uses include spatial analysis of global new ventures and merger proximities of production facilities and office locations. These applications spatially compare data on GIO's facilities, workforce, and assets to those of new-venture or merger candidates. Is there a fit geographically between GIO and other entities? Can the proposed consolidations be beneficial? What are the savings from proximities?

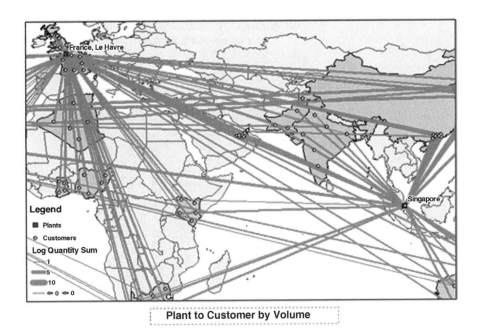

Figure 1.7   GIO's Supply Chain Routing of Containers from Plant to Customer in Africa, South Asia, and Australia

Application of GIS to company strategy at GIO can be analyzed through matrices, such as the simple one illustrated in Figure 1.8 categorizing certain parts of the holding company and its many subsidiaries where GIS/Spatial is applied. In this matrix, the life-cycle stages are the columns, while the rows represent functional business sectors. The number of stars reflects the amount of GIS application. It's clear that GIS finds its way into most cells. At GIO, GIS has moved far from a "silo" and diffused widely into most of the business sectors, life-cycle stages, and subsidiary companies.

Given GIS's prevalence, the company has a surprisingly small GIS Central Group of a dozen experts, located in one of the subsidiary technology companies. That group interacts with twenty-five other GIS employees who are scattered in many of the dozens of GIO operating companies. The GIS Central Group does management, planning, and provides the expert spatial consulting for all the companies, as well as coordinating with the spatial employees worldwide.

The company is pushing the technology limits, in areas such as sub-surface geologic mapping, web-based applications, 3-D maps, data warehousing, and advanced spatial analytic tools for business planning. Overall, GIS is considered by GIO top management to be very strategic in taking on GIO's competition at many levels.

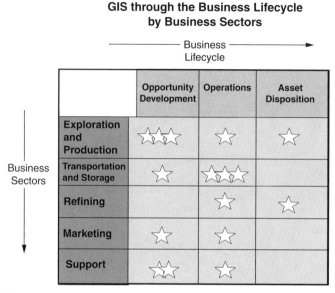

Figure 1.8   Matrix of GIS Applications at GIO by Business Sector and Life-Cycle Stage

THE SPATIAL RE-EVOLUTION

In the past few years, GIS and spatial developments in business have come at a rapid pace, leading to "re-evolution" of earlier business paradigms for GIS. This section looks back at key milestones and then considers several waves of new developments sweeping across GIS and spatial technologies that include RFID, sensors, Lidar, spatial web services, open source software, and event-driven architecture. This section sets the basis for some technology themes of the book.

Historical Antecedents

The history of GIS and spatial technologies in business goes back only about fifty years and only in a major way since the 1990s. However, antecedents go back to non-computerized map overlays in the early twentieth century. A *spatial overlay* is the process of exactly superimposing of several map layers such as terrain, hydrology, geology, and agriculture. The layers can be viewed together, and the relationships of their features analyzed (Wade and Sommer, 2006). Using exact scales to match up layers, Jacquiline Tyrwhitt did this in her *Town and County Planning* textbook in 1950 (Clarke, 2003). Waldo Tobler's article in 1959 conceptually foresaw using a computer to accomplish cartography from inputting data to producing maps (Tobler, 1959). In the

Figure 1.9   ESRI Inc. Founder and President, Jack Dangermond. *Source:* Copyright © ESRI. All rights reserved. Used by permission

1960s early computer programs such as SYMAP and CALFORM could overlay layers and produce maps using mainframe computers and on bulky, crude printers. The Canadian government was an early adopter in 1964 of primitive GIS and continued in subsequent decades to be a lead user. An academic milestone was the book *Design with Nature* by Ian McHarg, a professor at University of Pennsylvania. McHarg included plastic overlay sheets that demonstrated how overlays could shed new light on environmental design (McHarg, 1969).

In the mid to late 1960s, substantial progress was achieved on computer algorithms for GIS at the Harvard Laboratory for Computer Graphics and Spatial Analysis, including the use of arcs and nodes to build up boundary files (Clarke, 2003). In the late 1960s, Environmental Systems Research Institute (ESRI) was formed as a company and headed since its founding by Jack Dangermond (see Figure 1.9). Its mini-computer product ArcInfo, based on Harvard concepts, became the leading commercial GIS software package. Although ESRI's early markets were predominantly in government, this also marked the beginning of GIS and spatial applications for businesses. Later other software companies entered the markets, including MapInfo Corporation and Intergraph Corporation. During the Cold War, there were parallel and often secret developments in mapping and satellite technology by U.S. military planners who were reacting to the threat of nuclear war (Cloud, 2002; Charles, 2005). This stream of military R&D eventually led to the first development and deployment of satellite systems for GPS in the 1980s. The military history is less well known and was largely detached from the academic developments of those decades.

For the 1970s through the 1990s, GIS platforms progressed from bulky mainframes to mini-computers, pcs, and handheld devices. User interfaces changed from command-driven to Graphical User Interfaces (GUIs) in the 1980s. These transformations were driven by advances in the computing

TABLE 1.2   Moore's Law. Transistor Capacity of Intel Processor Chips, 1971–2006

Year of Introduction	Chip	No. of Transistors per chip	MIPS*
1971	4004	2,250	0.06
1972	8008	2,500	
1974	8080	5,000	0.64
1978	8086	29,000	0.75
1982	286	120,000	2.66
1985	386	275,000	5.00
1989	486	1,180,000	20.00
1993	Pentium	3,100,000	66.00
1997	Pentium II	7,500,000	1,000.00
1999	Pentium III	24,000,000	1,354.00
2000	Pentrium IV	55,000,000	9,700.00
2002	Itanium	250,000,000	
2003	Itanium 2	600,000,000	
2006	Dual-Core Itanium 2	1,100,000,000	27,000.00

*millions of instructions per second
Source: Intel, 2007.

power of the underlying component technology. There was a 450,000-fold increase in chip capacity and in processing power from the 1971 through 2006 (Intel, 2007) (see Table 1.2).

The expansion in power allowed GIS to run on much smaller devices or to run thousands of times more powerfully on the same device. Other technological advances impacting GIS were vastly improved monitor screens, higher-resolution printers, expanded networking lines and bandwidths, and more advanced telecommunications design and protocols.

GIS software, most of which was originally written in FORTAN, progressed in the 1990s to object-oriented (OO) languages such as C++ and Visual Basic. Object-oriented design emphasizes interchangeable components, interactive GUI interfaces, and greater ease of use. OO design also allowed GIS software to be more portable across computing platforms. As a result today's GIS software can be implemented as a family of products with the similar user interfaces extending from handheld devices to large-scale servers.

Networking changes in the late 1980s and 1990s transformed the distribution and reach of GIS. For large-scale applications, client-server architecture was introduced on conventional lines (non-internet). Most of the processing takes place on the server(s), which connect and share processing with the client's local system. Data can be stored on the central server, on specialized database servers, and/or on the client's system. Also, during this period, versions of all the leading software packages such as ESRI's ArcInfo and Intergraph's Geomedia were introduced for client-server platforms. Today, powerful client-server versions support advanced departmental applications often for specialized purposes. Client-server architecture was not designed for the internet whereas enterprise web services is. As the latter has become more prevalent, the client-server environment can be referred to as "traditional" (Sonnen and Morris, 2005), even though it is still in widespread use. The distinction of "traditional" versus enterprise/web-based will carry through the book as a theme.

Coupling Technologies

Coupling technologies such as GPS, RFID, and portable wireless devices became prevalent in the 1990s. A *coupling technology* is one associated with GIS that makes the combination more productive and efficient (see Table 1.3). For example, GIS by itself can produce maps based on existing datasets, but does not have the capacity to gather data in real-time. However GIS coupled with GPS can gather geo-referenced data, input it, combine it with existing datasets and produce real-time outputs. As another example, GIS in a field location formerly functioned on a desktop computer with dial-up networking. It is replaced by GIS coupled with a light, flexible, and physically transportable wireless device that is networked at higher bandwidth. The handheld computer in Figure 1.10 is supported by the ArcPad software from ESRI. It provides features for map viewing, data query, distance measurement, GPS navigation, data editing, limited spatial analysis functionality, and wireless communications. Data can be transferred back and forth between the ArcPad mobile device and a networked workstation with GIS by wireless, Bluetooth connections or a physical cable.

A list of some of the coupling technologies is given in Table 1.3.

Global Positioning Systems (GPS) technology, developed in the U.S. military beginning in 1973 and utilized for the first time in combat during Operation Desert Storm in 1991, was not made available for commercial use until shortly after the end of the Cold War in 1993 (Pace, 1995). However, the military at first broadcast a civilian signal that was only accurate to within 100 feet (NAS, 1997). In 1996, the Clinton Administration approved a higher level of GPS accuracy within several feet to be made available to anyone (NAS, 1997). GPS is based on a system of twenty-four Navstar satellites that were constructed by the Rockwell Division of Boeing (originally Rockwell International) and completely deployed in 1993. Each satellite completes a full low earth orbit every 12 hours. They are arranged in an orbiting formation so every point of the earth is in radio communications with at least four satellites at all times (NAS, 1997). GPS devices receive signals from four of the satellites that enables the device to determine its position anywhere in the world with a very high accuracy, commonly under one meter. Military GPS have even higher accuracies as low as a centimeter.

Radio Frequency Identification (RFID) technology started earlier than GPS. Invented by Léon Theremin in the Soviet Union in 1945, it was presented conceptually in a paper by Harry Stockman in 1948 (Landt, 2001), and

Figure 1.10   Handheld Computer Running ArcPad Software. *Source:* ESRI Inc.

further developed and tested in the 1970s and 1980s. RFID allows automatic identification of physical items which have tags (active or passive) that connect with RFID readers. Passive tags can be read within about twenty feet, while active tags can be read within several hundreds of feet and have larger memories. Its first commercial applications were in the late 1980s. It became widely deployed the 1990s after standards were developed and agreed upon (Landt, 2001). In the past few years, lead organizations such as the U.S. Department of Defense and Wal-Mart Inc. mandated its use for suppliers, and their "clout" has speeded up business adoptions. An RFID reader records the data on an item at a particular time and place, resulting in geo-referencing to the reader. It is not continually referenced, as with GPS devices, but occurs at discontinuous points when a tag goes by a reader. The advantage of RFID is that huge numbers of items can quickly be geo-referenced, inventoried, spatially analyzed, and mapped.

An RFID device has a processor, memory, and a radio antenna. Passive RFID devices do not transmit but can be read by radio signals in range of up

TABLE 1.3 Technologies Often Coupled with GIS

Technology	Importance for GIS in Business
GPS	Global Positioning Systems (GPS) is a technology that can determine exact point locations anywhere on the earth by communicating signals with four of the twenty four GPS satellites in an orbiting system. GPS combined with GIS allows real-time locational information to be mapped for business purposes.
RFID	Radio Frequency Identification (RFID) allows portable products of any type to be spatially registered and to carry data that can be accessed and updated remotely by RFID readers. Its use in business is that supply chains and inventory items can be RFID-tagged and their positional locations tracked and stored for GIS access (Richardson, 2003).
Sensors	Devices implanted into buildings, transport vehicles, inventory items, the landscape, and even people provide physical measurements of the environment, such as temperature, lighting, radiation, noise, heat, etc.
Mobile wireless communications	Allows field deployment of GIS technologies in mobile commerce. Useful in supporting the real-time field operations of businesses (Mennecke and Strader, 2003). Combines GIS, GPS, and wireless technologies.
Handheld Devices	Portable handheld spatial devices, such as Personal Device Assistants (PDAs), cell phones, handheld computers, and other mobile devices. For spatial purposes, it contains a GPS device and scaled-down versions of standard GIS software. Gives businesses field flexibility in inputting, outputing, modifying, analyzing, and utilizing data. Important in business sectors such as retail and utilities that have substantial field forces.
LIDAR	LIDAR (Light Detetion and Ranging) can estimate precisely the distance to a surface or object by bouncing laser pulses. The time delay from transmission to receiving the light signal determines the distance. Utilized in aircraft and ground stations for high-precision distance measurements.

to about 20 feet from an RFID reader. Active RFID devices actively transmit radio signals so the readers can be located at more distance—up to 300 feet. The costs of the tags and readers are falling rapidly. Readers have become quite affordable, many models at less than $1,000, and are widely distributed.

As an example of the importance of RFID, Wal-Mart in 2006 required its largest 300 suppliers to have RFID tags on its shipping crates and pallets. Each RFID tag stores an Electronic Product Code (EPC), which provides more information than the traditional bar code. In particular it provides codes not only for product description but also a code for the production lot at the time of manufacturing. This means that an item being shipped or stored can be associated with its detailed production, transport, and storage history. The transport and storage is the accumulated history of movements through readers, which is transmitted and stored in a database. Wal-Mart will track crates and pallets from the point of entering the Wal-Mart supply chain through distribution centers to individual stores (Williams, 2004). Whenever the item passes an RFID reader, not only the EPC but also the coordinate location of the reader is recorded. This supports mapping and spatial analysis applications in order to better plan and optimize the spatial movement and storage of inventory and improve transportation and optimal locating of inventory items.

Portable wireless devices were introduced for widespread commercial use in the 1990s and continue to expand in functionality and market penetration. They include handheld computers, mobile phones, PDAs (personal device assistants), and combined devices such as Blackberries. They support users in the field for data input and display, for instance utility field maintenance staff who need to view maps to locate and repair pipelines, control boxes, and underground facilities.

Wireless LANs are used to provide networking in a flexible local environment without cabling. It allows personnel to capture or update spatial information into devices often portable ones, unfettered by cabling restrictions.

LIDAR creates vivid earth imagery that may be used for weather forecasting and analysis, regardless of whether there is spatial analysis. Its displays are useful for viewing earth events for business and government analysis and decisions.

Networked sensors collected a variety of environmental information, usually at a fixed location. They can measure the magnitude and volume of of environmental or human events at the sensor's location. For instance, climatic data from a network of weather sensors in a region can be input in real-time into a GIS to produce continuous weather maps. Sensor-based data can be used for supporting decisions in business and government (Meeks and Dasgupta, 2005). In short, many of the Geo-location devices share spatial and non-spatial uses.

Broadband as the Foundation for Web Services

Another shift was the advent of web services and service-oriented architectures over the past decade (see Table 1.4). The shift is supported by the expanding internet capacities shown in Table 1.1 and by the widening bandwidths of internet transmission (Austin and Bradley, 2005). Larger bandwidth implies that greater volumes of information can be transferred per unit of time (Dodd, 2005). An important bandwidth division point occurs between narrowband and broadband, which generally means bandwidths higher than that of T1 transmission lines (Dodd, 2005). The dividing point is at 1.54 million bits per second (mbps).

TABLE 1.4   **Broadband Penetration Rates by Country**

Rank	Country	Broadband Subscribers Per 100 Persons (1/2004)	Households Using Broadband as Percent of Total Households (12/2003)	Percent of Population with High-Speed Internet Access (2002)
1	South Korea	24.0	70.5	21.3
2	Hong Kong	17.0	50.3	14.6
3	Canada	15.0	36.2	11.5
4	Iceland	14.5	NA	8.6
5	Taiwan	12.5	43.2	9.4
6	Denmark	12.0	25.7	8.6
7	Belgium	11.5	24.7	8.4
8	Japan	11.0	28.0	NA
9	Netherlands	11.0	NA	6.5
10	Switzerland	11.0	23.1	NA
13	United States	10.0	22.5	6.5

Source: Reprinted by permission of Harvard Business School Press. From The Broadband Explosion by Robert D. Austin and Stephen P. Bradley (eds.), Boston, MA 2005.

Today's broadband has capacity much higher than that, for instance cable modem services support 6 mbps. T3 lines have capacity of 44.7 mbps, more than the average individual user can take advantage of (Dodd, 2005). Broadband is rapidly becoming more prevalent, including several nations that had more than 50 percent of households connected to broadband in 2003. Many advanced nations had over 20 percent (see Table 1.4).

The growth rates of conversion to broadband are high, so it can be expected within several years to be the dominant transmission mode in developed nations. This trend favors spatial web services, which require rapid and high volumes of information transfer, i.e. in the broadband range.

Spatial Web Services

Spatial web services are those that can be delivered to the user over the web. They are delivered over the Internet Bus, which refers to the high-speed internet or intranet available throughout the enterprise. As seen in Figure 1.11, the organization can put its spatial software on an enterprise server, which creates maps, performs spatial analysis, and sends outputs across the Internet Bus. Also, database servers with data stores are connected to the Internet Bus. Spatial web services managed by outside service vendors are linked to the bus. The maps and other spatial output are transmitted over the Internet Bus to reach users who have access to thin client systems, i.e. ones without much of their own capacity, or thick client systems, ones that have their own software packages and databases. At the lower left of the diagram is a connection to business enterprise systems such as ERP, CRM, and Supply Chain.

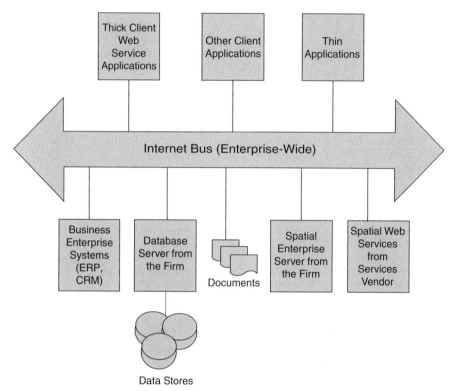

Figure 1.11   Spatial Web Services Provided by Enterprise-Wide Internet Bus

This framework utilizes the protocol of *Service Oriented Architecture* (SOA). SOA differs from traditional client-server protocols in supporting a set of loosely coupled and interoperable application services that are independent of the hardware platforms and programming languages. The most common web services version of this is based on Simple Object Access Protocol (SOAP). It supports SOA as a web service based on the Extensible Markup Language (XML) web protocol. SOAP allows application programs to coordinate with each other across the Internet Bus, even though they utilize different operating systems, programming languages, and technologies. Thus it supports the integration of business applications, allowing sharing of resources and lower cost.

Open Source Software

Another important trend is *open source* software, which has grown since the late 1990s. Open source refers to software development by a community of developers who contribute to publicly available software code. It may or may not have copyright or patent protections, but if protected, the licensing makes the software freely available. Probably the most famous open source software is the Linux operating system, which has entered the mainstream pc operating system market with a small but growing share. Open source development is becoming more important for spatial and GIS software, although no Linux-like software has yet become a leader. An example is MapServer software, developed at University of Minnesota, which allows development and rendering of maps for the web (MapServer, 2007). It's not a full GIS software but has many basic spatial features and tens of thousands of users.

The open environment was also stimulated by the product and legal approach taken by the internet companies Google, Yahoo, and Microsoft when in 2005 they released their free spatial software, Google Earth, Yahoo! Maps, and Microsoft Virtual Earth. The firms opened up their code for outside development, by releasing the APIs. An *Application Program Interface* (API) is a group of protocols, tools, and code modules that allow developers to build applications consistent with the original software, although the firm may retain some limited controls. The outside programmer can use the API elements as a set of building blocks to develop applications that enhance or expand the original software. An example for GIS is a property development company in Portland, Oregon, that utilizes the Google Earth API, combined with its own property database to display satellite imagery of its properties along with their value, tax status, square footage, and year built.

Event-Driven Architecture

Along with SOA and open source, another web trend for GIS/Spatial is event-driven architecture. *Event-driven architecture (EDA)* refers to developing applications in which software events in certain combinations or sequences trigger sending of messages in an asynchronous manner to software modules at remote sites that are unaware the messages are coming (Silwa, 2003). Asynchronous refers to transmission of messages at different times, while synchronous is at the same time. It is "de-coupled," in the sense that the event, sender, and recipient are not previously connected. Middleware serves as the intermediary to which event-messages are sent and allocates the messages to software programs that have subscribed to be notified (Silwa, 2003). EDA is a decoupled, asynchronous architecture that complements SOA's loosely coupled synchronous architecture.

In GIS and spatial business applications, an example of EDA is for a transportation firm that sends out notifications when a vehicle is errant from its course. It can set up a combination of event criteria that define an errant vehicle, e.g. it is more than 5 miles outside its travel buffer zone and at a speed more than 10 miles per hour above the speed limit for more than a half hour. If the vehicle goes errant, the notification is automatically sent to a subscription list of office managers, customers, and security personnel. A current weakness of EDA is lack of widely accepted standards, which means that it runs best where all the programs involved are linked to the same middleware (Silwa, 2003).

In summary, GIS and spatial technologies have advanced tremendously over the past fifty years. Not only have capacities of the underlying component technology increased vastly and the internet revolutionized approaches to transmitting information, but new coupling technologies such as GPS, RFID, LIDAR, and Sensors have extended the combined functionality. Many of the key developments for business took place since the web's advent in 1989, so widespread adoption of spatial technologies in business is fairly recent. Even if a technology diffuses rapidly, companies and their people are often slower to adopt it due to prior investments, measured adoption approaches, and resistance to organizational change.

The overall changes in the IT context of the evolution of GIS and spatial technologies are summarized in Figure 1.12.

GIS parallels this IT timeline. It commenced in the Batch Era in the late 1960s and progressed through the Online Era of the 1980s and Distributed Era of the 1990s and into the first decade of this century (IDC, 2005). The year 2005 was a key turning point in GIS history, marking the start of the map services era, with free dynamic online processes for the general public, as typified by Google Earth and Microsoft Virtual Earth.

In summary, spatial technology trends have transitioned from mainframe to client-server to web services and event-driven architectures; from larger to smaller computing devices; from batch processing to interactive, real-time processing; from command-driven user interfaces to user-friendly GUI ones; from separated departmental data to data shared enterprise-wide or multi-enterprise-wide; from lower to higher quality standards of spatial information; and from traditional, stand-alone GIS software to GIS coupled with a group of associated technologies.

THE SPATIAL INDUSTRY

This section considers the spatial industry, which.comprises GIS vendor firms, distributors, data providers, spatial service providers, firms for the associated technologies (GPS, RFID, LIDAR, sensors), consultants, and integrators. Overall, the industry revenues are estimated in the range of $20 billion, with a further estimated $40 billion in government spatial data collection (based on Sonnen et al., 2005; Daratech, 2005; and Longley et al., 2005). The main components of the industry may be divided into (1) GIS software and add-ons, (2) geolocation technologies, (3) web-based enterprise-wide applications and infrastructure, and (4) spatially-enabled enterprise database products.

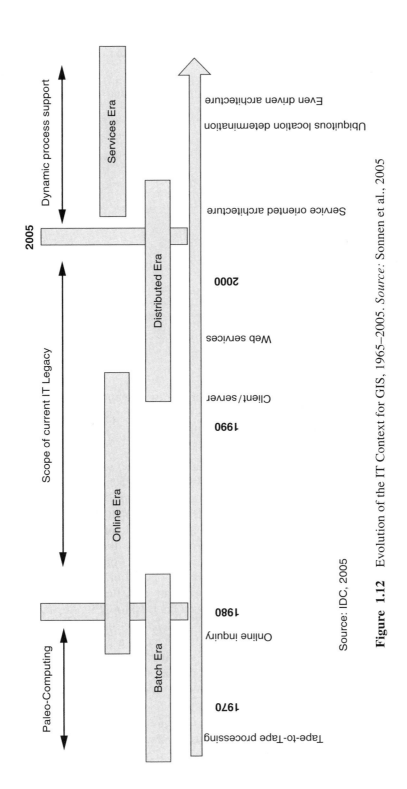

Figure 1.12 Evolution of the IT Context for GIS, 1965–2005. *Source:* Sonnen et al., 2005

Source: IDC, 2005

TABLE 1.5   GIS/Spatial Software Worldwide Revenues from Leading Vendors

Vendor Firm	GIS/Spatial Revenues, 2004, in millions of dollars	Percent of Market, 2004	Annual Growth Rate 2002–2004
ESRI	445.0	22.6	2.0
Intergraph	376.9	19.2	−0.3
Autodesk Inc.	261.3	13.3	24.1
MapInfo	97.7	5.0	15.4
AOL - Mapquest	67.0	3.4	6.1
Microsoft	56.0	2.9	16.7
GE Energy	18.8	1.0	−53.1
Group 1 Software Inc.	11.7	0.6	9.4
ObjectFX	10.0	0.5	11.1
PCI Geomatics	8.1	0.4	53.0
Other	612.2	31.2	5.6
TOTAL	1,964.7	100.0	5.6

Source: Sonnen et al., 2005

(1) GIS Software and Add-Ons

GIS revenues from the ten leading core software vendors in 2004, shown in Table 1.5, reflects that four companies, ESRI, Intergraph, Autodesk Inc., and MapInfo control 60 percent of the market.

1. *ESRI*, the long-time and largest general-purpose software and services vendor, introduced ArcGIS 9 in 2005 as its new lead product family.The family offers GIS software ranging from enterprise applications at the high end to software for portable devices, and including map server options. The products are built in object-oriented components that allow them to function in a variety of environments. It licenses web server software software to firms as ArcGIS Server. For enterprise-wide architecture, ArcGIS is provided as component libraries residing on the ArcGIS Server. Outsider developers can gain licensed access to the ArcObjects components through ArcGIS Desktop, Engine, and Server. ESRI also has divisions that provide selective and large-scale applications consulting as well as management of a client's web services under ArcWeb Services and other offerings. ESRI has been a technology leader in GIS software design. ArcPad software is offered to mobile users, and Business Map and Business Analyst Online to medium- and small-sized enterprises.
2. *Intergraph Corporation* provides software to middle- and large-sized government organizations and businesses. It also sells hardware to support the software. It focuses on vertical markets including homeland

security, government, power and utilities, manufacturing, and transportation. Its leading product family, Geomedia, is offered in web, client-server, and desktop versions.

3. *Autodesk Inc.* especially serves the utility, manufacturing, building, and infrastructure sectors, and partners with Oracle for enterprise-based applications. Its software has tools for engineering, design, planning, and managing large land-based assets. Autodesk heavily serves the utilities industry, where engineering exactness and asset tracking is essential. It extended its products into location-based services to support small and middle-sized businesses in their mobile workforce and field operations. Its major client base comprises government organizations and large infrastructure-related firms. Autodesk grew rapidly from 2002 to 2004, the result of its emphasizing the areas of homeland security and government infrastructure that benefited from the post 9/11 build-up.

4. *MapInfo* markets software to users ranging from individuals to medium-sized organizations. Its lead product is the full-featured GIS software package, MapInfo Professional. Other products are in enterprise applications, geodemographics, and street mapping data. Mostly it sells to medium-sized businesses and emphasizes marketing, banking, insurance, utility, and government applications. MapInfo, which since 2007 is a division of Pitney Bowes, has not yet introduced data management engines, map servers, or mobile device products. It is sometimes known as PB MapInfo.

The GIS software industry also has hundreds of smaller, more-specialized firms that often work in partnership with leading vendors. An example is PCI Geomatics (number ten in the Table 1.5), a Canadian firm that offers services in remote sensing, digital photogrammetry, terrain analysis, radar analysis, and data visualization software development, as well as mapping products to support these areas.

All told the GIS software industry in 2004 totaled about $2 billion in revenues (IDC, 2005). IDC estimates that the segment of industry that provided associated services in 2004 was $8 billion (IDC, 2005). These firms provide design, development, consulting, facilities management, and outsourcing to implement, manage, and enhance the core software.

The industry also includes a segment of systems integrators, software distributors, and software retailers. There are many partnerships and interrelationships among these enterprises (Daratech, 2004), as seen in Figure 1.13. Daratech estimated the total GIS industry and services in 2004 at $8.5 billion, with a somewhat lower services component of $6 billion. It includes specialized spatial hardware vendors with revenues in 2004 of $650 million (Daratech, 2004). An example of a specialized hardware vendor is Trimble Inc. which manufactures and markets a variety of small- to large-sized GPS devices.

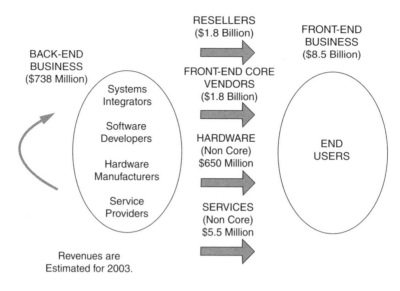

Figure 1.13   Model of the GIS Marketplace, 2003

Systems integrators support the planning and integration of the groups of spatial and other technologies. They establish processing flows, data flows, and software and networking coordination, when varied hardware and software products are applied in combination. This is often in conjunction with data providers and networking platforms. Systems integrators are especially valuable for large-scale projects, which must realize complex configurations of hardware, software, and applications. Here, the systems integrator will be present throughout the project to advise management. Among the steps in a large project that the integrator consults on are the feasibility study, conceptual design of hardware and software, requests for proposals (RFPs), specifications, quality assurance, developing, and building interoperability between different vendors, implementation, and training (Daratech, 2005). In sum, the integrator acts in a high-level technical and management consulting role.

If the project management is fully delegated to an outside party, then outsourcing occurs. Although not yet prevalent for GIS, outsourcing is on the rise and is covered in Chapter 10. The integrated arrangement of GIS and associated components, human resources, and processes needs to be stressed, and will be seen throughout the book and its cases.

(2) Geolocation Technologies

These technologies, GPS, RFID, wireless LANs, cellular networks, Lidar, Sonar, and networked sensors (Sonnen et al., 2005) have already been introduced. They advanced greatly in the present decade and new ones are likely to be introduced (Sonnen et al., 2005). Many smaller, specialized firms in the spatial industry and some larger ones provide and support these devices. Since these technologies are heavily utilized in military and intelligence, this side of the spatial industry is allied with the defense industry.

(3) Web-Based Enterprise-Wide Applications and Infrastructure

Many businesses have already developed IT infrastructures that support enterprise applications such as Enterprise Resource Management (ERP), Customer Relationship Management (CRM), Data Warehousing, Supply Chain Management (SCM), and Electronic Commerce (Gray, 2005). The development of these systems was stimulated by the Year 2000 necessity to re-design large legacy systems to avoid the feared failure of built-in clock algorithms in many of them. Another stimulus to such systems was the more robust web and the trend of the underlying networking towards higher bandwidths.

Vendors of many of these large-scale business systems are adding spatial modules or interfaces to GIS software. An example is the ERP leading vendor SAP, which has introduced spatial connectors. In 2006, there were five technical interfaces that connected ESRI ArcGIS and ArcIMS software with SAP (ESRI, 2006):

(1) SAP remote function calls (RFCs) between SAP and ArcGIS
(2) third-party connectors
(3) the SAP GIS Business Connector
(4) enterprise application integration from both SAP and third parties
(5) direct connections in prototype stage between SAP and ESRI software

Each of the connectors has pluses and minuses. For instance, the Belgian utility firm Pidpa uses ArcIMS to create a website called GeoLink that connects ERP and GIS data. The application is for utility monitoring and maintenance applications known as SCADA. Pidpa is examined as a case study in Chapter 4.

(4) Spatially-Enabled Enterprise Database Products

Enterprise database software has spatially-enabled versions that create a platform strong on database functionality, yet providing extensive spatial functionality as well. This approach to GIS emphasizes seamless incorporation of spatial functions into the backbone databases of the enterprise (Lopez, 2005). It is particularly suitable for large-scale applications involving extensive data and huge user bases across large organizations (i.e. millions of concurrent users). Since that profile is already being well served by enterprise databases for many corporate functions, using the same database with a spatial extension is appealing. These large scale databases tend to be supported by the IT department, not a separate GIS department. It is spatial with an IT flavor to it, emphasizing huge processing and efficiency (Francica, 2005; Lopez, 2005).

Two major database providers, Oracle and IBM, have spatially-enabled database products. In the general database software marketplace in 2004,

Oracle had 34 percent of the market, followed by IBM at 29 percent (Standard and Poors, 2006). Since the database market leader is Oracle, it is not surprising that the firm has led in introducing versions of the database software with spatial functionality.

The recent version of the Oracle database enhanced with spatial functions is Oracle Spatial 10g (Francica, 2005; Lopez, 2005; Oracle, 2005). This database has moderate GIS functionality. Although the GIS functionality is somewhat less than for mainstream GIS software, Oracle Spatial 10g offers potentially greater integration with enterprise software and applications, especially for firms that have already adopted Oracle as a standard. However, for certain areas such as business intelligence and ERP, Oracle Spatial 10g's functionality may exceed standard GIS software (Francica, 2005). The mainstream IT connectivity in the enterprise arena makes Oracle Spatial 10g competitive with traditional GIS software offerings for high-volume, huge-user-base applications. Companies can even have both, Oracle Spatial 10g underneath for generalist applications and one or more traditional GIS software packages running on top for particular specialties (Lopez, 2005). There are also service and consulting firms that provide software add-ons, services, and integration for the web-based Enterprise Applications. The architecture of spatial database applications are compared further in Chapter 8.

Overall, the emerging spatial market includes desktop uses of GIS, traditional client-server GIS software, and web-based enterprise applications (Sonnen et al., 2005). As seen in Figure 1.14, the established GIS market has a high spatial focus and medium to high integration complexity (Sonnen et al., 2005). "Integration complexity" refers to how complex it is to integrate GIS with other systems and applications. Established GIS is an older segment that is informed by a lot of geographical knowledge and a strong and

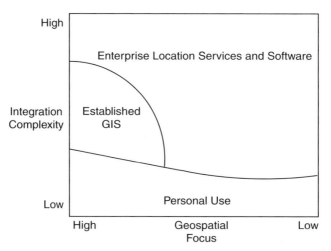

Figure 1.14 Model of Geospatial Markets in 2004. *Source:* Sonnen and Morris, 2004

dedicated workforce of GIS professionals, but less expansive architecture. A second part of the GIS market consists of spatial software for personal use that may be implemented on desktops, laptops, and PDA devices. Its spatial focus varies from high to low. Users range from traditional GIS experts to emerging business users. Its integration complexity is low, but it offers user convenience and flexibility. The emerging market for web-based enterprise applications, seen in the upper right, serves users with mostly middle to low spatial focus, and the applications are medium to high in integration complexity. The most rapid growth in businesses is for the latter group of users, as a number of the case studies will demonstrate.

STRATEGY, COMPETITIVE ADVANTAGE, AND GIS

Companies are successful or unsuccessful in IT depending on how they set up business models, deploy strategies to take advantage of their core competencies, and move ahead of the competition (Applegate et al., 2007). Successful firms need to understand and plan for (1) strategic opportunities and (2) strategic risks (Applegate et al., 2007). Opportunities exist at all times, but are accentuated when firms and industries are undergoing rapid changes, such as happened in the Dot.Com era of the late 1990s. Earlier sections of the chapter have indicated that the early twenty-first century is a time of rapid change and innovation for GIS and spatial technologies in business. The current pace of change is seen by the advent in the past five years of the enterprise web platform for GIS; the advent of widespread RFID uses in firms and industries, often combined with spatial analysis; the appearance of free consumer web packages such as Google Earth; and the increasing sophistication of the large-scale spatial databases such as Oracle Spatial. As in earlier times of change, successful firms will spend time to assess risks and come up with strategies that move the company forward versus its competition. Although the details of strategic and competitive GIS/Spatial are covered in Chapter 12, this section briefly considers the strategic grid and spatial strategic alignment models, and examines them in the context of GIS. The latter is a spatial strategy model for the current period of rapid change and innovation. It underscores why the web integration platform is important in understanding spatial strategies. Sperry Van Ness, a commercial real estate firm, exemplifies as a case how a competitive web strategy for GIS can be successfully implemented.

Two models of strategy are considered. The McFarlan Strategic Grid, seen in Figure 1.15, encompasses the two dimensions of (1) impact on operations, and (2) how strategic it is for the business. The grid can be applied to GIS applications, which may or may not impact business operations and strategy. For instance, Global Integrated Oil's GIS depends on spatial analysis to model its upstream exploration, especially the geological aspects of petroleum deposits and exploration. For GIO's geologic spatial analysis, it's highly strategic and it has a strong impact on operations, i.e. the firm's global explorations could

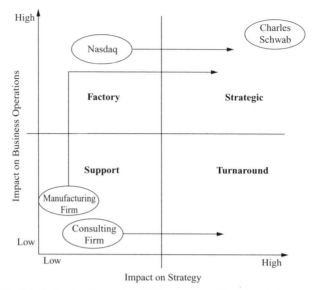

Figure 1.15   McFarlan's Strategic Grid. *Source:* Reprinted by permission of Harvard Business Review. This article was originally published under the title, "Information Technology Changes the Way You Compete," by F. Warren McFarlan in May/June 1984. Copyright © 1984 by the Harvard Business School Publishing Corp.

not be done well today without it. It's clear that GIO's application falls into the Strategic Grid's upper-right cell, i.e. GIO can't get along without it. This model is returned to in Chapter 12.

The second model (Hagel and Brown, 2001) offers a way to organize thinking about spatial strategy. It reasons that the web services architecture increases strategic competitiveness. Firms that have tended to shed their former proprietary and closed approaches to the internet and instead developed interaction with multiple other firms through the web and internet can realize net benefits. Web services can be accessed globally, to combine the best data and software applications available that are affordable and function well together (Hagel and Brown, 2001).

The final chapter will demonstrate through testing with all twenty research cases in the book that the presence of a web integration platform is strongly associated with how strategic GIS is to the company. The implication is that management of firms that can deliberately champion and effectively move forward in the new spatial web environment will tend to do better competitively.

SPERRY VAN NESS: GAINING COMPETITIVE ADVANTAGE FROM GIS

Sperry Van Ness, a private firm founded in 1987, is a rapidly growing commercial real estate brokerage firm with over 1,200 employees and commercial projects throughout the United States. It advises clients and brokers on over a billion dollars annually in retail, industrial, office, multi-family, and land sales transactions. The company has deployed web-based spatial applications that support marketing and sales efforts by its national sales force of 800 people, who are referred to at Sperry as "Advisors." Sperry's Advisors represent the sellers and buyers of commercial properties that range in price from $3 million to $50+ million. Usually the owners are sellers but sometimes are buyers. The top Advisors are hard working, highly paid at often well into six figures, and critical to Sperry's success as a company.

The GIS was developed over the past four years by a manager and team of three technical specialists, a group also responsible for Sperry's IT. The team followed a non-traditional approach for GIS, adopting Microsoft software including MapPoint and MS Virtual Earth on a web platform available both on the company's internet and intranet. GIS user training was emphasized and offered online through the commercial Raindance Conferencing service, which provides combined web and phone training conferences to the Advisors and Advisor Support Center (ASC) staff that can be flexibly deployed across time zones.

The goal of the GIS was to provide the Advisors and Brokers with maps, photos of properties, property sales descriptions, and relevant demographic information in a very user-friendly format. This allows them to showcase online or in person the properties for sale and "tour" prospective investors on the web around sets of prospective properties. For face-to-face meetings with clients, Advisors can use the system to very quickly prepare fancy printed sales material in person. Sperry Van Ness is unique among national brokerage firms in implementing a broker marketing plan along with its investor marketing plan. Its ethos is to encourage cooperation of parties engaged in commercial real-estate transactions. Its three main spatial systems are the following:

1. General public viewing website. A publicly accessible part of the corporate site that lists the firm's properties for sale nationwide, it enables the user to locate properties on a map, see a photo of the property, get basic sales data and the building history, and examine supporting demographic data. An example of the property description and mapping web pages for a similar service is shown in Figure 5.4.

2. Online Publisher, a proprietary and fully featured software package that serves the Owners, Advisors, and the Advisor Support Center (ASC) staff, includes all features from the public site, plus report generation in a highly polished look. Further, it allows the Advisor to "see" out of the property at oblique views, i.e. at 30-degree angles. For any one property, the user can select five viewing angles, a capability called "immersive, birds-eye imagery." The multi-view perspective allows the broker, prospective buyer, and Advisor to imagine themselves inside the property and get a sense of surrounding views, obstructions, and

surrounding neighborhoods. This unique feature, as well as the 1-hour speed in putting together finished packages, sets Sperry apart from the competition. In commercial real estate, speed of response is often of the essence, especially for sought-after properties.

This case demonstrates a firm that is located in the upper-left strategic cell of the McFarlan Strategic Grid, i.e. highly operational and highly strategic. Since Sperry's approach is totally based on an enterprise-web platform, it is correlated with strategic competitiveness as postulated by Hagel and Brown (2001). The firm's top management is enthusiastic about the use of GIS, even though they maintain a practical one- to three-year planning horizon on all facets of the company including GIS.

CHAPTER SUMMARY

Geographic Information Systems emerged as an important factor in the business world over the past ten years. The GIS trends are towards smaller devices, coupling of GIS with associated technologies, web platforms, and enterprise-wide applications. Some huge firms have adopted GIS across their enterprise, as illustrated by Global Integrated Oil, which uses it throughout its value chain and strategically in the upstream exploration and pipeline stages.

GIS and spatial technologies can be strategic and advance firms versus their competitors. Some background on strategy is presented, including the strategic IT grid and web services strategy. The strategic importance of GIS is linked to use of enterprise-web platforms versus traditional client-server. The case study of the medium-sized Sperry Van Ness commercial real estate firm illustrates how well-conceived, user-friendly design in a web environment can be very strategic in providing crucial maps and multimedia sales information to top sales people much faster than the competition.

REFERENCES

Applegate, Lynda M., Robert D. Austin, and F. Warren McFarlan. 2007. *Corporation Information Strategy and Management*, 7th Edition. Boston: McGrawHill-Irwin.

Ashley, Steven. 2003. "Next-Generation GPS." *Scientific American* 289(3): 34.

Astroth, Joe. 2005. "LBS—from Killer App to Killer Enabler." *Directions Magazine*, September 4. Available at www.directionsmag.com.

Austin, Robert D., and Stephen P. Bradley. 2005. "The Broadband Explosion." In Austin, Robert D. and Stephen P. Bradley (eds.), *The Broadband Explosion*, Boston, MA: Harvard Business School Press, pp. 3–20.

Barnes, Scottie, and Heather Gooch. 2004. "Tracking Orkin's Bottom Line." *Geospatial Solutions*, May 1. Available at www.geospatialsolutions.com.

Bisio, Ron. 2005. "Mobile GIS." *GeoWorld*, November.

Boar, Bernard H. 2001. *The Art of Strategic Planning for Information Technology*, 2nd Edition. New York: John Wiley and Sons.

Boas, Nancy. 2004. "Mapping ChevronTexaco's Memory." *CVX* First Quarter, pp. 16–21.

Bossler, J.D. 2002. "An Introduction to Geospatial Science and Technology." In Bossler, J.D. (ed.), *Manual of Geospatial Science and Technology*, London: Taylor and Francis, pp. 3–7.

Brewin, Bob. 2005. "No Silver Bullets." *Federal Computer Week* 19(13): 39. May 2.

CCSF. 2007. "GIS Education Center: Providing GIS Solutions for Industry and the Community at City College of San Francisco." Office of Workforce and Economic Development, City College of San Franciso. Available at ww.ccsf/ resources/geographic_information_systems, June 13, 2007.

Charles, Daniel. 2005. "Do Maps Have Morals?" *Technology Review* (June) 108(6): 77–79.

Choi, S.Y., D.O. Stahl, and A.B. Whinston. 1997. *The Economics of Electronic Commerce*. Indianapolis, IN: Macmillan Technical Publishing (p. 626 has the model of e-commerce market areas).

Clarke, Keith. 2003. *Getting Started with Geographic Information Systems*. Upper Saddle River, New Jersey: Prentice Hall.

Cloud, John. 2002. "American Cartographic Transformation during the Cold War." *Cartography and Geographic Information Science*, July.

Crosswell, Peter L. 2004. "Know the Past to Understand the Present and Future." *GeoWorld*, December, pp. 32–35.

Dangermond, Jack. 2006. "GIS: the Framework for Information Management." *Geospatial Solutions* 16(1): 18–19.

Daratech. 2004. *Geographic Information Systems Markets and Opportunities*. Cambridge, MA: Daratech.

Dodd, Annabel Z. 2005. *The Essential Guide to Telecommunications*, 4th Edition. Upper Saddle River, NJ: Prentice Hall.

Francica, Joe. 2004. "MetaCarta Inc.—Geographical Text Searching." *Directions Magazine*, March 11. Available at www.directionsmag.com.

Francica, Joe. 2005. "LBS: Are Consumers Ready to Blow This Market Open?" *Directions Magazine*, August 6. Available at www.directionsmag.com.

Francica, Joe. 2005. "Oracle Articulates Strategy to Special Interest Group." *Directions Magazine*, March 30. Available at www.directionsmag.com.

Galliers, Robert D., and Dorothy Leidner (eds.). 2003. *Strategic Information Management: Challenges and Strategies in Managing Information Systems*. Oxford: Butterworth-Heinemann.

Geoplace.com. 2005. "Wireless Carriers Extend E911 Deadline." November 21. Available at www.geoplace.com.

GeoWorld. 2005. "Industry Outlook 2005." *GeoWorld*, December, pp. 24–31.

Gewin, Virginia. 2004. "Mapping Opportunities." *Nature* 427:376–377.

Gray, Paul. 2006. *Manager's Guide to Making Decisions about Information Systems*. Hoboken, NJ: John Wiley and Sons.

Greenman, Catherine. 2000. "Turning a Map into a Layer Cake of Information." *New York Times*. January 20.

Hackbarth, Gary, and Brian Mennecke. 2005. "Strategic Positioning of Location Applications for Geo-Business." In Pick, James B. (ed.), *Geographic Information Systems in Business*, Hershey, PA: Idea Group, pp. 198–210.

Hagel III, J., and Brown, J.S. 2001. "Your Next IT Strategy." *Harvard Business Review*, October, 105–113.

Intel. 2003. "Moore's Law." December. Retrieved from www.intel.com.

Sonnen, David, Henry D. Morris, and Dan Vesset. 2005. "Market Analysis: Worldwide Spatial Information Management 2005–2009 Forecast and 2004 Vendor Shares." Framingham, MA: International Data Corporation.

Landt, Jeremy. 2001. *Shrouds of Time: The History of RFID*. Pittsburgh, PA: Association for Automatic Identification and Data Capture Technologies.

Levy, Steven. 2004. "Making the Ultimate Map." *Newsweek*, June 7, pp. 56–58.

Longley, Paul A., Michael F. Goodchild, David J. Maguire, and David W. Rhind. 2005. *Geographic Information Systems and Science*. Chichester, England: John Wiley and Sons.

Lopez, Xavier. 2005. "Business and Technology Trends Driving the Future of Geospatial Technologies: Oracle Corporation's Vision." Paper presented at Oracle Spatial Special Interest Group Meeting, Denver, CO, March 18.

Louwerse, Abraham and Hans van DerMaarel. 2004. "Going Mobile." Powerpoint presentation. Wharton Conference.

MapServer. 2007. "Welcome to MapServer." Minneapolis, Minnesota: University of Minnesota. Available at http://mapserver.gis.umn.edu (May, 2007).

Marble, Duane. 2006. "Who Are We? Defining the Geospatial Workforce." *Geospatial Solutions (May)*, 16(5): 14–21.

McFarlan, F.W. 1984. "Information Technology Changes the Way You Compete." *Harvard Business Review*, 62(3): 98–103.

Meeks, W. Lee, and Subhasish Dasgupta. 2005. "Geospatial Information Utility: An Estimation of the Relevance of Geospatial Information to Users." *Decision Support Systems* 38:47–63.

Meeks, W. Lee, and Subhasish Dasgupta. 2005. The Value of Using GIS and Geospatial Data to Support Organizational Decision Making, in In Pick, James B. (ed.), *Geographic Information Systems in Business*, Hershey, PA: Idea Group, pp. 175–197.

Murphy, L.D. (1996). "Competing in space: the strategic roles of geographic information systems." In *Proceedings of the Association for Information Systems*, AIS, Atlanta, Georgia.

Oracle Corporation. 2005. "Oracle Grid Computing." Oracle Business White Paper, February, 12pp.

Oracle Corporation. 2005. "Oracle Spatial 10g." Oracle White Paper, August, 7pp. Available at www.oracle.com.

Pace, Scott, Gerald P. Frost, Irving Lachow, Dave Frelinger, Donna Fossum, Don Wassem, Monica M. Pinto. 1995. *The Global Positioning System: Assessing National Policies*. Santa Monica: Rand Corporation.

Papp, Raymond. 2001. "Introduction to Strategic Alignment." In Papp, Raymond (ed.), *Strategic Information Technology: Opportunities for Competitive Advantage*, pp. 1–24.

Pick, James B. 2004. "Geographic Information Systems: A Tutorial and Introduction." *Communications of the Association for Information Systems* 14: 307–331.

Pick, James B. 2006. "Strategic Importance of Spatial Technologies and Enterprise-wide Spatial Web Integration: A Case Study Analysis." Paper Submitted to HICSS 2007 Conference.

Roush, Wade. 2005. "Killer Maps." *Technology Review* 108(10): 54–60.

Silwa, Carol. 2003. "Even-driven Architecture Poised for Wide Adoption." *Computerworld*, May 12. Available at www.computerworld.com.

Smith, Gary, and Joshua Friedman. 2004. "3D GIS: A Technology Whose Time Has Come." *Earth Observation Magazine*, November.

Sonnen, David. 2004. "Spatial Information Management: The Road to Enterprise Systems." Powerpoint presentation. Framingham, MA: International Data Corporation.

Sonnen, David, and Henry Morris. 2005. "ESRI: Extending GIS to Enterprise Applications." White Paper. February. Framingham, MA: International Data Corporation.

Sonnen, David, Henry D. Morris, and Dan Vesset. 2004. "Worldwide Spatial Information Management 2005–2009: Forecast and 2004 Vendor Shares." Market Analysis. Framingham, MA: International Data Corporation.

Sonnen, David. 2006. "Pervasive Spatial Information Management." *Geospatial Solutions* 16(1): 20–21.

Standard and Poors. 2006. "Oracle Corp." New York: McGraw-Hill Companies.

The Internet Society. 2006. Data available at www.isoc.org, 6/06.

Tomlinson, Roger F. 2000. "An Overview: The Future of GIS." *ArcNews*, Winter.

Tomlinson, Ralph. 2003. *Thinking about GIS: Geographic Information System Planning for Managers*. Redlands, CA: ESRI Press.

U.S. Census. 2006. "Data on Retail Trade Sales." Available at www.census.gov. 6/06.

Wade, Tasha and Shelly Sommer. 2006. *A to Z GIS*. Redlands, CA: ESRI Press.

Williams, David. 2004. "The Strategic Implications of Wal-Mart's RFID Mandate." *Directions Magazine*, July 29. Available at www.directionsmag.com.

CHAPTER 2

INFORMATION SYSTEMS AND GIS

INTRODUCTION

GIS has foundations in information systems, geography, and other disciplines. In order to understand and apply concepts of Geo-Business, the basic concepts of GIS and spatial analysis need to be explained. One of the starting points is the foundation role of Information Systems in GIS. Although GIS grew up in the public sector with prominent interest in the geographic side, today with the growth of GIS in business, there is more perception of GIS as an information system. Viewed as an IS, the concepts and principles developed in IS since the 1950s become more significant, including architecture, security, systems analysis and design, databases, knowledge building, enterprise systems, and scalability (Laudon and Laudon, 2007). The chapter's overview on information systems first reviews some elements of the concepts of information systems. Next the transformation model of information systems in business is described. Today it is a broad view that encompasses the entire organization, a theme that will be reinforced by considering enterprise systems in Chapter 4. Information systems support users at different levels in the organizational structure, from the low-level clerk up to the Chief Information Officer (CEO). Current systems are becoming increasingly interorganizational, for instance eBay's web auction system whose users frequently represent organizations. Another example is a firm's supply chain software system, which interacts with a dozen other companies' systems for supply chain.

Geo-Business: GIS in the Digital Organization, By James B. Pick
Copyright © 2007 John Wiley & Sons, Inc.

The chapter turns to GIS concepts and definitions. This builds more depth on the rudiments from Chapter 1, including spatial data, data capture, layering, spatial analysis, spatial web services, and the underlying geometry. It explains the process of moving from information with a locational reference, say locations of trucks in a fleet, to associating the reference with the earth i.e. through a coordinate system, and arranging the information in geometries on map layers. Then the information can be analyzed by standard modeling as well as spatial modeling and analysis, i.e. basing models on spatial locations and relationships. An example is a model to determine how many trucks in the fleet pass within 10 miles of major metropolitan areas of over one million population. At the end of this process the results can be mapped so users can visualize outcomes, summarized in tables, and/or fed into other business systems for further processing.

A chapter section examines the essential referent disciplines for Geo-Business, especially business, information systems, and geography, but also statistics, economics, marketing, operations management, and environmental studies. The human and organizational sides are very important including psychology, behavior, and organizations. For instance, the business GIS analyst shown in Figure 2.1 is using a GIS that is based on geography, IS, and systems concepts, but his perceptions, comprehension, and ability to communicate and share results refers to the behavioral and organizational realm. The connections are explained, so the knowledge base for business GIS can be perceived more broadly.

Figure 2.1 GIS Specialist at Work on a Business Problem

The case study of Baystate Health illustrates a medium-sized organization with a dynamic leader in GIS. It shows how GIS finds a place in a technology-laden environment and reinforces information systems, organizational, and GIS concepts.

Spatial data differ from some traditional business data. For instance, accounting data are include in balance sheets, income statements, and return on investments. This information is missing spatial-referencing. The section on spatial data starts by examining how spatial-referencing takes place. It covers essential rudiments of data capture, and coordinate systems. It carries the concept of spatial data further and examines how they are incorporated into data structures and databases.

The chapter then turns to elements of spatial analysis and spatial modeling. In analysis and modeling, spatial information is examined for its relationships, agglomerations, proximities, and trends.

OVERVIEW OF INFORMATION SYSTEMS

Information systems function in businesses to solve problems and help business decision makers. They have become critical at all levels in the organization. They are spreading through businesses, with increasing percentages of business workforces using them.

A broad model of information systems for business problem solving, seen in Figure 2.2, includes a range of entities. The diagram indicates the influence of each of these entities for IS systems to function well. People are essential to IS. They plan, develop, manage, and use information systems. They are also the decision-makers that IS supports. Without people, IS in business

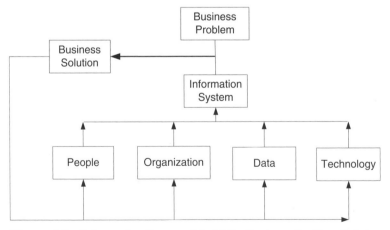

Figure 2.2   Information Systems Model for Business Problem Solving

would accomplish little. The organization is the broader social, behavioral, and strategic setting for the information system. For one thing, most of the people, technology, and data for the system are housed within the organization. Its size, structure, leadership, missions, and strategies influence how, why, and where the information system functions. The goals in the ultimate IS solution are usually to help the organization achieve better performance, productivity, or value.

Data from inside and outside the organization are input into the IS for processing. For instance, on the inside are accounting, financial, marketing, sales, human resources, legal, manufacturing, inventory, R&D, and administrative data. From outside the organization are economic, marketing, political, environmental, urban, technological, consumer-behavior, and demographic data. Data from the outside derive from governments, consulting firms, survey organizations, media, competitors to the extent possible, and other sources. The data are increasingly available online, allowing access from different locations globally.

The technology is critical to any information system. It includes computer hardware, communications networks, sensors, satellites, mobile devices, and data storage. It is assembled together to function as an integrated and reliable technology base. Today, some or all of the technology is increasingly located at an outsourcer, web service provider, communications carrier, or partner company. The rise of outsourcing is due to globalization and cost savings. With the internet and lower communications costs, some services dependent on technology can be moved to lower-cost settings including overseas.

A factor ever present with the technology is the increase in processing and storage capacity. Moore's Law predicts that processor capacity will double about every two years. For instance in Table 1.2, it was seen that processing capacity grew by about half a million times between 1971 and 2006, which is doubling every two and two-thirds years (Intel, 2007). Experts predict a continuing rapid rate of capacity increase (Hiremane, 2005). This parallels other rapid and continuing increases in technological capacities and throughputs. For instance in the communications realm, broadband bandwidths defined by the ITU as 1.54 million bits per second or higher apply to increasing number of business users and to the general population. For the general public in December of 2003, 70.5 percent of South Korean households have broadband, while the figures for Hong Kong (50.3 percent), Canada (36.2 percent), U.S. (22.5 percent), and Belgium (24.7 percent) are also high (Austin and Bradley, 2005). Measured slightly differently, by the percent of total population that had broadband, the results in 2006 were: Denmark (31.9 percent), Netherlands (31.8 percent), Switzerland (28.5 percent), Canada (23.8 percent), Japan (20.2 percent), the United States (19.6 percent), and Australia (19.2 percent) (OECD, 2007). These proportions can be expected to grow, with broadband becoming commonplace in economically advanced nations. Along with higher capacities, is a much wider acceptance and use of web-based technologies, based on the infrastructure to support it.

Another influential technological change is mobile technology. Cell phones increased to several billion worldwide and an estimated 200 million in the United States. Mobile communications are widely utilized in advanced countries and growing rapidly in developing ones. While the majority of older phones have limited data capability, new 3G services provide much greater data bandwidths, offering the potential for new applications. Besides cell phones, prominent mobile technologies include pocket pcs, personal device assistants (PDAs), GPS units, RFID equipment, iPod family of devices, medical monitoring devices, and many more.

Thus the technology element of IS continues to expand dynamically. In Figure 2.2, these four key elements discussed influence the information system. An *information system* collects, processes, stores, analyzes, and outputs data and information for a specific purpose (Laudon and Laudon, 2007). The type of system developed and built depends on the type of business problem, the decisions being made, the users, and the organization.

The output from the IS is intended to support a business problem as seen in the figure. If successful, the business problem will be solved and a business solution will be reached. If not successful in solving the problem, the system can be re-run, or other ways to solve the problem attempted. IS is only one of many tools that are used in business problem solving For instance, a customer is being tracked by a sales team using a customer relationship management (CRM) system. The data are accurate and the technology base works well. The system runs well and provides the sales force with some relevant information to help land the customer. However, if the customer decides to do business with another company, the problem is not solved. The point is that the goal of an information system is to provide support in the decision making process. However, there is no guarantee that the problem will be solved. Whatever the outcome, whether the problem is solved or not, the results are fed back to influence the IS in the future.

Having set this broad context for information systems, two other rudimentary concepts of IS are essential, the systems development process, and the process of data transformation into information and knowledge. The systems development process, sometimes referred to as systems analysis and design, supports the building of new information systems and the upgrading of existing ones. Every system currently in place and operating went through the systems development processes. The standard steps in developing a system are: planning, analysis, design, implementation, and maintenance (Laudon and Laudon, 2007; Satzinger et al., 2007). For instance, a small business is very disappointed with its scheduling system. Consequently in the field, its marketing people cannot keep track of their daily appointments with customers. The company gets a rough idea of some solutions, studies competitors, determines what the cost ranges may be and gets the buy-off from the company president (*planning*). It then looks in depth at alternative systems, checks with users, does careful comparisons of alternatives, and recommends the solution to management (*analysis*). The current system is considered as one of the alternatives. In *design*, the new system is carefully analyzed and specified in detail including user needs, inputs, outputs, data, data flows, process flows, and workflows Some features of the current system might be considered. In *implementation*, the new system is either built in-house or outsourced to an external provider to build. It is tested; users are trained; and it is turned on for use. The process then moves into an extended step of ongoing use of the system, often for many years (*maintenance*). There may need to be bug fixes, changes, repairs, and further training. At some point the system will age or deteriorate to the point that it is either replaced by a new one or undergoes a major upgrade.

Systems Development for GIS is the focus of Chapter 6. It is fortunate that the IS field has developed not only the concept of the stages just mentioned, but methods, techniques, and management approaches to systems development that carry over to GIS.

The final IS concept in this section is the process of data transformation to information and knowledge. *Data* are defined as raw facts that do not have context. For instance, this might be a set of thirty numbers or thirty cars. Neither of these has much value beyond the immediate facts. *Information* is fact that are organized so they have value beyond just being known. For instance, if the cars have been sorted into four brand groups, there is additional value and they become information (Haag et al., 2005). *Knowledge* is information that has a higher level of interpretation through being applied in a certain context. It requires business intelligence, models, and/or experience to have the increased value from information. For instance, the cars have now been tested for performance and the dealership has grouped them into performance quality categories. The added experience and greater context turns the information into knowledge. In Figure 2.2, data become information and knowledge as part of the processes through one or multiple cycles. After several cycles, the box labeled "data" actually becomes a mixture of "data, information, and knowledge." In the chapters upcoming, the business problems and decisions in cases and examples involve at times all three of these concepts.

GIS: CONCEPTS AND DEFINITIONS

This section expands on Chapter 1's initial introduction to GIS and spatial concepts. GIS both builds on the structure of IS concepts as well as on new ones that are particular to space and geography.

The major principles discussed for Information Systems hold true for GIS, which constitutes one type of information system. Referring again to Figure 2.2, a Geographic Information System might be present in the place of an Information System. For GIS, the same entities are present of people, organization, data, and technology. However, the influences are more specific in the following ways:

People. For a GIS, the people need to include some staff and/or outside consultants who are knowledgeable about GIS and spatial concepts. This might be GIS specialists with training and experience concentrated in GIS. It may be IS specialists, networking, and other technology people, who have received some training in GIS and serve partly as GIS staff. Or it might a skilled GIS and spatial group at an outsourcer. For larger companies, it is likely a combination of several of these.

Another set of people that need to be present are non-specialists in the organization, such as executives, managers, people in key GIS user departments, and other support units, who have enough exposure to GIS and spatial technologies to appreciate what they are and why they are useful to the organization. If such a group of GIS-aware people is not present, then awareness training might be needed.

The internal users, users in partner organizations, and customer-users of the system also need to be exposed to GIS and spatial technologies through training and communications. If the spatial application is more sophisticated to use, they would need more of this. For instance, if a multi-featured GIS application is implemented for a large building construction firm, the users including GIS analysts, data-base administrator, systems support people, and programmers, would need more training.

Organization. The organization for a GIS application has all of the ordinary IS roles that have been described. For GIS and spatial applications, the organization needs to give added emphasis to several aspects. First, since GIS is more recent in business, it needs to emphasize organizational learning and training. Second, it needs to provide sufficient support to the GIS specialist function described under People. GIS is often not as established in business as IS, which has been around for a longer time, so the GIS department or group needs sufficient resources to thrive. For instance, for two of the book's twenty research case studies, the GIS manager mentioned in the interview that he/she had not received adequate support from the organization and in one case reported that the IS department resisted GIS including maneuvering to reduce their resources. However, the good news is that mostly GIS was given organizational support and had a good working relationship with IS.

A third aspect for the organization is to gain understanding that GIS development cycle times may be long. This point is emphasized in Chapter 7. The reasons development duration may be lengthy include (1) the necessity to identify and gather spatial data, check it for errors, and often transform it for use, (2) the added time for spatial learning and training, (3) the coordination time between GIS and other associated departments such as IS, networking/communications, engineering, and marketing, and (4) the need sometimes to associate several spatial technologies together, such as server-based GIS, GPS, mobile devices, and sensors.

In short, the organization has all of the ordinary functions for IS plus a number of crucial ones more specific to GIS. This includes dealing with often large amounts of spatial data. In addition, the organization is often challenged by the novelty and rapid innovation pace of spatial technologies.

Data. The data part of the overall scheme has additional aspects with GIS and spatial technologies of locating, cleaning, transforming, and inputting spatial data—in addition to the normal processes to handle attribute data. Even though today many spatial datasets are available through the internet and web, problems remain. Those datasets may not be appropriate to the business problem. They may be restricted from use through copyright or licensing, or may be in a proprietary format that prevents use. They may be of low data quality, a topic covered in Chapter 8. Further, such a dataset may need to be transformed, in order to correspond to spatial data from other sources being used in the same GIS. In addition, for some business problems, the best spatial data may need to be newly collected—they don't already exist. Data can be collected through means of digitizing, geocoding, GPS, scanning aerial photos, and conducting surveys that are discussed in the section on understanding spatial data.

Technology. As emphasized in the first chapter, GIS and spatial technologies have dynamically changed during their over forty years of commercial use, and they continue to evolve. In even the past ten years, among the advances are: mainstream commercial use of RFID, consumer-web spatial services, spatial data warehouses, specialized spatial mobile devices, and geospatial virtual reality. IS technology has also advanced at a rapid pace. However, the specialized knowledge and capacity to plan for emerging spatial technologies needs to be present but often is reduced or missing in a traditional IS department.

Another special aspect of GIS and spatial technologies is the need to integrate them. They need to be integrated with each other, and with enterprise and other mainstream systems. This can sometimes be challenging. For instance, some leading enterprise systems such as ERP do not yet have built-in spatial capacity. Instead, there are specialized "connectors" between them and GIS software. However, often the "connectors" may be difficult to implement and operate, as will be seen in Chapter 4. In sum, the inclusion of GIS brings additional challenges to IT management, particularly the specialized need to track GIS's rapid advances and often heightened system integration challenges.

Most of the remainder of this chapter focuses on details of how GIS is constituted and how it functions. It will cover many of GIS's unique aspects, including coordinate systems, spatial layers, connection of layers to tables, spatial analysis, capturing of spatial data, spatial models, and GIS software.

One foundation IS concept that carries over very well in its principles to GIS is systems development. The five major steps outlined for IS apply to GIS and will form a basis for the coverage of spatial systems development in Chapter 6.

The discussion now turns to rudiments of GIS functioning. It starts with GIS location and coordinates, map layers and their relationship to attribute tables, and discusses what is spatial analysis and provides an example. This builds on the starting material in Chapter 1.

GIS Location and Coordinates

A GIS functions by the input of information that has a location. This is commonly done by identifying the X-Y earth coordinates of an object at a time and place. The most common coordinate system is longitude and latitude. A *longitude* is the east-west angle of a point starting at 0 degrees for the Greenwich, England, observatory. As seen in the figure, they are calculated by determining what meridian an earth point lies on. A meridian is a line on the surface of the earth extending from the North Pole to the South Pole, always at the same longitude. For instance, any point lying on north-south meridian that is at a 22.5° angle to the West of Greenwich, England, lies on the meridian of −22.5 degrees longitude.

The *latitude* is defined as the angle created by a vertex at the earth's geometric center and lines to the equator and a point on the earth's surface. This angle for the north pole is +90 degrees and for the south pole is −90 degrees. Lines circling the earth at a latitude are called parallels, for instance the circle at 45 degrees north of the equator is the 45th parallel (see Figure 2.3). This leads to any point of the earth's surface be identified as (X,Y), where X is the latitude and Y is the longitude.

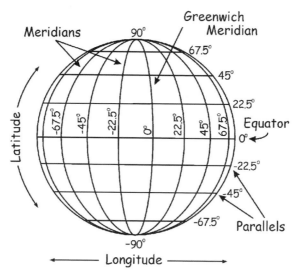

Figure 2.3   Concepts of Longitude and Latitude. *Source:* Bolstad, 2005

Figure 2.4   3-D Visualization of a Park in London, England, Using ArcInfo. *Source:* ESRI

A third dimension can be added for elevation, resulting in (X,Y,Z) co-ordinates. For GIS, three coordinates allow 3-D displays and analysis. For instance, a 3-D display of a park in London, England (Figure 2.4), shows details of the park layout and visualization of buildings surrounding the park, although more the distant buildings have simpler shapes. Such a display could be useful for architects, builders, and city planners. The calculations and processing of 3-D GIS are more intensive than 2-D and special algorithms and solutions are required (Smith and Friedman, 2004). Software vendors have released special software to support it, such as ESRI's ArcView 3-D Analyst (ESRI, 2007).

For maps in (X,Y) coordinate systems, how does the recording of a point location translate into a complex map? This is accomplished by building up two or more points into lines and polygons (i.e. areas). As seen in Figure 2.5, on the left side are a set of seven (X,Y) coordinates in the form of two numbers. The numbers represent the storage of points in a computer. The points are shown by the black points. A pair of points in turn forms the ends of a line. A group of points can form a connected set of lines, as seen to the left of the points. Finally a connected set of lines can form the boundary of a polygon. If the line segments are close enough together, the polygon will appear to curve smoothly. Having formed points, lines, and polygons (areas), they in turn can be combined in a set of layers to portray complex maps. In short, the (X,Y) point locations form the basis for constructing eventually any map shape.

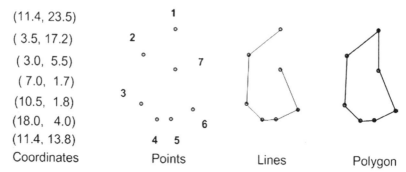

| (11.4, 23.5) |
| (3.5, 17.2) |
| (3.0, 5.5) |
| (7.0, 1.7) |
| (10.5, 1.8) |
| (18.0, 4.0) |
| (11.4, 13.8) |

Coordinates   Points   Lines   Polygon

Figure 2.5 Points, Lines, and Polygons

Map Layers and Their Relationship to Attribute Tables

Once points, lines, and polygons of interest are identified, they can be grouped into map layers.

As introduced in Chapter 1, a GIS starts by the input of attribute and spatial data. The attribute information is mostly numbers and characters; the spatial data are (X,Y) coordinates of points. The GIS functions by combining attribute data in attribute tables with corresponding spatial data in map layers. This was introduced in Chapter 1 as the generic GIS design shown in Figure 1.2. On the right side of the model in Figure 1.2, each map layer represents a map feature. The information in one layer can be in the form of either points, lines, or polygons.

For instance, one map layer consists of the points for a company's thirty-eight distribution centers. This layer would be added to the right in a diagram like Figure 1.2. On the left side of the model are the associated tables. In the example, the table might contain four attributes for each of the thirty-eight distribution centers. The attributes are: floor area (in square feet), number of items received per month, number of items shipped per month, and number of employees in a center. The table has thirty-eight rows (one for each center) and four columns (one for each attribute).

This is made clearer in Figure 2.6, that shows three layers in a GIS, the top one consists of seven polygons (areas) and an associated table having three attributes. The second layer consists of four points and has an associated table with four attributes, while the third layer of five lines has an associated table with two attributes. For the polygon layer, each polygon has its associated attributes in a row of the table. For instance Polygon 2's attributes A, B, and C appear in the row 2 of the table. The number 2 is referred to as the *feature ID*. It appears as the first column in the table, which serves to connect the layer with the table.

The same process applies for the points and the lines. For instance, Line 23 is associated with the attributes P and Q in the third row of the table, having Feature ID 23.

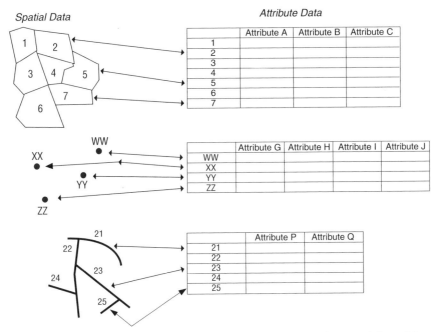

Figure 2.6   Relationship of Spatial Data and Attribute Data. *Source:* Adapted from West, 2000

This simple example can be extended to a larger GIS that may have thirty layers with dozens of attributes per layer. The same principle holds that for a layer, each spatial feature has a unique feature ID that also connotes the row of the table that contains its attributes.

Spatial Analysis—What It Is and an Example

A GIS functions by performing spatial analysis on the information stored in map layers and their associated tables. A simple business example is now presented on how the spatial and attribute data inform spatial analysis.

The business problem is to analyze spatial relationships involving a fast-food company XYZ Inc. in an urban area that has four sales districts and a network of major highways that are located nearby XYZ's fast food outlets. As seen in Figure 2.7, the GIS has two layers. The bottom layer contains the city's major highways. Associated with each major highway segment (represented by straight line, or curved line segments) are four attributes: number of gas stations segment, number of gas stations that sell soft drinks, the highway speed limit, and the total daily vehicle traffic for the segment.

The second layer consists of four areas (polygons), each representing a sales district for XYZ. Associated with each sales district are five attributes: monthly sales, number of employees, customer floor area, number of menu items, and soft drinks as percentage of sales.

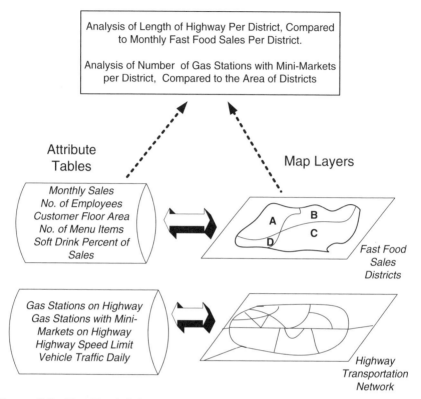

Figure 2.7 Fast Food Sales Regions and Transportation Network: Example of Spatial Analysis

In this example, spatial analysis for XYZ is shown in the box at the top of the figure. The first analysis compares, by sales district, the length of highway in the district versus the average monthly fast food sales in the district. When the highway map is superimposed over the sales district map, it is possible to determine the total length of highway segments within each of the four sales districts. This is referred to as *spatial analysis* because spatial features, not attribute features, are being compared and analyzed to determine an outcome. After the length of highway is computed within each district, it is divided by the average daily food sales per district. This yields the highway length per sales total, so that the districts can be compared to see if some districts are not realizing enough sales given the amount of highway.

The second analysis evaluates how much the presence of gas stations with mini-markets compares to the area of districts. XYZ would like to know if larger districts have more gas-station mini-markets. It consists of calculating, for sales district, the ratio gas stations with mini-markets to area. If the ratio is high, then XYZ's marketing department will give more emphasis to gas stations. It is spatial analysis because the GIS needs to compute the overlap of highway segments and sales districts.

This example demonstrates that even in a simple setting, spatial analysis can yield new insights into business problems. The insights are in addition to other standard analysis and models that could be run using just the attribute information i.e. non-spatial analysis. The chapter now returns to the broader perspective on GIS and addresses how it fits into academic disciplines. Baystate

LINKAGES TO OTHER DISCIPLINES

GIS began in the 1960s and 1970s in departments of geography, landscape architecture, cartography, and remote sensing (Longley et al., 2000a). Over the past two decades, it has branched into other academic disciplines particularly computer science (Longley et al., 2000a); statistics and geostatistics (Getis, 2000); land administration (Dale and McLaren, 2000); urban planning, regional sciences, public policy (Greene, 2000); natural resource, energy, and environmental studies (Harder, 1999); social sciences, medicine, and public health (Khan, 2003); and the humanities (Gregory et al., 2002). Since the 1990s, it has spilled over into the disciplines of business including management (Huxhold, 1991, 1995; Tomlinson, 2003), information systems (Huxhold, 1995), logistics, organizational studies (Reeve and Petch, 1999), real estate (Castle III, 1998; Thrall, 2002), retail management (Longley et al., 2003), marketing (Miller, 2007), and telecommunications (Godin, 2001).

These disciplines have all made conceptual contributions to GIS for business. As shown in Table 2.1, the concepts contributed are essential ones for this book including spatial analysis, systems analysis and design, decision support systems, visualization, geodemographics, cost-benefit analysis, strategic management, and web service models. It will be seen in the book that some of the key literature that supports business GIS comes from these other disciplines.

The blending reveals that GIS today goes across the spectrum of knowledge and relates to a wide variety of disciplines. This is reflected by some schools and universities that have elevated GIS to school-wide or campus-wide focus. The blending of knowledge also has implications for businesses. They also consist of a variety of departments drawing on distinctive knowledge bases. It means that in a business, people from marketing, IS, finance, and real estate have valuable ideas to contribute since their knowledge is part of the broader GIS and spatial knowledge. GIS problem-solving teams in a business can benefit by inclusion of people from several referent areas.

TABLE 2.1 Referent Disciplines for Concepts and Theories of GIS

Concept of Theory in GIS in Business	Referent Discipline(s)	Concept or Theory in GIS in Business	Referent Discipline(s)
Spatial Analysis	Geography, Regional Science	Networking Configuration	Telecommunications
Location Theory	Geography, Operations Research	Visualization	Psychology, Computer Science, Media Studies, Geography, Earth Sciences
Gravity Model	Geography	Geostatistics	Statistics
Remote Sensing	Geography, Earth Sciences	Customer Relationship Management	Marketing, Information Systems
Decision Support Systems	Information Systems	Adoption/Diffusion Theory	Marketing
Knowledge-Based Discovery	Information Systems	Market Segmentation	Marketing, Retail Management
Data Mining	Information Systems	GeoDemographics	
Location Based Services	Information Systems	CAMA and AVM Models	Real Estate
Value of II Investment	Information Systems, Economics	Cost-Benefit Analysis	Economics, Business
Electronic Business	Information Systems, Economics	Organizational Theory Strategic Management	Management, Sociology
Environmental and Geologic Time-Based Models	Natural Resources and Environmental Studies	End User Computing Systems Analysis and Deisgn	Information Systems
Epidemiological Spatial Models	Medicine and Public Health	Data Models, Web Service Structures	Computer Science
		Mapping with Incomplete Data	Humanities

CASE STUDY: BAYSTATE HEALTH

Baystate Health is a very large health-care system in New England. It is based in Springfield, Massachusetts, and has three member hospitals in central and western Massachusetts. There is a children's hospital and a variety of facilities for health services as well as health centers. GIS is part of the health geographics program that has been in place since the mid 1990s. The GIS applications started in the Department of Surgery. The department, an accomplished practicing surgeon, came to Baystate with responsibility to re-energize Baystate's research program. There the first Baystate GIS application was identified and implemented in injury prevention. A biostatistician was added who had a GIS certificate, followed by two GIS professionals. There is now a four-person department chaired by the chief surgeon, which makes this department unique among U.S. hospitals in its size and experience (Kolb, 2001).

GIS is utilized in a wide variety of applications within the Baystate system. They include:

Emergency planning. Baystate participates in multi-state regional emergency planning. In multi-state emergency exercises, Baystate has provided situational maps and other GIS support to the Regional Coordination Center.

Epidemiology. Epidemiology has been a long-time part of the GIS at Baystate, beginning as part the chief surgeon's emphasis on research. Early on, GIS helped in epidemiological and statistical analysis of breast cancer and injuries, and it extended to youth violence. Currently Baystate is collaborating with United Way in western Massachusetts to produce a CD of epidemiology to distribute to all health services in that part of the state.

Routing. GPS-enabled route optimization and route management are available for two delivery systems—homebound patients and lab specimens. Some in-house software additions have been made to commercial software.

Hospital floor plan maps. A disaster patient tracking system links the master patient database to floor plan maps of the hospital, which would support the hospital not just in finding a bed but in finding a bed located near the appropriate services.

Emergency services. Baystate's emergency services center utilizes GIS for dispatch and to study spatial patterns of former emergency patients, examining the services they received compared to their demographic and financial attributes. It has the goal to identify patients who should not be going to emergency rooms.

Human body. Baystate has designed and implemented a unique GIS for viewing the human body in 2-D and 3-D. It has been notably applied to understand the locations and statistically analyze the locations of colon polyps and lesions, including cancers, based on a new coordinate system for this study.

In accomplishing this wide set of applications, the Health Geographics team has collaborated with other Baystate departments and multiple external government and nonprofit organizations—in emergency planning, community health care, and epidemiology. Led by a surgeon-champion of GIS use, the team has acted as a change agent for the whole organization, moving it into a national leadership position in hospital GIS. Curiously, almost none of Baystate's administrative systems have so far been spatially-enabled, with the exception of some aspects of facilities management (floor plans). GIS has stayed on the medical and health side. This may be why GIS is not yet recognized as strategic by Baystate's top management, many of whom may be closer to the administrative and financial side of Baystate.

The case illustrates many of the chapter concepts. It demonstrates the influences seen and discussed for the GIS version of the model in Figure 2.2. It confirms the importance of people and the organization in achieving GIS solutions. Leadership is seen to have been essential for the build-up in only ten or so years to national prominence. The case demonstrates the significance of an interdisciplinary body of knowledge of GIS. At Baystate GIS benefited by people from diverse health-care departments being involved. There remains the potential to have the same impact on the business/administrative side of the organization.

UNDERSTANDING SPATIAL DATA AND MAPPING

This section examines spatial data and mapping. These are large topics that readers can find a lot more about in sources that focus fully on them (Brewer, 2005; Bolstad, 2005; Clarke, 2003; Heywood, 2006; Longley et al., 2006b).

Spatial data can come ready-made from governments, businesses, consultants, nonprofits, and portals. Among the prominent locations to obtain pre-set spatial data are the GeoData.gov (sometimes called Geospatial One-Stop), U.S. Census (www.census.gov), and The Geography Network (www.geographynetwork.com). *GeoData.gov* can help a user locate a data or map service, create a map, browse information regarding geospatial data, and cooperate on data acquisitions. The latter feature is a bulletin board for locating partners or seeking partners in acquiring spatial data. It's possible to use the "Marketplace Map" to indicate a certain geography is of interest for partnering, and a list will be produced of prospective partners for that geographic area. There is a grants area to find opportunities for geospatial funding. A sample map created by GeoData.gov's Map Viewer (see Figure 2.8) shows the transportation network encompassing Kansas City and Wichita, Kansas.

The *U.S. Census* site has a wealth of economic, demographic, and social information and maps for the United States. The maps extend down to small areas within cities and cover hundreds of variables. The user can create maps using the Census map service tools, or download data to use with a commercial software package. *The Geography Network* is a nonprofit spatial data portal that provides maps and data, both free and at cost, for geographies worldwide on subjects covering a vast range of topics, including geography, geology, environmental, social, and business. Some of the data areas are richer with data than others, for instance a wide range of environmental

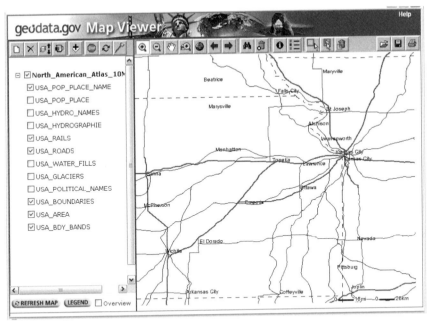

Figure 2.8   GeoData.gov Map Viewer Display of Transportation Network that Includes Kansas City and Wichita, Kansas. *Source:* GeoData.gov

offerings are provided, but the business ones are limited, likely due to the proprietary nature of much business data. The portal is sponsored by ESRI Inc. and supported by Sun for hardware. It allows sharing among private and governmental providers of data, web services, and other users globally.

In attempting to locate appropriate existing resources, "the trick is knowing where to look, what to do when you find what you want, and how to get the data into your GIS" (Clarke, 2003).

If commercial map sources do not provide an appropriate map or spatial data, then other means must be used to capture spatial data. Among the major ways are digitizing, scanning, using GPS devices, or utilizing satellite and remote-sensed data.

Digitizing

Digitizing manually transcribes an existing hardcopy map into digital form. As seen in Figure 2.9, a user moves a digitizing puck across the hardcopy map fastened to a digitizing tablet and follows click sequences to enter the points with (X,Y) coordinates. Digitizing is time-consuming and error-prone but might be necessary today if only the hardcopy map is available as a source.

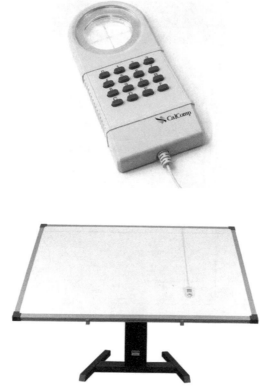

Figure 2.9 Digitizing Mouse and Tablet. *Source:* © GTCO CalComp, Inc., used by permission

Scanning

A hardcopy map can be entered using a scanner. After entry, software programs along with a mouse can be used to identify features on the screen, i.e. points, lines, and polygons. It is quick to scan a map, but the identification of features remains manual and time-consuming.

Use of GPS

GPS provides very accurate positioning by connecting to a system of twenty-four satellites that orbit the earth at middle range of about 12,000 miles. The GPS receiver receives signals from those satellites that are not blocked by the earth. Normal GPS accuracy is within a ten to twenty-five meter range, but when used differentially, i.e. with one device fixed and another moving around, the range can be sub-meter. An example of a GPS unit that is hardened for field use is seen in Figure 2.10. The GPS can read at timed

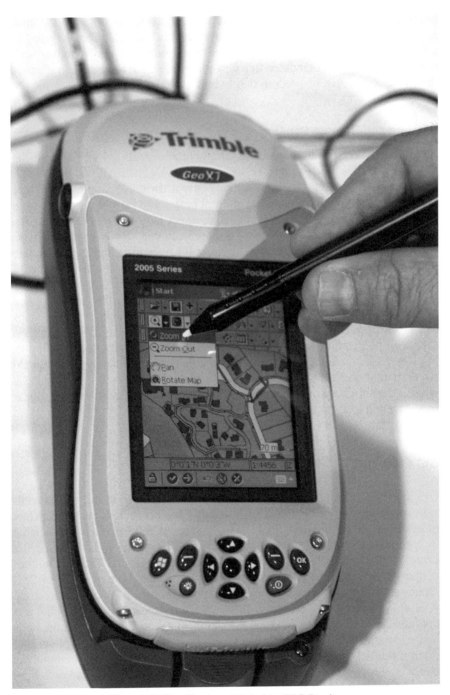

Figure 2.10   Hardened Trimble GPS Device

intervals or when the user requests. The (X,Y) location is stored in the unit, and depending on its design can be transmitted immediately or on return to a fixed workstation. GPS has become prevalent today in some countries such as the U.S. that have mandated that new phones need to to be able to identify their location precisely, predominantly by GPS capability.

Satellite and Remote Sensing

Satellite imagery became available commercially starting in 1972 with the Landsat satellites. Today such services as SPOT, INTELSAT, and the NOAA satellites provide extensive satellite imagery worldwide. Examples of satellite and aerial photography images at different scales and resolutions are seen in Figure 2.11 (Clarke, 2003). This provides exact land features that are often superimposed on feature maps, so both are available. The accuracy is high, but locating the correct imagery with the right resolution and type of image takes training and experience. Also, satellites are limited by land cover, so one cannot see beneath nature's canopies or into built structures.

Once spatial data have been entered into a GIS data-base, they are expressed in layers and processed in ways that have been discussed. The resulting maps can be displayed in hardcopy, on monitor screens, and in mobile devices. They can be displayed along with tables and other imagery such as photos. Figures 2.12 and 2.13 show several examples of map display. A handheld street map of part of the city of Redlands, California, is seen in Figure 2.12, while a digital photo of a feature and the corresponding satellite map appear in a screen display in Figure 2.13.

GIS ANALYSIS

GIS analysis techniques consist of methods that are used in the spatial analysis, modeling, and statistical analysis of a GIS. This section describes a few of the most common spatial analysis techniques. A full treatment is available in specialized sources (Mitchell, 1999; Getis, 1999; Lo and Yeung, 2002; Longley and Batty, 2003). Spatial analysis consists of analytical techniques that emphasize the map layers, portrayed on the right side of Figure 1.2. It relates and compares the features of the physical locations of objects in space (Getis, 1999; Longley and Batty, 2003). Since it draws from geography, it is not familiar to most IS researchers. Modeling and statistical analysis methods include many methods and techniques well known in business disciplines, but often modified to take into account spatial relationships. These methods are based on attribute and spatial data, portrayed on both sides of Figure 1.2. Specialized statistical methods that include space are referred to as geostatistics (Getis, 1999). Some desktop/laptop software packages include geostatistics modules, such as ArcGIS Geostatistical Analyst (Johnston, 2001).

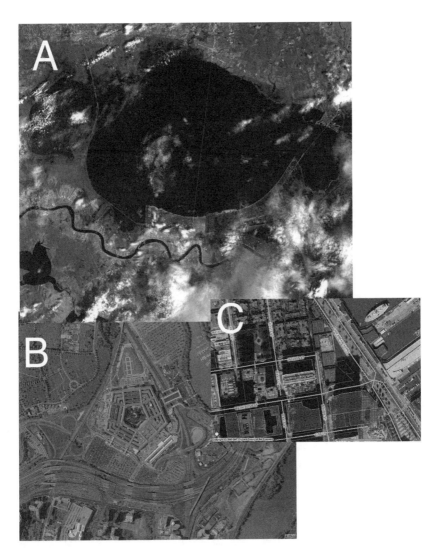

Figure 2.11 Imagery Used in GIS, (a) Landsat image, (b) Digital Orthophoto of Washington DC, (c) Aerial photography of San Francisco with vector GIS overlay. *Source:* (a) and (b) Courtesy of USGS, (c) City and County of San Francisco

Spatial Analysis

Since spatial analysis techniques compare spatial features, they can, for example, determine how many points are inside a polygon, how many line segments cross a polygon boundary, or how much polygons overlap each other. A practical example would be to ask how many highways and streets (lines) cross a zone of retail businesses.

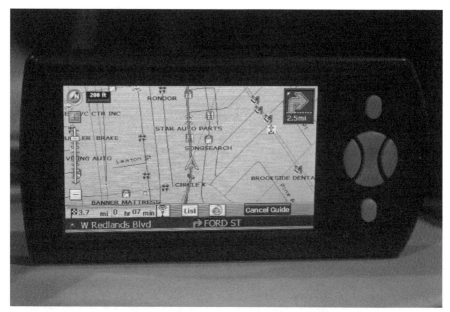

Figure 2.12   Handheld GPS Unit Showing Redlands Streets and Businesses

Figure 2.13   Digital Photo and Associated Satellite Image Displayed Together

Buffer Analysis

In buffering, GIS software forms bands on all sides of a point, line, or polygon, in order to perform analysis within the bands. A simple example would be to assign half-mile buffers on both sides of a highway, in order to query how many service stations are within the buffer.

Map Overlay Functions

Overlay consists of superimposing two or more map layers. Quite a few operations for map overlays are typically supported. One example is the union procedure, in which two polygon layers are combined to result in a third output polygon layer. The resultant layer has the identical geographic extent as the two layers that form it, and it concatenates the attributes from those two layers in its associated data-base (Greene and Stager, 2005). The polygons from the original two layers are cut up wherever they cross to form a larger set of polygons in the output layer as seen in Figure 2.14.

This diagram shows one layer that has census blocks and a second layer with three store sales areas. The resultant overlay on the bottom combines all these features. The attributes of each layer are combined into a resultant table (not shown). The advantages of overlay procedures include the ability for form new layers that can provide new insights. The business purpose in the example is to understand the complex pattern of census block attributes and how it relates to the sales areas (Greene and Stager, 2005).

Examples of more sophisticated spatial analyses include uses for industrial specialization and location quotient analysis in an urban labor market and for trade area analysis, based on a gravity model, which can examine customers' attractions to competing consumer destinations. Greene and Stager (2005) discuss the gravity model with respect to attraction of major opera houses in northern Illinois and southern Wisconsin.

Proximity Analysis

Proximity analysis assesses how close certain map features are to other map features. For instance, it can determine how many customers are in a grocery store's trade area.

Census Blocks   Store Sales Areas   Overlay of Census Blocks
                                                   and Store Sales Areas

Figure 2.14 Map Overlay Example. *Source:* Modified from Greene and Stager, 2005

Longitudinal Change Detection

This type of analysis compares maps over time, and assesses what significant spatial changes have taken place. For instance, real estate maps produced for a suburb on an annual basis can show variations in the spatial patterns of housing prices and their changes over time.

Modeling and Forecasting

Forecasting and simulation models can be built with spatial data, and the results displayed in map form. An example is a model that projects the population distribution of retail consumers within a county, based on starting year data. The future population distributions of retail consumers can be mapped, to inform businesses and the public.

Statistical Analysis

Statistical models are often applied to study the relationships of certain spatially referenced attributes to other attributes (Getis, 1999). They include correlation, regression, analysis of variance (ANOVA), cluster analysis, principles components, and t tests. Often the methods are corrected or refined for geostatistics (Getis, 1999). The input data, as well as the results, of many of these models can be represented as spatial displays. This enhances understanding of the geographical effects and influences. Although beyond the scope of this chapter, a specialized part of statistics, called geostatistics, takes especially into account spatial effects and interactions, such as spatial autocorrelation (Getis, 2000). An example is a regression forecast of the future spatial patterns of demand for advertising services in an urbanized area.

EXAMPLE: LOCATION QUOTIENT ANALYSIS FOR SITING

A common problem facing businesses is the decision on where to site new facilities that include retail outlets, distribution sites, factories, service offices, and administrative offices. The decisions are often influenced by concentrations of business facilities for the industry as a whole. For example, professional services firms often group together in the same urban zones to share workforce pools, services, and customers. Similar agglomeration is present for locational groups of hotels and restaurants. The location quotient (LQ) indicates the ratio of proportion of workforce in a particular industrial sector for an urban zone to the proportion of workforce in that industrial sector for the entire urban area. An LQ of 100 indicates the proportion of workforce in the zone is the same as that for the urban area, while an LQ of 400 indicates the zone's proportion is four times the urban area's (Greene and Stager, 2005; Greene and Pick, 2006).

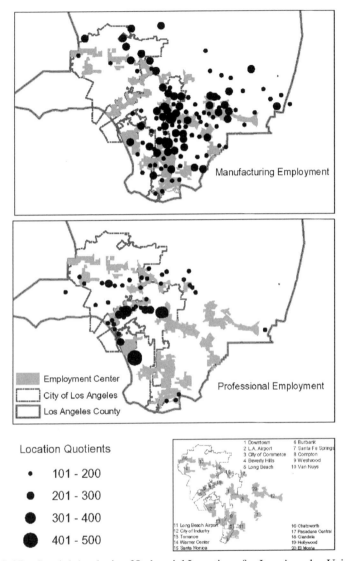

Figure 2.15   Spatial Analysis of Industrial Locations for Los Angeles Using Location Quotient. *Source:* Greene and Stager, 2005

LQ spatial analysis maps the levels of LQs for an urban area. For example Figure 2.15 shows LQs for manufacturing employment and professional employment for the Los Angeles urban area. A high-tech business that manufactures and provides professional services can use maps such as these to make decision on siting of its plants, R&D facilities, and office locations. For a large corporation with locations in hundreds of cities worldwide, LQ spatial analysis can lead to competitive advantage on a national or global scale.

NATIONAL SPATIAL DATA INFRASTRUCTURES

Governments have recognized the importance of spatial information by establishing National Spatial Data Infrastructures (NDSIs), sometimes referred to as Spatial Data Infrastructures (SDIs) (Masser, 2005). Governments can create national data infrastructures that apply to the nation as a whole. Early adopters of NDSIs are Australia, Canada, Indonesia, Japan, Korea, Malaysia, Netherlands, Portugal, Qatar, the UK, and the U.S. In the U.S, an NDSI vision was set forward by the Office of Management and Budget in 2002 (Masser, 2005). The lead agency is the FGDC (Federal Geographic Data Committee) in the U.S. Geological Survey the Department of Interior that supports the goals of the U.S. NSDI of data sharing, use and dissemination nationally of spatial data, and the interoperability of federal spatial systems (Masser, 2005). "The NSDI is a physical, organizational, and virtual network designed to enable the development and sharing of this nation's digital geographic information resources." (FGDC, 2007). Since much of the spatial data of businesses comes from government sources, the development and growth of NDSIs worldwide is a significant trend.

GEOWEB

The user-friendly environment that supports less technically skilled web-based users is called the *GeoWeb* (Dangermond, 2006; Lake, 2006). It has been defined as "a large, widespread, distributed collaboration of geospatial knowledge services that can be dynamically interrelated and orchestrated for application support" (Dangermond, 2006). The GeoWeb involves the spatial web services that are not just a group of isolated services acting separately, but services collaborating with each other and exchanging information in orchestrated steps. The GeoWeb is global and is not slowed by geographical or jurisdictional boundaries (Dangermond, 2006; Lake, 2006). Good examples of the GeoWeb have occurred in times of disaster. For instance, following Hurricane Katrina in 2005, emergency spatial information was available as a set of map web services. This made the information widely available to a disrupted and scattered citizenry as well as to hard-pressed emergency workers. Another example is the real estate industry, which has had strong adoption of a variety of map web services, including such organizations as book cases Sperry Van Ness, Prudential Preferred Realty, Trulia.com, and Fanny Mae Foundation. These and others overlap in their APIs, mapping data sources, and attribute data sources, and sometimes interact with each other. The upshot is that the way of doing business in real estate has changed, for instance many customers no longer need to take home tours. Figure 2.16 shows GeoWeb users in a corporation discussing a problem.

In the GeoWeb, map services are available for mapping, geocoding, gazetteer (online atlases), viewing terrain in 3-D, image processing,

Figure 2.16   GIS Specialists Working on a Problem

multimedia, sensor data, real-time monitoring, and cataloging of metadata (Dangermond, 2006; Lake, 2006). The services are able to collaborate and to exchange information. Behind this are agreements, standards, and procedures.

Along with movement in GIS and spatial applications towards the GeoWeb environment, mainstream IT is becoming spatially-enabled. An important dimension of this for enterprise systems will be seen in Chapter 4. ERP, CRM, and other large-scale backbone IT systems were originally introduced as non-spatial, but many now offer inherent spatial features or connectors to spatial software. Even with the spatial features, these mainstay applications are not centered on spatial, but rather on supporting the company's underlying business processes. The spatial features are available when needed to add to the support. Likewise, for spatial decision support systems, the spatial component is a complement to existing models. For instance in the LCI case in Chapter 3, underwriters nationally utilize models to price policies that include spatial features, but the system is principally IT-oriented. In fact, the underwriters usually prefer not to look at maps, but benefit through spatial analysis by having more accurate modeling outcomes. As spatial techniques are only one one of multiple components in these models, these are IT systems that are spatially-enabled rather than GIS (Barnes, 2001; Sonnen, 2006).

FUTURE TRENDS IN SPATIAL TECHNOLOGIES

Where is the evolution of spatial technologies heading? Among the future trends are the following (Buyya and Venugopal, 2005; Dangermond, 2006; Sonnen, 2006):

- GIS and spatial technologies will become commonplace in IT systems.
- Spatial Data Infrastructures (SDIs) will offer architectures to share geographic information nationally and internationally.

- The spatial centralized storage areas of enterprise systems in organizations will become larger and more efficient.
- More spatial and GIS software code will become openly available, leading to a more open source environment.
- Spatial standards will become more widely accepted, as well as vendor compliance with standards.
- Satellite, sensor, and other spatial data gathered in real-time will be pervasive and permeate real-time business systems.
- GIS-enabled and locationally-aware mobile technologies will become prevalent.
- For the web infrastructure, greater collaboration, range, and intensity of spatial web services will occur through movement towards the emerging concepts of semantic web, spatial agents, and Grid computing. Grid computing will be discussed in the end section of Chapter 5.

CHAPTER SUMMARY

The chapter has provided an overview of key concepts from Information Systems that form one of the bases for GIS in business. These concepts were related to GIS as a type of IS. The chapter then proceeded to provide more background on spatial functioning including the point location, coordinate systems, and forming map layers from points, lines, and polygons.

The linkages of GIS to other disciplines are important since a mixture of concepts and theories are brought to bear in the business context. The case study of Baystate Health concerns a successful health-care system that has introduced GIS through fine leadership, development of professional staff, carefully chosen spatial applications that are meaningful, and organizational collaborations internally and externally.

The chapter examines the key topics for any GIS of data sources, entry of spatial data, and spatial analysis. The latter is illustrated by a location quotient example. It ends by considering Spatial Data Infrastructures, the concept of GeoWeb, and the future trends in spatial technologies.

ACKNOWLEDGMENT

Part of the section on spatial analysis was published in an article of *Communications of the Association for Information Systems* (Pick, 2005). It is used with the permission of the journal.

REFERENCES

Aoyama, Yuko, Samuel Ratick, and Guido Schwarz. 2006. "Organizational Dynamics of the U.S. Logistics Industry: An Economic Geography Perspective." *The Professional Geographer* 58(3): 327–340.

ArcNews. 2004. "On Demand, In Demand—ArcWeb Services." Special Section. *ArcNews* 7(4): 40–46.

ArcNews. 2005. "New Version of ArcWeb Services Allows Users to Customize Services." *ArcNews* 27(2): 1–3.

ArcUser. 2000. "Choosing the Best Projection." *ArcUser*, 23.

Austin, Robert, and Stephen Bradley. 2005. *The Broadband Explosion*. Cambridge, MA: The Harvard Business School Press.

Bolstad, Paul. 2005. *GIS Fundamentals*, 2nd Edition. White Bear Lake, MN: Elder Press.

Brewer, Cynthia A. 2005. *Designing Better Maps: A Guide for GIS Users*. Redlands, CA: ESRI Press.

Brewin, Bob. 2005. "No Silver Bullets." *Federal Computer Week*, 19(13): 39, May 2.

Chen, Y.H. 2004. "Getting Ready for RFID." *OR/MS Today* (31)3, pp. 30–35.

Chilsholm, Patrick. 2005. "RFID." *Military Medical Technology*. Online Edition. http://www.military-medicial-technology.com/print_article.cfm?DocID=431.

Clarke, K. 2003. *Getting Started with Geographic Information Systems*, 4th Edition. Upper Saddle River, New Jersey: Prentice Hall.

Croft, John. 2005. "RFID: Be Not Afraid." *Overhaul and Maintenance*, Washington, D.C., April 1.

Dale, P.F., and R.A. McLaren. 2000. " GIS in Land Administration." In Longley, P.A., M.F. Goodchild, D.J. Maguire, and D.W. Rhind (eds.), *Geographical Information Systems*, Two volumes, New York: John Wiley and Sons Inc., 859–875.

Dangermond, Jack. 2006. "GIS Enterprise Architecture: Unifying the Utility." *GITA 2006 Proceedings*.

ESRI. 2005. "About ArcWeb Services." Available at www.esri.com.

ESRI. 2006a. "ArcGIS." Redlands, CA: ESRI Inc.

ESRI. 2006b. "ArcGIS 3D Analyst." Redlands, CA: ESRI Inc.

ESRI. 2007. "MapObjects-Windows Edition." Available at www.esri.com.

FGCD. 2006. Federal Geographic Data Committee Website. Reston, Virginia: FGCD. Available at www.fgcd.gov.

Galuszka, Peter. 2005. "Lessons from Baghdad." *Chief Executive*, Vol. 208, May, p. 48.

Getis, A. 2000. "Spatial Statistics." In Longley, P.A., M.F. Goodchild, D.J. Maguire, and D.W. Rhind (eds.), *Geographical Information Systems*, Volume 1, New York: John Wiley and Sons Inc., pp. 239–251.

Godin, L. 2001. *GIS in Telecommunications*. Redlands, CA: ESRI Press.

Gregory, I., K. Kemp, and R. Mostern. 2002. "Geographical Information and Historical Research: Integrating Quantitative and Qualitative Methodologies." *Humanities and Computing*.

Greene, R.P., and J.C. Stager. 2005. "Techniques and Methods of GIS in Business." In Pick, J.B. (ed.), *Geographic Information Systems in Business*, Hershey, PA: Idea Group, pp. 36–55.

Greene, R.W. 2000. *GIS in Public Policy*. Redlands, CA: ESRI Press.

Guerrero, Ignacio. 2005. "Emerging Technologies in the Geospatial Industry." In *Proceedings of the Annual Conference of the Geospatial Information and Technology Association (GITA)*, GITA: Aurora, CO.

Haag, Stephen, Maeve Cummings, and Amy Phillips. 2005. *Management Information Systems*. New York: McGraw Hill.

Harder, Christian. 1997. *Arcview GIS Means Business*. Redlands, CA: ESRI Press.

Harder, Christian. 1999. *Enterprise GIS for Energy Companies*. Redlands, CA: ESRI Press.

Heywood, Ian. 2006. *An Introduction to Geographical Information Systems*, 3rd Edition. Upper Saddle River, NJ: Prentice Hall.

Hiremane, Radhakrishna. 2005. "From Morre's Law to Intel Innovation—Prediction from Reality." *Technology@Intel Magazine*, April, 3–8.

Huxhold, William E. 1991. *An Introduction to Urban Geographic Information Systems*. New York: Oxford University Press.

Huxhold, William E., and A.G. Levinsohn. 1995. *Managing Geographic Information Systems Projects*. New York: Oxford University Press.

Johnston, K., J.M. Ver Hoef, K. Krivoruchko, and N. Lucas. 2001. *Using ArcGIS Geostatistical Analyst*. Redlands, CA: ESRI Press.

Karini, Hassan A., and Amin Hammad. 2004. *Telegeoinformatics*. Boca Raton, FL: CRC Press.

Keenan, P. 2005. "Concepts and Theories of GIS in Business." In Pick, J.B. (ed.), *Geographic Information Systems in Business*, Hershey, PA: Idea Group, pp. 1–19.

Kolb, Karen. 2001. "Medical Center Improves Care, Prevention Programs with GIS." *ArcUser* 4(3): 24–25.

Laudon, Kenneth C., and Jane P. Laudon. 2007. *Essentials of Business Information Systems*, 7th Edition. Upper Saddle River, NJ: Prentice Hall.

Lo, C.P., and K.W. Yeung. 2002. *Concepts and Techniques In Geographic Information Systems*. Upper Saddle River, NJ: Prentice Hall.

Longley, P.A., M.F. Goodchild, D.J. Maguire, and D.W. Rhind. 2000a. "Introduction." In Longley, P.A., M.F. Goodchild, D.J. Maguire, and D.W. Rhind (eds.), *Geographical Information Systems*, Two volumes, New York: John Wiley and Sons Inc., pp. 1–20.

Longley, P.A., M.F. Goodchild, D.J. Maguire, and D.W. Rhind (eds.). 2000b. *Geographical Information Systems*, Two volumes. New York: John Wiley and Sons Inc.

Longley, P.A., and M. Batty (eds.). 2003. *Advanced Spatial Analysis: The CASA Book of GIS*. Redlands, CA: ESRI Press.

Maguire, David J. 2006. "*New Approaches for GIS-based Modeling and Analysis.*" *GITA 2006 Proceedings*.

Masser, Ian. 2005. *GIS Worlds: Creating National Spatial Data Infrastructures*. Redlands, CA: ESRI Press.

Miller, Fred. 2007. *GIS Tutorial for Marketing*. Redlands, CA: ESRI Press.

Mitchell, A. 1999. *The ESRI Guide to GIS Analysis Volume 1: Geographic Patterns and Relationships*. Redlands, CA: ESRI Press.

Moore, John. 2005. "RFID's Positive Identification." *Federal Computer Week* 19(11): 53, April 18.

OECD. 2007. "OECD Broadband Statistics to December 2006." Directorate for Science, Technology, and Industry. Paris: Organisation for Economic Co-operation and Development. Available at www.oecd.org/sti/ict/broadband on June 15, 2007.

Oliva, Lawrence M. 2004. *IT Security: Advice from Experts.* Hershey, PA: CyberTech Publishing.

O'Sullivan, David, and David Unwin. 2003. *Geographic Information Analysis.* Hoboken, NJ: John Wiley and Sons.

Pick, James B. 2004. "Geographic Information Systems: A Tutorial and Introduction" *Communications of the Association for Information Systems,* 14: 307–331.

Ray, J. 2005. "Spatial Data Repositories: Design, Implementation, and Management Issues." In Pick, J.B. (ed.), *Geographic Information Systems in Business,* Hershey, PA: Idea Group, pp. 80–112.

Reeve, D.E., and J.R. Petch. 2002. *GIS, Organisations and People: A Socio-Technical Approach.* London: Taylor and Francis.

RFID Journal. 2003. "Military Edict: Use RFID by 2005." *RFID Journal,* October 3. Available 5/12/05 at www.rfidjournal.com.

RFID Journal. 2003. "U.S. Military to Issue RFID Mandate." *RFID Journal,* September 15. Available 5/12/05 at www.rfidjournal.com.

Satzinger, John W., Robert B. Jackson, and Stephen D. Burd. 2004. *Systems Analysis and Design,* 3rd Edition. Boston: Thompson Course Technology.

Smith, Gary, and Joshua Friedman. 2004. "3D GIS: A Technology Whose Time Has Come." *Earth Observation Magazine,* November.

Sonnen, David, and Henry D. Morris. 2005. "Oracle 10g: Spatial Capabilities for Enterprise Solutions." IDC White Paper. Framingham, MA: International Data Corporation.

Sugumaran, Ramanathan, Shiram Ilavajhala, and Vijayan Suguraman. 2007. "Development of a Web-Based Intelligent Spatial Decision Support System (WEBISDSS): A Case Study with Snow Removal Operations." In Hilton, Brian (ed.), *Emerging Spatial Information Systems and Applications,* Hershey, PA: Idea Group Publishing, pp. 184–202.

Sun Microsystems. 2005. "RFID Keeps U.S. Troops Well Stocked." Available 5/12/2005 at http://www.sun.com/solutions/documents/articles/go_rfid_dod.xml.

Tao, Vincent. 2003. "The Smart Sensor Web." *GeoWorld,* 16(9): 28–32.

UCGIS. 2007. University Consortium for Geographic Information Science. Website. Available at www.ucgis.org.

U.S. Geological Survey. 2002. Geographic Information Systems. Washington, D.C.: U.S. Geological Survey.

CHAPTER 3

SUPPORTING BUSINESS DECISIONS

INTRODUCTION

Spatial technologies are growing rapidly and becoming more web-dependent and competitive. Information systems today support the enterprise almost from top to bottom as an essential element (Gray, 2006). GIS rests on the IS foundation and as well on geospatial concepts and methods. IS and GIS are linked together through common elements such as database, networking, systems development, and IS organizational and management principles. On the other hand they differ in GIS's recognition of location, mapping, and IS's greater scope. GIS and IS have in common their support for business decisions.

GIS and spatial technologies have a crucial role in supporting people in businesses to make decisions. This resembles IS's longer established role in business decision-making. The IS field has well-known systems for decision-support including decision support systems (DSS) and business intelligence (BI) (Marakas, 2002; Power, 2002; Gray, 2006). For GIS, there are the relatively new concepts of spatial decision support systems (SDSS) and spatial business intelligence. An example of these concepts is models and data that help bank managers overseeing a rapidly expanding branch network to make better decisions on locating some branches, while closing, merging, or relocating others. These decisions are based on spatial displays and analysis of the customer base, the competition, and branch locations.

This chapter concerns GIS and spatial technologies applied to business decision-making. It starts with the concepts of decisions, decision support

Geo-Business: GIS in the Digital Organization, By James B. Pick
Copyright © 2007 John Wiley & Sons, Inc.

systems, and spatial decision support. A case study of spatial decision support in the U.S. division of a global bank is given. The chapter then looks at spatial decision support systems and spatial business intelligence (spatial BI), seeking to explain their concepts, models, and applications. It finishes with a case on spatial decision-making in a large U.S. insurance firm.

GIS TO SUPPORT DECISION-MAKING IN ORGANIZATIONS

Businesses depend on continual decisions. Executives guide the enterprise in deciding on long-term strategies, while middle managers decide on tactical initiatives to achieve middle range project goals. Knowledge workers make decisions to analyze business problems, conduct research, develop products, and generate creative decisions to put the enterprise in the forefront. Operations supervisors and managers focus on proximate decisions to operate particular business processes or sub-processes. For any organization, decisions constantly appear and need to be acted upon (Marakas, 2002).

In IS, decision support systems (DSSs) have been available since the 1980s and continue to evolve into new versions that incorporate the web, intelligent agents, and mobile technologies. A DSS is a software package that has a database, model base, knowledge engine, and user interface that are programmed to support management decisions (Marakas, 2002; Gray, 2006). The concept of DSS is necessary to review first, before moving to the major topic of SDSS.

A DSS is best suited for *semi-structured* or *unstructured* decisions (Gorry and Scott Morton, 1989; Marakas, 2002). A *structured decision* implies that the steps to reach it are logical and can be automatically calculated. For instance, the accounting calculations to produce a company balance sheet are logical and automatic. A person does not have to make the decisions, and the steps can be delegated to a computer.

An *unstructured decision* occurs in situations where the objectives of a decision conflict with other decisions, the alternatives for a decision are not clear, and/or the impacts of a decision are not known (Power, 2002; Marakas, 2002). An unstructured decision cannot be exactly calculated because its mechanisms are not known or it is too complex to model. For example, the decision on the strategy of a political campaign cannot be automated into fixed steps. Between structured and unstructured decisions are semi-structured ones, which can be partially calculated but not entirely. Some parts of the decision can be automated, so human intuition must comes into play. An example of semi-structured is the decision on how much to spend to construct a new warehouse. A DSS addresses semi-structured or unstructured decisions by sizing up the problem, selecting the appropriate model from a group of models referred to as the model base, and running the model which accesses data from the database (Turban and Aronson, 2001; Marakas, 2002).

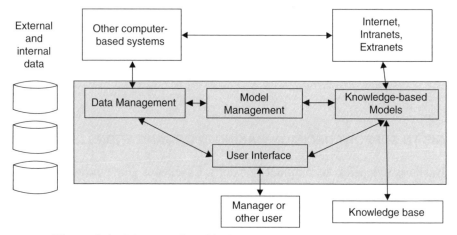

Figure 3.1   Diagram of a DSS. *Source:* Turban and Aronson, 2001

A DSS depends on a database management system that manages the storage, retrieval, and security for the data. As seen in the schematic diagram in Figure 3.1, the model management system makes available one or more models from a stored set of them. They can be quite varied (Turban, 1995; Marakas, 2002). Some important ones are optimization, simulation, and what-if (see Table 3.1). Depending on the decision being made, the model base determines which model to invoke, gathers the relevant data, and accesses a knowledge-based model if appropriate. A knowledge-based model includes a *knowledge engine* that applies logical reasoning based on rules, tasks sometimes called expert systems. It stores and utilizes logical rules, constraints, and heuristic principles (Marakas, 2002). The rules are extracted from human experts and stored in the knowledge base. The last major component, the user interface (sometimes called graphical user interface or GUI) provides the interactive interface for the user to communicate back and forth with the DSS. Through the user interface the user can interact with the data management, model management, and knowledge-based modules. It is crucial because the typical DSS user, a manager or executive, has limited time to communicate and is usually not a technical expert. As an example of a DSS use, a telecommunications manager who needs to estimate customer demand interacts with the user interface to call up an exponential-smoothing forecasting model from the model base which in turn invokes the data management system to draw data from a customer database. The basic components of a DSS are relevant to the chapter since they carry over to SDSS.

A decision support system assists in decisions at varied organizational levels, from the top executive down to supervisors of factory processes and clerical groups. As seen in Figure 3.2, executive management makes strategic

TABLE 3.1   Types of Decision Support Systems Models

Category	Process and Objective	Representation Techniques
optimization (few alternatives)	find best solution from few alternatives	decision tables, decision trees
optimization (many alternatives)	find best solution from many alternatives by iterative improvement	mathematical programming, network models
analytical solution to optimization	find best solution in one step by formula	some inventory models
simulation	mimic reality to find a "good" solution (perhaps best)	wide variety of models in nearly all fields
heuristics	use practical rules to find "good" solution	expert systems
predictive models (forecasting)	forecast the future based on assumptions	forecasting models, Markov models
"what if" models	vary assumptions to assess effects on outputs/sensitivity analysis	financial modeling

Source: Turban, 1995

Manglik, 2006

Figure 3.2   Organizational Hierarchy for SDSS and Spatial BI. *Source:* Manglik, 2006

decisions that are long-term and have enterprise-wide impacts. The data provided to top executives tend to be aggregated and integrated across the company. For instance, a CEO accesses the historical time series of data on all the firm's customer service requests in North America versus Europe, in order to gauge company-wide responsiveness. The executive-level data are often external, since the executive needs to environmentally scan and assess facts and forces outside the firm. Executives, who often have limited time and reduced hands-on experience, need a friendly user interface. Such a sub-category of DSS focusing on top executives is referred to an *executive information system.*

Middle managers, with responsibility for divisions, departments, or regions, make periodic decisions that relate mostly to tactical initiatives affecting their organizational unit. They need partially aggregated data, and they review reports that are often periodic. In addition to deciding on business processes in their unit, their swath of decisions also cuts across other units, so they sometimes require integrated information. Knowledge workers make decisions in business planning, forecasting, R&D, and creative areas, with little direct impact on operations. They base their decisions on a range from specialized to aggregate information, which may be internal or external depending on the analytic problem. Finally, operational supervisors and managers need support for real-time decisions involving a business process or sub-process in their unit. For instance, a utility field supervisor benefits by decision support on how to pattern the next week's maintenance tasks on a segment of pipeline. The data are specialized, recent, and keyed to the unit's immediate needs.

Other types of systems besides DSS impact all of these levels, so the role of DSS needs to be pinpointed more. By cross-classifying the level of management activity with the structuredness of the decision (Table 3.2), DSS is seen to be especially strong in supporting semi-structured decisions at the strategic, management levels, and knowledge levels (Gorry and Scott Morton, 1989; Marakas, 2002). DSSs may fail when confronting unstructured decisions, because their model base cannot provide an appropriate model leading to decisions based on experience and "gut instinct."

In summary, DSSs can support a variety of managers in making semi-structured and/or somewhat unstructured decisions. A DSS can support an individual or group in decision-making. The latter type of system is known as a GDSS—group decision support system (Marakas, 2002). Unlike transactions processing and management information systems, the DSS has the capability to respond to surprises and unprecedented situations, and can support simultaneous decision-making at different organizational levels and geographies in the company.

Business Intelligence (BI) is closely related to DSS, but is broader and draws from more diverse sources. A BI is a combination of data gathering, data storage, and knowledge management with analysis and modeling tools that provides complex enterprise-wide corporate and competitive information to decision makers (Gray, 2006). The BI gathers more far-reaching and diverse information and tends to be focused on more complex situations than a DSS.

TABLE 3.2   Classification of a DSS

Decision Type	Structured	Semi-Structured	Unstructured
Management Activity			
Operational Control	Inventory control	Securities trading	Decision on cover photo for monthly magazine
Knowledge Management	Consulting report on standard production process	Research on market changes for fast foods in a region	R&D on emerging technologies
Management Control	Load balancing of production lines	Establishing marketing budgets for new products	Hiring of management personnel
Strategic Planning	Physical plant location	Analysis of acquisition of capital assets	Determining what R&D projects to undertake
Support Needed	Transaction Processing Systems, MIS	DSS	Executive Information System (EIS), human reasoning and intuition

Source: Reprinted and adapted from *A Framework for Information Systems* by A. Gorry and M. Scott-Morton, MIT Sloan Management Review, Vol. 13, 1991, pp. 56–79, by permission of the publisher. Copyright © 1971 by Massachusetts Institute of Technology. All right reserved.

Like DSS, BI has components for data management, model management, knowledge management, and a user interface. Its knowledge management function is broader and more powerful than for a DSS. In the book, we regard DSS and BI as close relatives that share many features and constitute the ends along a continuum of decision systems. A further distinction separates the vendor products in DSS, BI, SDSS, and spatial BI. Vendor products fall along the DSS-to-BI range described, but recently vendors have tended to prefer their products to be called "BI." In the book, when vendor products are discussed, the vendor's own terminology (DSS or BI) is respected.

A *spatial decision support system* (SDSS) is a DSS that provides locational decision support where there is a geographic or spatial component in the decision-making (Keenan, 2005; Jarupathirun and Zahedi, 2005). Likewise a *spatial business intelligence system* (spatial BI) is a BI that provides locational decision support where there is a spatial element in the decision-making. The generic SDSS seen in Figure 3.3 falls in between GIS and DSS (Huerta, Navarrete, and Ryan, 2005). The same added components of spatial analysis and spatial boundary layers apply to Spatial BI, which falls between GIS and BI.

An SDSS combines GIS and DSS features. It may be formalized into a single system or product, or reside in a combination of two or more loosely

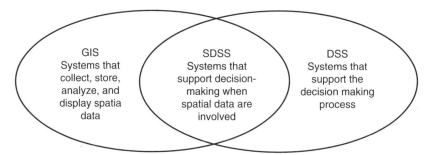

Figure 3.3   GIS, DSS, and SDSS. *Source:* Huerta, Navarrete, and Ryan, 2005. Copyright 2005, IGI Global, www.igi-pub.com, reprinted by permission of the publisher.

coupled products. In the latter case, a DSS vendor may offer a product that interfaces with a GIS package. Later in the chapter, the BI product WebFocus and loosely coupled GIS product ArcGIS are described.

A conceptual model of a typical SDSS (Figure 3.4) enlarges the DSS model from Figure 3.1 by adding spatial analysis and spatial data components. The spatial analysis model performs the specialized spatial functions discussed in Chapter 2 such as buffer, overlay, proximity estimates, distance measurement, longitudinal change analysis, spatial statistics, and spatial econometrics. These techniques perform computations based on locations and geographic surfaces. The spatial data are the points, lines, and polygons arranged in boundary layers from Chapter 2.

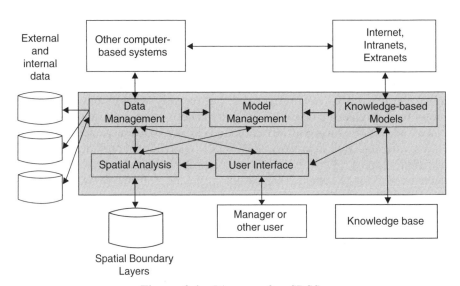

Figure 3.4   Diagram of an SDSS.

SDSS may be viewed along the continuum of GIS to SDSS to DSS (see Figure 3.3). Thus some SDSSs may resemble a GIS more than a DSS, while others are closer to DSS but with spatial features. In Chapters 1 and 2, it was emphasized that GIS is defined as having analysis capabilities. This version of an SDSS (in the left-middle in Figure 3.3) has an enlarged analysis component of GIS that serves for decision support.

Historically, a line of GIS and products has grown and developed without recognizing formal DSS concepts or DSS products. This line has led to today's GIS decision-modeling products. For example, ArcGIS's Model Builder feature allows the user to build a model interactively and visually by designing the model layout of attributes and their relationships, and testing if the model components work together. It produces spatial analysis and maps, based on the model's logical flows (ESRI, 2006).

The spatial decision systems derived from the GIS side are important and dominant for certain companies and industries. This chapter's large commercial bank case illustrates the GIS approach. Another example of the GIS approach to decision support occurs in the utility industry discussed in Chapter 9. The GIS-derived decision support assists utility engineers in planning and design of networks and facilities. Also, GIS assists decision-making in site selection, meter readings, fleet management, outage management, demographic analysis, and logistics. In health care, Kaiser Permanente, a national hospital chain headquartered in California, follows GIS for decision support, basing decisions on spatial analysis and modeling to classify in-service areas, profile disease patterns of regions, analyze optimal distribution of health care resources such as physicians and MRI equipment, and spatially assess facility siting. What decision support approach should a company practically adopt—(1) that derived from DSS and BI products or (2) that from GIS products? It depends on such factors as staff training and education, how inherently geographical the decision problems are, prior adoption of GIS or DSS/BI software that can be built upon, the organizational reach of the system (departmental versus enterprise), and the cost. It is recommended that a firm trying to decide on the appropriate approach perform a cost-benefit analysis of the alternatives, a topic in Chapter 7. Large organizations and technically inclined ones might adopt both approaches for different business units and projects.

The history of spatial decision support has unfolded over four decades. DSS was conceived with pioneering work in the late 1960s and 1970s, much conducted at MIT, where Gorry and Scott Morton (1971) originally identified non-structuredness as crucial and outlined its framework given in Table 3.2. The GIS approach began in the mainframe era of the late 1960s and evolved through client-server into modern forms. The parallel evolution of GIS and DSS systems (Jarupathirun and Zahedi, 2005) is shown in Table 3.3. An early SDSS paper introduced the GADS (Geodata Analysis and Display System), an IBM training system for routing decisions that included maps. Starting in the mid 1970s (Nagy and Wagle, 1979), decision support based on GIS evolved and became recognized in the GIS and GI Science fields. In the

TABLE 3.3 Parallel Stages in Evolution of GIS and Decision Support Systems (DSS)

	time	
Mobile GIS	▲	**Mobile DSS**
Intelligent GIS (e.g. personalizing GIS based on users' abilities and needs)		**Intelligent DSS** (e.g. intelligent agents for helping in decision making
Web-based GIS (e.g. using GIS for helping web-users find locations, directions or distances)		**Web-based DSS** (e.g. using DSS for helping web-users in their financial decisions or choice of products)
Advanced GIS (including spatial databases, spatial statistics models, and interactive interfaces)		**Decision Support Systems** (including model bases, databases, interactive and user-friendly interfaces)
GIS for Map Processing (e.g. off-line map generation)		**Transaction Processing Systems** (e.g. off-line report generation)

Source: Jarupathirun and Zahedi, 2005. Copyright 2005. IGI Global. www.igi-pub.com, reprinted by permission of the publisher.

1980s and 1990s, advanced visualization was incorporated into GIS. SDSS was included as a research and curricular component in the first U.S. Center for Geographic Information and Analysis, founded at University of California Santa Barbara in 1990.

By the mid 1990s, web-based DSS and GIS had become available and improved rapidly over the last decade. Subsequently, SDSS and spatial BI have become internet-enabled and often implemented on the enterprise-wide internet bus (Figure 1–11). In recent years, these systems have become available in mobile devices and in conjunction with coupled spatial technologies. Expert systems, which emphasize rule-based logic, appeared originally in the 1960s from research on artificial intelligence, and are now incorporated into DSS, SDSS, BI, and spatial BI as part of the knowledge management component (Marakas, 2002). Intelligent agents are software packets, often having artificial intelligence features, that act on behalf of the user to perform repetitive computer-related tasks (Marakas, 2002; Wikipedia, 2006). Some SDSS and spatial BI systems have incorporated intelligent agents (ESRI, 2006; Sugumaran et al., 2003, 2004, 2005). Known in simple terms as "wizards," intelligent agents can relieve the decision user of the need for complex coordination and command sequencing of data, models, and software.

However, for expert systems and intelligent agents, there is a tradeoff. Although they relieve the user of expert knowledge and complex coordination, they also shield him/her from knowledge and control of the detailed decision processes (Jarupathirun and Zahedi, 2005). Today there are a variety of spatial decision-making approaches, ranging from commercial to in-house, from standalone to coupled packages, and from the GIS modeling approach to SDSS and spatial BI. The future evolution of spatial decision-making support is uncertain, but is likely to move in the direction of the web/internet, mobile, and coupled spatial technologies.

CASE STUDY OF SPATIAL DECISION-MAKING IN A LARGE PERSONAL/CORPORATE BANK

This case concerns spatial decision-making at the U.S. division of Large Personal/Corporate Bank (LPCB), a global company headquartered in Europe. The U.S. division has grown rapidly in the Northeast and some Sunbelt locations. With an emphasis on personal and corporate customers, its expansion is driven by its branch network, which numbers in the mid hundreds. The support for spatial decision-making at LPCB is focused on helping middle managers and knowledge specialists understand the trade areas, customer profiles, and marketing potential in the areas where its branches are already located and new potential branch zones.

LPCB's GIS team consists of a manager and two specialists. It resides organizationally in the personal banking division, where it is part of the office of branch location strategy. The firm's IT group provides loose support to the GIS team's hardware and software needs. The GIS team's software from ESRI and MapInfo resides on a small client-server network that is not web-based. The decision-support approach taken is to utilize the analysis and modeling tools of commercial GIS software packages, but in certain projects to run a commercial location planning software package, that loosely interacts with the GIS. The GIS team in the U.S. has limited contact with GIS teams in other countries, which vary in size and sophistication.

The bank's GIS decision-support applications are trade area analysis for branches and ATMs, market demographics and competitor analysis, branch-related campaigns, location allocation, forecast of market potential for LPCB securities, and mapping to support executives in their strategies.

(1) Trade Area Analysis

The bank collects extensive customer data down to the Census block-group level, which are utilized to gain understanding of what branch a customer is assigned to, at which bank he/she opens accounts, the volume the customer is transacting, and where transactions originate. A block group is a U.S. Census small-area geographic designation that contains about 1,500 residents. It is common that a customer will open an account at one location but make all his/her transactions at others. The analysis takes this into account and gives a picture of the customer market around branches, so decisions can be made on retaining, in-filling, re-aligning, and closing branches and ATMs.

(2) Market Demographics, Competitor Analysis, and Customer Satisfaction

Detailed analysis can be done of LPCB's market share and the location of competitors' versus LPCB's branch locations. It pinpoints where there are high-value customers who are not served. Customers' ratings of customer service are analyzed with attention to spatial clustering. For instance, a very busy branch may have low customer service scores because of the waits and delays. This analysis can point to remedies such as locating new branches or adding to the existing branch's capacity.

(3) Branch-Related Campaigns

LPCB frequently conducts campaigns to target the locations of new prospects and markets. Spatial analysis helps to focus and speed the campaigns. A GIS team member stated, "If you hit the right people in the right areas, you get the best return on the dollar." GIS is also used to assess the strength of a branch manager relative to a particular campaign in his/her area.

(4) LPCB Securities

Securities and insurance sales representatives at the bank utilize geographic planning tools to gain insight on the market potential for their products. The bank's internal geographic allocation of securities/insurance people and resources can be assessed versus the nearby market potential.

(5) Mapping Support for Executives on Strategy

Senior management at LPCB/USA are supported by spatial analysis regarding the bank network, the market potential of products and services, and the competition, in order to gain a general understanding of the bank's situation and its opportunities.

The SDSS approach for LPCB/USA consists of GIS with enhanced analysis, rather than SDSS or spatial BI software. The GIS approach is broad-based. It utilizes customer, competitor, and demographic data, financial traffic patterns in branches, and business patterns in shopping centers, It ties all the items together to support and resolve decision-making. GIS is regarded as providing an objective and broad-based view that serves as a "third party voice" among many contributors to the decision process. Decision support focuses on marketing managers, regional managers, and some specialists.

The decision support is especially important for allocations and re-alignments of branches. Here bank managers have become increasingly dependent on the objectivity of spatial analysis. GIS has become a formal part of business procedures for decisions on whether or not to open new branches. It's also crucial to ATM locational decisions. The GIS team's inputs go into every branch decision, but the team is not the "power broker," rather it is up to senior management to pick and choose what information they want and ultimately the decisions. At the same time, a secondary role of the GIS team is to provide senior management with an overall perspective on the branch network.

Although senior management has not yet recognized GIS in the bank's strategic plan, GIS has moved up in importance indirectly through its impact on critical strategic factors of branch expansion.

SPATIAL DECISION SUPPORT SYSTEMS

This section further explains SDSS, examines an academic conceptual model of SDSS, considers the visualization aspect, looks at its prevalence and the barriers to SDSS use, and considers an example of SDSS for typhoon insurance.

In the general model of SDSS (Figure 3.4), it is helpful to add human dimensions to the components of spatial analysis, spatial data, and the user interface, going beyond the software to consider the spatial tasks people undertake, user abilities to succeed with the tasks, user goals, and performance. Companies and their people often have less familiarity with spatial applications, so the user's motivation and his/her fit with the tasks is critical for success. In the LPCB case, for example, there was positive motivation by the GIS team and a good fit between the spatial analysis methods and the branch marketing tasks that needed to be performed.

The conceptual model by Jarupathirun and Zahedi (2005) in Figure 3.5 is useful in enlarging the perspective to include the user, motivation, and performance/utilization. The GIS Technology at the upper left represents the map functions, modeling tools, and data management that appeared on the left side of Figure 3.4. The tasks that utilize the technology may range from simple to complex based on the user's spatial abilities. The abilities may be an individual's or a team's, as in the LPCB case. In Figure 3.5, user motivation starts with self-perception of the tasks ("intrinsic incentive") which leads to goal commitment and establishment of a goal level. The amount of commitment and aspiration in turn influences SDSS performance and utilization. All this comes together in "task-technology fit," which measures whether the SDSS performance and utilization are commensurate to the size and complexity of the decision tasks being confronted. Success depends on a good balance of task and technology (Jarupathirun and Zahedi, 2005).

The user's incentive, motivation, and goal setting are often overlooked factors in considering spatial decision support. In the LPCB case, the team's positive incentives and motivation, and clear goal setting helped it to succeed.

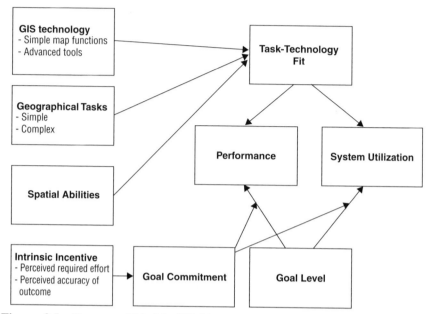

Figure 3.5   Conceptual Model of SDSS Task-Technology Fit. *Source:* Jarupathirun and Zahedi, 2005 Copyright 2005, IGI Global, www.igi-pub.com, reprinted by permission of the publisher

This area calls for an expanded research effort to understand how it occurs and what its amount of impact is. Business management needs to gain awareness of it and work at motivating/incentivizing GIS workers and teams.

An important model component is the user's spatial abilities. Does he/she have the natural ability to visualize maps and spatial relationships? Has he/she received sufficient training and education in spatial software and technologies? The total amount of user ability needs to be assessed and steps taken to bring the user or team up to a satisfactory amount. Studies have been done of people's inherent spatial ability to visualize and how that impacts decision-making, Overall, the task-technology fit model (Jarupathirun and Zahedi, 2005) is useful in broadening the dimensions of SDSS to extend to the human spatial ability, motivation, and performance.

SDSS and Visualization

Visualization refers to the visual display of spatially arranged elements. The user can better understand spatial relationships and assimilate new concepts through visualization (Gonzales, 2004; Gershon and Page, 2001). People think and communicate visually (DiBiase, 1990). This is evident today in the prevalence of video, multimedia, and digital imagery. Visual understanding helps in decision-making. Visualization can be emphasized and the outcomes of spatial analysis made more meaningful through display of buffers, contours,

TABLE 3.4   Classification of Spatial and Non-Spatial Information Systems

	Visualization		Analysis	
	Spatial	Attribute	Spatial	Attribute
Non-Spatial Information Systems				
Transaction Processing Systems		X		
Management Information Systems		X		X*
Decision Support Systems		X		X
Spatial Information Systems				
Consumer-Based Spatial Web Sites	X	X	X*	X*
Geographic Information Systems	X	X	X	X
Spatial Decision Support System	X	X	X	X

Note: *the analysis capabilities are limited when compared to decision support systems
Source: Copyright 2005, IGI Global, www.igi-pub.com, reprinted by permission of the publisher

graphics, and overlays; in 2D or 3D; and including satellite imaging, digital photographs, or animation.

Spatial visualization is not a standard aspect of transaction processing systems, management information systems, or decision support systems. Table 3.4, modified from Jarupathirun (2005) illustrates in the left-hand column that spatial visualization is typical of consumer-based spatial web sites, GISs, and SDSSs. The two right-hand columns indicate that spatial analysis is not typical of transaction processing systems, MIS, and DSS, but is available in the three categories of spatial systems, although less so for spatial websites. These classifications underscore that spatial visualization is one of the defining characteristics of an SDSS and along with spatial analysis distinguishes SDSS from DSS.

Experimental studies for over a decade have shed light on how visualization helps for certain tasks depending on the profiles of users (Smelcer and Carmel, 1997; Swink and Speier, 2000; Mennecke et al., 2000; Gershon and Page, 2001; Kraidy, 2002). An early experiment (Smelcer and Carmel, 1997) indicated that users performed faster problem solving with maps versus tables. For both maps and tables, the time to solve problems grew as the difficulty of the task increased. However, when users were tested on map-versus-table understanding of proximity and adjacency geographic relationships, maps encouraged short problem-solving time, whereas tables led to dramatically increased time (Smelcer and Carmel, 1997). For a geographic tasks of containment, maps and tables performed the same. The practical implication of this study is that for low-difficulty tasks, users performed the same for maps and tables, but for greater task complexity, maps make a difference. This suggests the advantages of SDSSs over DSSs for situations of high complexity.

In another experimental study (Swink and Speier, 1999), subjects' performance of working with a GIS was evaluated for different degrees of task problem size, data aggregation, and data dispersion. The subjects' spatial-cognitive skills were assessed by a "spatial orientation-card rotations test" (Swink and Speier, 1999). They showed that spatial orientation skill leads to superior quality of decisions. The user's ability to understand data dispersion led to superior decision quality. At the same time, the user performance with GIS declined as the problem size grew. Although many cognitive factors were left out, the study is useful in supporting that different users have different inherent levels of spatial abilities.

An elaborate study (Mennecke et al., 2000) showed that experts are more accurate than novices in utilizing GIS to perform geographic tasks. Experiments on 240 subjects, students and professional planners, measured cognitive fit, map interpretation, and reading. The students and professionals showed more efficiency with SDSS compared to maps, when they worked on complex problems, However, the professionals were more accurate yet less efficient than students. In all, the investigation confirmed that there were decision gains from SDSS compared to paper maps, particularly for more complex projects.

These and other studies of spatial visualization and cognition reveal gains from GIS and spatial analysis versus tables and paper maps. They also show differences in abilities for specific profiles of users and types of tasks. They inform the topic of SDSS and spatial decision-making by highlighting the user's cognition and abilities as among the key success factors.

Prevalence of SDSS

Given the potential benefits of SDSS, it is crucial to ask how prevalent it is. In lieu of any published data, examining the book's research case studies can provide an indication, even though they do not randomly represent a full population of firms with spatial applications. For this discussion, the firms are divided into three size categories, and the results compared by size and industry.

For the ten large firms, only three had formal SDSSs. None of the three used a standard SDSS or spatial BI package, but rather they utilized the modeling and analysis features of standard GIS software for decision support. Global Integrated Oil used standard GIS for decisions on facility location, drill siting, and leasing locations. URS applied customized ESRI ArcGIS product for decisions on managing groundwater and hazardous substances, while Rand McNally applied Plan-o-grams and GIS software for decisions on routing of sales reps, schedules, and product choices. The large Property and Casualty Insurance Firm had an SDSS package that was written in-house and based on simple knowledge rules. The SDSSs only interacted minimally with other major business systems such as ERP, Customer Relationship Management, and Supply Chain. In large firms, the users of spatial decision support were mostly by managers and specialists, with reduced use by executives or operational people.

For the five medium firms, there was moderate use but not of formal software. None of these firms had formal SDSSs and only one of them supported decisions with enhanced GIS. However, all of the medium-sized firms indicated that spatial data and programs support decision-making in areas including inventory management, sales, advertising, newspaper circulation, and hospital services. The users were similar to those of large firms—mostly managers, and lesser use by executives and clerical staff.

For small firms, there is moderate decision support, but no formal SDSSs, although one company provided SDSSs for clients in the form of GIS software enhanced by macros and add-ons. Users at the client organizations were managers, administrators, specialists, operations, and clerical people.

In sum, a sample of case companies had widespread use of spatial software and programs for making decisions, but the use was largely not based on formalized decision models. Where there was formalized spatial decision support, it tended to be from GIS with strong decision modeling, rather than from SDSS or spatial BI. Users tended to be mostly managers and specialists, but there was some use by executives at large firms and clerical/operations people at small ones.

Given the reduced formalized use of spatial decision support and BI indicated, it is important to focus on costs and benefits, and ask what precludes the formalized approaches from being adopted.

In the standard cost categories, formalized decision support accentuates he costs of training, licensing, and consulting. More training is needed because BI software skills are drawn from business and information systems fields, more than geography and GIS. A concern was expressed about the "declining depth of both conceptual knowledge and practical skills in computer science/information technology among those individuals entering the geospatial workforce" (Marble, 2006). SDSS and spatial BI are more easily adopted by users trained in decision support systems and business intelligence, coming from information systems and quantitative business degree programs. Use of strong decision modeling components in a GIS also requires some of this business understanding.

Licensing also potentially increases cost. SDSS and spatial BI products are expensive—often $10,000 or much more per single-user license that commonly is on top of GIS licensing cost. Start-up issues for spatial decision support can be mitigated by skilled consultants, but they are expensive. On the benefit side, it may be more difficult to justify the expense of formal spatial decision support, because of its lack of a track record and less tangible pluses. Since the SDSS users tend to be managers making tactical and sometimes strategic decisions, it is harder to quantify the benefits.

A further reason formalized SDSS and spatial BI has not yet become prevalent relates to their early growth stage. Richard Nolan (1973; 1979) proposed six stages of information systems growth, as measured by growth of computing budget. They are as follows: (1) initiation (acquisition of the technology), (2) contagion (intensity in developing use and growing user base), (3) control (reaction to contagion by imposition of accounting controls), (4) integration (orientation towards user services), (5) data administration (tight control of organizational computing resources, but some "slack" present to develop systems with added value), and (6) maturity (final state of costs under control and rising benefits). The stage theory is still relevant today,

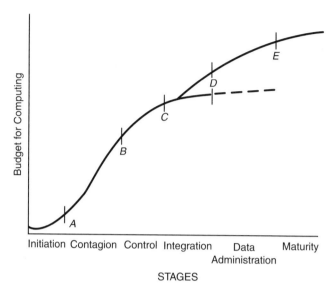

Figure 3.6 Nolan's Stage Theory—1979 Version. *Source:* Reprinted by permission of Harvard Business Review. This article was originally published under the title, "Managing the Crisis in Data Processing" by Richard L. Nolan in March/April 1979. Copyright © 1979 by the Harvard Business School Publishing Corp.

and is here applied to SDSS and spatial BI (see Figure 3.6 adapted from Nolan, 1979). In the figure, the case-study responses would assign the SDSS and spatial BI to late Stage 1 awaiting Stage 2. As a new form of product having only been introduced five to ten years ago, it has not yet caught on. By contrast, some newer spatial products have already reached contagion (Stage 2), such Google Earth and related "mash-ups" covered in Chapter 5, and navigation systems in cars.

Although the Nolan model was criticized as being only classificatory without dynamic transition (King and Kraemer, 1984), it is useful in the context of this book to gauging the maturity of spatial technologies. Stage theories derived from Nolan's work are in prominent use today including for strategic information systems (Galliers and Sutherland, 2003) and enterprise systems (Ross et al., 2006). This book is mainly intent on classifying maturity stages, and does not seek to explain the cause of transitions.

Example of an SDSS – Predicting Typhoon Insurance Risks in China

An example of SDSS is one designed to make decisions regarding the insurance risks of typhoons in China (Li et al., 2005). This SDSS is a prototype developed by academic researchers in close consultation with industry. It illustrates advanced SDSS applied to a difficult business problem. Typhoons are a severe threat in certain areas of the world, including Guangdong Province in China, a huge area of 70,312 square miles that borders the Pacific Ocean for 2,105 miles. This SDSS focuses on typhoon applications for Guangdong. The province's prior typhoon losses were huge, involving billions of U.S. dollars and thousands of deaths.

From an insurance standpoint, the goal of insuring against severe hazards is to pool together a portfolio of premiums that would be unacceptable individually, but can be insured as a group. The traditional pricing approach is "claims-based methodology," which prices by deterministic calculations, based on normal typhoon activity, population profiles, construction patterns, and past insurance coverage and losses (Li et al., 2005). The problem with this methodology is that insured firms have underestimated the loss potential from severe meteorological hazards such as hurricanes and typhoons. One solution is to utilize GIS combined with mathematical, statistical, pricing, and other modeling tools. Adding the spatial component brings the model closer to recognizing the true environmental threat.

The SDSS architecture consists of an in-house user interface and central control module that connect to a set of modules for statistics, math, spatial statistics, expert systems, and insurance pricing. As seen in Figure 3.7, the SDSS also has a database, as well as a GIS-COM library that supports programming features of the system. The SDSS has the capability of producing standard business graphics and written reports. Examples are seen in Figure 3.7 on the right.

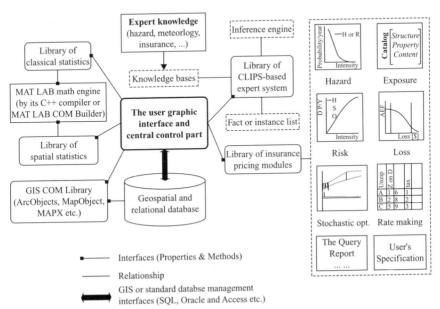

Figure 3.7 Architecture of SDSS for Insurance Pricing of Typhoons. Note: Object-oriented Component Object Modeling (COM) is the interface protocol. *Source:* Li et al., 2005

The SDSS modeling takes into account the following hazard and insurance phenomena (Li et al., 2005):

1. *Spatial-temporal patterns of natural hazards.* Based on distributions of the natural hazard's past frequency, location, and intensity, correlations can be utilized to predict future hazards and rank geographic areas on hazard vulnerability.
2. *Spatio-temporal variation of exposure.* The exposure of property, people, and facilities to hazards can be traced by the SDSS in time and space. Total exposure can be summed up for the province, its regions, and smaller zones (Li et al., 2005).
3. *Past claims and their correlation by categories of policies.* Although the occurrence patterns of past claims are not highly reliable in predicting vulnerability, they are a useful accessory indictor.
4. *Uncertainty and other factors.* The sources of uncertainty include inaccuracies in the data, weaknesses in the models chosen, and faulty execution of the models.

Based on these modeling principles, five models constitute the model base of the SDSS (Li et al., 2005):

1. *Hazard occurrence model.* This expert systems model predicts the spatio-temporal patterns of typhoons based on weather theories and historical data. It creates simulated typhoons, which are stored in the hazard database.
2. *Comprehensive risk analysis model.* It analyzes comprehensive risk for entire portfolios of exposed assets based on deterministic or stochastic simulations. Also, the model can identify geographic hot spots.
3. *Zonal correlation model.* It calculates spatial correlations between zones that are vulnerable to the typhoon. This model determines insurance rates across multiple zones.
4. *Loss analysis model.* The insurance rate for a zone can be computed through a series of steps. The model computes comprehensive loss, consisting of the direct losses from the typhoon hit, and secondary losses from off-shoots of the typhoon itself, such as peripheral storms, floods, and wind damage.
5. *Rate making and pricing.* Based on the specific exposure of an insured in a certain zone, the model estimates the insurance rate and consequently the premium amounts.

An example of the use of this SDSS is the dashboard seen in Figure 3.8 consisting of a map and associated graphs and tables for the fourteen regions of Guangdong Province. "Dashboard" is a concept utilized in high-end DSS or BI of an interactive and carefully designed display with dials, graphs, charts,

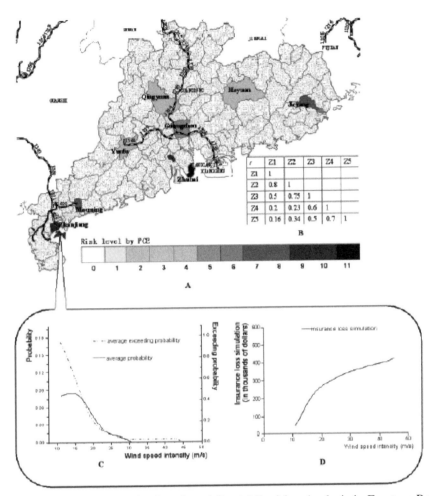

Figure 3.8 Insurance Risk Levels and Spatial Decision Analysis in Fourteen Regions of Guangdong Province, China. A. Map of relative insurance risk levels of typhoons for fourteen regions of Guangdong Province, China. B. Spatial correlation between hazard regions. C. Wind speed intensity probability analysis for Zhanjiang region. D. Insurance loss versus wind speed intensity for Zhanjiang region. *Source:* Li et al., 2005

like a car dashboard, but in this case used for executive decision-making. For instance, the figure shows a table of spatial correlations between hazard regions (B in Figure 3.8), a plot of the probability of wind speed intensities for one region in the province (C in figure), and a plot of insurance loss by wind speed intensity for the same region (D in figure).

In short, this SDSS can be applied to complex analysis of meteorological and hazard patterns, and insurance pricing. The model set includes statistical, math, and expert systems models. Outputs can be mapped, graphed, or presented in tables. Although the example is a prototype, SDSSs such as this are implemented in some insurance firms. In terms of the chapter, this case illustrates a custom-programmed SDSS, with strong and specialized analysis and modeling capabilities. The benefit of a SDSS compared to a DSS is that the digital geography of typhoons and their damage profiles for particular land areas can be analyzed spatially, leading to improved accuracy in estimation of hazards and risks, better decisions on pricing and premiums, and ultimately lower cost for the customer.

SPATIAL BUSINESS INTELLIGENCE SYSTEMS

Spatial business intelligence (spatial BI) is a combination of data gathering, data storage, and knowledge management combined with modeling, and spatial analysis tools that provide complex corporate and external information to decision makers (Gray, 2006). As mentioned earlier in the chapter, spatial BI differs from SDSS in its greater breadth and ability to draw from more diverse data sources. Since business intelligence is broader, it also tends to be utilized across the enterprise (Manglik, 2006). Users are typically higher up organizationally than for DSS, and somewhat more squeezed on their time. A few examples of spatial BI will illustrate its somewhat broader reach.

1. Routing by Sears. GIS and BI are loosely coupled to support decisions on managing the locations and routing of delivery personnel and repair technicians throughout a vast network of millions of homes (ArcUser, 2005). The BI helps Sears to forecast demand for servicing and decide on resource allocation spatially, leading to better productivity for field personnel. The full Sears case study appears in Chapter 7.

2. In cellular telecommunications, spatial BI has been applied in Holland to decide on the best locations of cell phone towers to maximize calling utilization, reduce dropped cell phone calls, and to plan cell tower capacities (Gonzales, 2004). The BI user has access not only to standard charts, tabular spreadsheet-like calculations, and thematic mapping, but can also analyze messaging hot spots and density surfaces of users. Its layering allows overlays of provincial and local administrative boundaries (Woonplats), in order to enhance decision-making involving local jurisdictions. The BI also can overlay satellite imagery of land surfaces and digital elevation models over cellular layers (Gonzales, 2004).

3. In real estate, current and historical property sales can be analyzed For instance, the BI displays the proximity of sales and sales agents. This supports decisions on the best geographic allocations of agents and averts duplication of sales effort for one property, or zones that lack agent coverage. Satellite imagery is provided for overlay by ESRI's ArcWeb Services (Gonzales, 2004).

The examples demonstrate the broad reach and diverse information sources of spatial BI.

WebFocus from Information Builders

Information Builders is an example of a leading purveyor of BI software including the spatial BI. Standard, non-spatial WebFocus utilizes Microsoft Excel for data manipulation and graphics. The "Spatial BI" add-on module enhances WebFocus with access back and forth with the ArcGIS package. Rather than combining the software into a single product, separate BI and GIS "engines" can be connected and coordinated (Figure 3.9). A BI dashboard displays Excel graphics, spreadsheets, and pivot tables, text files in .pdf format, and maps from ArcGIS. The practical example in Figure 3.10 shows, on the right of the screen, a WebFocus table listing information on high-value insurance policies for an area in Florida having the most risk. On the left a map shows the geographical distribution and size of these policies. The user of the ArcGIS package has the converse benefits of being able to invoke WebFocus modeling features, tables, and graphs.

The WebFocus and ArcGIS databases are coordinated in a seamless way. The WebFocus database feature of accessing different databases and operating systems in a single query assist the user. The loosely coupled arrangement allows the strengths of each software package to complement the other.

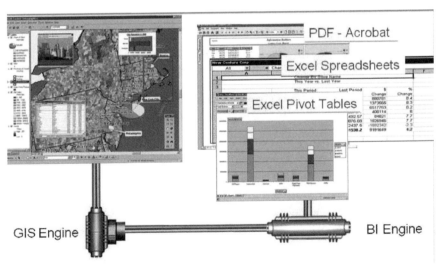

Figure 3.9 Overall Design of BI from Information Builders and ESRI. Note: This Spatial BI offering combines WebFocus from Information Builders and ArcGIS from ESRI Inc. Maps interact with Excel, .PDF, and .HTML features. *Source:* Information Builders, 2006

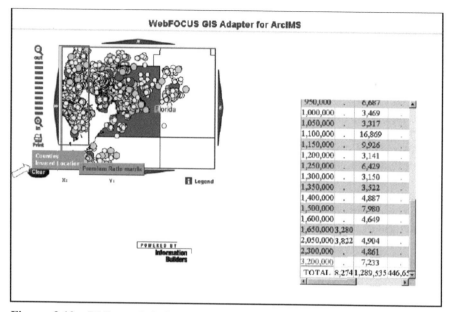

Figure 3.10   BI Example in Insurance with Web Focus from Information Builders. This example Uses WebFocus and ArcGIS from ESRI to locate and display the geographical distribution of high value insurance policies in a portion of Florida who are most exposed to risk. The user can toggle between the spreadsheet report and map, to refine the analysis. *Source:* Information Builders, 2006

Another advantage is that business users can work from the BI interface they are used to, while GIS users, typically with geo-science and environmental backgrounds, can remain on the familiar GIS side.

A weakness of this "coordinated" approach is that the vendors have to keep the two software packages in balance, as new versions appear and user needs change. Also, the user must learn three packages (WebFocus, Excel, and ArcGIS).

Map Intelligence

Map Intelligence BI software depends on Microsoft Excel for tables and graphs, and data manipulation. It can be run with ArcGIS from ESRI or with the desktop GIS product of MapInfo. As seen in Figure 3.10, Map Intelligence Software is set up as a dashboard. The dashboard and map display are synchronized (Gonzales, 2004). "Any data manipulation such as limits, filtering, or chart slicing that are applied in the dashboard are automatically reflected in the mapping application" (Gonzales, 2004). Data are passed back and forth, e.g. spatial map data can be displayed on the dashboard, to highlight trends and give sharper analytic focus.

On the server side of the architecture, data are sent back and forth between the Map Intelligence application server and a map server, commonly ESRI's ArcIMS. This design illustrates service-oriented architecture (SOA) running on a small enterprise-wide internet bus, concepts introduced in Chapter 1. It implies that Map Intelligence BI capabilities can be made available on the web throughout the user's enterprise, although the client components must be installed. This BI design provides access across the wide reach of the web.

Although the two BI examples coordinate branded BI and GIS software in distinctive ways, both architectures allow a breadth of applications and wide reach from diverse data sources.

CASE STUDY OF LARGE INSURANCE COMPANY

Large Insurance Company (LIC) is one of the biggest property and casualty insurance firms in the U.S. It includes personal insurance, commercial insurance involving property, casualty, and workers compensation, and a smaller set of other insurance lines. LIC has utilized GIS software for decision-making for over a decade, but does not have a formalized SDSS. The most significant decision support is for commercial underwriting. It is a critical decision function that the whole company depends on for profits, so GIS software with modeling features provides powerful decision support. The GIS manager pointed out that if GIS were removed from underwriting, the firm would be much less responsive on short notice to underwriting requests. The critical role of GIS for decision-making was highlighted in the two World Trade Center bombings, for which the firm had insured clients in the buildings in both cases.

The company has a small GIS team of seven located in Commercial Lines, but also receives periodic loans of support people from IT such as database analysts and a network analyst. The main applications of spatial technologies at LIC are to manage capacity planning at property locations, support casualty decisions, perform risk analysis to evaluate businesses for property insurance, support underwriters in deciding on the property risks, and take actions and manage in catastrophes. The GIS software is not currently internet- or intranet-based, but supported through a nationwide client-server network.

In the instance of the catastrophic Hurricane Katrina in 2005, LIC had insured in the area. Spatial analysis and mapping helped to quickly respond to the hardest hit areas of flooding and wind damage. Data were drawn from government and commercial sources, including FEMA, and flood maps. After Katrina hit, the firm was able to develop a complete picture of the depth of water throughout the metropolitan area. The disaster was of a scale that could not be predicted ahead of time, but the catastrophe response team was able to accurately predict damages afterwards.

LIC's users consist of (1) underwriters and underwriter assistants, who utilize GIS daily for location-based risk assessment; (2) the senior management team that uses it for capacity planning and exposure analyses; (3) the catastrophe management unit, that needs GIS for modeling of weather conditions, responses to the needs of insured in catastrophes and reporting sent to reinsurance firms, i.e. companies that accept and balance industry-wide risks; and (4) the GIS team.

As with the typhoon insurance example, GIS feeds information into the risk rating and premium pricing systems. Underwriters are highly dependent on it. For example in fire insurance, the underwriter cannot price policies without knowing the distance of a location from fire hydrants or other water supply.

For its main spatial area of Commercial, LIC does not have formalized SDSS or spatial BI, but rather uses GIS software enhanced with modeling of locations and ratings. Over 1,000 commercial underwriters depend strongly on GIS with modeling capabilities. The GIS is programmed to help the underwriter make rule-based decisions, based on locational characteristics. This represents the enhanced GIS approach to decision support described earlier.

In personal lines, there is a commercial SDSS that follows simple, rule-based logic. The basic model for personal underwriters is that the system tells the user what he/she can or cannot offer, based on locational characteristics. It takes a home address, geocodes it, determines the X-Y coordinates, and then invokes a flood analysis module to determine nearby flood, earthquake, or other hazard zones.

The two World Trade Center (WTC) bombings illustrate how far LIC has come in its capability to support its insured in a disaster. In the original 1993 WTC bombing, the firm had insured commercial policyholders in the tower that was bombed, but the firm could not determine using the traditional legacy mainframe at that time, what insured businesses and people were in the building. Instead of having a list to act on, LIC's catastrophe group had literally to go to the building, find out by walking around what companies were in it, since the towers were still standing from only a garage bomb, and check the tenants against LIC's master list.

In the 9/11 terrorist disaster in 2001, LIC's catastrophe team requested from the GIS team the list of which insured parties were in the two towers. Within minutes the GIS team produced a list of every LIC policyholder in the building. Within hours, there was a picture of the insured's' losses. The reason for the change was recognition by the CEO after the 1993 bombing that it would be strategic to develop a complete and detailed mapping and inventory of all insured clients throughout the country. As a result, in 9/11, quick decisions were made and insured clients suffering huge losses were responded to nearly immediately.

In sum, LIC has developed its national spatial decision support to the point that it has become essential for decision-making in the underwriting and disaster areas, with moderate decision importance in other areas. The dominant form of support is GIS software enabled to run models based on data for weather, climate, insured capacity, location of clients, risk assessment, and pricing.

CHAPTER SUMMARY

Spatial decision support has developed into an important tool for businesses. Companies face decisions on a daily basis. Traditional tools of DSS and business intelligence can be enhanced with spatial components, or GIS analysis can be built up to offer robust decision modeling. The formal SDSS and spatial BI tools are scarce in businesses, but likely to expand as they become more affordable and user-friendly and as spatial teams in firms are better trained. Overall the SDSS/Spatial BI area is in an early growth stage, but is positioned to move into the subsequent stage of rapid growth. Several case studies in banking and insurance illustrate that well-thought-out and focused spatial decision support can yield competitive benefits. As seen by LIC, it may take unpreparedness for a disaster to startle the firm into advancing its spatial decision support.

REFERENCES

Agarwal, P. 2005. "Ontological Considerations in GIScience." *International Journal of Geographical Information Science*, 19(5): 501–536.

Andriendko, N.V., and G.L. Andrienko. 2001. "Intelligent Support for Geographic Data Analysis And Decision Making In The Web." *Journal of Geographic Information and Decision Analysis*, 5(2): 115–128.

ArcUser Magazine. 2005. "Mapping Better Business Strategies: Integrating GIS and Business Intelligence." *ArcUser Magazine*, 8(3): 10–14.

Bhargava, H.K., and D.J. Power. 2001. "Decision Support Systems And Web Technologies: A Status Report." Proceedings of Americas Conference on Information Systems, Boston, MA, August 3–5, pp. 229–235.

Carlsson, C., and E. Turban. 2002. "DSS: Directions for The Next Decade." *Decision Support Systems*, 33(2): 105–110.

Casey, M.J., and Austin, M.A. 2002. "Semantic Web Methodologies for Spatial Decision Support." Proceedings of International Conference on Decision Making and Decision Support in the Internet Age (DSIage2002), July 4–7, U.C.C, Ireland.

Crossland, M.D., B.E. Wynne, and W.C. Perkins. 1995. "Spatial Decision Support Systems: An Overview of Technology And A Test Of Efficacy." *Decision Support Systems*, 14: 219–235.

Fonseca, F.T., M.J. Egenhofer, P. Agouris, and G. Camara. 2002. "Using Ontologies for Integrated Geographic Information Systems." *Transactions in Geographic Information Systems*, 6(3): 231–257 .

Frank, A. 2001. "Tiers of Ontology And Consistency Constraints In Geographical Information Systems." *International Journal of Geographical Information Science*, 15: 667–678.

Galliers, Robert D. and A.R. Sutherland. 2003. "The Evolving Information Systems Strategy, in Galliers, Robert D. and Dorothy E. Leidner, *Strategic Information Management: Challenges and Strategies in Managing Information Systems*. 3rd Edition, Butterworth-Heinemann, pp. 33–63.

Gonzales, Michael L. 2004. *Spatial Business Intelligence*. Ultimo, Australia: Integeo Corporation.

Gonzales, Michael L. 2004. "More than Pie Charts." *Intelligent Enterprise*, November. Available at www.intelligententerprise.com.

Goodchild, M.F. 2000. "The Current Status of GIS and Spatial Analysis." *Journal of Geographical Systems*, 2(1): 5–10.

Gorry, A., and M. Scott-Morton. 1971. "A Framework for Information Systems." *Sloan Management Review*, 13: 56–79.

Gray, Paul. 2006. *Manager's Guide to Making Decisions about Information Systems*. New York: John Wiley and Sons.

Holland, William S. 2005. "The Fifth Dimension of GIS: Spatially Enabled Business and Analytic Intelligence." *ArcUser*, 8(3): 16–19.

Huerta, E., Navarrete, C., and Ryan, T. 2005. "GIS and Decision-Making in Business: A Literature Review." In Pick, James B. (ed.), *Geographic Information Systems in Business*. Hershey, PA: Idea Group Publishing, pp. 20–35.

Jarupathirun, Suprasith, and Fatemeh Zahedi. 2005. "GIS as Spatial Support Systems." In Pick, James B. (Ed.), *Geographic Information Systems in Business*. Hershey, PA: Idea Group Publishing, pp. 151–174.

Jarupathirun, Suprasith, and Fatemeh Zahedi. 2007. "Exploring the Influence of Perceptual Factors In The Success of Web-Based Spatial Decision Support Systems." *Decision Support Systems*. Article in press and available at www.sciencedirect.com.

Keenan, Peter B. 2003. "Spatial Decision Support Systems." In Mora, Manuel, Guiseppi Forgionne, and Jatinder Gutpa (eds.), *Achievements, Trends, and Challenges for the New Decade*, Hershey, PA: Idea Group Publishing, pp. 28–39.

King, John Leslie, and Kenneth L. Kraemer. 1984. "Evolution and Organizational Information Systems: An Assessment of Nolan's Stage Model." *Communications of the ACM*, 27(5): 466–475.

Li, Lianfa, Jinfeng Wang, and Chengyi Wang. 2005. "Typhoon Insurance Pricing with Spatial Decision Support Tools." *International Journal of Geographical Information Science*, 19(3): 363–384.

Longley, Paul A., Michael F. Goodchild, David J. Maguire, and David W. Rhind. 2005. *Geographic Information Systems and Science*. Hoboken, NJ: John Wiley and Sons.

Malczewski, Jacek. 1999. *GIS and Multicriteria Decision Analysis*. New York: John Wiley and Sons.

Manglik, Anupam. 2006. "Increasing BI Adoption: An Enterprise Approach." *Business Intelligence Journal*, 11(2): 44–52.

Marakas, George. 2002. *Decision Support Systems*, 2nd Edition. Upper Saddle River, NJ: Prentice Hall.

Marble, Duane F. 2006. "Who Are We? Defining the Geospatial Workforce." *Geospatial Solutions*, 16(5): 14–21.

Mennecke, B.E., M.D. Crossland, and B.L. Killingsworth. 2000. "Is A Map More Than A Picture? The Role of SDSS Technology, Subject Characteristics, and Problem Complexity On Map Reading and Problem Solving." *MIS Quarterly*, 24(4): 601–629.

Murphy, Lisa D. 2005. "Geographic Information Systems: Are They Decision Support Systems?" Proceedings of 28th Hawaii International Conference on System Sciences.

Nasairin, Syed, and David F. Birks. 2003. "DSS Implementation in the UK Retail Organisations: A GIS Perspective." *Information and Management*, 40:325–336.

Nolan, Richard. 1973. "Managing the Computer Resource: A Stage Hypothesis." *Communications of the ACM*, 16(7): 399–405.

Nolan, Richard L. 1979. "Managing the Crisis in Data Processing." *Harvard Business Review*, March/April, pp. 115–126.

Pick, James B. 2005. *Geographic Information Systems in Business*. Hershey, PA: Idea Group Publishing.

Power, Daniel J. 2002. *Decision Support Systems*. Quorom Books.

Ray, Julian J. 2005. "A Web-Based Spatial Decision Support System Optimizes Routes For Oversize/Overweight Vehicles In Delaware." *Decision Support Systems*. Article in press. Available at www.sciencedirect.com.

Ross, Jeanne W., Peter Weill, and David Robertson. 2006. *Enterprise Architecture as Strategy: Creating a Foundation for Business Execution*. Cambridge, MA: Harvard Business School Press.

Sengupta and Bennett. 2003. "Agent-based Modeling Environment for Spatial Decision Support." *International Journal of Geographical Information Science*, 17(2): 157–180.

Shim, J.P., M. Warkentin, J.F. Courtney, D.J. Power, R. Sharda, and C. Carlsson. 2002. "Past, Present, and Future of Decision Support Technology." *Decision Support Systems*, 33(2): 111–126.

Sikder, I., and A. Gangopadhyay. 2002. "Design and Implementation of a Web-based Collaborative Spatial Decision Support System: Organizational and Managerial Implications." *Information Resources Management Journal*, 15(4): 33–47.

Sikder, Iftikhar U., and Aryya Gangopadhyay. 2003. "Distributed Data Warehouse for Geo-spatial Services." Chapter 8 in Gerald Grant (ed.), *ERP and Data Warehousing in Organizations: Issues and Challenges*, Hershey, PA: IRM Press, pp. 132–145.

Sikder, Iftikhar, and Aryya Gangopadhyay. 2004. "Collaborative Decision Making in Web-Based GIS." Chapter 6 in Khosrow-Pour, Mehdi (ed), *Collaborative Decision Making in Web-Based GIS*, Hershey, PA: Idea Group Publishing, pp. 147–162.

Smelcer, J.B., and E. Carmel. 1997. "The Effectiveness of Different Representations For Managerial Problem Solving: Comparing Tables And Maps." *Decision Sciences*, 28(2): 391–420.

Sugumaran, R., J. Meyer, and J. Davis. 2004. "A Web-Based Environmental Decision Support System (WEDSS) for Environmental Planning and Watershed Management." *Journal of Geographical Systems*, 6:1–16.

Sugumaran, Ramanathan, Shriram Ilavajhala, and Vijayan Sugumaran. 2005. "Experiences with Implementing a Spatial Decision Support System for Planning Snow Removal Operations." Proceedings of the 11th Americas Conference on Information Systems, Omaha, NE, August 11–14, pp. 1668–1676.

Sugumaran, V., and R. Sugumaran. 2003. "Spatial Decision Support Systems Using Intelligent Agents and GIS Web Services." Americas Conference on Information Systems. Tampa, FL, August 4–6, pp. 2481–2486.

Swink, J., and C. Speier. 2000. "Presenting Geographic Information: Effects of Data Aggregation, Dispersion, and Users' Spatial Orientation." *Decision Sciences*, 30(1): 169–195.

Tarantilis, C.D., and C.T. Kirandoudis. 2002. "Using a Spatial Decision Support System For Solving The Vehicle Routing Problem." *Information and Management*, 39(5): 359–375.

Tomlinson, Roger. 2003. *Thinking About GIS: Geographic Information Systems for Managers*. Redlands, CA: ESRI Press.

Tsou, M.H., and B.P. Buttenfield. 2002. "A Dynamic Architecture for Distributed Geographic Information Services." *Transactions in GIS*, 6(4): 355–381.

Turban, Efraim, and Jay E. Aronson. 2001. *Decision Support Systems and Intellegent Systems*. 6th ed. Upper Saddle River, NJ: Prentice Hall.

Turban, Efraim. 1995. *Decision Support and Expert Systems*. 4th ed. Upper Saddler River, NJ: Prentice Hall.

West, Larry. 2000. "Designing End-User Geographic Information Systems." *Journal of End User Computing*, 12:3: 14–22.

West, Larry, and Traci J. Hess. 2002. "Metadata as a Knowledge Management Tool: Supporting Intelligent Agent And End User Access To Spatial Data." *Decision Support Systems*, 32:247–264.

Winter, Stephan. 2001. "Ontology: Buzzword or Paradigm Shift in GIS Science." *International Journal of Geographical Information Science*, 15(7): 587–590.

CHAPTER 4

ENTERPRISE APPLICATIONS

INTRODUCTION

A long-term trend for business has been towards mainstream business systems that serve critical business functions including manufacturing, supply chain, finance, accounting, human resources management, marketing, and sales. They form building blocks for companies and enable processes to function smoothly, supported by databases, data warehouses, networking, and internet infrastructure.

In the 1990s, integrated systems appeared known as enterprise resource planning (ERP) systems that supported groups of functions or even all of the functions. ERPs are expensive and difficult to implement, but contribute to the robust "back office" needed in many industries for competitive positioning.

A business system that is growing in importance is a *customer relationship management system* (CRM). A CRM supports a firm in finding and communicating with customers, meeting their needs, and developing long-term relationships with them. As consumers have become more discerning and quality-conscious, companies and industries have become customer-centric. The new way to achieve what the "friendly local merchant" used to provide is through motivated customer-care staff who utilize customer-centric systems. Rather than "hard sell" or "direct marketing," the focus is on the key concept of building the company-customer relationship. An example is a CRM that supports a customer loyalty program. Prospects are tracked; committed customers are identified and asked to join loyalty programs; and benefits are provided to loyal customers to retain them.

Geo-Business: GIS in the Digital Organization, By James B. Pick
Copyright © 2007 John Wiley & Sons, Inc.

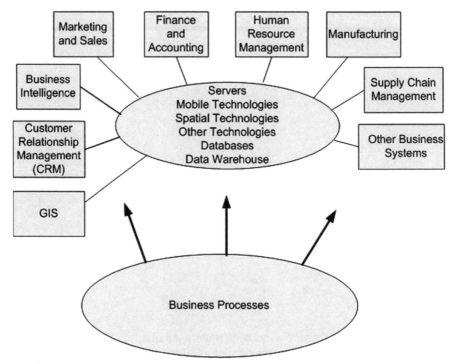

Figure 4.1 The Framework of Enterprise Applications

These are examples of enterprise applications that serve the whole organization. Figure 4.1 shows a group of enterprise applications that rely on a technology base, shown in the center. GIS is one of this group. Alternatively, GIS software could also be built into enterprise applications software, but so far it is only an inherent part of some databases and data warehouses.

Enterprise systems and the central base depend in turn on the underlying business processes. For instance, a human resource management (HRM) system, part of an ERP, runs on a server using information stored in a database. It is accessed by 250 users on PCs, laptops, and mobile wireless devices. Underlying the application and technology are the HRM business processes. For instance, four HR process steps are needed to advertise for a management level position. The advertising is also spatial, since searches are influenced by geographies, such as West Coast or California-only. The GIS component is not a part of the HRM application, as seen in Figure 4.1. The GIS and HRM system can work together through connector software. This diagram and its concepts are returned to later in the chapter. Through their richness of data and coordination, enterprise systems, some spatially-enabled, contribute to the strategic competitiveness of firms.

The advantages of the enterprise-wide approach are scalability, accessibility, connection to external systems, ability to collaborate and cross-share information, security, better management, and maintainability (see box).

Features of an Enterprise-Wide Approach to GIS and Spatial Technologies

Scalability. The enterprise approach makes it easier to scale up GIS and spatial technologies from relatively few to hundreds of thousands of users. This is important when a company is growing rapidly or when user demand leads to a rapid adoption increase.

Supported and accessible everywhere. In a global economy, enterprises have extended their market reach. An enterprise approach implies that a spatial application can be made widely available geographically and organizationally.

Connection to external systems. Companies' systems are becoming more collaborative. They are interacting with the government and nonprofit sectors. For instance, a firm's supply chain system involves dozens of business and government suppliers and procurers. The firm and its providers need to interconnect with organizations up and down the chain.

Ability internally to collaborate and cross-share information. Major functional systems are interrelated in their business processes. Marketing projects depend on budgetary accounting, as well as manufacturing specifications to produce products being marketed. These imply collaborative systems that share information.

Security. Enterprise systems tend to run on a common technology base, instead of having dispersed islands of technology around the organization. Hence the firm can focus on security and protection of the common base.

Better management. Consolidating systems into major functional modules makes the enterprise system more understandable and manageable. The tendency in industry to utilize well-known commercial enterprise applications means they are easier to manage over the long term.

Maintenance. Having fewer and larger enterprise applications that are well-known simplifies the maintenance burden over the long run.

Taken together, these features characterize the enterprise approach (Ross et al., 2006).

The enterprise spatial perspective has only appeared in recent years in business (Keating et al., 2003; Thurston, 2003; Sonnen and Morris, 2005). This chapter examines the cutting edge of large, enterprise-wide spatial applications. However, 63 percent of the book's twenty research case study firms do not have enterprise-wide spatial applications. In fact, only one case, Rand

McNally, had widely integrated GIS and enterprise spatial applications (see Table 4.1). Five out of twenty firms had integrated GIS and supply chain management. The least prevalent coupling was between GIS and ERP (only Rand McNally out of twenty firms). This may be due to the high cost and technical difficulties in linking them up. In the sample, three-quarters of the firms having integration of GIS and enterprise software were large ones. This is not surprising, since large companies tend to have the resources to afford the high cost and skills necessary to implement, manage, and maintain enterprise software.

The heavy adoption of ERP and other enterprise applications among larger firms encourages them to consider coupling and integrating them with GIS software. An alternative pathway leading to GIS integration would be to build GIS directly into enterprise software, as has already occurred with some enterprise databases and data warehouses.

The chapter emphasizes the role of GIS and spatial technologies for enterprise business applications. As pointed out in Chapter 1, GIS is expanding across the enterprise. GIS today is able to work together with and enhance the set of enterprise business applications. The chapter first examines ERP-GIS integration, which is illustrated by the Pidpa electrical-utility case. It then turns to CRM-GIS integration, exemplified by the Chico's apparel case. The chapter discusses supply chain and its relationship to GIS, RFID, and GPS, and then examines data warehousing and GIS. The capstone Nesa case at the end demonstrates how a firm can integrate most of the enterprise applications with GIS.

GIS AND ENTERPRISE RESOURCE PLANNING

ERP is an enterprise-wide, complex software application having multiple major business applications that share a common database and/or data warehouse. Information flows automatically throughout the ERP structure (Gray, 2006). A basic ERP is limited to key functional systems of marketing and sales, finance and accounting, human resource management (HRM), and manufacturing (Figure 4.2). For this ERP design, other applications such as business intelligence and GIS, are implemented as separate software applications outside the ERP, that coordinate with it. In a comprehensive ERP, more modules are purchased from the ERP vendor and included inside the ERP (Figure 4.3).

The motivations for moving to ERP include the following (Gray, 2006):

- *Historical.* Y2K problems. At the turn of the twenty-first century, companies were forced to perform software fixes to chronology bugs for the whole enterprise. For many firms, it was easier to replace all or nearly all their business functional systems with ERP software, rather than find the bugs.

TABLE 4.1 Case Study Results on GIS Linked to Enterprise Systems (Results shown only for the eight out of twenty case-study firms that link GIS and enterprise systems)

Case Study Firm	Extent that GIS is linked to ERP	Extent that GIS is linked to CRM	Extent that GIS is linked to Supply Chain Management	Extent that GIS is linked to Data Warehouse/Data Mining
Global Integrated Oil	No.	No.	A little. One very small project in the additives company of GIO. Maps show suppliers, processing plants, customers, and company locations.	A little. One focused project used data mining and GIS. ESRI GIS and fuzzy logic used to search data for upstream applications.
Large Commercial Bank	No.	No	No.	Yes. GIS Group extracts data on value of customers from the data warehouse, and geo-references it.
Rand McNally	Yes. Rand McNally has an internally developed ERP. Spatial functions link the ERP with direct store delivery coverage and routes, and inventory management.	Yes. In large sense, GIS are a part of CRM. Plan-o-grams (shelf layouts) created for customers. These linked with area demographics.	Yes. GIS helps in understanding parts of SCM flows. Used for inventory management and forecasts.	Yes. Large data warehouses are accessed with data mining to create input data that are scaled for GIS-based products.
Sears	A little. In marketing.	A little. CAMS (Customer Allocation Management System) allows managers to provide services where customer densities are low.	No.	No.

(Continued)

TABLE 4.1 (*Continued*)

Case Study Firm	Extent that GIS is linked to ERP	Extent that GIS is linked to CRM	Extent that GIS is linked to Supply Chain Management	Extent that GIS is linked to Data Warehouse/Data Mining
Large U.S. Property and Casualty Insurance	No.	No. GIS team works with catastrophic response team to give locational information to customers.	No.	Yes for data marts. Note: A data mart is smaller than a data warehouse and specialized for what user can access.
Chico's	No.	Yes. A CRM package is used for direct mailings and customer information. Through linkage with GIS software, mapping and spatial analysis supports the CRM.	No.	No.
Baystate Health	No. Slowly getting there.	No. Baystate has a CRM, but not yet been linked to GIS.	No.	No.
Sperry Van Ness	No.	Yes. GIS and Microsoft CRM 3.0 integrated for commercial real estate by adding maps and aerials.	No.	No.

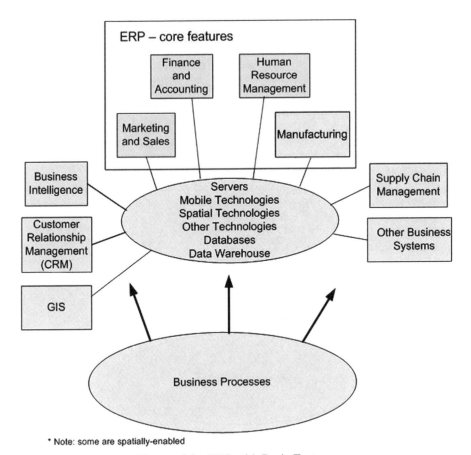

Figure 4.2   ERP with Basic Features

- *Reduced cost of commercial versus in-house software.* As well-tested, commercial ERP software became available, it was regarded as cheaper to purchase and adapt it to the firm's business processes, rather than to continue a heavy custom-programming effort.
- *Lack of compatibility of "silos" of separate business functional applications.* Each functional silo, e.g. marketing or manufacturing software, might work well by itself, but interfacing a silo with other business applications was too expensive. The silo problem remains a challenge for GIS software.

ERP software from SAP, the world's largest vendor of ERP, is present in over 50,000 installations, with more than 10 million users in 120 nations (Gray, 2006). Among its leading products are SAP R/3 and mySAP.com. SAP R/3, designed to run in a client-server environment, has four core modules

ERP – full featured

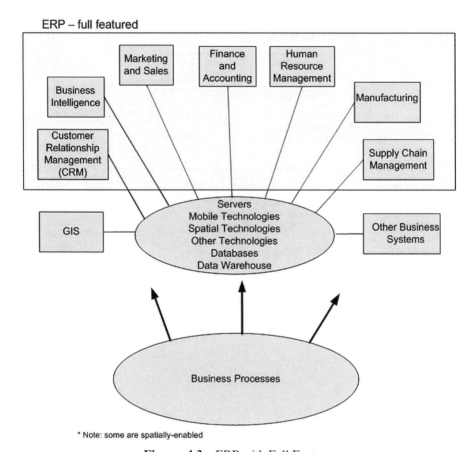

* Note: some are spatially-enabled

Figure 4.3 ERP with Full Features

(finance, sales and distribution, human resources, and manufacturing) and over ten optional modules. Each module supports hundreds of business processes (Gray, 2006). SAP R/3 is designed to integrate all of the modules in a client-server environment. It is better adapted to a hierarchical organizational structure (Gray, 2006). mySAP.com is based on internet enterprise bus architecture with web access for users.

ERP systems are expensive, usually costing many millions of dollars. They take several years to implement, and involve extensive training. Although employees often resist its roll-out, in the years after ERP is installed and running, the benefits accrue, in particular greater efficiency, fewer personnel, shorter cycle time for products to reach customers, better financial management, and fewer people (Gray, 2006).

ERP II operates on the internet enterprise bus platform described for GIS in Chapter 1. Based on SOA, XML, and other web protocols, it can interface with web-enabled business software, such as CRM, supply chain, and BI.

It also interacts with web-enabled GIS and web map services, which are discussed in Chapter 5. The advantages of ERP II include flexibility, a wider user base, and greater ease in open sourcing to third-party software modules. In the ERP II environment, the user's job is made easier by web portals, intelligent agents, and voice recognition (Gray, 2006).

ERP and GIS software can be connected together, which takes advantage of key strengths of each type, and yields a stronger integrated result for the user. The ERP software is enriched by map displays and spatial analysis, while the GIS package benefits by access to deeper and broader attribute data. ERP and GIS software can be integrated by several alternative means (ESRI, 2006):

Remote Function Calls (RFCs). The ERP software and GIS software invoke each other's remotely callable functions. Calling software is usually developed by third-party vendors.

Third-party connectors. Connectors are built by third party vendors that directly connect packaged front-end and back-end systems. An example is iWay Control Builder from Information Builders. This alternative, although expensive, offers an application solution that usually provides good performance and scalability (ESRI, 2006).

Passive middleware. ERP and GIS are connected at the level of passive middleware, that runs on top of the operating system (ESRI, 2006). This solution works as long as users stick to generic ERP and GIS, and don't try to customize their processes. An example is the SAP's GIS Business Connector. Both ERP vendors and third parties market these products.

Customized Enterprise Application Integration (EAI). An environment of standards, platforms, and connector software together supports enterprise integration between ERP and GIS. An example is SAP Exchange Infrastructure, which performs this comprehensive integration between SAP and ArcGIS software.

In the list, the bottom two types are more customized and expensive, but also involve less design and implementation cost (ESRI, 2006). In short, ERP has a huge user base, is very expensive, and can yield improved efficiencies and competitiveness in back office applications. GIS, in the form of a separate software application, can be coupled with ERP to achieve "best-of-breed" synergies. ERP-GIS connections are undergoing rapid development, and nearly complete integration might be achieved in the future. The Pidpa case demonstrates the synergies of well-conceived ERP-GIS integration.

CASE STUDY OF ERP AT PIDPA, BELGIAN WATER UTILITY

Pidpa, a Belgian water utility firm based in Antwerp, is among the largest drinking water firms in the Flanders portion of the country. It supplies

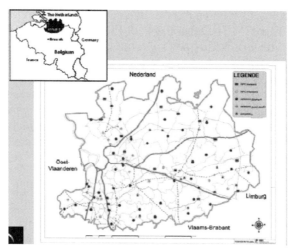

Figure 4.4 Pidpa's Water Distribution Locations in Antwerp Province, Belgium. *Source:* Reynaert, 2005

drinking water throughout Antwerp Province. Figure 4.4 shows the firm's water production centers and distribution network. Pidpa's water comes mostly from groundwater, which is sometimes polluted adding to the firm's emphasis on water quality. Pidpa samples the water quality at a multiple network points. The sampling is supported by a lab information management system (LIM) that does continual quality checking. The Scada (Supervisory Control and Data Acquisition) system automatically controls its water distribution network. Pidpa also has hydraulic modeling software, and AutoCAD-based Synoptiek software that allows for designing detailed sketches on its water distribution network. The network has more than 7,500 miles of water mains and produces over 72 million cubic meters of water yearly.

Pidpa adopted a full-featured implementation of SAP/R3 ERP, shown in Figure 4.5, which includes SAP's four standard modules, plus others for control, asset management, funds management, project systems, and plant maintenance. The firm adopted the ArcGIS family of products, combined with ArcFM, a spatial module from Miner&Miner/Talvent for the engineering management of utilities. The GIS database is managed by ESRI's data management software, ArcSDE. The web-server software ArcIMS supports web and mobile users.

Pidpa performed in-house programming for its web viewer and for its SAP-to-GIS connection. It commissioned ESRI Nederland B.V. to custom-program GeoLink, a web viewer for the GIS database based on ESRI's ArcIMS HTML viewer. It provides web viewing of maps and data from the SAP ERP, Scada, and CIS, a customer information system. Costs to develop GeoLink were limited due to the presence of a solid GIS and SAP architeiture. A benefit to

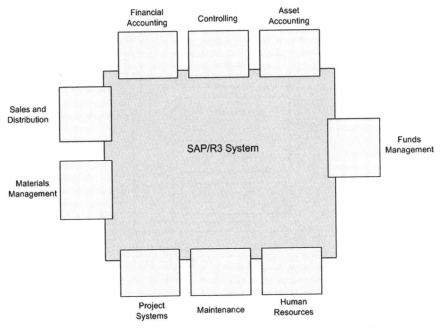

Figure 4.5   Pidpa's ERP System. *Source:* Reynaert, 2005

users is that GeoLink can act as a web portal to access diverse information relevant to Pidpa's customers and employees. In sum, Pidpa's GIS system, seen in Figure 4.6, is largely standard with the exception of the GeoLink web browser.

Although GeoLink solved the need for web viewing, a custom approach was adopted for integration of SAP and GIS data. Pidpa custom-programmed its own "third party connector," but it limited the integration to eight business scenarios that users rated as essential.

One scenario in the GIS-ERP connection is "calamity point," which Pidpa calls a water-utility maintenance problem that is not quickly fixable, but rather long-term in nature. Calamity points are marked and accumulate over time. They serve a strategic purpose for management, when it plans for renewal of major segments of the network (Reynaert et al., 2004). A set of calamity points is shown along a water distribution line in the top of Figure 4.7. The user can highlight a calamity point as seen in dark shading at the top of the map and request the software to provide automatically from SAP's maintenance module a listing of the service orders for fixing it, which are shown at the bottom.

As seen in Figure 4.8, besides invoking SAP tables, the GeoLink web browser can also automatically call up Scada summary tables, CRM information, and scanned water-network schematic drawings from Synoptiek.

In summary, Pidpa succeeded in implementing a full-featured ERP, GIS, CRM, and commercial Scada utility software, along with GeoLink, a

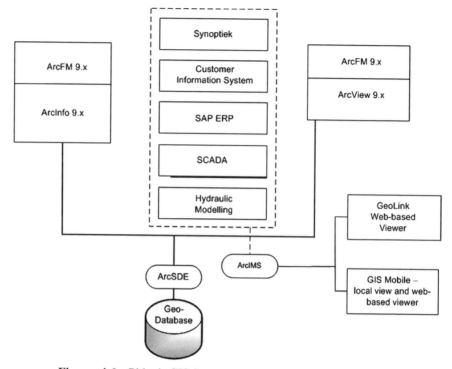

Figure 4.6 Pidpa's GIS System Design. *Source:* Reynaert, 2004

customized web map browser. It is designed so users can click on map features and gain access to information from the other enterprise business and utility systems. Pidpa plans to modify the GeoLink map browser to enable use by field workers who have mobile devices. Further, it hopes to increase the extent and power of integration between GIS and the other systems.

GIS AND CUSTOMER RELATIONSHIP MANAGEMENT

Customer Relationship Management (CRM) refers to a business strategy or application intended to improve customer satisfaction and in turn to grow revenues and profits (Oracle, 2006). CRM also encompasses software packages to achieve this and the transformation of an organization through new thinking about customers (Oracle, 2006; Gray, 2006; Fjermestad and Romano, 2006). Customers who sometimes feel neglected benefit by the personal attention and customized services provided by CRM. Direct, personal interactions between the company and customer, termed "touch points," build and reinforce the customer relationship (Oracle, 2006; Gray, 2006). CRM helps in this process by streamlining targeted information and providing it to the customer

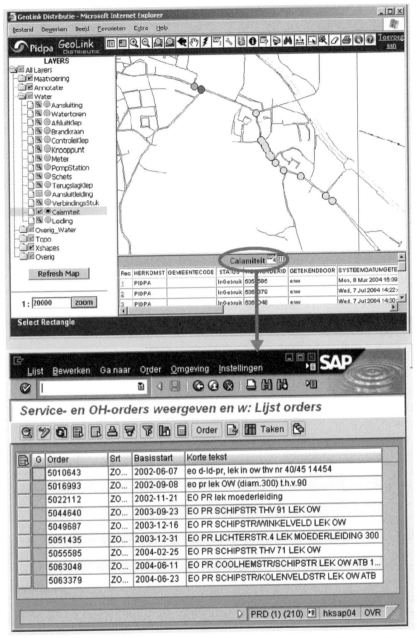

Figure 4.7   Pidpa: User Selection of Calamity Point in GeoLink Browser Showing Link to SAP Work Orders. *Source:* Reynaert, 2005

SAP: Equipment Tree
for a functional location

SCADA summary table

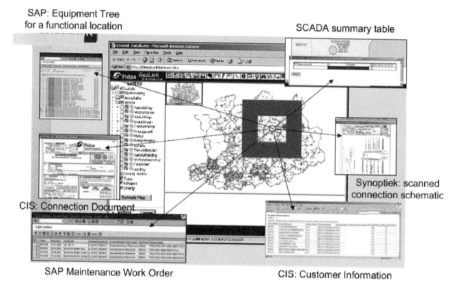

Synoptiek: scanned
connection schematic

CIS: Connection Document

SAP Maintenance Work Order

CIS: Customer Information

Note: CIS = Customer Information System

Figure 4.8   Pidpa's Links of GIS with Major Business Systems. *Source:* Reynaert et al., 2004

and customer-service employees. Most CRMs have business intelligence features, so analysis and modeling can be done to support better decisions for the customer.

CRM emphasizes the "best" customers, i.e. those most remunerative to the firm. It's a rule of thumb in marketing that a fifth of the customers provide four-fifths of the profits (Gray, 2006). Helped by CRM support, customers gain loyalty that can be reinforced for years or a lifetime. The benefits of CRM to the company are to: (1) identify good customers, (2) develop greater customer satisfaction and loyalty, (3) close more deals more quickly, and (4) improve market segmenting, which results in better targeting of customers (Oracle, 2006; Gray, 2006). Understanding the location of customers, facilities, employees, and assets can enhance the benefits.

Specific functions of CRM are to improve customer service (e.g. give call center and customer agents much more information on customer history) and strengthen personalized marketing by the sales force, i.e. sometimes referred to as sales force automation. This encompasses design of marketing campaigns and capture of information on customers, sources, and regional demographics (Oracle, 2006).

CRM software is available from vendors that include Oracle's Siebel Systems, M2M's Onyx Software Corporation, and Microsoft. Additionally, CRM is offered as a module in most ERP products, such as SAP's R/3 and mySAP.com. Oracle is a leading, full-featured vendor that offers client-server and hosted web services products through its Siebel products. M2M's Onyx is a medium-sized CRM vendor that emphasizes professional markets. CRM software has the following features: (1) product management, (2) sales capability in the field and on the web, (3) collaboration (with partners and internally), (4) marketing automation, (5) customer service, and (6) business intelligence (Gray, 2006). BI, covered in the last chapter, provides analysis and modeling to help managers cultivate and handle customers better.

CRM software, only a decade or so old, is still in a low maturity stage, and has tended to have a high failure rate, as much as 50 percent or higher according to the Gartner Group (Gray, 2006). To overcome these problems, CEO Janice Anderson of Onyx (Financial Services Technology, 2006) points to four key ways to achieve success with CRM: (1) Develop customer information in the CRM that can support many business units and products. This enables diverse sales people to cross-sell products to a customer. (2) Customize the customer's solution to his/her individual needs. The customer does not want a solution that replicates every competitor's CRM. (3) Adapt the information and uses of the CRM to changes in markets and customers. CRM design and implementation might take significant time, during which customer needs change rapidly, so when rolled out the solution might appear old-fashioned. (4) Integrate the CRM in real-time with other major business systems. This comes back to the chapter's enterprise framework in Figure 4.1, which shows the integration of CRM with eight or more major business application modules (Financial Services Technology, 2006). Another mistake is that a company can rush to implement CRM without developing its customer strategy (Gray, 2006). Furthermore, privacy issues with CRM can develop when personal information is used for purposes other than originally intended, without appropriate permission from the customer. An example in a spatial context is that customers and their personal information might be identified through easy recognition of their mapped locations. Privacy issues are covered in Chapter 11.

Spatial systems enhance CRM functions by recognizing location. Spatial analysis refines benefits of CRM to the customer as follows (Winslow and Lea, 2002):

Data collection and enhancement. GIS can be helps in error-cleaning customer data. The process of geocoding addresses and mapping customer data can reveal errors in the data. For instance, a map shows the same customer at multiple principal residences or it displays many headquarters for a single business customer. These can be checked and corrected, on the ground if necessary. Spatial analysis can be useful in imputation of missing values. If a customer has missing attributes, certain values can be estimated by taking averages of customers who are geographically adjacent. In a different setting, imputation of missing values is done for small areas by the U.S. Census.

Business intelligence. BI is useful in CRM for data mining, modeling, and forecasting. As indicated in Chapter 3, many BI techniques can be spatially enhanced. Data mining is a method for looking for certain characteristics or data relationships in a large-scale dataset, a process strengthened by including spatial location of entities. Forecasting is often strengthened through spatial statistics and spatial econometrics. For instance, the error in regression forecasting models for housing prices can be reduced by including location (Wachter et al., 2005).

In the telecommunications industry, spatial BI can sustain customer relationships by reducing cell phone churn (Winslow and Lea, 2002). Cell phone markets suffer from rapid turnover of customers who are disappointed by dropped calls, poor service, and malfunctioning equipment. Users come to depend on always having good outdoor reception regardless of location. Using GIS and data from GPS-enabled customers, spatial BI can analyze how the customer's locations are correlated with his/her demographics, the time of day of use, and call volume in the area (Winslow and Lea, 2002). "By analyzing the customer's locations, the risk of losing a particular customer can be predicted months ahead" (Winslow and Lea, 2002). As a consequence, attention can be given to checking and correcting that customer's usage problems, and special customer service can be applied such as offers of new cell phone plans or providing promotional maps showing the growth of existing cell-service areas.

Site Evaluation Models

Corporate customers in many industries can be assisted by site evaluation models. Although the models can be run non-spatially, they are improved through GIS. In the real estate industry, customers are interested in visualizing the siting aspects of their properties, as seen in the first chapter's Sperry Van Ness case study. In banking, site evaluation can be done of branch locations, such as the last chapter's LPCB case, or real estate site evaluation services can be provided for high-value customers. Spatial analysis can model optimal siting of business facilities, utility lines, and transport corridors.

Distribution of Resources

The workforce and investments being applied to enhance customer relationships can be modeled spatially. For instance, sales force automation seeks to allocate a sales force in the best way to identify customers and develop relationships. Map layers of the locations of the sales force and its customers can be overlaid and compared. Misallocations can be corrected. Such overlays are useful also in call centers in the telecommunications industry. Call-center operators can visualize the location of customers phoning in, relative to nearby service facilities (ESRI, 2006).

To accomplish these benefits, CRM and GIS interact as separate software packages. GIS and CRM are tied together by software connectors developed in-house or by third-party vendors. For example, Paz Oil, an Israeli consumer oil and gasoline firm, implemented SAP's CRM module connected to ESRI ArcGIS software. Paz has 260 filling stations that also include convenience stores. Its subsidiary Pazomat provides fuel to customers that have fleets of vehicles. The fleets have gas-tank-mounted devices that read the fuel levels and transmit the information to Pazomat's IT system. The GIS and SAP's CRM module are linked together through the integration hub of SAP's NetWeaver XI (SAP, 2006). Pazomat can view maps that display the locations and fuel levels of customers' fleet vehicles, allowing Pazomat to adapt to the spatial distribution of customer gasoline demand throughout its network.

The interaction of GIS and IT with CRM can be examined through a two-way matrix that has the process stages of customer relationship as columns and factors of CRM as rows (Gray, 2006). The four stages are (1) identifying prospective customers, (2) differentiating customers by their values and needs, (3) interacting with the customer, and (4) customizing a response. As seen in Table 4.2, modified from Gray (2006), the process stages are linked to CRM sub-factors and corresponding IT and GIS uses.

For instance, identifying customers can be supported by cookies, customized websites, and product personalization. At the end stage of customization, with CRM fully implemented, the IT "heavy-hitters" of ERP and e-commerce can be brought into play to deliver maximal information both to customers and their relationship managers.

The matrix has been modified to include GIS shown in the bottom row. In the identification stage, GIS can provide personalized maps to customers, while in the differentiation stage, spatial BI can be applied to refine customer groupings. For instance, cluster analysis results can be mapped to distinguish customer groups. In the interaction stage, web and wireless interactions can be enhanced through maps and analysis. Maps can be made available to customers on their cell phones to assist them with a retail service. Finally in the customization build-out at the end GIS can be coupled with ERP, CRM, and other powerful enterprise systems.

In summary, CRM is an approach to give attention and personalized interest to customers. GIS helps CRM better realize this relationship building by incorporating location and spatial processes.

CHICO'S CASE STUDY: GIS AND CRM IN A CUSTOMER-CENTRIC FASHION COMPANY

Chico's is a women's apparel chain that emphasizes customer service and appeals to a "mature" (forty-five-year-plus) market. Founded in 1983, by 2006 Chico's had store, catalog, and web sales that totaled $1.4 billion, and employed 11,000 persons. Its rapid growth is shown by addition of

TABLE 4.2 GIS and IT Factors in CRM

Process Factor	Identification	Differentiation	Interaction	Customization
CRM goal	Identify individual customer	Evaluate customer value and needs	Build a continuing relationship	Fulfill customer needs, generate profit
Traditional mass marketing	Not done	Clustering	Call center	Sales, services
CRM sub-function	Customer profiling	Individual level analysis	Call center management for individual. Customized auto response	Sales force automation, marketing
IT used	Cookies, website, personalization	Data mining, organizational learning	Web applications, wireless communication	ERP, e-commerce
GIS used	Personalized mapping	Spatial BI	Spatial web, spatial wireless	GIS and spatial technologies (GPS, RFID) seamlessly linked to CRM, ERP, and e-commerce

Gray, Paul. 2006. Manager's Guide to Making Decisions about Information Systems. New York: John Wiley and Sons.

150 stores in 2007 (Chico's, 2006). It has always emphasized customer loyalty and direct marketing (Roussel-Dupré, 2002). This is highlighted by its Passport Club which requires $500 in cumulative purchases for membership. There are 1.7 million permanent members of the Passport Club and 334,000 members for its less expensive White House/Black Market chain of stores (for thirty-five-year-plus age group). The members of the clubs provide 80 percent of Chico's revenues. Members' Passport credit cards provide personalized service, discounts, coupons, and birthday gifts. The Passport customer gives detailed information in her application that includes home address. Subsequently her home location is geocoded. Geocoding is the process of applying GIS software to convert street addresses into X-Y coordination locations. Hence, the customer home locations appear as points on a map layer.

The purchase information of customers from all the stores is uploaded weekly from the store's point-of-sale databases and consolidated into a national database that is provided to the GIS team to analyze. It includes each Passport customer's residence and principal store location, demographic information, purchase history, and the socioeconomic profile of her home small geographic area (U.S. Census block group).

Chico's sales approach is characterized by sales personnel who offer an attentive and personalized approach to customer care. Typical customers demand new apparel frequently so there are rapid inventory turns. The philosophy is that employees act as if they work for a small local store, e-mailing customers, being friendly to customers, and even calling them by first names. Chico's has capitalized on its loyal customer base by implementing a successful CRM supported by GIS. These systems enhance responsiveness to customers and improve Chico's employees' knowledge of them.

The CRM and GIS systems also support real estate analysis of new and existing store sites. The CRM information is used for decision-making on opening, closing, or changing store locations. The AnySite software from MapInfo can analyze the relationship between the current store location preferences of customers and prospective real estate locations. For instance, if a new store site is being evaluated, customers can be mapped color-coded by their primary store preference. If an area reveals a mixture of colors with no clear store preference, that points towards the need to locate a new store in that area. The map also shows topographic and man-made barriers such as rivers, highways, and hills that may influence whether or not, and where a new store is designated. The amount of "cannibalization" (i.e. a new store taking away sales from old ones) can be predicted, and steps taken to adjust to the correct amounts of merchandise at each outlet. It can even make adjustments, so that employees at an old store are not unduly deprived of bonuses, once the new store arrives and draws away business.

Chico's MIS system is housed in central, large IBM servers at its Fort Myers, Florida, headquarters and Georgia distribution center, that connect with decentralized application servers located at store sites. The company does not yet use an ERP system, but one is planned for rollout in 2008. Instead there are a group of specialized application packages, many leading ones for the retail industry (Chico's, 2006). For CRM, Chico's uses the Connected Retailer from NSB, which supports CRM as well as store merchandising, planning, allocation/replenishment, and sourcing. MapInfo Professional GIS software is run alongside the Connected Retailer and utilizes the same database of customer information.

The CRM and GIS support a number of key features that relate to Chico's customer-centric focus.

> *Direct mailing.* An estimated 5 million items are sent monthly to customers, including event promotions, coupons, and catalogs (Roussel-Dupré, 2002). The CRM refines this mailing through analysis that gives the optimal customer audience for a particular mailing.
>
> *Unified customer database.* Prior to the CRM, each sales channel had its own customer information system. The CRM gathered them into a uniform customer database that supports cross-organizational flows of information (Roussel-Dupré, 2002).
>
> *Business intelligence for CRM.* Chico's was able to perform analytics to make customer relationship processes more efficient and to understand customer patterns better. For instance, Chico's was able to determine that its best customers on the average shopped in a Chico's store every four to five weeks. Through CRM and GIS, it was able to find out where customers shopped and what they bought at particular locations. In Florida, Chico's many stores have a seasonal customer flow. A woman Passport member from Chicago vacationing in Florida may purchase two tops in Florida, a transaction that can be compared with her purchase profile back home.
>
> *Forecasting.* The CRM enables the firm to predict, based on historical records, how the customers residing in an area would respond to a sales promotion. GIS is used to map the results.

Chico's CRM/GIS initiative has worked. Before the CRM, Passport members represented only 9 percent of Chico's revenues, while three years after implementation, they accounted for 80 percent. During each store visit, a Passport member spends 40 percent more than a non-Passport/member (Roussel-Dupré, 2002). GIS has reinforced CRM, by taking into account where customers shop, what they buy where, and what is the geography of customer relationships. The strategic success of CRM coupled with GIS is tied to its synchrony to Chico's key value of developing and sustaining customer loyalty.

GIS AND SUPPLY CHAIN MANAGEMENT

Supply chain is the flow of goods and services in an organization. Goods originate in raw materials, are transported, assembled into components, further assembled into finished products, distributed, sold, and sometimes returned. Supply chain management uses modeling and analysis techniques to improve performance and functioning of the corporate supply chain (Gray, 2006). Information systems including GIS are important in controlling and coordinating the supply chain, and enhancing its efficiency and profitability.

The factors in supply chain management (Gray, 2006) are:

1. *Planning*. The products or services must be designed, and the multiple steps planned out to end up with the finished result. The IS to support the supply chain must be developed to enhance communication, efficiency, and accuracy. Along with this, the GIS and spatial technologies must be planned.
2. *Sourcing*. Sources for raw materials and components need to be determined, and optimized for cost, shipping distance, and availability.
3. *Manufacturing/creating*. How will the components be manufactured into a product? The process of component assembly needs to be determined.
4. *Delivering*. The approach for the final delivery of products to customers must be worked out. This includes whether the product will be delivered pre-assembled or as parts. Delivery must be coordinated with the customer's schedule.
5. *Returning*. If a product is not acceptable to the customer, return of the product to an earlier step in the supply chain must be planned. A returned product rarely can be sent back along the same forward route from which it originated. The returned items are in smaller quantity, and usually go back via different geographic routes. Often return is done through a third party, that can wait until a sufficient lot size is accumulated to cost-effectively reverse-ship the items.

IT supports information flows that inform, analyze, and optimize the physical flows. IT for "planning" (Factor 1 above) consists of determining the end demand for the finished product, and then working backwards to estimate the demands upstream in the chain. A second type of software program, "implementation," supports Factors 2 through 5. The focus is to reduce the length of time for manufacture and deliveries and make adjustments so demand targets are met at each step. Often there are multiple suppliers in the chain, that lead to poor estimates, misunderstandings, and underperformance. If the supply chain is internal to a firm, the same problems can occur, although there is the advantage of being under a single management structure.

Supply chain has a close relationship with levels of inventory (Gray, 2006). If demand forecasts lead to overproduction, the surplus might have to be abandoned, given away, or written off, while underproduction in the chain results in disgruntled customers.

Supply chain software is available as modules in ERP packages such as SAP. The ERP approach has the advantage of tight, seamless exchange of supply chain with the other major business systems, but the minus of reduced flexibility in modifying the supply chain parameters for a particular client. Supply chain is also available as standalone software from such vendors as Logility Inc., Catalyst International, Aspen Technology, and Clarus Corporation. Supply chain software can reside inside or outside of ERP (compare Figures 4.2 and 4.3), and can consist of commercial or in-house programs.

The problems and challenges for supply chain success are (1) trust among suppliers, manufacturers, distributors, customers, and information vendors; (2) employee resistance (supply chain often involves displacement and loss of jobs); (3) lack of training in the start-up phase (supply chains rarely run "out-of-the-box," they need tuning, adjustments by parties involved, and re-tuning); (4) consumer preferences that lead to new product designs which imply modified supply chain; and (5) errors in forecasting demand. Demand fluctuates depending on environmental conditions, political regimes, transportation strikes and delays, economic ups and downs, and other factors, so it rarely can be accurately estimated (Gray, 2006).

GIS and spatial technologies contribute to more efficient and faster supply chains. Any item moving in the supply chain with recorded geographic coordinates can be more accurately tracked through a combination of GIS, RFID, and GPS. Examples of how GIS contributes are as follows:

Spatial analysis of supply, manufacture, and delivery points. Transport and shipping durations can be better modeled by incorporating geography (ESRI, 2006). Consider a supply chain in a region impacted by an earthquake. Vehicle transportation is halted or slowed due to physical barriers and dangers. Shipping is impacted due to harbor and dock damages. Airports are temporarily closed. However, zones vary considerably in their extent of transportation disruption. Spatial analysis can estimate the geographical pattern of damages and delays for different transport modes, and can include location to better estimate how supply-chain transport timing will be altered.

Spatial distribution of customers in the supply chain. Customers are the source of supply chain demand which is hard to predict. The present and future locations of end customers who receive goods are a critical aspect of demand. Their geographical prevalence in sales areas helps to determine the allocation and timing of the final supply routes to sales locations.

RFID and GPS can receive input data on the spatial locations of supply-chain items and transport vehicles, which are combined with attribute data and utilized by GIS to perform spatial analysis. RFID-tagged items are read as they pass fixed reader locations in the supply chain. An ID on the tags allows records to be accessed on a remote server. If the readers are spatially referenced, mapping can be performed. Businesses are beginning to make use of RFID, but the proportion going further to apply GIS is presently small.

The example of the U.S. military points to growing use. The military is the leading organization using RFID and GPS in supply chain. It imposed RFID requirements for all its suppliers by 2005. It demonstrated the wartime strategic value of these technologies in the Iraq War where the military utilized RFID and GPS to input location data into real-time GIS to assist in battlefield decisions (Galuszka, 2005).

RFID was introduced in Chapter 1, with the Wal-Mart example. Although the focus of this book is on the private sector, the military use of spatial supply chain is included, since it is at the leading edge and points to where many businesses are heading. However, there should be caution that not everything from the military carries over to business.

The U.S. military's huge and complex supply chain includes 43,000 suppliers. Correct inventory must be supplied to hundreds of thousands of personnel, and life and death might depend on it. For instance, a combat unit that is quickly running out of ammunition and food must have delivery at a particular place by a given time.

The military spent over $100 million to implement RFID as a standard by 2005, as a part of Secretary Rumsfeld's modernization of military technology (Galuszka, 2003). In the Iraq War, the U.S. military was the first one to use RFID for supply chain in combat. Military commanders were able to monitor the supply-chain flow of equipment and supplies in real time (Military Medical Technology, 2005). RFID tags were affixed variously at the individual item, box, carton, and pallet levels.

For higher-value ordnance, active tags were used at the item level that can be read by fixed RFID readers within a 150-foot radius. All shipping containers have active tags that indicate in detail what is inside, and can be read by military satellites that pass by every 6 to 12 hours. Hence, all the supply-chain inventory having active tags can be viewed and analyzed. In Iraq, hardened RFID readers, spaced at 120 guarded locations, collect information on the contents of passing supply convoys instantaneously (Galuszka, 2005). At U.S. Central Command (CENTCOM) in Tampa, GIS maps of the war zone show the shipping containers and high-value items, as well as aircraft, drones, vehicles, and fighting action on the ground. When an item is moved in a vehicle, GPS can track the vehicle and its contents in real-time.

The benefits to the military are multiple. (1) In a dynamic battle situation, supplies can be moved to the right place quickly. (2) Cargo can be dropped or sequestered in a "secret" location and picked up later. (3) What is typically a "just-in-time" supply chain can be changed to "sense and respond," which refers to flexibility to change the supply chain while operations are underway (Galuszka, 2005). For example, a combat unit under pressure could escape with limited gear, while leaving equipment and RFID-tagged supplies behind, which are tracked by satellite to be picked up later. Hence, receiving supplies at an exact time and location becomes somewhat less important. (4) The supply chain contents become "visible" meaning that the contents of all the items in the chain are visible system-wide without opening packages, containers, or pallets (Sun Microsystems, 2006). (5) Inventory management is improved, which leads to reduced supplier fraud and pricing errors, and better theft detection and control of returns.

This advanced military system does not eliminate some problems. Predicting demand remains difficult, with the risks of over- or under-production. In the Iraq War, there was initially severe shortages of body armor and armored hummers. There were also problems in faulty RFID readers, inaccuracies of reading, and gaps in satellite reception. Nevertheless, this military supply chain based on RFID and GPS has been successful in and out of combat. GIS is coupled with RFID and GPS to provide visualization and spatial analysis.

Although Wal-Mart as an industry leader trails the military, its requirements set in 2006 of having its largest suppliers attach RFID to shipping crates and pallets supports similar potential to the military, but under different operational constraints. There is a leveraged effect for suppliers to adopt RFID upstream and downstream in this huge supply chain, and other major retailers are following Wal-Mart's example. It will be helped by the anticipated drop in pricing of passive RFID tags from 25 cents to under 1 cent based on the expanded volumes expected within a few years (Williams, 2004).

In summary, the supply chain represents a major business system. As items move geographically through it, location information can be detected by RFID and GPS and spatially analyzed through GIS. The IT control and management of the chains is made more accurate, while they can also be more quickly altered and reconfigured. The U.S. military led the way in achieving a cutting edge spatially-enabled and combat-ready supply chain, while Wal-Mart and other leading companies are not too far behind.

SPATIAL DATA WAREHOUSES AND DATA MINING

The data warehouse is an alternative form of data storage from the conventional operational database. It is oriented towards a view of data that is subject-oriented, rather than application-oriented. Subject-orientation refers to objects that represent the key elements of decision-making in business, such as customers, markets, products, and employees (Laudon and Laudon, 2006). By contrast, the traditional operational database focuses on the functional areas of the business, such as sales, finance, and manufacturing. Another feature is that the data warehouse retains older data so it can look at change tendencies over time. The operational database regularly purges older data for deletion or archiving. Since the philosophy is to store everything, the size of storage can be potentially huge, a true "warehouse." The

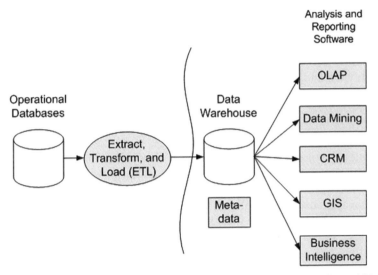

Figure 4.9   The Data Warehouse and Its Data Flows. *Source:* Gray, 2006

data are nonvolatile, i.e. after being stored, they remain the same over time. This lends stability to the data in a data warehouse (Inmon, 1992). The data warehouse concept also favors summarized data, which are useful in decision-making and also become nonvolatile. Granularity distinguishes the individual data items from the summaries, i.e. the most granular refers to raw data, while less granular is summarized data (Gray, 2006). An example of summarized data is a summary of account totals for March, 2007, for a business department.

At certain time points, data are moved from operational databases into the data warehouse for permanent, long-term storage. In a large organization, often data are input from a wide collection of databases on the inside and outside. The process of error-checking and entering these data is known as ETL (extraction, transformation, and load). As shown in Figure 4.9, data enter the data warehouse from the operational databases. Once inside, they can be accessed by a variety of analysis, statistical, data mining, and GIS software (Gray, 2006; Laudon and Laudon, 2006). Also shown are metadata, which keep track of the detailed descriptions of the records and entities in the data warehouse.

Data warehouses have been particularly useful for the applications of data mining, direct marketing, online analytical processing (OLAP), business intelligence, CRM, and supply chain management.

Data mining seeks answers to business problems directly from the raw and summarized data and from data relationships in the data warehouse. The answers are not pre-determined but often discovered through exploratory methods (Gray, 2006). A variety of data mining techniques are utilized which are beyond this book's scope: intelligent agents, expert systems, fuzzy logic, neural networks, exploratory data analysis, and data visualization (Tan et al., 2005; Gray, 2006). All these methods are able to intensively explore large amounts data and/or relationships, and to identify potential answers to complex business problems.

Direct marketing uses techniques that segment customer data based on market distributions. They are examined further in Chapter 5. *Online Analytical Processing* (OLAP) is a set of rules for accessing and processing multidimensional data. OLAP rules, covered in Chapter 8, enable accessing data based on simple and efficient steps rather than complex models.

Data warehousing and GIS form a strong analytical combination. The GIS provides spatial analysis and visualization of geo-referenced data in the data warehouse. For instance, it can enrich the uses of data warehouse information for utilities infrastructure; energy exploration, production, and distribution; traffic accident analysis; large scale auto insurance risk analysis; management of fleets of vehicles; and business intelligence for decision-making (SQL Server Magazine, 2002; Farley, 2004; Location Intelligence, 2006).

For data warehouses in auto risk insurance, maps can be produced that take spatial views from the usual ZIP code geography down to hundreds of small areas within the ZIPs (Location Intelligence, 2006). This allows underwriters to set more refined policy pricing. Another example is the City of Portland's spatial data warehouse for city and regional traffic accident data which has fourteen dimensions and sixteen years of data. As a result, users of the city's system have access to interactive mapping of all the accident locations during a decade and half, which accompany accident reports and give added insight for decisions (SQL Server Magazine, 2002).

GIS and spatial analysis can be in use for data warehouses at various steps along the data flows shown in Figure 4.9, a topic of Chapter 8. Data warehouses, which constitute an important part of enterprise architecture, can be spatially-enabled and have proven valuable for many larger-sized firms.

CASE STUDY: NESA, DANISH ELECTRICAL UTILITY

Nesa, a medium-sized Danish electrical utility firm, has not only installed a group of enterprise systems including a GIS; an ERP system; and Scada, an enterprise-wide process control system; but it has implemented SmartLight, which allows consumers to automatically control outdoor lighting. Coming at the end of the chapter, the Nesa case demonstrates an enterprise philosophy and approach.

Nesa has over one million residential, business, and government customers and a large share of the Danish electrical utility market. Its IT mission is to "support and improve the competitive power and the business basis of Nesa" (Nesa Annual Report, 2006). To achieve the mission, Nesa decided to focus on leading software packages to support major business applications, rather than on lesser-known software from smaller vendors or on in-house applications. Its large vendors include SAP for ERP, ESRI for GIS, Siemens from CRM, and MDSI for management of mobile workforce. Through an enterprise approach, Nesa's goal is to achieve a high extent of internal and external integration. It hopes that the software consistency and standards can lead to better customer service in concent with its vision to meet customer needs and create value and relationships with them (Nesa, 2006).

A general schematic of Nesa's IT application configuration rests on a bottom level of communications and process control (see Figure 4.10). At the lower right, the Scada process control refers to a type of utility software that provides integrated monitoring and control of the entire electrical utility network. For instance, if a part of an electric transmission line fails, Scada registers the failure, assesses what the impacts are, takes automatic corrective action, and notifies managers about the problem and its potential impacts.

At the middle level in Figure 4.10 is the ERP back-end system that includes the modules of material management, payroll, maintenance and service, project management, finance, and control (Engsbro and Westmose, 2005). The ERP system and its modules run on top of a data warehouse. Alongside the ERP are separate GIS software packages (ArcGIS and ArcFM) and computer-aided design software (Auto CAD and Grid Design). Arto CAD software provides computer-generated drawings for engineering design, e.g. design of a utility transformer station or a power plant. It is linked through a standard interface with GIS.

At the top of the figure are software applications close to the customer, including financial applications of trading and portfolio analysis, management of the mobile workforce (MDSI and SRMON), telephone and voice systems, the SAP CRM module, printing and distribution, web software, SmartRead software for automated meter reading, and SmartLight for automated lighting. SmartRead automatically reads and transmits customer utility meter information into the SAP Customer and Maintenance modules. As seen in Figure 4.11, the SmartRead meters at the customer premises feed this information to SmartRead monitors through wireless communications. This innovation saves the firm the high costs and inaccuracies of regular meter reading by service technicians. Rather, a technician visits the meter only if it needs to be maintained. For the SmartRead system, GIS displays the design maps of network transmission flows.

Nesa has been innovative in designing and implementing a system called SmartLight (Engsbro and Westmose, 2005) (see Figure 4.12) for automated monitoring and control of outdoor lighting. Street lamps outfitted with SmartLight devices are connected through a power line and wireless links to the Customer Information Center. The Center allows Nesa managers and users

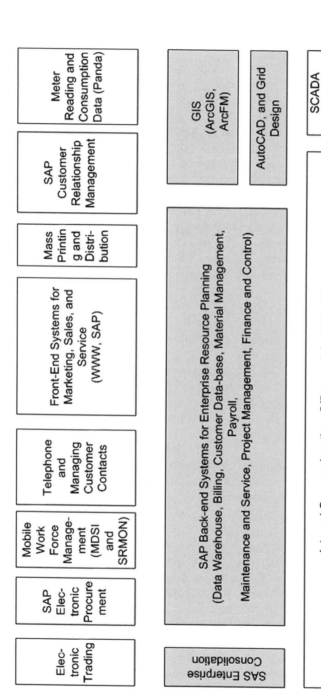

Figure 4.10 Nesa's Corporate IT Application Configuration. *Source:* Engsbro and Westmose, 2005

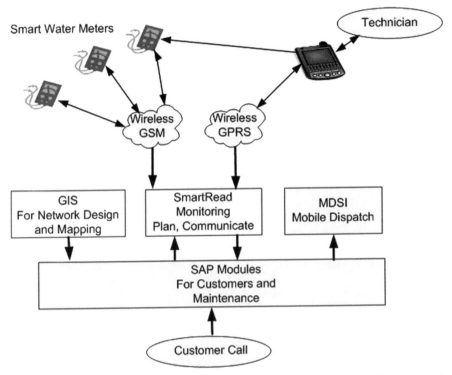

Figure 4.11 Nesa's IT Processes for SmartRead System. *Source:* Engsbro and Westmose, 2005

to control over a half million street lamp units. SmartLight has the following features:

- Field teams through real-time flows of information know the conditions of lighting fast and accurately.
- Through remote lighting options, the customer automatically adjusts and controls large groups of street lamps.
- Customers can easily learn about a street lamp's repair status by phoning or e-mailing the Info Center.
- Customers can see the street lamps' technical details in real time including maps of lighting functioning in geographical areas.

Advantages are improved efficiency, reduced cost, and an automatic documentation archive, which can be provided to customers, citizens, the government, and contractors. The role of GIS is to summarize lighting

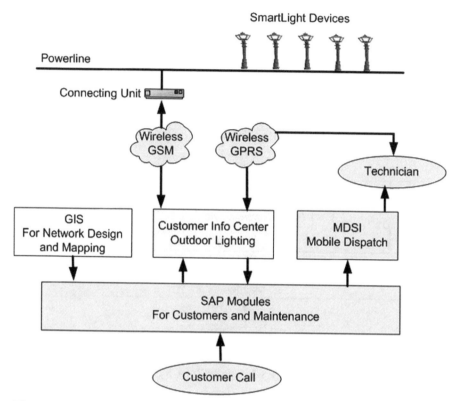

Figure 4.12 Nesa's IT Processes for Outdoor Lighting Customer Information Center. *Source:* Engsbro and Westmose, 2005

performance into maps, conduct spatial analysis and modeling of changes and trends, and give Nesa employees and customers real-time access to lighting maps.

Nesa has the SAP CRM module and other front-end systems for marketing and sales that are shown in Figure 4.10. GIS interacts with them to provide mapping and spatial analysis of prospects, customers, and Nesa facilities. At the nesa.dk, customers can download maps, such as underground cabling for their sites, which are useful for construction projects.

In sum, Nesa taken an enterprise approach with leading software packages including many of the enterprise applications emphasized in this chapter. They work together in an integrated manner with GIS. GIS is called into play for those user needs where mapping and spatial analysis are relevant and useful. The company's IT goals of efficient and effective customer support, system integration, and standardization are being met. At the same time, the architecture allows new applications such as SmartLight to be brought into the enterprise framework to take advantage of its synergies.

CHAPTER SUMMARY

Enterprise applications are mainstays that control the "back office" of businesses. They support and provide control for the operational business processes. Major enterprise applications covered in this chapter are ERP, CRM, Supply Chain Management, and Data Warehouses. GIS is also an enterprise system which can function in a collaborative, coupled environment with the other business enterprise applications. At the underlying storage level of databases and data warehouses, spatial features can be built in.

The contribution of spatial technologies to enterprise applications is to refine the accuracy of performance of the applications by recognizing location of customers, facilities, assets, transport vehicles, and other business phenomena. GIS also provides visualization and exploration benefits to understand enterprise information and make better decisions. Three chapter case studies have illustrated how spatial technologies can yield these benefits, and the ways that GIS is connected to work together with other enterprise applications. The challenge is to design spatially-enabled enterprise architectures that provide added value to corporate users and customers, and are flexible enough to change with the rapid technology advances in this field.

REFERENCES

Chilsholm, Patrick. 2005. "RFID." *Military Medical Technology*. Online Edition. http://www.military-medicial-technology.com/print_article.cfm?DocID=431.

Codd, E.F. 1995. "Twelve Rules for On-Line Analytic Processing." *Computerworld*, April 13.

Dyché, Jill. 2002. *The CRM Handbook*. Boston: Addison-Wesley.

Engsbro, Lars, and Poul Westmose. 2005. "The Changing Role of IT." Paper presented at Sapphire 2005, Copenhagen, Denmark, April 26.

ESRI Inc. 2006. "How ESRI Technology Interfaces with SAP's ERP Software." *ArcNews*, Winter 2002/2003. Available at www.esri.com.

ESRI Inc. 2006. *NESA Deploys a Complete Business Solution: Denmark's Largest Electricity Company Implements Enterprise GIS*. Redlands, CA: ESRI Inc. Available 8/11/06 at www.esri.com.

ESRI Inc. 2006. *ESRI and SAP*. Redlands, CA: ESRI Inc. Available 8/11/06 at www.esri.com.

ESRI Inc. 2006. *Spatial Data Warehousing*. Redlands, CA: ESRI Inc. Available 8/11/06 at www.esri.com.

ESRI Inc. 2006. "American Suzuki Motors Corporation: Internet Mapping Helps Customers Find Stores." Case Study available at www.esri.com.

Farley, Jim. 2004. "Oracle 10g: A Location-enabled Platform for Enterprise GIS and Core Business Applications." *Earth Observation Magazine*, April. Available at www.ecomoline.com.

Financial Services Technology. 2006. "Don't Box Me In. Interview with Janice P. Anderson of Onyx Software." *Financial Services Technology*, No. 2.

Fjermestad, Jerry, and Nicholas C. Romano Jr. (eds.). 2006. *Electronic Customer Relationship Management*. Armonk, NY: M.E. Sharpe Inc.

Francica, Joe. 2005. "BC Hydro Integrates ERP Solutions with GIS." *Directions Magazine*, March 19. Available at www.directionsmag.com.

Galuszka, Peter. 2005. "Lessons from Baghdad." *Chief Executive*, Vol. 208, May, p. 48.

Gray, Paul. 2006. *Manager's Guide to Making Decisions about Information Systems*. New York: John Wiley and Sons.

Greenberg, Paul. 2004. *CRM at the Speed of Light*, 3rd Edition. New York: McGraw-Hill.

Houwen, Peter, Wayne Hewitt, Ben Ralph, and Colin 't Hart. 1999. "The Keys of Successful SAP/ESRI Interfacing." *ArcUser*, October–December. Available at www.esri.com.

Inmon, W.H. 1992. *Building the Data Warehouse*. New York: John Wiley and Sons.

Jukic, Nenad. 2006. "Modeling Strategies and Alternatives for Data Warehousing Projects." *Communications of the ACM*, 49(4): 83–88.

Keating, Gordon N., Paul M. Rich, and Marc S. Witkowski. 2003. "Challenges for Enterprise GIS." *URISA Journal*, 15(2): 23–36.

Kramer, Gail, and Stuart Nisbet. 2006. "The Practical Union of OLAP Analysis and Geographic Mapping." *ArcUser*, January/March. Available at www.esri.com.

Laudon, Kenneth C., and Jane P. Laudon. 2006. *Essentials of Management Information Systems*. Upper Saddle River, NJ: Prentice Hall.

Marakas, George. 2002. *Decision Support Systems*, 2nd Edition. Upper Saddle River, NJ: Prentice Hall.

McKinney, James. 1999. "GIS Solutions for SAP R/3." Paper presented at Sapphire 1999, Nice, France.

Mohraz, Karim. 2000. "Geographical Analysis in SAP Business Information Warehouse." Proceedings of the 8th ACM International Symposium on Advances in Geographic Information Systems, Washington, D.C.: Association for Computing Machinery, pp. 191–193.

Moore, John. 2005. "RFID's Positive Identification." *Federal Computer Week*, 19(11): 53, April 18.

Morales, Diane K., and Steve Geary. 2003. "Speed Kills: Supply Chain Lessons from the War in Iraq." *Harvard Business Review*, November, pp. 16–18.

Nesa Inc. 2006. *2005 Annual Report for Nesa*. Gentofte, Denmark: Nesa Inc.

Nogueria Barrionuevo, Rodrigo. 2002. "A SAP and GIS Integration." *Imagem Sensoriamento Remoto*, June 21.

Oracle Corporation. Oracle Spatial Database 10g. Available at www.oracle.com.

Osterland, Andrew. 2000. "Blaming ERP." *CFO.com Magazine*. Available at www.cfo.com.

Reynaert, Bart, Patrick Vercruyssen, and Rene Horemans. 2004. "GIS and Beyond: Looking to SAP through the Geo-Window." Paper presented at ESRI International User Conference, San Diego, August, 18 pp.

Reynaert, Bart. 2005. "GIS and Beyond: Integration with SAP Improves Business Processes." *ArcUser*, 8(3): 20–23.

Rittman, Mark. 2006a. "GIS-Enabling Your Oracle Data Warehouse." *DBAzine.com*, April 18. Available at www.dbazine.com.

Rittman, Mark. 2006b. "An Introduction to Oracle Warehouse Builder 10g." *DBAzine.com*, August 19. Available at www.dbazine.com.

Ross, Jeanne W., Peter Weill, and David Robertson. 2006. *Enterprise Architecture as Strategy: Creating a Foundation for Business Execution*. Cambridge, MA: Harvard Business School Press.

Roussel-Dupré, Stephanie. 2002. "What are your Customers Telling You?" *Integrated Solutions for Retailers*, March.

SAP. Salzburg AG. "SAP Customer Success Story: Utilities." Available at www.sap.com.

SAP. Paz Oil Company Ltd. 2006. "SAP Customer Success Story: Oil and Gas." Available at www.sap.com.

Schnur, Mark T. "Mapping Data in SAP-Business Warehouse." Paper available 8/11/06 at www.esri.com.

Sonnen, David, and Henry Morris. 2005. "ESRI: Extending GIS to Enterprise Applications." White Paper, February, Framingham, MA: International Data Corporation.

Sun Microsystems. 2005. "RFID Keeps U.S. Troops Well Stocked." Available 5/12/2005 at http://www.sun.com/solutions/documents/articles/go_rfid_dod.xml.

Swoyer, Stephen. 2005. "RFID Keeps Customer Service Stellar, ROI Strong. BI case Study." *Business Intelligence Journal*, Fall, pp. 35–38.

Tan, Pang-Ning, Michael Steinbach, and Vipin Kumar. 2005. *Introduction to Data Mining*. Boston: Addison-Wesley.

Thurston, Jeff. "GIS/IT Integration Maximizes Enterprisewide Benefits." *GeoWorld*, 16(7): 34–37.

Van Berkel, Jan. 1997. "Data Warehouse—Where to Locate GIS." Proceedings of 1997 ESRI User Conference. Available 7/2005 at gis.esri.com/library.

Wachter, Susan, Michelle M. Thompson, and Kevin C. Gillen. 2005. "Geospatial Analysis for Real Estate Valuable Models." In Pick, James B. (ed.), *Geographic Information Systems in Business*, Hershey, PA: Idea Group Publishing, pp. 278–300.

Wallace, Butch, and Eric Fulcher. 2004. "Bridging the Gap Between GIS and ERP at Alagasco." Paper 1642. Proceedings of 2004 ESRI User Conference. Redlands, CA: ESRI Inc. Available at www.esri.com.

Williams, David. 2004. "The Strategic Implications of Wal-Mart's RFID Mandate." *Directions Magazine*, July 29. Available at www.directionsmag.com.

Winslow, Jon, and Anthony Lea. 2002. "Customer Relationship Management: Location Maximizes Return on Investment." *GeoWorld*, 15(4): 32–34.

CHAPTER 5

CUSTOMER-FACING GIS: WEB, E-COMMERCE, AND MOBILE SOLUTIONS

INTRODUCTION

Today's consumers are increasingly dependent on web and mobile technologies. The spatial aspects of this trend are the focus of this chapter. Comparison is made of traditional client-server architecture with that of spatial web services and mobile technologies. Impacts of the new architectures on companies, users, customers, and the general public are considered. The chapter shows the benefits of these more accessible and flexible approaches through discussion, examples, and case studies.

After a comparison of the architectures, spatial web services are examined from a business and strategic standpoint. Contrasting uses are evident in the examples of Edens & Avant and the Delaware Department of Transportation. Mobile services offer dynamic handheld spatial content for employees or consumers anywhere, anytime—working, in the field, traveling, or at leisure. DS Waters' field workers sell water products depending on spatial for location and routing, while Seaspan International, a Canadian tugboat/barge firm, uses mobile mapping systems for navigation, dispatch, and fleet management.

The MotionBased case demonstrates how combined web and mobile services can expand into a new market niche, in particular monitoring and mapping of training results of high-performance athletes. The section on

Geo-Business: GIS in the Digital Organization, By James B. Pick
Copyright © 2007 John Wiley & Sons, Inc.

consumer web services gives the history and impacts of the expansion of mapping on the web, that includes mashups and open source applications.

The spatial web service and mobile architectures impact electronic commerce and mobile commerce. This has occurred more for business-to-customer (B-to-C) than in business-to-business (B-to-B) e-commerce. Examples include MasterCard and Zillow.com. The trends influence markets through gains in efficiency. Everyday examples of the spatially-enabled smart trolley and pedestrian mobile navigation demonstrate micro-market efficiencies.

Movement from client-server towards the web services and mobile environments depends on having standard technical definitions and concepts. As with the advent of other technologies, such as PCs, cell phones, and video conferencing, standards for the spatial web take time and effort of standards bodies to gain critical mass and acceptance. This is especially necessary when the technology involves global sharing of information in real time. The spatial standards and protocols from GIS vendors, the OGC, ISO, and other leading standards organizations set a good basis for standardization and are increasingly adhered to. The chapter talks about the role of several of the leading spatial web standards, although full coverage of multiple standards is beyond the book's scope.

ARCHITECTURAL APPROACHES TO SPATIAL TECHNOLOGIES

This section examines and compares the major architectures for spatial applications of client-server, web services, and mobile services (sometimes called location-based services). This does not exhaust the alternative architectures, but they are the most common. Standalone architecture was already introduced in Chapter 2. Grid computing, a promising architecture for the future, is examined later in the chapter.

Client-Server

Client-server architecture in its simple concept, as shown in (a) in Figure 5.1, consists of software resident on a server that accesses data in a database or data warehouse. The server, or servers, communicates information across the internet to multiple clients. The client may have little or no software and data of its own (referred to as *thin client*) or may have moderate to high amounts of software and data (called a *thick client*). The clients vary in arrangement with the server for processing and data. Some clients are self-supported; some process software applications in collaboration with server software; and others depend on processing by server software (Dodd, 2005).

Take an illustration of ABC Company that follows the client-server concept in Figure 5.1(a). The firm might have specialized servers, one for networking, one for applications software, and one for data. Its fifty clients vary, with

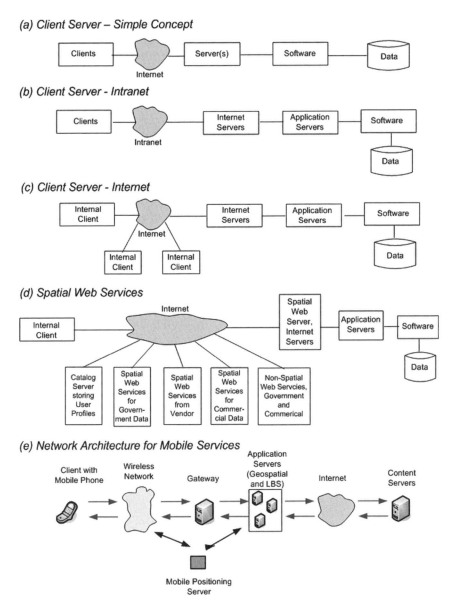

Figure 5.1 Client-Server, Spatial Web Services, and Mobile Services Architectures. *Source:* Modified from Lopez, 2004

its engineers utilizing thick clients, while its clerks and customer-service people use thin ones. Client-server's strengths are: (1) it concentrates data and software in the server(s) rather than duplicating it on client computers, (2) it scales from a small single-server arrangement with few clients to multiple servers and clients, and (3) it still provides local functionality if they need it.

The network can consist of a variety of types, protocols, and physical media, which are not discussed here (Dodd, 2005). However, the movement is from older forms of wide-area-network protocols towards the internet's TCP/IP protocols.

Internet for internal users in an organization is referred to as the *intranet*. It follows the client-server model and is shown in (b) in Figure 5.1. In this case, the server or servers and the clients are restricted to one organization. In the illustration, they are all from ABC Company. This type of network offers greater security and the ability to utilize proprietary software and data with lower risks of loss, piracy, and intrusion (Dhillon, 2007). Spatial applications and data can reside on ABCs servers or on client systems. A disadvantage for spatial applications is that the data from the vast public sources that reside on government or third party sites would have to be imported and stored on the intranet, rather than being directly accessible. For some organizations, the intranet offers a secure spatial architecture that appeals such as in defense, the military, and intelligence, and to businesses that emphasize R&D on proprietary products.

Many firms get around this by allowing its users access to both the internet and intranet. Another alternative is to offer the *extranet*, a variation on the intranet that allows approved outside users to have access. Client-server for the internet is seen in Figure 5.1(c). This is similar to the intranet, but opens up the TCP/IP-based network fully to publicly accessible servers. This model has the advantages of vast access to information and processing, while being exposed to enlarged security and privacy risks and greater potential for maintenance problems or failure. This model can support web services for users and customers, as well as other types of transactions and information exchange.

The spatial web services architecture, seen in (d) in Figure 5.1, is a subset of client-server internet in (c). An organization has a specialized server for spatial web services, and other application servers. The internet is open to the world as in (c), but now it particularly includes access to a variety of spatial web servers. The potential for collaborations, processing sequences, and exchanges of the organization's spatial web servers and these multiple public spatial servers and other web servers is the underlying driver of this approach.

The last variant shown in (e) in Figure 5.1 is Mobile Services (Location-Based Services). It is an open internet environment of the host organization and other public spatial web servers. In this case a gateway connects one or more of the host's servers through a wireless network to mobile clients (Lopez, 2004). This architecture has the pluses of spatial web services from (d), and the added advantage of access to spatial web services for mobile users who move around dynamically in space. The wireless network opens up greater security problems, as radio transmission of wireless is more vulnerable to intrusion than other transmission modes (Dodd, 2005). Another disadvantage is the ergonomic problem of spatial displays on handheld mobile devices.

TABLE 5.1   Comparison of Web Services and Client-Server Models

	Web Services Model	Client-Server Model
User Management		
User profiles	**X**	X
Security and access control	X	**X**
Clients		
PCs (standard and browser-base apps)	**X**	**X**
Mobile devices (cell phones, PDAs, etc.)	**X**	X
Middleware		
API-based middleware interactions	**X**	X
Interactions with multiple servers	X	**X**
Servers		
Web servers	**X**	**X**
Proprietary servers	NA	**X**
X = Fully supported		
X = Partially supported, with constraints		

Note: API is Application-programming interface.
Source: Ismail et al., 2005.

Maps can be seen but complex ones at larger scales can only be viewed by moving around smaller window portions of the map.

What then are the differences between the client-server and web services models? As summarized in Table 5.1 (Ismail et al., 2005), the client-server model has robust physical security and access controls, partly due its earlier advent allowing more time for the security procedures and standards to become accepted. Since the web services environment is more open to the public, potential intrusion and threats are greater, in contrast to a more restricted client-server model, that reaches its extreme in a fully closed intranet (Dhillon, 2007). Another difference is how users are added. For client-server, user set-up is done in a proprietary way to grant a client user access to the host's server(s). In the illustration of ABC Company, the firm arranges for a client Smith to be set up to begin use. However, for web services, Smith's user profile resides on a catalog server, which enables her quickly and automatically to be connected to other web services (Ismael et al., 2005). Another difference is that mobile devices are better supported in the web services environment. The traditional client-server doesn't include radio transmission nor special servers suitable for mobile devices.

The client-server model often has multiple servers that work together to provide information, so the model needs middleware to coordinate the host servers. Middleware is software that connects software applications or components, such as between servers or between the client and server. The web services model also has moved in that direction as services become more mainstream and enterprise-based. On the other hand, the openness of the web services approach is based partly on availability of software code to developers through APIs. An Application Programming Interface (API) is a "set of interfaces, methods, protocols, and tools that application developers use to build or customize a software program" (Wade and Sommer, 2006). For client-server the code is more likely to be proprietary (Ismail et al., 2005). Finally, proprietary software and data servers are more prevalent for client-server, in contrast to the openness of software and data for web services. In short, the traditional client-server approach is more secure and proprietary, while its variant, web services, is open, flexible for access, and less secure. The two models have similar underlying technology components, but they are set up, organized, controlled, and restricted differently.

Web Services

This section delves deeper into web services. It discusses more about the way web services functions, its business advantages, and gives two examples. Three key elements in understanding web services functioning are the user profiles stored on a catalog server, the ways to access web services, and the orchestration of web services. A user profile is the characteristics needed to set him/her up for access to a server. This includes the user preferred login IDs and passwords, authorizations to access websites, user preferences such as map styles, appearance of imagery, calendar, and characteristics of the user's mobile devices (Ismail et al., 2002). For traditional client-server, the computer service staff gathers the user profile and sets it up. For web services, the user profile is stored in a standard format as the Universal User Profile (UUP). Numerous UUPs are stored on special *catalog servers*, many located at service providers such as Microsoft. NET Passport or AOL Magic Carpet (Ismail et al., 2002).

The user's perspective is seen in Figure 5.2 which doesn't show the full web services architecture but only the user's view of web services. The Catalog Server has numerous UUPs including the user's (face symbol shown). As a complex chain of web service procedures take place, each web service in turn checks with the catalog server, locates the user's UUP, and obtains the permissions and user profile for that service to proceed. Since this is done automatically without the user's human intervention, multiple service tasks can be done very rapidly.

The orchestration of web services refers to the series of access steps that comprise complex web services (Ismail et al., 2002; Zhao et al., 2007). The processes are governed by protocols, mostly ones from the Open Geospatial Consortium (OGC). Some of the important protocols for web services are discussed later in the Standards section.

The second key function is for the user to find a desired web service. This can be done in several alternative ways (Zhao et al., 2007): (1) by the user searching a registry of web services located on a special web server, (2) by an indexer, a software agent that searches systematically through websites for services, or (3) by peer-to-peer searching, in which case there does not have

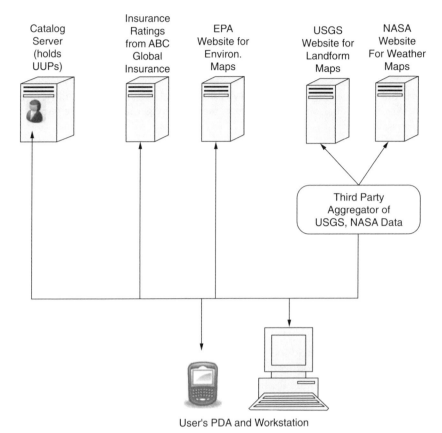

Figure 5.2 User's Perspective on Web Services. *Source:* Modified from Ismail et al., 2004

to be a centralized registry or an indexer, but rather the query information is passed along through each node in the network, eventually returning hits back to the requester.

The last key function is orchestration, which refers to the series of access steps that comprise complex web services (Ismail et al., 2002; Zhao et al., 2007). The processes are governed by protocols, mostly ones from the Open Geospatial Consortium (OGC). Some of the important protocols for web services are discussed later in the Standards section.

This is done through service chaining, sometimes called orchestration. An example of a sequence of web service calls is seen in Figure 5.3 that determines land susceptibility to landslide in a risk model (Zhao et al., 2007). The orchestration can involve more complex processes involving multiple pathways, and steps that loop back based on logic (see Zhao et al., 2007). The user may or may not be involved in directing this orchestration. The benefit

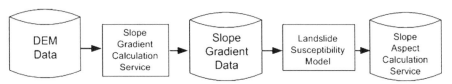

Figure 5.3   Orchestration of Web Services for Model of Land Susceptibility. Copyright 2007, IGI Global, www.igi-pub.com, reprinted by permission of the publisher

of complex orchestration is that, analogous to a macro in a spreadsheet, many services can be automatically accessed, information processed, and data accessed, leading to a complex end response based on a sequence of heterogonous services, all without the end user being aware.

From a business standpoint, spatial web services unlocks the potential of legacy systems, offers new approaches to problems and can uncover revenue sources. One of the well-known advantages of web services for IT has been its ability to "unlock" the information in legacy-based systems. Large-scale legacy systems are older enterprise applications that run on large servers programmed in an inflexible way, so it is costly to enhance or rewrite them. The problem is much greater when several legacy systems need to work together.

Web services can be added as a layer of software located on top of such a legacy system(s) that connects the legacy's inputs and outputs to web service applications. It may not be feasible to realize on the web the full functionality of the legacy system by this approach, but if the most important legacy processes can be opened up to web services, that greatly expands the access to the legacy data and the flexibility of use. Upgrading of the web services can be accomplished relatively quickly and inexpensively.

Although large-scale, traditional GIS software is newer in general that its IT legacy counterparts, the same philosophy can apply. A web service for a proprietary, traditional GIS, in certain cases, can "open up the silo to enterprise IT architecture" (Uleman, 2006).

If a company has converted its IT to a web services architecture, it is even easier to spatially-enable it. New programming language standards especially Geographic Markup Language (GML) from the Open Geospatial Consortium are designed for the spatial enablement of web services. Consider the following example from Uleman (2006). An set of steps to process a home utility repair were implemented as a web service as follows.

- Validate the service agreement
- Assign a repair person
- Contact the homeowner
- Examine the home without service
- Repair the problem

Spatial processing steps can be written in GML to modify the process as follows (the GML steps are in italics):

- Validate the service agreement
- Assign a repair person—*based on physical proximity*
- Contact the homeowner
- *Plan the repair person's routes based on the assignment*
- Examine the home without service
- Repair the problem
- *Monitor the repairs in the neighborhood and city, and detect unusual spatio-temporal clusters of repair problems*

Here, by adding GML code, spatial-enablement can occur quickly and flexibly.

What are the pluses and minuses of the spatial web services approach? Among the pluses are: speed, low cost, flexibility, wide accessibility, and user friendliness. The minuses include the following: (a) Limited spatial functionality. The features currently available for spatial web services are more limited than for traditional GIS software. For some APIs such as Google Map, they are highly limited. (b) Size of spatial data. Some high-resolution satellite imagery and maps with thousands of polygons may be cumbersome to transport on the internet, even with broadband. However, this can sometimes be overcome by compressing the format of the imagery or map. (c) Because spatial analysis functions are not yet standardized in the real world, spatial analysis involving multiple web services in succession may not be consistent. This problem can be gradually resolved by more widespread acceptance of standards.

This example demonstrates the flexibility and ease of adding spatial web services. Yet it is often difficult or an organization to change its IT and networking traditions. How does an organization proceed to adopt spatial web services? Hagel (2007) strongly recommends that an organization do this as a *staged development* approach. Systems development, the focus of the next chapter, involves a series of stages leading to implementation. Hagel recommends that a company develop a small spatial web service application initially, gauge user responses, make improvements, and gain institutional confidence, before advancing to broader and more complicated applications. Dell Computer, which is often touted as successful in non-spatial web services, followed this approach in implementing web services for its inventory management systems (Hagel, 2007). It started with a small project, and proceeded in gradually more complex stages. Dell further convinced its suppliers to simultaneously follow identical stages.

Hagel cautions against trying to reach too far and too fast with spatial web services. Rather there needs to be a strategy of implementing in practical short-term steps, while keeping in mind a full long-term solution (Hagel, 2007).

An example of spatial web services is Edens & Avant (E&A), a medium-sized shopping center developer that serves nineteen Eastern states and over 170 shopping centers, with assets of over $3 billion. E&A built a spatial web service for its retail customers who seek shopping-center space that allows them to analyze and compare shopping centers in order to choose a location. Online, the customer can see the layout of the center, proximity to competitors, road maps, shortest routes, drive times, local geography, demographics, and the market size. The application utilizes ESRI's Business Analyst, RouteMAP, the ArcIMS spatial web server (Beitz, 2001). An E&A customer can look through hundreds of possible locations and weigh characteristics of the shopping center, demographics, distances, appearance, and layout (see example in Figure 5.4). E&A cites the benefits to retailers of saving time in siting decisions and being able to coordinate multiple sites. Another benefit is for E&A leasing representatives, who now have to think proactively about the same spatial choices that confront their customers. The E&A example shows how web services can combine a lot of data from the Business Analyst and other sources with powerful routing algorithms, and yet be very user-friendly and accessible to users.

A second example is a spatial web services for SDSS at the Delaware Department of Transportation. It manages the movement of oversize and overweight vehicles throughout the state (Ray, 2005). The design seen in Figure 5.5 depends on extensive routing, street, bridge, and overpass height data stored in a spatial database. The three programming modules are written in XML (a web-based function for transporting data) and J2EE Servlet (a web-compatible version of the Java language). The location management module analyzes characteristics of vehicles at particular locations, while route management considers possible routes that are feasible for these huge vehicles in getting to a destination. In the core module, the algorithm for control and route evaluation makes the optimal decision on the best route. The information is output through a system interface to a spatial web server that provides maps and data to users throughout the DOT and in transport companies. The system has been successful and has led to lower processing costs to estimate routing, reduced permitting time, and safety benefits (Ray, 2005). The system was developed within the rubric of existing IT infrastructure. It runs alongside other web services applications and can be easily modified. Delaware DOT illustrates that spatial web services can fill new organizational niches inexpensively yet have considerable analysis and modeling capability.

CONSUMER WEB SERVICES

The introduction of Google Map in February of 2005 had major impact not only on spatial map services but on the entire geospatial industry. Although not the first such service, Google Map's appeal, ease, world coverage, and

North Delray Commons
Delray Beach, FL

555 NE Fifth Avenue
Delray Beach, FL 33483
Miami-Fort Lauderdale-Miami
Beach, FL CBSA

• 34,087 square feet
• Major retailer: Publix
• Over 1,000 residential units
within a three mile radius of the
property expected over the next
several years
• Average household income of
$76,348 within three miles
• Traffic count on Federal
Highway is 26,000 cars per day.

www.edensandavant.com

Demographics

Distance	1 mi	3 mi	5 mi	10 mi	15 mi
Population	10,682	66,943	161,703	481,008	944,738
Households	4,715	29,339	75,700	211,603	401,442
Avg HH Income ($)	93,850	77,540	78,267	86,234	80,525

Figure 5.4 Edens & Avant Spatial Web Services: Property in Port Plaza Shopping Center, New York. *Source:* Edens & Avant, 2007

free cost moved it to immediate prominence and opened a new geospatial era for public consumers. Google Map can display nearly the entire earth with satellite imagery. For urban areas it has limited features such as place names, parks, rivers, landmarks, streets, and hospitals. Users can toggle around the map and zoom in and out. They can get directions to addresses. A powerful feature is the business search, that builds on Google's strength in search

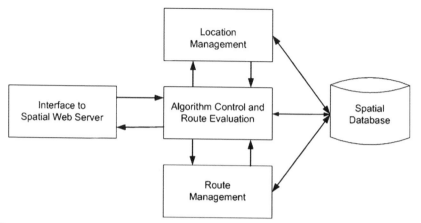

Figure 5.5 Logical Components of Routing System for Oversize, Overweight Vehicles in Delaware Department of Transportation. This article is available electronically as in press, August 15, 2005, from Decision Support Systems, Julian Ray, Copyright Elsevier 2005.

technologies. A search for say, accountants in Canton, Ohio, will show with map pushpins the locations of accountants, and web links to information about them. Businesses can create free listings so users can pinpoint them, and they can create "free coupons," a small pop-up printable advertisement. What was surprising was the success of this new "lightweight" product with everyday consumers. The examples given in the last section were user-friendly web services for consumers, but ones with considerable analytic and mapping capability designed by professional staff and consultants. Google Maps and other consumer map services are different in their ease of development. That was made possible by the company's simultaneous release of the free API (Application Programming Interface) for Google Map. The API enabled any user to modify code and customize display not only the standard Google map layer but additional map features, a phenomenon known as mashups. The consumer can superimpose data from one or more web sources on standard imagery (Roush, 2005). The term "mashup" comes from hip-hop music, in which digital equipment can blend one song's vocal line with background music from another tune (Ramsey, 2006).

This success of consumer spatial web can be explained by the theory in information systems of the Technology Acceptance Model (TAM). This theory attributes the acceptance of a technology to two main components: "perceived ease of use" and "perceived usefulness" (Davis, 1989, 1993). The consumer offerings of the spatial web have both components. It can be argued that desktop GIS is more complex and not so user friendly, hence the widespread adoption of the web services.

Microsoft, which before Google had offered less popular map services called Map-Point Location Server and Microsoft Streets and Trips, followed suit in 2005 by introducing Microsoft Virtual Earth, and Yahoo introduced Yahoo Maps the same year, both with the APIs available for free. Google shortly added a slightly more sophisticated mapping service, Google Earth, which provides a 3-D view of the earth and additional basic mapping capabilities.

Since the APIs were freely available, a vast number of developers as well as everyday amateurs have stepped in and developed customized versions of these services, re-marketing them. Tens of thousands of mash-ups have appeared, some of which have gained prominence and considerable visitor base. The explosion in these offerings opened up a new niche of spatial consumer users and ignited the interest in mapping across broad reaches of the internet public.

Consumer mapping has weaknesses and drawbacks. One is reduced spatial functionality. For instance multilayer displays have been limited and such software functions as coordinate systems and projections are not present. However, this is somewhat improved by third-party firms such as PlaceBase that provide more functionality (Vermes, 2006). Mainstream GIS software vendors have felt a wake-up call from this consumer mapping explosion. ESRI has introduced ArcWebExplorer which competes in the free, low-end market space, but with more spatial features and even some analysis. This is a very dynamic business area that is only at the start of its product curve. This section now turns to an example of a low-end spatial consumer services and a somewhat more sophisticated, free web service from a non-profit.

Trulia.com

Trulia.com is a residential real estate search engine that gives free real estate pricing and other information in the current real estate market. Maps and graphs display information including average home prices by size of home, market price trends, community demographics, neighborhood popularity, comparable listings, and much more. One feature is a map display that allows the user to see all the listed properties for sale. When visitors click on a property pushpin, the listing price appears alongside corresponding real estate descriptions (see Figure 5.6). "Heat maps" are Google mashups that show the levels of current pricing for a larger city or county. Trulia's friendly and well-designed user interface makes the best of the functionality constraints of the Google Earth API.

DataPlace.org

A second example is DataPlace (www.dataplace.org), an initiative of KnowledgePlex, that is sponsored by the Fannie Mae Foundation, a nonprofit interested in providing mortgage and housing information to the public. It is a spatial web service that provides housing and demographic information and maps across the United States by city, community, and census tract. The data sources are the U.S. Censuses of 1990 and 2000, federal home mortgage

Figure 5.6 Trulia Real Estate Search. *Source:* Trulia, 2007

data, and special federal tabulations on housing needs by income level of households. Users can create extensive city, neighborhood, and area profiles by housing, demographic, income/employment, and mortgage lending data. They can be mapped thematically, as seen for year 2000 housing vacancies in Evanston, Illinois (Figure 5.7). Using the hundreds of variables available, a user can accumulate a spatial tapestry of a neighborhood or community. This application was created with the support of a nonprofit entity and initially intended for an audience of affordable housing community specialists.

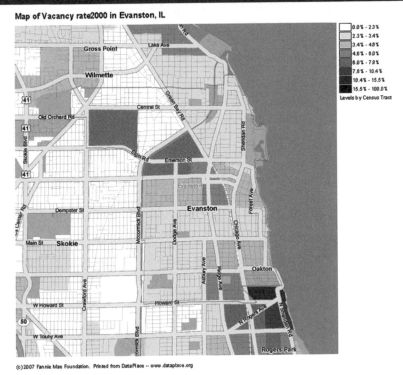

Figure 5.7   DataPlace.org Map of Vacancy Rate in Evanston, Illinois. *Source:* DataPlaceTM. 2007. World Wide Web (http://www.dataplace.org/map/?z=1), February 26, 2007

The mapping software came from PlaceBase Inc. that has deep expertise in geospatial web platforms and databases. In contrast to Trulia, DataPlace emphasizes nonprofit-private collaboration.

MOBILE SERVICES

Mobile services (also referred to as Location-Based Services or LBS) are a wide variety of services that provide access to locational and associated attribute information for users of portable locational devices. Spatial mobile devices communicate with server networks by GPS, RFID, Wi-Fi, and WiMax (Astroth, 2005). A device can have an active or passive GPS unit built in, allowing it to determine within feet its X,Y coordinate location. The X,Y coordinate location can be transmitted to a mobile server through Wi-Fi or WiMax communications. A device with an RFID tag can have its location read by a nearby RFID reader and the reader updates information on a server with the reader's X,Y location.

Mobile services benefit a range of businesses by providing a mobile employee with maps, web-based information, knowing where he/she is located, communicating instantaneously, and receiving field data inputs, resulting in enhanced responsiveness to customers in the field. While computer users are more fixed in location, the users of mobile services are in dynamic physical movement. Some business examples of spatial uses are employees involved in monitoring assets in the field, logistics, navigation, real estate, marketing, sales force, and electronic marketplaces.

A common model for mobile services is shown in Figure 5.1e. A web service network is connected via a gateway to a wireless network, which communicates with mobile devices. If the mobile device has GPS or other georeferencing, it can transmit locational data for mapping back to the server. In some situations, data are transmitted manually between the field and server network. There are multiple alternative mobile networks that are beyond the scope of the book (Dodd, 2005). Several examples of them are:

- A network of portable RFID readers that transmits inventory information through a wireless network to a gateway and then to a client-server network. An application server analyzes the inventory characteristics and records the location of the inventory for spatial analysis.
- OnStar or NavStar devices in cars, which communicate via a wireless network to a client-server network connected to a spatial server.
- Enhanced 911 (E-911) network. In an emergency, a cell phone which is GPS-enabled sends the coordinate location of the phone through a cellular network to a 911 Public Safety Answering Point (PSAP), which routes the call to the closest location to the caller for dispatch of emergency services.

In mobile networks relevant to this book, the messaging needs to include spatial information. This might be the coordinate location of the mobile device that is detected by GPS, RFID, and sensors. Spatial information in the form of maps and spatial analysis outputs can flow to and from the mobile device. Non-spatial information usually accompanies the spatial information. For instance, a field utility worker may transmit back to the server network the X-Y coordinates of utility assets that need maintenance, along with a text description of the repairs required. Other types of common messaging for mobile systems include address verification and matching, driving directions, voice messages, and proximities.

Some of the qualities desired for a mobile device network (Lopez, 2004) are:

- *Mobile*. The mobile device can connect to the mobile network anywhere, anytime.

- *Real-time.* The mobile devices transmit information instantaneously.
- *Scalable.* The mobile network can grow in size considerably without exceeding its technical limitations.
- *Sufficient performance.* The network can handle a sufficient number of mobile messages to suit the business goal.
- *Interoperable.* The information from mobile devices can be reliably transmitted across gateways and enter a client-server or other network.
- *Open.* The standards and protocols are widely known, such as HTTP, XML, Wireless Markup Language (WML), or Multimedia Markup Language. The common standards allow the different parts of a mobile network to work together well.
- *Secure.* Security features protect the network from intrusion, information theft, or shutdown.

In designing a spatial mobile network, these qualities need to be prioritized for the business problem and weighed against the costs.

An emerging development in spatial mobile services is *location-awareness*. This refers to automatic reporting to a customer of information related to his/her current location. For instance a customer in a downtown city neighborhood can request hotel information from his/her GPS-enabled mobile device and it will signal what hotels are within a quarter mile and also have rooms available.

Some vendors of mobile services are listed in Table 5.2. They provide mobile infrastructure equipment and software, GPS and other positioning features, software for spatial analysis and mapping of mobile data, services and content to mobile devices in the field, and web portals for business and individual customers (Lopez, 2004). The practical development and operation of spatial mobile networks involves working with combinations of these vendor categories.

This section on mobile services now turns to two mini-cases of spatial mobile services: DS Waters and Seaspan.

DS Waters

DS Waters, based in Atlanta, is one of the largest bottled water delivery companies in the U.S. having 5,500 employees and revenues of over $1 billion. Its brands include Crystal Geyser, Sparkletts, Belmont Springs, and Sierrra Springs. Its employees had previously used combinations of cell phones, radios, and pagers to communicate with dispatchers and supervisors in the field. There were often delays of hours in responses (ESRI, 2005). Another problem was payroll. Based on paper timesheets turned in by the field delivery people, weekly payroll processing was time-consuming, costly, and full of errors.

TABLE 5.2   Major Vendors by Category for Mobile Services

Infrastructure Software Providers
Provide databases, application servers, positioning servers, and enterprise applications.
IBM, Lucent, Microsoft, Motorola, Nokia, Oracle, and Sun

Network and Handset Positioning Vendors
Give positioning technology in the network structure or GPS positioning technology into handsets and other mobile devices.
Alcatel, Cambridge Positioning Systems, Ericsson, Lucent, Motorola, Nokia, Qualcomm, Siemens, Trimble

Specialty Tools for LBS
Offer mapping, spatial analysis, routing, and geocoding software for deploying mobile services
ESRI, Autodesk, Ionic, Intelliwhere, MapInfo, Telcontar

Mobile Services
Provide branded custom mobile services.
Mapping, driving, and yellow pages
    MapQuest, Vicinity, Webraska, Yahoo
  Satellite imagery services
    GlobeXplorer
  Real-time traffic
    SmartTraveler, TrafficMaster
  Geocoding and gazetteer
    Whereonearth

Content Providers
General
  Governments (federal, state, local)
Geographic
  TeleAtlas, Geographic Data Technologies, Navigation Technologies
Demographic and business
Acxiom, Claritas, InfoUSA, Polk

Wireless and Web Portals
Wireless carrier portals
  Verizon, AT&T, British Telecom, Vodaphone
Wireless ASP portals
  InfoSpace
Telematics portals
  OnStar from GM

Source: Lopez, 2004.

DS Waters implemented a mobile system based on cell phones that feeds delivery and payroll data to a gateway and into spatial web servers, similar to the model in Figure 5.1e. An application server can produce reports and maps for supervisors and field workers (ESRI, 2005). The cell phones are ruggedized and utilize the WorkTrak mobile software that includes web display of delivery routes (see Figure 5.8).

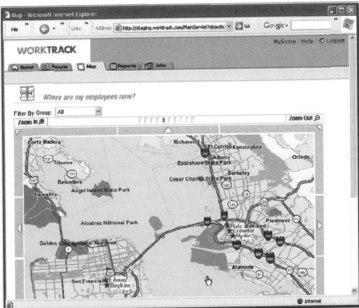

Figure 5.8 Cell Phone and Mobile Web Service which Track Deliveries at DS Waters. *Source:* ESRI, 2007

After a pretest on 100 water-cooler installation people, the system was put into use with 2,000 delivery and maintenance employees nationwide (ESRI, 2005). As the day goes along, the field person enters his/her shift, break, and service-job information at stop points (ESRI, 2005). After transmissions are received at the dispatcher's console, the dispatcher can re-deploy the technician based on maps and reports. After finishing each job task, the field employee receives text information on his/her cell phone regarding the specifics of the next job.

Although the system was planned to track and analyze all the field workers' detailed productivity daily and weekly, the managers in charge found out instead that it produced information overload (ESRI, 2005). Instead, the key management use has turned out to be checking on exceptions for individuals or on bottleneck situations.

DS Waters estimates the average time saved per employee is 20 minutes daily which adds up in added productivity to $3 million per year (ESRI, 2005). The example demonstrates the net benefits of a spatial mobile model, and also shows that pre-planned uses may need to be modified.

Seaspan International Ltd.

Seaspan International Ltd. is a part of the Washington Marine Group, one of Canada's largest shipping and marine companies. With forty-six tugs and several hundred barges, Seaspan is one of the largest marine hauling companies in the Pacific Northwest (Miller, 2005; Seaspan, 2007). The tugs and barges are contracted by shipping firms, developers, other companies, provincial and federal governments, and enterprises on islands. They haul ore, logs, building supplies, and mining and other equipment (Miller, 2005). The routes are mostly along the Fraser River but cover the entire Canadian and U.S. west coasts.

Seaspan's tugs, such as the one in Figure 5.9, are dispatched from Vancouver. Previously dispatchers communicated with the tugs by radio phone and mapped their locations by moving magnetic markers on a map board. On the boats, all the paperwork was done by hand. Washington Marine's CEO made the decision that the system had to be upgraded to digital dispatch. The captains were demanding this, and it was expected to increase competitiveness. The new system was implemented as a prototype within ninety days, in consultation with ESRI Canada. The architecture of the mobile system is seen in Figure 5.10. The data head is usually able to communicate to shore by a cell phone wireless network, but if the vessel is too far from shore, it automatically switches to a satellite network (Miller, 2005). The spatial application server at the dispatch center stores and provides maps, logs, traffic, and other information. At the dispatch center, large projectors display maps and data on dual screens. External information can be accessed through content servers on the internet. Privileged users including managers and families of the crews in the tug fleet also have web access.

Figure 5.9 Seaspan Tug Hauling a Barge Offshore Canada. Photo courtesy of nix-pix, licensed under Creative Commons Attribution-NoDerivs 2.0, source http://www.flickr.com/photos/nix-pix/161461860/

On the tug, the captain can select an assignment by viewing information on the data head and confirm job assignments through messaging with dispatch. Once confirmed, the job starts immediately, but the captain can also end it in circumstances such as bad weather, which simultaneously stops the customer from being charged. A second phase of the project links the time records and contract management to the billing and financial system.

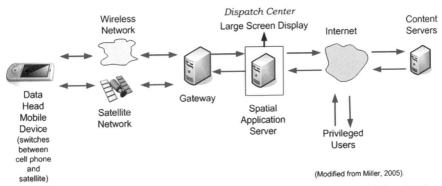

Figure 5.10 Architecture of Seaspan's Mobile Network. *Source:* Miller, 2005

Figure 5.11   Map Showing Ship Located in Vancouver Region and Assigned Tugs. Photo courtesy of nix-pix, licensed under Creative Commons Attribution-NoDerivs 2.0, source http://www.flickr.com/photos/nix-pix/71735723/

The system lets dispatchers and managers view Seaspan's tugs and barges from the dispatch center or online. (an example appears in Figure 5.11). Other information available include ocean currents (from an external content server), GPS-based vessel speeds, tug voyage history, accident reporting, tug logs, and static orthophotos (Miller, 2005). An unexpected benefit stemming from the post-911 security environment is that all ships within 200 miles of shore in the U.S. and Canada must have a functioning transponder. Hence the locations of all competitor tugs and barges in this shore range are now known and can be overlaid on Seaspan's maps.

In this example, a visionary CEO asked for a cutting edge spatial mobile system. In spite of some management resistance, it was successfully and quickly implemented and has improved safety, efficiency, and competitiveness.

CASE STUDY: MOTIONBASED TECHNOLOGIES

MotionBased Technologies started as a Sausalito, California, based small firm to perform performance analysis of high-endurance athletes, such as marathoners, long-distance bikers, hikers, and competitive sailors. The firm was purchased in 2005 by Garmin, a GPS equipment company, and continues as a Garmin division. An athlete customer utilizes a Garmin GPS device during a practice session, recording his/her route (X-Y coordinates), elevation (Z coordinate), and heart rate. A special technical contribution of the company was to cross-reference the athlete's X-Y GPS coordinate with a national elevation database, Global Mapper. A new Garmin device used by some runners also provides body cadence in rotations per minute.

After an athlete completes a practice route, the athlete uploads the information to MotionBased's website. At the site, the athlete can use the "dashboard" to view metrics of their practice route. For instance, for a marathoner, it can analyze running speed versus elevation incline and heart rate throughout a practice run. The site can also simulate activities on a variety of types of maps such as street, topo, or elevation, depending on the type of sport. The athlete maintains a record of his/her performance history on the same route and different routes. Also, the athlete can compare his/her performance with that of other athletes taking the same route.

There are a range of levels of legal rights that the athlete can retain or grant to MotionBased regarding his/her performance history. MotionBased does not receive fees except for a small proportion of its clients who pay a small monthly fee for extra features. The start-up company ran at a loss, while the value to Garmin was to acquire MotionBased's web services skills and some proprietary software design. The web application is programmed in Java and uses the MySQL database.

For map services, MotionBased utilizes the APIs for both Google Maps and ESRI's ArcWeb Services. Many of the base maps from these services come from the base map providers TeleAtlas and NavTeq. MotionBased's goal is to provide performance athletes with pertinent visual and tabular information that they can analyze outside of the training sessions. The firm also seeks to feed back more information to the athlete during performance, so he/she can also make comparisons during actual practice to his/her performance profile.

This case illustrates a combination of web services and mobile services. The proprietary original design was done by the three founding employees in a year or so, and the design remains easily extensible and flexible. It is a good example of the advantages of spatial web and mobile services and it took place in an environment with no legacy systems to hold things back.

E-COMMERCE

The move towards spatial web and mobile services is influencing markets and e-commerce. This is seen in cases and examples in the chapter. For instance, the information available to Edens & Avant's East Coast retail customers influences the locations of shopping centers they choose to locate in. For MotionBased, a market for a new service has been created.

This section considers the two leading e-commerce models of business-to-consumer (B2C) and business-to-business (B2B). It asks the question how can the new models of spatial web and mobile services influence B2C and B2B. It finishes by considering two examples: MasterCard's ATM Locator and Zillow.com.

Business–to–consumer e-commerce involves using the Internet for retail selling of products and services to individual customers (Laudon and Laudon, 2007). Some highly successful and commonplace examples of nonspatial B2C e-commerce are airline reservations, which are increasingly done through travel or airline web services, and book sales by Amazon.com, BarnesandNoble.com, and services, which replace visits to bookstores.

GIS and spatial technologies influence B2C in the following ways:

Customers can:

- find the locations and driving directions for elements of B2C including retail outlets, shopping centers, service outlets
- do map comparisons of locations of items being sold such as homes
- examine the influence of the natural environment on products and services
- examine locational proximities
- spatially view characteristics of places, travel routes, cities, neighborhoods, points of amenities, hazards, before deciding on a service or product
- run spatial models and forecasts, geostatistics, and SDSSs to evaluate products and services

Businesses can:

- do the same spatial viewing and study as customers
- understand the characteristics of customers through geodemographics and other spatial methods
- price products and services with models that include space
- study the spatial array of their own retail and sales facilities and those of competitors in order to reach customers and serve them better

For B2C, GIS and spatial technologies introduce new dimensions of thinking and understanding of products, services, and markets for buyers and sellers.

Business-to-business (B2B) e-commerce refers to markets and sales of goods and services between businesses (Laudon and Laudon, 2007). A highly successful B2B is the Milacron website for companies buying and selling in the plastics processing industry (Laudon and Laudon, 2007). On its site market exchanges occur for some of the products and services in this industry such as buying and selling machinery, tooling, and related supplies.

EBay.com is another example of a website that constitutes a market for buying and selling a vast range of products and services, albeit mostly for individuals, rather than businesses. Its exchanges include B2C and B2B. It also supports direct exchanges between two consumers, termed C2C.

GIS and spatial technologies influence B2B in the following ways:

Businesses involved as a party in a B2B exchange can:

- do map comparisons of locations of items being sold such as machinery, agricultural products, commercial properties
- examine the influence of the natural environment on products and services
- spatially view characteristics of places, such as factory neighborhoods, dump sites, agglomeration of hospital services, fast-food labor pools before deciding on a service or product
- run spatial models and forecasts, geostatistics, and SDSSs to evaluate products and services
- examine locational proximities
- view regulatory and legal jurisdictions and boundaries
- study spatial differences in costing and pricing

Businesses hosting a B2B web service can:

- have user features that divide customer pools of buyers and sellers into local, regional, or national sub-pools
- have models of routing for deliveries of goods being bought or sold, so customers can be better informed about delivery times
- present informational data on products and services that are strongly tied to geography such as real estate and wine regions
- analyze geography of customers, so as to advertise their B2B service to prospective businesses in underserved regions

For B2B, the influence of spatial web services depends partly on how inherently geographical the product or service is. Maps and spatial results can be made available for reference purposes to all the market parties.

Two examples demonstrate how spatial web services can influence e-commerce.

MasterCard

MasterCard, the second largest payment system in the U.S., serves 25,000 member banks worldwide. In 2003, MasterCard decided to develop a web service to help its hundreds of millions of card customers to locate an ATM anywhere in the world. The MasterCard Global ATM Locator service now provides maps and descriptions of 900,000 ATMs worldwide that are in the Cirrus ATM Network, owned by MasterCard, as well as other ATMs. Prior to this, MasterCard had two different locator systems with limited information that frequently differed on locations (Chen, 2005).

The web service locator application is based on Google Map and uses street information from TeleAtlas (MasterCard, 2007). A customer can request that it forward a text message of directions to access the ATM location to the customer's cell phone. If the customer's phone has GPS, he/she doesn't have to enter current location. The service also indicates the physical handicap status of sites. Overall, the result is that accuracy has improved by 50 percent (Chen, 2005). It has hundreds of thousands of hits per day. The service not only makes customers' credit card use more efficient, but also helps banks and other credit card issuers build customer ATM volume. The spatial dimension has altered the B2C model for credit card use at ATMs, by increasing customer and banking information and efficiencies.

Zillow.com

Zillow.com is a leading consumer real-estate site founded by Richard Baton and Lloyd Frink, former Microsoft and Expedia executives. From its start in 2005, Zillow has become one of the leading real estate sites. Zillow.com has 52 million estimates of house prices in the U.S. and the number is growing. The estimates, referred to as Zestimates, are seen in Figure 5.2. They vary in accuracy when compared to actual sales prices (O'Brien, 2007). For instance, only 65 percent of its estimates have been accurate within 10 percent of actual sales price (O'Brien, 2007). The site provides listing prices, sales prices, Zestimates, and information on properties. The mapping gives overhead satellite views with real estate plots superimposed, showing pricing. Its "heat map"

Figure 5.12 Zillow.com Z-Estimate of Property. *Source:* Zillow.com® Zestimate™ valuations

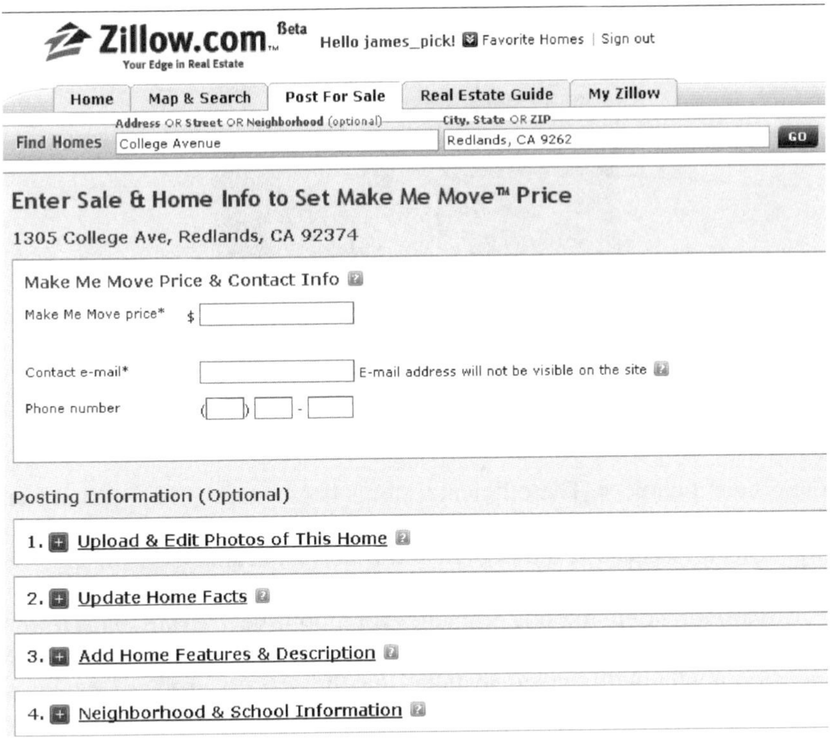

Figure 5.13 Example of Zillow.com Make Me Move Page. *Source:* Example of Zillow.com® Make Me Move™ Price Page

feature produces a thematic map for cities showing the "hot areas" in housing values per square foot. A new feature "Make Me Move" allows a seller to list a price that is sufficiently above the area's sales norm to incentivize the seller to move. The seller can add additional facts and information (see Figure 5.13). If a seller goes ahead with a Make Me Move, a special symbol will appear on the map so that buyers can contact that seller.

Real estate markets are known to be asymmetric, i.e. one party (the seller) has a lot more information than the other (the buyer) (O'Brien, 2007). Zillow.com has a goal to even this out with large amounts of information available for buyers as well as sellers. Zillow is a spatial web service that is changing the e-commerce market for real estate. If this model were applied for buyers and sellers of commercial real estate, it would represent a B2B example. The Sperry Van Ness case from Chapter 1 comes close to this, but the difference is that it is not widely known across the whole commercial real estate market.

Market Efficiency

One of the dimensions of spatial e-commerce seen in the examples is market efficiency, i.e. how buyers and sellers can utilize spatial information to make

Figure 5.14   Smart Trolley: Using a Cart Computer While Shopping.

more efficient choices. The efficiency stems from geographical insights and from better use of space (analogous to better use of time). The geographical insights occur because of the visualization and spatial analysis from GIS, and the locational sensing and tagging of objects by GPS, RFID, and sensors.

Two examples of marketing efficiency for mobile devices are *smart trolleys* and *pedestrian navigation* with cell phones. Smart trolleys in supermarkets have a computer with screen installed on the grocery trolley (see Figure 5.14). The trolley can sense grocery shelf items having RFID passive tags. Most smart trolleys also have bar code readers so the shopper can read bar codes of items not tagged by RFID. In either case the trolley's computer displays pricing and other information about the store items. Some trolley models let a customer enter a shopping list in advance through their home computer. Customers with a smart trolley can also organize aisle trips. A map on-board displays the best route through the aisles (Senne, 2005), a time-saver in mega-grocery stores!

For some smart trolleys, customers with preferred-customer cards receive special discounts and are directed to sales areas based on their buying patterns. For smart trolley shoppers, there is self checkout, with a lot of the items already pre-entered during the store trip. The cost for a store to convert to smart trolleys is over $100,000, but there are multiple benefits for the store and customers. For the store, checkout is quicker and the employer tasks are automated. Also, the store has another way to advertise products, and can get better response to its preferred-customer cards (Senne, 2005). For the customer, the benefits are the time savings and better choices to gain value in purchases. In the example, spatial knowledge increases market efficiency for buyers and sellers.

Analogous to NavStar and other car navigation systems, pedestrian navigation systems inform city dwellers about locational information. This approach is based on a cell phone having GPS navigation, precise to thirty feet or less; an electronic compass that orients the pedestrian; and mapping web services. One example in Japan is the GeoVector service, which partners the U.S. firm

Figure 5.15   Cell Phone Used for City Navigation and Information, Tokyo. *Source: Geo Vector*, 2007

GeoVector with the Japanese cellular carrier KDDI; Japanese networking firm NEC Magnus; Mapion, a map service; and Sony Ericsson that produces handsets. As seen in Figure 5.15, a pedestrian in Tokyo can select a type of destination, for instance banks, and point the phone in a direction. The list of banks located in that direction appear on the screen along with the distances and other information, and maps can be displayed to indicate routes to get there. Spatial features are increasing the customer's knowledge of retail markets in the city and improving the efficiency of the market.

STANDARDIZATION

The final section examines standards in GIS and spatial technologies. It considers some of the key spatial-web service standards, and why they are important.

In its early history, GIS tended to be standalone or departmental. There was much less networking and interoperability. Spatial software standards depended on the GIS major vendors. Today, there are many software alternatives, types of spatial web service providers, mobile service firms, networking and communications models, and sensor and other data gathering technologies. Consequently, there is growing need for spatial and GIS standards as well as for great acceptance of the standards.

Overall, the geospatial industry is moving towards more standardization (Daratech, 2004; Croswell, 2005). Along with this trend is movement towards greater interoperability and openness of software and data. *Interoperability* refers to spatial applications that work across different systems and organizations. *Open systems* refers to the ability of a user or developer to have free or affordable access to spatial software, software code, and spatial and attribute data. The benefits of an interoperable and open environment include: (1) ability to operate applications on a variety of technology platforms and databases, (2) integration of spatial and non-spatial applications, (3) collaboration among spatial technologies, (4) ease in sharing and using geographic data, (5) greater commonality in development methods and tools in the GIS community (ESRI, 2003).

Standards are set by leading vendors and by important standards organizations. ESRI Inc. has been a business leader in setting industry standards, especially for storage of spatial data. For flat-file storage of spatial data, its shape file (.SHP) norm has become the leading standard. ESRI went further with a more advanced spatial storage type of geodatabase (.MDB) that has also become an industry standard. In spatial databases, Oracle is the most important industry standard leader for middle- and large-sized applications. In addition to its mainstream non-spatial Oracle relational database standards, the Oracle Spatial 10g database has set standards for access to spatial data that are influential. Other important software and database vendors such as Intergraph, MapInfo, Microsoft, and IBM have also contributed some industry-based standards.

The major standards-setting organizations influencing GIS and Spatial Systems (see Table 5.3) are governmental agencies and nonprofits. Several of them support generic standards, such as the American National Standards Institute (ANSI), the European Committee for Standardization, and the International Organization for Standardization (ISO). ANSI has set programming and processing standards that have influenced the development of the computer and IT industries. The ISO has not only established many significant computer and IT standards, but has a sub-group, ISO TC 211 with the mission to provide standards in digital geographic information (ISO, 2007).

Among the organizations setting spatial standards, the most important and active one has been the Open Geospatial Consortium (OGC). The Federal Geographic Data Committee has set a goal of setting standards for a national digital spatial infrastructure for the U.S. and has made some progress towards that but is less influential in practical standards for spatial developers and users.

Two key standards organizations, the OGC and ISO, have been the most influential for the spatial industry. Their standards are particularly important for the web services and mobile services environments.

The OGC, founded in 1994, has grown from eight charter members to 336 corporations, universities, nonprofits, and governments. By 2007, it had nineteen standards listed that particularly related to interoperability and openness,

TABLE 5.3 Leading Organizations for Spatial Standards

Name	Type	Website
American National Standards Institute	standards	www.ansi.org
European Committee for Standardization	standards	www.cen.eu
Digital Geographic Information Working Group	standards	www.dgiwg.org
Federal Geographic Data Committee	standards	www.fgdc.gov
Global Spatial Data Infrastructure	interoperability	www.gsdi.org
International Hydrographic Organization	standards	www.iho.shom.fr
International Organization for Standardization	standards	www.iso.org
Organization for the Advancement of Structured Information Standards	standards	www.oasis-open.org
Open Geospatial Consortium	specifications	www.opengis.org
Open Mobile Alliance	specifications	www.openmobilealliance.org
World Wide Web Consortium	standards	www.w3.org
Web Services Interoperability Organization	interoperability	www.ws-i.org

Source: Modified from ESRI, 2007.

i.e. apply to the new services era. Among the most important of these are the six standards seen in Table 5.4.

Geographic Markup Language (GML) is the best-known modeling language applied to geographic systems on the Internet. GML statements coordinate geographic features and analysis. Web Catalog Service (CAT) specifies common web-server catalogs for user profiles are set up across the heterogonous servers on the web. The Web Map Service (WMS) defines standards of how single and overlaid map views can be arranged and function on the web, overcoming the problems of spatial data coming from diverse sources.

The influence of the OGC standards on spatial web services is seen in the model of the web service standards shown in Figure 5.16 (modified from Zhao et al., 2007). It shows the spatial data at the bottom feeding up to data access services and integrative spatial web services. GML applies to this whole middle section of the model as the spatial language. The spatial catalog mentioned earlier is governed by the CAT standard at the upper right. Gazetteer serves as a geographic dictionary. Finally, the web services feed up to the spatial clients and their applications. It is evident that OGC standards fully encompass the web services environment. Not surprisingly its standards have been the most important in this realm.

The ISO's TC211 standards group has been influential in setting the ISO 19115 standard for metadata. Metadata describes digital geographic datasets. It is crucial for cataloging them, as the population of datasets continues to grow

TABLE 5.4 **Important OGC Standards**

OGC Standard	Abbreviation	Content
Geographic Markup Language	GML	The Geography Markup Language (GML) is an XML encoding for the transport and storage of geographic information, including both the geometry and properties of geographic features. GML is also an ISO standard.
Simple Feature Access Parts 1 and 2	SFS	This standard specifies both a common architecture (Part 1) and SQL schema (Part 2) that supports storage, retrieval, query and update of geospatial features with simple geometry via the SQL Call Level Interface (SQL/CLI), an ISO standard. There are also COM and CORBA binding specifications. Simple Feature Access Part 1 and Part 2 are also ISO standards.
Web Catalog Service	CAT	Defines common interfaces to discover, browse, and query metadata about data, services, and other potential resources.
Web Coverage Service	WCS	Supports electronic query, description, and retrieval of geospatial data as "coverages" – that is, digital geospatial information representing space-varying phenomena, such as imagery and gridded data. Returns the result in a standard format, such as GeoTIFF.
Web Feature Service	WFS	Enables a client to retrieve and update geospatial data from multiple Web Feature Services. The specification defines interfaces for data access and manipulation operations on geographic features, using HTTP as the distributed computing platform. The payload encoding is GML and is independent of how the data are stored.
Web Map Service	WMS	Defines the operations for requesting, creating, and displaying registered single and superimposed map views of information input concurrently from many heterogonous sources. Includes how to get information on map type and content from a server.

Source: OGC, 2007.

for web services. In the grid computing environment that accesses numerous spatial datasets globally, accurate metadata is even more a critical factor. Also influential are ISO 19125-1 and 19125-2 for Simple Feature Access. This is a SQL schema for digital storage, retrieval, update, and query of both spatial and non-spatial features, and corresponds to OGC's SFS standard.

In summary, spatial standards have become essential in the increasing internet-based and services environment for GIS. Major vendors and standards

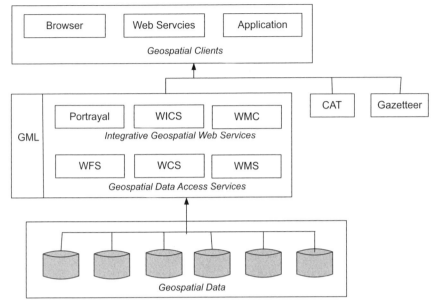

Figure 5.16   OGC Standards for Spatial Web Services. Copyright 2007, IGI Global, www.igi-pub.com, reprinted by permission of the publisher

organizations have made progress in providing a robust set of spatial standards, and they are growing in adoption.

Grid Computing

As a final topic, Grid Computing represents a future framework that offers greater processing power and a worldwide reach of collaborative services beyond what is present today. Grid Computing refers to "flexible, secure, coordinated resource sharing among dynamic collections of individuals, institutions, and resources—what is referred to as the virtual organization" (Foster et al., 2001). It depends on open standards and protocols, that enable access to unprecedented amounts of resources across the internet. Rather than file-sharing, in the Grid environment, there is a collaboration of multiple web services working together across virtual organizations worldwide (Foster, 2001).

A framework for Grid Computing, seen in Figure 5.17 (Buyya and Venugopal, 2005) has resources and databases located globally. The users access resource brokers, which in turn can access resources directly or link to grid information services that provide specialized help in accessing the resources. The information services have specialized strengths in discovering appropriate resources. A user accesses a sequence of resources and information services into order to solve his/her problem.

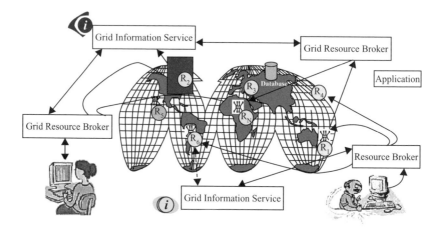

Figure 5.17 Global Grid Computing Environment. *Source:* Rajkumar Buyya, University of Melbourne, Australia

Grid Computing is especially good at solving giant problems like disaster management, financial simulation, and environmental simulation for world regions. Because it can search everywhere for resources, it excels at locating slack resources. Although Grid Computing is applied currently by large governmental organizations, big science projects, and larger technical companies, it is expected to become more widely available in the next fifteen years. It offers GIS potential for worldwide data sharing, greater processing power, and combinations of spatial and non-spatial web services to achieve more sophisticated outcomes.

CHAPTER SUMMARY

The trend in GIS is towards the spatial internet bus from Chapter 1. This includes movement towards web services, mobile services, and spatial e-commerce. This chapter examines this growing area of spatial applications. Starting with the architecture of the major models for GIS and spatial, it next covers in more depth the business and commercial sides of spatial web services.

Consumer spatial web services and mobile services are revolutionizing the public's awareness of spatial technologies and providing many benefits as well as opening up new niches. The MotionBased case study illustrates the architecture, business advantages, and practicalities of spatial web services and mobile services. A specialized customer base can get their own data through GPS and receive analysis of it through an interactive web service. The environment is flexible and customer-friendly.

The new internet-based spatial service environment is influencing e-commerce especially B2C. It brings new dimensions to electronic markets and creates efficiencies. The examples of MasterCard and Zillow.com demonstrate how e-commerce markets are changed by spatial applications. Mobile services such as smart trolleys and portable locators create new efficiencies both for customers and businesses.

Standards are key to the success of GIS and spatial technologies. Although they have been around from the start of the IT industry, in the web-based, open, and interoperable environment today, they are critical. Vendors and standards organizations have progressed in establishing a robust spatial set of standards for the current era that are gaining increasing acceptance. The future will depend on having even stronger and more widely accepted standards. The Grid environment represents the future promise of even more open standards and protocols that allow users to access the extensive data and powerful processing, and combinations of computing resources worldwide that cut across administrative and political boundaries.

REFERENCES

ArcNews Online. 2003. "GIS Standards and Interoperability." *ArcNews Online*, Spring. Redlands, CA: ESRI Inc. Available at www.esri.com.

ArcNews. 2005. "DS Waters Increases Efficiency and Profits with GIS and LBS." *ArcNews*, Summer. Available at www.esri.com.

Beitz, David Z. 2001. "GIS Assists Site Location in the E-Commerce Age." Proceedings of the 2001 ESRI User Conference. Redlands, CA: ESRI Inc. Available at www.esri.com.

Buyya, Rajkumar, and Srikumar Venugopal. 2005. "A Gentle Introduction to Grid Computing and Technologies." *CS Communications*, 29(1): 9–19.

Chen, Anne. 2005. "MasterCard Cashes in on Web Services." *eWeek*, February 7. Available at www.eWeek.com.

Davis, Fred D. (1989). Perceived usefulness, perceived ease of use, and user acceptance of information technology. *MIS Quarterly* 13(3), 319–340.

Davis, Fred D. (1993). User acceptance of information technology: System characteristics, user perceptions, and behavioral impacts. *International Journal of Man-Machine Studies*, 38, 475–487.

Dhillon, Gurpreet. 2007. *Principles of Information Systems Security*. New York: John Wiley and Sons.

Dodd, A.Z. 2005. *The Essential Guide to Telecommunications*, 4th Edition. Upper Saddle River, NJ: Prentice Hall.

ESRI 2005. "GIS Standards and Interoperability." *ArcNews*, Spring. Available at www.esri.com.

FGCD. 2006. *Federal Geographic Data Committee Website*. Reston, Virginia: FGCD. Available at www.fgcd.gov.

Foster, 2001. "The Anatomy of the Grid: Enabling Scalable Virtual Organizations." *The International Journal of High Performance Computing Applications*, 15(3): 200–222.

Hagel, John. 2002. "Edging into Web Services." *McKinsey Quarterly*, November, 5–13.

Ismail, Ayman, Samir Patil, and Suneel Saigal. "When Computers Learn to Talk: A Web Services Primer." *McKinsey Quarterly*, November, 15–21.

Lopez, Xavier R. 2004. "Location-Based Services." Chapter 6 in Karimi, Hassan, and Amin Hammad (eds.), *Telegeoinformatics: Location-Based Computing and Services*, Boca Raton, FL: CRC Press.

Maguire, David J. 2005. "Enterprise Geographic Information Servers: A New Information System Architecture." In *Proceedings of the Annual Conference of the Geospatial Information and Technology Association (GITA)*, GITA: Aurora, CO.

Markoff, John, and Martin Fackler. 2006. "With a Cellphone as My Guide: Digital Search Meets the Real World in the Streets of Japan." *New York Times*, June 28, p. C1.

Miller, Alex. 2005. "Business Panel Discussion. Seaspan Case Study." Presentation at ESRI User Conference, San Diego. Redlands, CA: ESRI Inc.

Open Geospatial Consortium. 2005. Open GIS Specifications. Wayland, MA: Open Geospatial Consortium. Available at www.opengis.org.

Puckorius, Timothy J. 2005. "Will Virtual Earth Scale Up the Spatial Market?" *Geospatial Solutions*, 15(9): 30–33.

Ray, Julian J. 2005. "A Web-based Spatial Decision Support System Optimizes Routes for Oversize/overweight Vehicles in Delaware." *Decision Support Systems*, in press.

Reed, Carl. 2004. "The Spatial Web." White Paper. Wayland, MA: Open Geospatial Consortium. Available at www.opengis.org.

Reed, Carl. 2004. "Integrating Geospatial Standards and Standards Strategies into Business Processes." White Paper. Wayland, MA: Open Geospatial Consortium. Available at www.opengis.org.

Seaspan. 2007. Seaspan Ship Management website. Available at www.seaspanmanagement.com.

Senne, Steven. 2005. "New Computers Make Grocery Carts Smarter." *USA Today*, May 3.

Stankiewicz, Amy. 2005. "A View from Above." *Geospatial Solutions*, 15(7): 30–35

Zhao, Peisheng, Genong Yu, and Liping Di. 2007. "Geospatial Web Services." In Hilton, Brian (Ed.), *Emerging Spatial Information Systems and Applications*, Hershey, PA: Idea Group Publishing, pp. 1–35.

CHAPTER 6

SPATIAL SYSTEMS DEVELOPMENT

INTRODUCTION

The book has considered multiple ways that GIS and spatial applications are benefiting businesses and organizations. Cases and other examples have demonstrated these advantages, such as Sperry Van Ness in commercial real estate and Chico's in customer relationship management. The focus has been on the features of contemporary spatial systems and how their applications are helping businesses and their customers. However, another side of the entire GeoBusiness field concerns how those applications are designed and developed. This chapter's central theme is designing and developing spatial systems, rather than operating them. Some of the content of this chapter draws from the fields of information systems and project management, which go back further than GIS. The chapter builds the central theme by first examining the frameworks and methods for planning and designing spatial systems. It discusses the well-known system development life cycle (SDLC) applied to GIS and spatial techniques. The small but growing knowledge of spatial design is included. The implementation phase consists of building, testing, and activating the GIS application. Frequently development teams will decide to outsource implementation to external parties. The alternative type of end user development of professional and scientific spatial applications is discussed. The outcomes may be decision support systems, software for R&D, or professionally-oriented models. An example is a epidemiologist in a pharmaceutical research center who produces spatial models and mapping of disease diffusion. End users are highly skilled and can create spatial models

Geo-Business: GIS in the Digital Organization, By James B. Pick
Copyright © 2007 John Wiley & Sons, Inc.

that significantly help in decision support or discoveries. However, most of the chapter focuses on formal development of business spatial applications by the GIS and IT groups in organizations that use formal development methods and project procedures.

The case study of a small GIS consulting firm, Engineering Systems in Los Angeles, focuses on how the firm follows these system development steps as an outsourcer in working with client users who are mostly from local government.

SYSTEMS DEVELOPMENT FOR GIS

A GIS system must be conceived, planned, and taken through a series of analysis, design, testing, and implementation steps to actually reach the point that it is "turned on" and put into use. Many problems and mistakes can occur along the way that might lead to a faulty system, the wrong system, or a system that works but is too expensive. A major tenet coming from both the IS and business-planning disciplines is that of systems development phases. It is commonly accepted that a GIS can be better planned if the process is divided into steps. A standard set of systems development phases applied to GIS is presented in Figure 6.1. A brief discussion is given now of the phases, and a more detailed discussion follows.

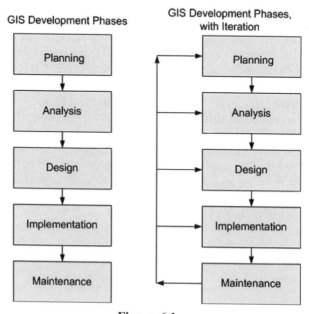

Figure 6.1

The *Planning* phase involves conceptualizing the system, doing broad planning, and justifying the need for a GIS. It ends by the decision of top management on whether or not to commit to the project. The *Analysis* phase emphasizes discovery and information gathering, leading to identifying a set of alternatives. Feasibility and cost-benefit are weighed before prioritizing a list of alternatives that is presented to top management. For instance, a large insurance firm is analyzing what GIS would be best to implement for underwriting and environmental modeling applications. It needs to gather information on the sources of data, types of architectures (client-server, web), and types of analytical tools to solve the problems. In the process, it discovers a third GIS use for the firm—marketing. It determines four alternatives to be feasible and beneficial, and presents them in priority order to top management for an executive decision on whether to go forward with one of them.

In *Design*, the system and data specifications are worked out in much more detail. It involves diagramming, researching, and specifying of the fine points of the prospective system. Users are extensively consulted on details of what is being designed. *Implementation* is the phase of actually building the spatial application, based on the detailed design. The design group has a key decision to make here of whether to build it in-house, purchase it commercially, or outsource it. In this phase, the in-house and customer users are trained in how to use the system. The actual cutover to the new spatial system takes place and the system is *turned on*.

In the *Maintenance* phase, the system is up and running, but users are continuing to have issues and problems including training, correcting bugs, and requesting features be added that were left off the original system. These problems are addressed, often over many years. The final disposition of the system involves its abandonment or replacement. In the latter case, the replacement is the result of a new systems development process.

The systems development phases are iterative. In other words, at any time during development, it may be necessary to return to an earlier phase or phases and go through the phase(s) again. For instance, as seen on the right of Figure 6.1, a new RFID system for inventory may have had a fine design and the system was built well, but the implementation was botched because the users were mostly not trained at all, and resisted the new system as being too difficult. Using the iterative method, the SDLC can return to the implementation phase, focusing this time on success in the sub-phase of training, and can complete this phase the second time with turning on the revised system for now well-trained users.

An alternative set of phases for GIS system planning by Tomlinson (2003) comprised ten stages (see Table 6.1). The book's systems development phases are compared on the right side. The work by Tomlinson focuses mostly on planning, analysis, and especially the design phase. It is informed by practical experience in implementing GIS systems and is referred to in discussing those phases.

TABLE 6.1   Tomlinson's Ten-Stage GIS Planning Process, Compared to Systems Development Phases

Tomlinson Planning Stages	Systems Development Phases
1. Consider the strategic purpose	1. Planning
2. Plan for the planning	
3. Conduct a technology seminar	2. Analysis
4. Describe the information products	
5. Define the system scope	
6. Create a data design	3. Design
7. Choose a logical data model	
8. Determine system requirements	
9. Consider benefit-cost, migration, and risk analysis	
10. Make an implementation plan	4. Implementation
	5. Maintenance

Source: Tomlinson, 2003.

Methodologies, models, and tools are available from the information systems, economics, and software engineering professions and disciplines that can be useful for GIS development (Satzinger et al., 2007). *Structured design* is a well developed system and software design method that advocates breaking the system into modular parts. Sometimes the modules are arranged in a hierarchy known as top-down design. It has the advantage that the whole design and high-level steps can be better understood. Associated with structured design is structured programming, which is an approach to computer programming of breaking a program into modular sub-programs. The sub-programs can be better focused and also can be re-used, to save time.

A high-powered, software-driven design method known as *Computer-Assisted Software Engineering* (CASE) is implemented by using software tools known as *CASE tools*. CASE tools support storing common metadata in a *data dictionary*, a repository for the entire system's development team. The CASE tools also have features for diagramming the processes, data flows, and data modeling of a system. Among the well-known diagrams are *data-flow diagrams* (DFD) that show processes and data flows, *entity relationship diagrams* (ERD) that portray the relationships between data entities, *structure charts* that give the big picture of object-oriented design, and *class diagrams*, that show the hierarchical relationships of object types.

Another category of methods includes *rapid application development (RAD)* and *rapid prototyping*. In RAD, the system development phases are performed more rapidly. They can be performed simultaneously and/or iteratively, rather than being done sequentially. RAD favors CASE tools and prototyping to speed up the steps. Prototyping refers to moving very quickly to produce a limited final product for the user to test and critique. It has the advantage that mistakes and errors in design can be picked up by the user, fed back, and improved quickly. The final prototype, once approved, needs to go through some or all of the more formal systems development phases for thorough testing and finish prior to implementation.

The case study firm Motion-Based Technologies used a combination of RAD and prototyping to build its web-based spatial applications for high-performance athletes. As a start-up, the firm's experienced web programmers wanted to move quickly. They could do so since the small firm had an informal, flexible atmosphere without systems project procedures and controls. The feedback was limited since the firm was small, so internal improvements have come mostly from live users.

For the project management dimension of systems design, *project management software* is utilized that can track the tasks, workers, costs, and critical pathways for a project. Cost-benefit methods, explained in Chapter 7, such as ROI and net present value, are utilized in the planning phase as well as to measure actual net benefits in the maintenance phase.

The actual use of the systems development methods and tools for GIS and spatial technologies is limited in industry, as will be shown later by reviewing the twenty research cases. This may be due to: (1) the history of GIS development occurred mostly in the public sector which is not as well versed in the techniques; (2) in a company, the GIS design team is often located in a small independent group with members drawn from non-business backgrounds; and (3) fewer big-corporation design methods and techniques are imposed for GIS, since GIS is rarely a visible profit center for larger companies. The positive aspect is that nearly all of these development tools apply to GIS and are widely available and documented extensively (Satzinger et al., 2007).

There are two major approaches to systems development—the traditional approach and the object-oriented approach (Satzinger, 2007). Both approaches go through the five phases that have been outlined. The traditional approach is based on structured design and structured programming. Two of the major diagrams utilized are the data flow diagram and the entity relationship diagram. The problems with the traditional approach often concern lack of consistency in explanations of it. Also, it is difficult to use for modeling highly object-oriented solutions.

Object-oriented (OO) system development takes a very different view. The key item is the *Object*, which is defined as an item in the computer system that has attributes and behavior and is capable of sending and responding to messages. In *object-oriented spatial systems development*, a set of interacting objects is designed to work together to accomplish goals. The object replaces the processes, programs, and data entities from the traditional approach at the application level, although individual objects have more focused programmatic elements and use of data. The OO approach has the advantage that the object is easier to think of as relating to the real world. Also, objects can be re-used in different programs more easily than for traditional processing procedures. For instance, a firm has the spatial objects for customer, product, and store that are reusable, naturally meaningful, and can include location.

Either the traditional or the object-oriented approach can be suitable for designing spatial systems. The traditional is more appropriate for systems that are slowly changing and have complex geographical layering, while object-oriented is better for more rapidly changing, interactive systems with simpler layering. The phases of systems development apply for both approaches, and the discussion below does not distinguish between the two.

PHASES IN SYSTEMS DEVELOPMENT FOR GIS

This section goes into more detail on each phase.

The Planning Phase

In the project planning phase, the spatial problem or opportunity that needs a solution is identified. The phase then defines it further and looks at its feasibility, budget, staffing, scheduling.

Recognition of the problem may derive from management, professional GIS or IS staff, users, or customers. For instance, a retail executive in a mid-sized firm is concerned that his stores are not located in the most rapidly growing market areas. At a meeting, his IS manager mentions that GIS is used by some competitors to identify growing markets by small-area. Another illustration is drivers in a small trucking firm, who ask their management for a sophisticated GPS-based truck navigation system.

Once identified, the problem must be checked for feasibility and budget. Can it be accomplished technically within the capabilities of the organization and/or providers? Is it affordable? An example of these issues is seen with ABC Blinds Inc., the fictional name for a $2 million–revenue small business in California. The firm has the idea to implement GIS for marketing using a commercial GIS package, but key questions remain: Can its single outside technical-support person understand and apply GIS for the marketing problem at hand? Can ABC afford mainstream commercial GIS software or services?

The next substeps are to determine staffing and scheduling of the project. Scheduling needs to take into account project difficulty, sub-tasks, availability of personnel, and the critical steps necessary for project completion. Staffing is a challenge for most organizations anticipating GIS projects. This challenge is partly the sectoral one of "knowledge gap," i.e. a situation in the labor market where a technology advances faster than the capability of businesses to find staffing for it (Tomlinson, 2003). This has applied generally to the GIS field over the past ten years (Marble, 2006). One response would be to allocate budget and time for training of internal staff. At the societal level, the knowledge gap points to a need for universities to build up more GIS programs across a variety of disciplines (Marble, 2006).

GIS Systems Development by Professionals and Scientists

For the GIS field, the staff who design, build, and implement spatial systems come from a variety of backgrounds that relate to the history of GIS. From its early days, GIS has been interdisciplinary, drawing in people from geography, environmental sciences, architecture, landscape architecture, computer science, engineering, public administration and government. Some of these users are engaged in scientific and professional spatial work, such as in corporate R&D centers, universities, and government research organizations. They contrast with personnel for the growing GIS markets in the private sector, who come from such fields as business, management, marketing, information systems, and geographic information sciences.

Systems development for the scientific users falls into the category of "end user development." Such users still accomplish the stages of systems development and use some of its methods such as prototyping and software testing, but they proceed as individuals or small groups through less structured and often iterative steps, and lack the formal controls of a professional development team. For example, a faculty ecologist at a university has developed a system to produce thousands of maps of ecological habitats worldwide. The mapping system is controlled by object-oriented programs that technical staff in her lab developed in consultation with the university's scientific programming unit. The ecologist is expert in spatial modeling of habitats and draws on lab assistants who are have become trained and experienced in GIS software and programming. The users for the software are eight scientists and graduate students, who produce scientific reports and papers.

This example illustrates an important type of systems development, but one that tends less to follow the formal phases and controls mostly examined in the chapter. This professional or scientific GIS user often has substantial knowledge of GIS software, models, data, and tools. Their systems tend to be at the level of DSS. Today, there continues a significant community of such professionals, who contribute important spatial discoveries and insights. However, in the corporate world today, GIS staff tend more to be business, IS, and applied GIS specialists, who develop transaction-processing, MIS, and enterprise systems that serve larger groups of users under tighter performance requirements. It is this latter group that utilize the formal development approaches and methods discussed in most of this chapter.

The training challenge for a business applies across all levels of GIS and spatial workers and users, starting with the GIS manager and including staff, users, and customers (Tomlinson, 2003). Since the technology is moving fast, even an experienced GIS manager must plan for his/her own training. Training deficits can undermine the system later in development. "One of the primary causes of under use of GIS is lack of staff training" (Tomlinson, 2003). At the worst, not sustaining skilled GIS staff or outsourced capabilities can eventually cause the company to regard the GIS as a failure and abandon it. Training also is important for end user developers, but is more specialized.

The planning phase culminates in a proposal to top management to go forward with a proposed project. If approved, the team commences work on the project.

The Analysis Phase

Analysis involves information gathering, discovery, visiting and hearing the users' needs, developing the spatial system requirements, prioritizing the requirements, and assembling a proposal for full design and implementation. A systems development team is assembled for this project, to take it from analysis all the way to an implemented solution. The project team is usually composed of a team leader, GIS and IS analysts, and a technical person who will play a greater role later on. The team leader might be the company's GIS manager, but often is appointed by that manager. Analysis is varied as seen by the multiple approaches used by the case companies.

One example is Baystate Health, where the staff of four GIS professionals, headed by the GIS technical manager, constitutes the spatial development group. The professionalism of a GIS staff is rare for hospitals. This technical group also has as its director a surgeon and chair of Baystate's Surgery department, who provides organizational leadership and lends subject-matter expertise to some of the GIS applications. The staff uses both formal and informal systems development approaches. The formal approach is helped by one staff member who worked for ten years at a leading GIS software vendor firm, which required formal protocols.

In Analysis, information is gathered in different ways depending on the project type and its needs. Frequently, if there is an existing system, it is analyzed and evaluated. It is run, tested, and its pluses and minuses evaluated. This allows weaknesses to be addressed in the requirements for a new system. A variety of stakeholders are surveyed, questioned, and consulted on their concerns and advice, including top executives, middle managers especially in user departments, users inside the company, and external customer users. This step is well known to be perhaps the most crucial (Laudon and Laudon, 2006; Satzinger et al., 2007), since the present users and customers will be among the most important eventual judges of the implemented spatial product.

Information is gathered from other diverse sources, including industry and vendor literature, consultants, other companies that are not directly competing, and websites that provide spatial services. The composite of this information and knowledge is not just stored, but is analyzed, synthesized, and prioritized. For example, a middle-sized private home security firm intends to upgrade the firm's GIS and GPS navigation systems for its fleet of agent vehicles. It has interviewed its agents for their critiques of the existing system, received an expensive consulting survey on the pluses and minuses of commercial systems, and received detailed feedback on the candidate system from a user firm in another country that is not competing. The project team goes through this mass of information, and connects together themes and conclusions, discarding some information as unreliable. It distills the mass down to eighteen prioritized key points.

It is useful in analysis, if time and resources allow, to build a small prototype of the most essential part of the new system. This prototype will show dramatically where there are weaknesses in the project and its requirements. Better yet is to involve users in reviewing a prototype.

URS Corporation, a large integrated, engineering design services company with a global reach, serves as an outsourcer to develop its clients' government and environmental GIS systems. URS GIS specialists develop specifications and design, following by a prototype. To the user, the prototype resembles an actual system minus error-trapping and finished data-base structure and functions well to serve workflow. However, it has "dummy" data. The client tests the system and gives more requirements, a process that may go through several iterations. There may be creep in the project scope. Only after agreement is reached with the client on the prototype is the finished system built.

A variation of early prototyping for GIS (Tomlinson, 2003) is termed a "Technology Seminar" (see box.).

The Technology Seminar for GIS Planning

Tomlinson (2003) proposes to hold a "Technology Seminar" very early in planning a GIS project. This concept is not too different from Joint Application Development (JAD), which is a group-meeting technique often used in systems development for middle- and large-sized organizations (Laudon and Laudon, 2007; Satzinger et al., 2007). A Technology Seminar is called by the GIS manager early in a project with the goals to provide some training, to increase understanding of GIS and spatial applications, and to have the group develop recommendations for requirements of a GIS product or products. The size of the Technology Seminar group ranges from a dozen for small organizations to thirty or more for large ones (Tomlinson, 2003). The group consists of key GIS-user department heads, some key staff users, the CIO, some middle managers, and a few executives.

The agenda for a Technology Seminar is the following (Tomlinson, 2003):

- GIS definition
- GIS terminology
- Functions of a GIS. This might include demonstrating examples of spatial hardware and software for exposure and training, not giving bias.
- The planning process: steps and responsibilities
- Initial identification of first requirements for the new or updated GIS system

The key question for such a Technology Seminar is what information is needed for you from the spatial system? (Tomlinson, 2003). The information may not be a map, but could be lists distilling the outcomes of spatial analysis. When the group coalesces on a project deliverable, it can be identified and recorded along with its requirements and the name of the principal person who proposed it. The session format precludes a person's manager from overruling or influencing the proposals from his/her staff. After the session, the project deliverables are checked to make sure they are in synch with the company's strategic plan and then they are prioritized. Another key question afterwards is, which user(s) or user department(s) will benefit? It is recommended that a Technology Seminar be held at the very beginning of analysis, and experience has shown it to be beneficial in discovering what the user really needs (Tomlinson, 2003).

Another key part of analysis is to recommend how the GIS application will be built and by whom. The alternatives are (a) build it in-house with staff from the GIS and/or IS departments, (b) build it through end-user development by high-level professionals or scientists located in user departments of the organization, (c) purchase the software commercially, and (d) outsource part or all of the construction to an outside provider.

Building in-house (a) requires that a team of technically skilled programmers, software engineers, or GIS specialists be available or be hired. In end user development (b), a skilled expert develops and builds a specialized application. This might involve spatial modeling, statistics, scientific programming, or decision support. End user development often involves less formal development steps, high analytical skills, and products that have a professional or scientific set of users. Purchase of the GIS software (c) can lead to quick implementation, but careful study is required to ensure that there is a good fit with user needs. The outsourcing alternative (d) reduces the technical burden, but often involves higher costs for software, hardware, training, and maintenance. Sometimes, this choice applies more broadly by not only having the outsourcer do construction but also get involved with analysis and design. Outsourcing has become more common for spatial projects, but has pluses and minuses that are covered more in Chapter 10. Analysis ends by the project team presenting its top recommended alternative, along with justification and high-level requirements to top management for its review and approval.

Design

In this phase, the complete design and full set of requirements are developed and created. It includes designing the architecture of the application, physical hardware including networking, design of the data model, design of the spatial application, identifying the best sources of digital data, checking on digital standards, planning data conversions, detailing the tabular, graphical, and spatial outputs, and outlining the spatial cartography. These tasks combine GIS, IS, and business knowledge and skills, often blending them together. Organizationally, it involves communication between staff in the three areas,

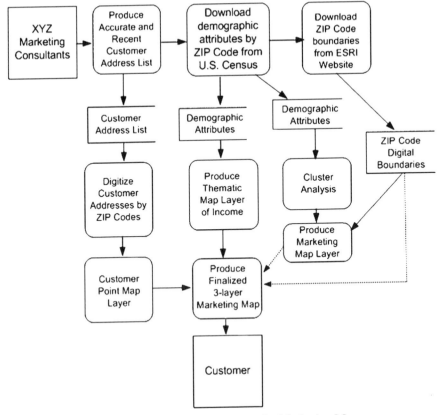

Figure 6.2   Data Flow Diagram for Marketing Map.

and better yet, staff from all three areas working together on the design team. For a small firm, or in an outsourcing situation, having every area represented on the team may not be feasible.

The *architecture* design for the spatial application often is expressed by diagrams, charts, and tables. For the traditional approach to systems development, well-known design diagrams are the *data flow diagram* (DFD) and *entity-relationship diagram* (ERD). The data flow diagram (see Figure 6.2) shows the components that are sending and receiving input and output (square symbols on the figure), the processing steps (squarish symbols with the curved corners) and data stores (C-shaped symbols), and the data flows (lines with arrows).

The process represented in the figure is the building of a three-layer marketing map to be output to the customer. The map is being built by XYZ Marketing Consultants. There are four paths vertically on the diagram, the left two producing two of the layers, and the right two paths produce the third

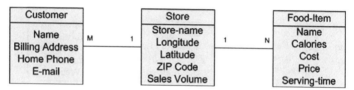

Figure 6.3   Entity-Relationship Diagram Example.

layer. For instance, the left column gathers the customer address list, stores it, digitizes it to ZIP codes, and produces the map layer showing customer point locations. At the end the finalized three-layer marketing map is produced for the customer.

The DFD can represent the spatial and non-spatial processing and storage steps. For instance, one data store holds the "customer address list," which is non-spatial, while another one stores the "ZIP Code digital boundaries," i.e., the spatial data. Although not shown here, the DFD is also capable of portraying the processing and storage of combined attribute and spatial data, such as happens with the object data model (see Chapter 8).

The DFD method has the advantage that any processing symbol, for example, "Digitize Customer Addresses by ZIP Codes," can be "exploded" into a whole DFD diagram with its own more detailed process, data flow, and storage symbols, which is located one level below. If all the process symbols at this level were exploded, there would be nine more detailed diagrams at the level underneath that shown in Figure 6.2. The process of developing a multi-level DFD is available to readers (Valacich et al., 2004; Satzinger et al., 2007).

An ERD shows the relationship between data entities, such as "Customer," "Store," and "Food-Item" (see Figure 6.3). Each entity has attributes. In some cases entities can be spatial, for example the attributes of point location (Latitude, Longitude or other X, Y coordinates), line coordinates, polygon coordinates, and other spatial units, etc. The relationship between entities A and B may indicate for each A there is one B (1 to 1); for each A there are many Bs (1 to n); there are many As for each B (m to 1); or there are many As for many Bs (m to n). These relationships are known as *cardinalities*. They can be helpful in design of spatial systems.

In the figure, the entity "Store" is spatially referenced to a point by Latitude and Longitude. It also indicates its relationship to the spatial category of ZIP Code. The other entities, "Customer" and "Food-Item," are not spatially referenced. The cardinalities are indicated by the labels on the connecting lines. Customer and Store are M:1, while Store and Food-Item are 1:N.

DFDs and ERDs constitute robust diagramming techniques that can be applied broadly to design spatial systems. They are also available as features in CASE tools. The multi-layer aspect of DFDs, and the connections between DFDs and ERDs can be automatically linked in a CASE tool. In the alternative Object-Oriented Systems Development Approach, there are other types of diagrams not covered here (Satzinger et al., 2007) that may be more or less useful than the traditional approach for modeling spatial development, depending on the type of problem.

The *physical design* of the spatial system is another major part of this phase. It includes the following components:

- Computing hardware and performance
- Network design and performance
  - Internet and web design and protocols
- Spatial hardware
  - Digitizers, high-resolution printers, plotters
  - GPS, RFID, and sensor hardware
  - LIDAR hardware and other airborne hardware
- Mobile devices
  - Cell phones
  - PDAs
  - Tablet and pocket pcs
- Spatial software
  - General purpose commercial software
  - Database software
  - Software for spatial hardware and mobile devices
  - Custom application software
- Capacity planning for future expansion of hardware base
- Backup hardware
- Plan to interface hardware with the corporate network including enterprise systems

The physical design needs to support the logical design. It should be carefully analyzed to confirm that all of its parts are compatible with, and connect well with each other and with the organization's existing physical infrastructure. An example of the challenge is a small delivery company that acquired GPS units for its fleet of vehicles, only to find out too late that it was difficult to import the GPS coordinate files collected in the field back into its commercial GIS software. It had to hire a consultant to write software that accomplished this conversion. The firm's logical design was fine, but at first it did not work with the physical devices.

Design for the acquisition of spatial data is essential. Digital sources of spatial data are quite varied and include government, commercial vendors, and in-house. Government data are often free or nominal in cost for the U.S. but can be quite expensive in European and other countries. Commercial data vary in price and quality including the extent of metadata and documentation available. Government and commercial data sources are described and often can be tested at spatial data portals, such as the U.S. Census Bureau (www.

census.gov), ESRI's Geography Network (www.geographynetwork.com), or the U.S. government's Geospatial One-Stop (www.geodata.gov). In-house data are often proprietary spatial data that have been digitized, collected by GPS, or collected and scanned from airborne systems.

For example, Kaiser Permanente, the California-based healthcare firm, examined in Chapter 10, applies GIS for travel-time analysis, site selection, regulatory reports, a library of reference maps for members posted on intranet, spatial web services for members, support for an ambulance service in the Bay Area, epidemiology research studies, sales and marketing, and finance/accounting. For these applications, government, commercial, and in-house data serve as input to the GIS. The finance/accounting data and epidemiology data are proprietary and in-house. The travel-time analysis is based on street-map data from commercial vendor TeleAtlas and the PEMS data on freeway performance measurement from a state government-university consortium (PEMS, 2007). The data for map services for members come from a commercial service. The data for the intranet library of reference maps are mostly in-house and proprietary such as member locations, but utilize some government data. Kaiser's GIS is not put in one central repository but resides in many locations keyed to specific projects throughout the firm.

For any spatial data, its characteristics are critical to examine. As seen in Table 6.2, the most important factors are scale, resolution, map projection, and error tolerance (Tomlinson, 2003). Map scale is critical. First of all, the

---

TABLE 6.2   Criteria to Evaluate Spatial Data in System Design

- *Scale.*
  The map scales need to be not too large, which makes data storage unacceptably large, and not too small which lowers resolution and weakens the business purpose. Scale needs to be compared so map layers have the same scale and remain accurate.

- *Resolution.*
  Resolution is closely tied to scale. It shows the smallest map features that can be identified for a certain scale. Thus it needs to be fine enough to satisfy the business problem solving with the given map.

- *Map Projection.*
  The map projection of each map needs to be known and accurate. There needs to be a check done that the conversions can easily be done into a common projections for all the layers on a map.

- *Error Tolerance.*
  The error tolerance is an estimate of the maximum error that can be tolerated for particular business problem. Once the tolerance is determined, the project team needs to estimate the cost to achieve that tolerance. There are methods available to analyze the major error types and how they relate to the problem at hand, in order to estimate cost.

Source: Tomlinson, 2003.

extent that map scale is limited in accuracy is based on the scale and accuracy of original map source. The current map cannot have larger scale or greater accuracy. If scale for a certain application needs to be small to conform to other layers in a map, a larger scale map can be stored for separate display (Tomlinson, 2003). The map resolution needs to be considered relative to the business problem. For instance, a thematic map portraying levels of market penetration in eight national sales regions can get by with low resolution, whereas a map that shows where utility gas lines cross under residential properties must have high resolution.

Design of data standards and data conversion depends on the sources of data and what is needed internally by the planned system. There are over thirty GIS data interchange formats (Tomlinson, 2003). Among the most important are .DLG (digital line graph), TIGER (from U.S. Census Bureau), and .DXF (the interchange format between CAD and GIS systems). The project team needs to consider if the in-house GIS software will accurately and efficiently convert data to the correct internal format from data being imported by one of these standards. The challenge of data standards and conversions extends to associated spatial technologies, such as RFID, sensors, and data being transferred over the internet and web. The book covered the major spatial web standards in Chapter 5, but it's beyond the scope to cover the multiple standards and conversions. The main point is that the spatial project team analyzes and resolves standards, compatibilities, and data conversions as part of design.

Design for controls and security has the goal to assure the system has integrity and safety to an appropriate and affordable level. GIS security, covered in Chapter 11, involves strengthening the technical security, as well as the formal and informal controls. The techniques of doing this range from passwords and firewalls to hiring practices and provisions for security education and training.

Prototyping can be applied to very quickly design, build, and test parts of the system or a whole system. Design team member and users can evaluate system functionality and performance. Some tools are available for spatial prototyping. For instance, ModelBuilder by ESRI (ESRI, 2000) has tools to allow rapidly building a model by adding graphical symbols to a flow diagram (see Figure 6.4), and testing them with real data (see Figure 6.4). It can be utilized during design to test the feasibility of a business spatial model.

Cartographic design focuses on cartography, the art of giving appealing and readable appearance to maps which was mentioned in Chapter 2. GIS software packages have built-in cartographic frameworks, but they are not high-level cartography keyed to the particular GIS problem at hand. Cartographic design can be improved by having a design-team or consulting cartographer add requirements for cartography. Some software packages allow the cartography to be replicated for an entire project. For example, ESRI's geodatabase feature allows a cartographic format to be entered which will

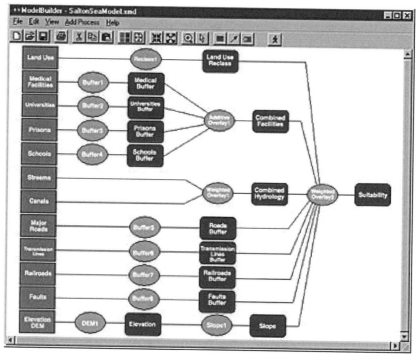

Figure 6.4   Copyright © 2007 ESRI. All rights reserved. Used by permission.

enforce consistency across all maps in the project, even new ones. In short, the cartography can be specified as part of the design.

The Implementation Phase

In Implementation, the system is built, tested, and put into use. The spatial system is constructed, based on all aspects of detailed design. This can be done in-house or outsourced. Spatial and attribute data are acquired and loaded into databases, data warehouses, or directly into tables in the GIS software. For this substep, some data conversions may be needed. Hardware and networking installations or upgrades take place and the entire physical system is connected together. Other spatial technology components including GPS, RFID, sensor, mobile devices are acquired, installed, and tested.

URS Corporation, discussed earlier, gets first an OK on a prototype and then builds the finished system. For implementation, the team runs and extensively reviews and critiques the finished system on its server. Next, the tested system is put on the client's server host in Beta version for the client to test and request any final changes. Only after this is the system implemented for the client's users.

The internal users and customers need to be trained. It can be done by web-based training, in-house or external training workshops. It is a critical factor for success, since users' responses ultimately determine system success. As mentioned, users may be unfamiliar with GIS and spatial concepts, so they need extra time and attention (Tomlinson, 2003; Marble, 2006).

The new system is "turned on." For replacement of an existing system, a process of cutover from the old to the new system takes place. The old system sometimes runs concurrently, which gives users reassurance that they can fall back on the old system if necessary.

The Maintenance Phase

The final phase supports the smooth running of the spatial system for years following the implementation. It includes the following: (1) maintaining smooth system functioning, (2) adding enhancements, (3) debugging errors discovered after implementation, and (4) providing continuing training and supporting the users (Valacich et al., 2004; Satzinger et al., 2007).

For users, this phase opens up the benefits and productivity gains of the new application. On the other hand for developers, maintenance may be dull, punctuated by sometimes ugly system repairs and debugging. It has been known for decades that job motivation of maintenance staff is among the lowest of systems professionals (Couger and Zawacki, 1980). The manager of GIS needs to foresee this problem, and attempt to offset it with incentives for maintenance staff, regular rotations in and out of maintenance, or enhancing its work.

The Maintenance phase ends in one of several ways. The GIS or spatial system can be replaced through implementation of a new system stemming from the development process. Referring to Figure 6.1 on the right, there is a loop back to start a new development cycle beginning in the Planning phase. It goes through all the phases leading to the new system. As seen in the diagram, the looping back may only go back several phases, in which case the new system is referred to as an upgrade. Another ending to Maintenance is through abandonment of the system. It might occur due to a shift in company strategy away from spatial technologies, or as an offshoot to corporate merger or restructuring.

CASE STUDY FINDINGS ON SYSTEMS DEVELOPMENT

This section next turns to the book's research case studies to assess what systems development approaches are actually used in the real world by the sample of twenty companies. The sample of 20 provides findings on the following:

1. Was systems development done in-house or mostly outsourced?
2. If in-house, were formal phases taken, or were informal steps followed?
3. What was the composition of the systems development project team?
4. Was the system development approach traditional or object-oriented?
5. Were there differences by the size of company in the approach taken?

Was systems development done in-house or mostly outsourced?

Regarding Question 1, only two firms of twenty had most of the development done through outsourcing. The Large Credit Bank had very limited GIS initiated. In the main credit bank, development was outsourced entirely to a small firm and limited in scope to spatial analysis of the markets for branches and mapping of the bank headquarters campus. The newly acquired banks utilized some GIS already and sought more. It was as yet unclear if their further spatial systems development would be outsourced. For LCB, outsourcing appears to be the result of benign neglect of the spatial area, rather than outsourcing for competitive benefits.

The second firm that mostly outsourced GIS development was Kaiser Permanente. Examples of major spatial systems development outsourced were enhancements to the minimum-travel-time system, full design, and implantation of the service area mapping application. For the latter, outsourcing was deliberately chosen by the GIS managers and supported by top management. The justification was that the GIS department in-house consisted of only one person, the manager who although talented as a designer and implementer clearly was over-extended to conduct the bulk of development himself at the scale of a middle-sized company. Instead the approach was for the GIS manager to initiate development, get it on the right track through analysis, and then turn it over to outside consultants to do the heavy design and programming. Another route Kaiser could have gone would have been to build up a skilled GIS staff reporting to the manager. However, the outsourcing approach utilized has been generally successful, and underscores that outsourcing can be worthwhile and beneficial, if planned carefully.

The other eighteen firms utilized primarily in-house development and implementation. Although Sears contracted its ESRI GIS applications to outside consultants, the bulk of all the spatial programming was done in-house by the programming group in IT. Global Integrated Oil includes contractors on some of its projects, but the bulk was done in-house by a combination of GIS, IT, and business specialists. The Large Insurance Firm began its GIS project design and programming with an outside contractor, was dissatisfied with the results, and brought all GIS development work in-house. Two of the firms in the sample, URS and Engineering Systems, primarily do in-house GIS development acting as the outsourcer for other firms. Engineering Systems is discussed later as the chapter case study.

If in-house, were formal phases taken, or were informal steps followed?

For the eighteen firms doing in-house development, ten utilized formal systems development phases and methods. Their approaches can be examined in Table 6.3. Some trends are evident: (1) The GIS team mostly leads in systems development, sometimes partnered with the IS group. For Southern Company, IT leads, while for smaller firms of Sperry Van Ness and Engineering Systems, GIS and IT are merged. This is not surprising given the specialized knowledge for GIS. (2) The formal steps resemble the five phases discussed in the chapter. (3) Three firms, Large Insurance Co., URS, and Sperry Van Ness, include Prototyping as part of their formal procedures. It is not surprising since for different reasons, each of them had time-pressure to get things done.

What was the composition of the systems development project team?

It's less clear how systems development is done for the eight case companies with an informal systems development process. For Prudential Preferred and Lamar Advertising, there seem to be GIS staff or business staff who take a lead in initiating ideas, some of which gather strength for development projects. At Chico's ideas come spontaneously from the small four-person GIS group. The informal development has been successful for most of these firms using it. It needs to be studied more to understand what makes it work well.

Was the systems development approach traditional or object-oriented?

For firms using formal systems development approaches, they were all traditional. Motion-Based Technologies utilized informal steps for systems development but for implementation centered on the Java language, making use of its object-oriented features. One of the reasons for the dominance of traditional is that systems development came mostly from the GIS group, which largely lacked training or experience in OO development methods or languages.

Were there differences by the size of company in the approach taken?

The formal approach is far less common for small companies (one-third), compared to large and medium ones (60 percent). An explanation is that small firms are at earlier maturity stages, are hard-pressed from day to day, and are often short-handed, so formal procedures and controls are less prevalent.

TABLE 6.3   Case-Study Firms Using Formal Systems Development

Name	Size	Who does systems development	Steps taken (formal or informal)
Global Integrated Oil	L	Groups within the company design, develop, deploy applications. Combination of GIS, IT, and business employees and contractors.	Development process depends on group composition. There is a standard internal project management process: (1) scope, (2) evaluate alternatives, (3) build, (4) deploy, and (5) look back.
Large Insurance Co.	L	Originally, GIS team outsourced design to external consulting firm. Now it's done in-house.	Steps: (1) research with selected group of underwriters reviewing good and bad of original design. Over 1-year period, GIS mangers and several others in GIS group wrote it in faster format, programming in C++. Used prototyping. Implemented basic functionality in one big application, and later improved it over time.
Rand McNally	L	GIS group leads if project for internal use. If project to be commercially packaged and sold, Rand McNally's programming group is the lead.	Steps: (1) R&D, (2) Conceptual design, (3) Requirements/prototyping, (4) Development, (5) Construction, (6) Review, (7) Maintenance. Details vary project-to-project. IT group has more rigorous requirements and tighter quality control than GIS Group.
Sears Roebuck	L	CAM application development is done by the GIS Group, SST application by 24-person IT programming management team, and ESRI GIS applications contracted to outside consultants.	Development process involves a training program. Field users provide input in the requirements stage. Development takes into account many details. Prototyping and screen designs used.
Southern Company	L	Usually developed by IT development unit in Southern Company Services. Sometimes developed in a subsidiary unit, but IT development unit needs to "in the loop" systemwide.	A "business driver" meets with a business analyst and they together clarify the need. With more digging for details, a business case is developed. Approval and funding OK are needed. Preference for commercial software ("off-the-shelf"). If built in-house, there is a highly disciplined approach. Project manager who communicates milestones.

TABLE 6.3 (*Continued*)

Name	Size	Who does systems development	Steps taken (formal or informal)
URS	L	The users are from client.	URS GIS specialists work with client to develop specifications. User needs to know quickly how the application works. A detailed design documents gives design requirements early on ("Quick and dirty straw man"). Implementation. If hosted by URS server, the prototype is run on the server with client data. Beta version includes "logins, error trapping, and permissions for data access." Everyone on the project team reviews and critiques it, and the Beta version is put on the client's server.
Arizona Republic	M		Steps: (1) conceived based on user needs, (2) designed by DP staff in GIS group, (3) developed by DP staff in GIS group, (4) implemented. Prototyping sometimes done.
Bay State Health	M	Staff of GIS professionals are principal conceivers, designers, developers, and implementers.	Staff uses both formal system design methodology and ad hoc methodology.
Sperry Van Ness	M	Avoid the bureaucracy. Customize for a project with particular players. Go to the customers of the applications. Ideas pour in from e-mail and marketing advisors will call in.	Skilled prototyping approach. Build the first full-blown version in 3 months. Avoid 6–10 months of iterations. Steps: (1) determine what we want to accomplish, (2) determine who uses it, (3) determine what you want to do with it, (4) go do it through prototyping, (5) roll it out, (6) adjust and fix.
Engineering Systems	S	ES believers GIS is a significant component of the IT system, and GIS and IT need to work together.	For clients, needs and requirements analysis. Do a JAD session with senior person from each division. JAD team meets monthly for 1–2 hours. Do technical design based on business needs, not just spatial data. How do we help the sure meet business goals. Develop the data model. Data conversion. Detailed database design. Implementation plan. Specifications for each step. Budget specs. Maintenance. Sometimes an Indian outsourcer is used for data conversion.

In summary, the twenty research case studies help to understand the real-world environment of systems development for GIS and spatial technologies. Although it's a limited sample, it suggests that most companies for GIS utilize a traditional systems development approach, that large- and medium-sized firms adopt formal phases for development, and that the GIS group plays a major or the lead role in development, although the associated IT group tends to conduct in-house programming and technical implementation.

CASE STUDY: ENGINEERING SYSTEMS

Engineering Systems (ES) is a small, Los Angeles–based GIS consulting firm that employs fifteen people. Its primary customer base consists of local and county government agencies in California and Virginia, with secondary emphasis on private companies. Examples of its clients include San Bernardino County, City of Downey, and Metropolitan Water District in southern California; and the Town of Vienna, City of Falls Church, and Fairfax County in Virginia. ES provides GIS planning, development, and implementation consulting services. The projects are usually multi-year, some as long as ten years, with ES personnel often located at the client's site. ES acts as a selective outsourcer for GIS, and it works together with the staff of the client organizations. For instance, for both Fairfax County and City, ES has worked for several years to develop and monitor the quality of the GIS for Fairfax's IT services department, including mapping that shows the update and maintenance of land parcel records (see Figure 6.5). Recently, ES has done a limited amount of its work for high-tech spatial client companies, such as one that helps manage supply chain logistics and AVL (automatic vehicle location) for container boxes once they have arrived at seaports. Some of the work requires highly accurate maps, for instance sub-meter accuracy for line maps for utilities (gas, water, sewer and storm water).

ES has adopted a strategy to emphasize accuracy for all of its work. It reasons that a new client that just wants to view low-resolution mapping of tabular information may later require high accuracy. For instance, one very large utility client initially did not care what side of the street utility poles were located—it just wanted to see a schematic map. But eventually that company realized that they required higher accuracy and the poles placed within several feet of accuracy for their application to be functional. There is, of course, a geometric relationship between accuracy and cost. Careful design is required to analyze costs and benefits to optimize a system.

ES has successfully developed its own internal GIS system at its office in downtown Los Angeles, but the bulk of its GIS development and the focus of this case study is on the GIS development for its outside clients.

ES follows the standard steps of systems development, that resemble the steps covered earlier. However, it always tries to start its development

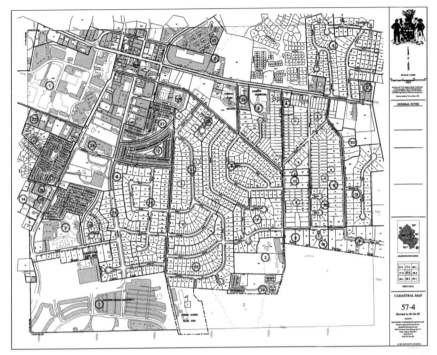

Figure 6.5 Engineering systems map of land panel update and maintenance for Fairfax Country, Virginia.

engagement with a client with a Joint Application Design (JAD) session. JAD is a systems development method that speeds up the gathering of the system requirements. Instead of being spread out over months, JAD compresses this gathering into several intensive meetings that include the client users, all the key stakeholders, and the project team members. The participants are pulled away from their normal daily activities, so they can focus on rapid sequences of gathering facts, building system models, making decisions, checking on policies, and verifying the results (Satzinger et al., 2007).

At the starting JAD session, ES invites a senior person from each division or major department, who can make things happen during the session and later on. Requirements gathering is done by drilling down deeper with each division represented at the JADs. The JAD team meets every month if possible to continue through subsequent design phases.

Design emphasizes determining the business needs and then performing the technical spatial design based on those needs—not the other way around. The data model is developed with an emphasis on the relational data model, which helps to avoid data redundancies, a topic taken up more in Chapter 8.

A detailed implementation plan is developed along with detailed tasks and budget specifications. Since most of the projects ES gets involved with are large-scale, sometimes huge, the entire project may take up to ten years or longer. Thus the project schedule is broken into five-year periods, with tactical one-year objectives.

The largely government clients frequently have needed data conversions. This is because data come in from a variety of external agencies and internal departments. ES is today known for its expertise in data conversion.

However, ES has experienced its share of projects that failed. One large utility client, one of ES's first ones in the early 1990s, had invested $30 million in a Geo-Info System (fictitious name) to try to integrate GIS information on the utility physical network with its customer information system. Unfortunately, the utility firm insisted on testing a prototype Geo-Info System on an entire large county. Not enough focus was given to demonstrating payback on the huge investment at the time. ES was called in at a late stage to try to salvage a dying Geo-Info System. Its intervention resulted in a few product demonstrations, but it was too little, too late. Geo-Info was abandoned and its converted parcel data given to the collaborating county, which has found it so valuable that it forms the basis of its county enterprise GIS system. The data were also sold to cities that comprise that county. ES spent the next four years successfully scaling down the project to a more practical level at a fraction of the initial cost. An unfortunate event as the dying system was nearing completion was that the utility company hired away almost half of ES's employees.

ES learned a lot from this early client failure and now spends more time on making sure that there are business reasons for any new GIS system. ES sees GIS development as different from IS development in the following ways: (1) The IS unit performing ordinary IS development is unaware of the visualization capability of their data and the benefits it can bring to services. (2) GIS can serve as a centralizing force across the systems in a company. It can reach across and serve to integrate a variety of isolated database systems, displaying related information as easy-to-understand graphics (3) Different levels of management regard the same spatial data through different lenses. For example, upper-middle managers in companies tend to view data as a way to analyze the business. Lower level managers view it as a technical tool, while the CEO feels that all the areas are equally crucial. Spatial components within the data allow a consolidated approach for users to view the same data through different graphic perspectives.

ES also strives to design client spatial systems that see beyond the initial limited system for the starting client. It believes that the consultant/outsourcer needs to always keep one eye on the potential for broader applications across the enterprise. Often users will get used to their first application success and ask for more, or spread the word to others. ES wants to plan and make this more possible by designing systems that can be scaled up and expanded.

Finally, a crucial part of consulting or outsourcing projects is the end stage, i.e. how the consultant pulls away from the project and encourages the client to function independently. ES emphasizes training client-company support and maintenance people, so ES can drop these and feel confident the system will continue to function well. ES helps the client firm find and hire skilled GIS personnel. By taking these steps, ES backs away from supporting GIS and retreats to its original status as planning consultant to clients for future projects.

ES has had dozens of successful projects for its governmental clients since its founding and the early mishap with the utility client. Its better and better capability to provide a strong systems development and implementation framework for its clients is now one of its mission strengths. As represented by JAD, ES tries to directly involve the key stakeholders and users at the start in the planning of GIS projects, and continue to gain their "buy-off" on the project as it progresses. The firm leverages its systems development knowledge and technical skills to offset weaknesses in a particular client. Since ES's team works very closely with the client's project team, even working physically at the client premises, ES does run a risk of losing some of its best field personnel, as happened early on with the utility firm and continues to happen from time to time. ES not only illustrates the strength of a formal systems development approach, but also demonstrates outsourcing, from the outsourcer's perspective.

CHAPTER SUMMARY

Systems development of GIS and spatial technologies is a crucial part of business success with them. The reason is that an organization cannot just rest on what GIS system it has now, but needs to continue to improve, update, and expand. The chapter gives background on the approaches to systems development, the phases of systems development projects, who does this, why the users are crucial, and what some of the methods, techniques, and models are.

The cases in the book give some guidance about how GIS and spatial applications are being developed and implemented in the real world. Based on this limited sample, development has been mostly formal except for small businesses. The approach is mostly traditional rather than object-oriented. Development tends to be spearheaded by the GIS group. Outsourcing to outside firms has a fairly small presence in the sample, but two of the case companies are outsourcers. The Engineering Systems case has provided insight into the benefits of a formal, traditional approach, and highlights the JAD technique, which early on brings together users, key stakeholders, and the systems project team for rapid analysis and design. The case also gives insight into the perspective of the outsourcer and recommends to businesses that they maintain some of their own GIS capabilities, as the outsourcer can only do so much, while some or all of the support eventually gets returned to the client.

REFERENCES

Bowman, Scott. 2005. "Building an Enterprise GIS in a Limited Fiscal Environment." *ArcUser*, 8(1): 10–11.

Bowman, Scott. 2005. "Evaluating Enterprise GIS Requirements." *ArcUser*, 8(1): 12–13.

Couger, J. Daniel, and Robert A. Zawacki. 1980. *Motivating and Managing Computer Personnel*. New York: John Wiley and Sons.

Dangermond, Jack. 2006. "GIS Enterprise Architecture: Unifying the Utility." GITA 2006 Proceedings.

ESRI 2000. "ModelBuilder for ArcView Spatial Analyst 2." ESRI White Paper, May. Redlands, CA: ESRI Inc.

Gray, P. 2006. *Manager's Guide to Making Decisions About Information Systems*. New York: John Wiley and Sons.

Gray, P., and H. Watson. 1998. *Decision support in the data warehouse*. Upper Saddle River, NJ: Prentice Hall.

Kearney, Pat. 2003. "Looking for Quality Geographic Data?" *GeoWorld*, 16(9): 38–40.

Laudon, Kenneth C., and Jane P. Laudon. 2007. *Essentials of Business Information Systems*. Upper Saddle River, NJ: Prentice Hall.

Malinowski, E., and E. Zimanyi. 2003. "Representing spatiality in a conceptual multidimensional model." In Proceedings of the 12th annual ACM international workshop on geographic information systems, Washington, DC: ACM Press, pp. 12–22.

Marble, Duane F. 2006. "Who Are We? Defining the Geospatial Workforce." *Geospatial Solutions*, May, pp. 14–21.

Spollen, Joseph F. 2006. "GIS Program Development: If At First You Don't Succeed—Try Again." Proceedings of the Geospatial Information and Technology Association, Conference 29, Aurora, CO: Geospatial Information and Technology Association. Available at www.gita.org.

Valacich, Joseph S., Joey F. George, and Jeffrey A. Hoffer. 2004. *Essentials of Systems Analysis and Design*, Second Edition. Upper Saddle River, NJ: Prentice Hall.

Viswanathan, N., J.B. Pick, W.J. Hettrick, and E. Ellsworth. 2005. "An analysis of commonality in the twin metropolitan areas of San Diego, California and Tijuana, Mexico." *Journal of Socio-Economic Planning Sciences*, (39) 57–79.

West, Lawrence A. 2002. "Designing End-User Geographic Information Systems." In Tonya Barrier (ed.), *Human Computer Interaction Development and Management*, Hershey, PA: Idea Group Publishing, pp. 53–70.

THE VALUE OF INVESTING IN GIS

GIS AND GEOGRAPHIC INFORMATION—THEIR VALUE

In considering GIS and spatial technologies, a business needs to ask the question, are there net benefits coming from their use? That answer should determine whether the company goes forward or not with GIS and spatial applications. To assess the question, management needs to know what categories of costs and benefits are present, how to measure them, what methods to employ in deciding whether there is net payoff, and what are the external and intangible factors. The chapter considers how a cost-benefit analysis is different for GIS and spatial systems compared to standard IT cost-benefit analysis which has been studied more (King and Schrems, 1978; Devaraj and Kohli, 2002).

The payoff from GIS is influenced by the effects of time. For example, a medium-sized company invests a half million dollars over one year to re-develop its client-server GIS into web-based service-oriented architecture and implement it. When should the payoffs be measured? After a half year? Three years? It's even more difficult to compare the investments, mostly made early, to the payoff if the value of the dollar is eroding over time through inflation. The technique of Net Present Value (NPV) is presented that allows time and inflation factors to be taken into account. The chapter discusses the steps a firm can take to conduct cost-benefit analysis. The books' cases demonstrate that large firms tend to utilize more formal methods for determining the payoffs from GIS, while small ones usually do it informally, sometimes by "seat of the pants." Some studies have shown that IT investments do

Geo-Business: GIS in the Digital Organization, By James B. Pick
Copyright © 2007 John Wiley & Sons, Inc.

not yield net measurable benefits. This issue, referred to as the "productivity paradox" (Brynjolfsson, 1993; Lucas, 1999), is taken up regarding GIS investments.

Case studies of Sears and Norwich Union are considered. Sears developed extensive methods for cost-benefit analysis, while the Norwich Union case demonstrates how unexpected benefits can occur from discovering the value of spatial data.

Why perform cost-benefit analysis for GIS? Three of the important reasons are as follows (King and Schrems, 1978; Worrall, 1994):

1. Cost-benefit (C-B) analysis assists in planning for an organization. Planning involves tradeoffs between competing demand for organizational investment and resources. C-B analysis can help in deciding between competing demands. GIS becomes one of the competing demands and must rise high enough in planning priority to compete.

2. Cost-benefit analysis is useful in auditing. The organization may decide after a GIS system has been put into effect to perform a retrospective C-B analysis, to audit what occurred. The auditor determines whether or not the investment paid off, and suggests changes.

3. To prepare and support participants in political decision-making. This is less formal and more rapid than the planning uses in 1 and 2. It is done with less complete information, but is more commonplace than the other reasons (King and Schrems, 1978). Often budget decisions are partisan and depend on the power structure of the players involved. However, in that environment the parties who know the C-B details may do better.

SETTING THE CONTEXT FOR COST-BENEFIT ANALYSIS

The stage and context needs to be set at the start to do a C-B analysis. As a C-B project is launched, the following four factors are useful to clarify early on (King and Schrems, 1978):

1. *Statement of purpose.* This statement indicates whether the C-B analysis is being utilized directly to make a decision, to provide background data for a decision, or to politically influence decision-making. It is important to ascertain, since the methods, quality of the data, and the reporting of findings differ by purpose.

2. *Time simultaneity.* The C-B analysis must indicate whether the C-B analysis pertains to a future GIS system, involves a current GIS system, or is retrospective. Any time point may be useful for C-B.

3. *Scope.* The C-B analysis may be comprehensive in examining all possible costs and benefits. On the other hand, it may be severely limited

in scope, for instance, it may only manipulate a single cost item, as part of a sensitivity analysis, to see how it affects the benefit outcomes.

4. *Criterion.* The last contextual factor is the method that is used to compare the costs and benefits, after they have been calculated. A problem is that costs and especially benefits may not be measurable in monetary terms. For instance one benefit of a new spatial web site is to improve the company's brand image. However, the analyst is not able to convert this to monetary values. If there are intangibles, they may or may not factor into the criterion. *Intangible* is defined as not convertible into a currency value.

The criterion may be a quantitative index measure, graphical comparison, or involve a lengthier model. The criterion definition needs also to state whether or not the values of the costs and benefits are to take into account inflation and opportunity costs through net-present-value calculations. Also, the criterion definition needs to indicate if intangibles are excluded or included.

Among the challenges in GIS cost-benefit analysis is that GIS tends to have higher costs than for conventional information systems, due to its considerable data acquisition and data management needs. This is because a GIS is based on both attribute data and spatial data (Huxhold, 1991; Clarke, 2001). The extra time and effort, versus non-spatial IT, stems from the need to do the following:

Gather boundary data and associated attributes

Convert the data to digital form

Design or configure topological data structures and link non-spatial with spatial data

Maintain GIS boundary files and data

Estimates indicate data collection for GIS may constitute 65 to 80 percent of the total cost for systems development and implementation (Huxhold and Levinsohn, 1995; Obermeyer, 1999; Tomlinson, 2003). Further, the attribute and digital boundary data need to be linked together. These linkage tasks add to costs, relative to non-spatial IS. Another difference has to do with GIS's feature of visualization (Jarupathirun and Zahedi, 2004). In this respect, GIS is comparable to a multimedia business application, which may have higher costs, due to its visual aspects. GIS tends to have a higher proportion of intangible benefits than a non-spatial IS. In some cases, it may be possible to build models that convert the benefits into a tangible benefit, but the organization does not commit the money to accomplish the conversion.

Another difference is that GIS applications often depend on outside data providers who create risk in two ways: (1) lack of commitment to an ongoing

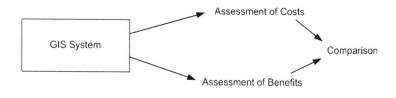

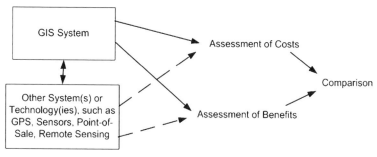

Figure 7.1 Comparison of Cost-Benefit for a Simple GIS System to a GIS System Closely Coupled with Another System or Technology

cycle of data import, conversion to proper format, and linkages within and between complex spatial datasets; (2) external data supply may be interrupted which might render the GIS system worthless. For instance, a chain of hospitals models and maps the traffic patterns that affect patients' access. The highway data are provided by a state university consortium. However, the consortium loses its funding, leading to shut-down of the data flow. IT also has these problems, but the cycles of data refresh are usually less complex and often there are more options if one data source shuts down.

Another distinctive aspect of GIS from Chapter 1 is that GIS is frequently coupled with other software systems and technologies. The systems and technologies such as GPS with which GIS is coupled appear in Table 1.3. As seen in Figure 7.1, because of this coupling, the cost and benefit calculation for any one of them may be more difficult.

Figure 7.1 demonstrates that the assessment of costs and benefits of an uncoupled GIS system can be done by performing a straightforward assessment of that system's costs and benefits, followed by a cost-benefit comparison with a criterion such as break-even analysis. However, the cost-benefit analysis becomes more complicated for a GIS coupled with another system or technology such as handheld computer, RFID, or GPS. For multi-component, linked systems, it is difficult to disaggregate the costs and benefits of the GIS from those of the other technologies. Additionally, the two coupled components may be at different stages of development, which complicates NPV and break-even analysis.

For a multi-component system, the marginal cost of investing in one spatial component to add to an existing system may be at a much lower cost than the total cost of implementing the full system from scratch. This must be weighed against the level of benefits for the two alternatives.

THE COSTS AND BENEFITS OF GIS

This section discusses the categories of costs and benefits of a geographic information system. Costs and benefits may be divided into tangible i.e. able to be converted into monetary amounts and intangible i.e. not convertible to monetary values (King and Schrems, 1978; Obermeyer, 1999; Karikari and Stillwell, 2005). Costs for information systems including GIS are predominantly tangible, while benefits are a mixture of tangible and intangible. For instance, the cost of a GIS managerial employee can be estimated by the tangible value of his/her salary and job benefits. However, the most significant benefit of the employee is his/her effective leadership and decision-making, outcomes difficult if not impossible to convert into dollar amounts.

Costs

The costs of a GIS can be classified into the categories given in Table 7.1. The costs are all tangible and possible to estimate. (Note: intangible costs are not considered here.) However, some problems often occur in calculating the costs, and there is a risk of excluding others that might be relevant. Many common errors prevalent in cost accounting create pitfalls (King and Schrems, 1978), such as not identifying hidden costs, counting costs twice, or omitting important costs. An example of hidden costs would be costs located at other places in the organization that are not being counted against the GIS. For instance, the development of a GIS system depends on the ideas of the GIS team leader, who spends a lot of time in discussion with analysts and managers in Central IT. However, the overhead of the time spent by the GIS team leader with Central IT is not included in the costs. Omitted costs are ones that are not obvious, but are in fact dedicated to the project. For example, space, site, and utility costs are commonly omitted, but may be important particularly in expensive locations, such as downtown Chicago.

Risk management has tangible and intangible costs. Among the tangible costs are security and insurance. Security reduces risk and insurance invests in mitigating its impacts. There are also intangible costs associated with risks. If a customer-centric GIS fails, such as a web service that provides routing

TABLE 7.1   Tangible Costs of a GIS

Hardware
Software
Data collection (internal)
Collection or purchase of external data
Staff
Transformation of manual maps and data into digital format
Systems development and implementation Business process change
Project management
Web services
Maintenance costs for hardware and software
Maintenance of data
Supplies
Training
Outsourcing (e.g. GIS applications programming)
Consulting
Licensing
Security
Insurance
The internet, other networks, communications interfaces
Space, site, and utilities

Modified and expanded from Huxhold, 1991; Worrall, 1992; Obermeyer, 1999; and Tomlinson, 2003

to customers, corporate image and reputation may be muddied but the costs can't be quantified. Other examples of risks for spatial systems that may incur intangible costs are privacy intrusion, reduced safety (e.g. if criminal targets appears on public maps), user resistance, and added intelligence of competitors through public maps. In many circumstances, there is a low probability of cost, but it could be substantial.

Benefits

The benefits of GIS and spatial technologies are more difficult to measure than costs (King and Schrems, 1978; Obermeyer, 2000; Worrall, 1994; Tomlinson, 2003; Karikari and Stillwell, 2005; Maguire et al., 2007). The reason is that benefits are expressed as an informed, ready, efficient, and decisive organization, which is hard to measure, since there are many beneficiaries, time lags, and intervening causes (Table 7.2). Benefits may also be expressed in terms of greater information value, but the value of information is difficult to measure because it depends on timeliness, its users, and what decisions it is influencing (Ahituv, 1989; Ragowsky et al., 2000). Another problem with measuring benefits has to do with quantity versus quality. How do you

TABLE 7.2   Benefits of GIS (Tangible and Intangible)

Tangible

Total salary and benefits lowered through reducing the workforce
Improved productivity
Improved performance
Greater accuracy
Higher value of assets
Cost reduction (through employees performing their tasks more efficiently)
Cost avoidance in the future (projected greater workload per employee)
Time saving in searching, manipulating, and processing maps and data.
Expansion of revenues (achieved through improved data quality, speed, efficiency)

Intangible

Improved decision making
Effectiveness of managers and executives
Reaching strategic objectives
Environmental scanning
Visualizing complex data
Improved siting of offices, branches, factories, and other facilities
Timeliness of information and quicker response
Volume and quality of information
Better capability to sell products (by spatial web services, manual maps)
Improved customer service

Identification of missing revenue sources (e.g. in government, identification of properties
  not being taxed)
Better environmental scanning
Reduced error
Reduced liability (e.g. GIS for security monitoring)
Improved brand image

Modified and expanded from Huxhold, 1991; Obermeyer, 1999; Stein and Nasib, 1997; Devaraj and Kohli, 2002; Tomlinson, 2003; and Karikari and Stillwell, 2005.

measure the value of a GIS that produces fewer, high-resolution maps versus one producing numerous low-resolution ones?

Although more challenging to measure than costs, benefits can be calculated. Suggestions on ways to compute them are the following:

1. Disaggregate larger benefits into smaller pieces, which may be more amenable to quantification. Consider an example. An advertising firm has identified the benefit of better knowledge of its products through presentations to its customers that rely on GIS. However, the overall better knowledge cannot be made tangible. Nevertheless, if the presentation process is broken down into a set of small control items, such as number of maps, length of the average presentation, number of sales agents making presentations, the benefits of GIS may be more amenable to assignment of dollar values, although it is still not easy.

2. The C-B analysis can be restricted to only tangible costs and tangible benefits (Smith and Tomlinson, 1992; Obermeyer, 1999). If that result indicates net benefit, then the intangible benefits may be regarded as an added plus. Another variation on this approach is to perform a break-even analysis for a future time point, just restricted to tangibles (King and Schrems, 1978). If costs exceed benefits, the negative value of benefits minus costs can be compared against positive intangible benefits. They may be close enough to yield a compelling argument for implementation.

An example of benefits calculation is for Lamar Advertising Company, which is the second largest billboard company in the United States. Lamar depends on nearly 200 sales managers, who sell billboard contracts to advertising companies and their client firms. The managers benefit by well documented reports that include maps indicating potential billboard locations relative to traffic flows and other features. The benefits of GIS are mainly improvement in closing contracts, and also improved marketing planning. Tangible benefits can be estimated by seeking expert opinion to gauge the percentage improvement in contract closings from introducing GIS. This change in percentage can also be measured since closing percentages were measured before GIS was introduced and afterwards. The percentage improvement can be multiplied by annual sales to determine the dollar benefit annually. Finally, intangible benefits include a better corporate image for Lamar and better responsiveness of sales managers.

Benefits calculations can be helped in some cases by creating simulation models of corporate revenue-generating or profit-generating activities that measure the sensitivity of adding GIS. The difference before and after is an estimate of tangible benefit.

PREVALENCE OF COSTS AND BENEFITS IN CASE STUDY COMPANIES

The book's research case study companies indicate overall patterns in cost-benefit analysis. Although a small sample, it gives some insight into overall industry trends in spatial costs and benefits. Two-thirds of the companies indicated that the level of net GIS benefits, i.e. benefits minus costs, was high. This supports a finding that for these companies GIS and spatial technologies are paying off. Only one firm, Large Credit Bank (LCB) indicated low net GIS benefits. LCB is a very large bank with a monoline product line in the credit card area, but has acquired several medium-sized regional consumer banks. IT in the credit bank is dominated by legacy systems. Although the acquired banks are users of GIS for branch siting, the benefits are restrained due to a top management in the big central unit that doesn't understand GIS and is resistant to it.

Only the largest firms, Sears, The Southern Company, GIO, URS, and Large Insurance Company, used formal methods of cost-benefit analysis. The methods were ROI and Net Present Value (NPV). The GIS managers in the large firms pointed out that these methods were company-wide standards applying to all corporate projects, and were not chosen specifically for GIS. The Southern Company did thorough NPV analysis broken out for each major cost category, for every operating company, and for the Southern-wide aggregate. This level of detail is helpful to upper-middle management in budgeting for, and tracking Southern's ambitious enterprise-wide spatial initiative. The largest firms, GIO and Sears, singled out very large GIS projects as having more rigorous cost-benefit models and complex financial analysis. It is firms of such size that would tend to have financial staff available to conduct such studies.

Across all firms, there was good agreement on the cost categories of personnel, software, hardware, and data (see Table 7.3), all of which appear in Table 7.1. The near agreement on costs to be considered probably stems from their more tangible nature. Furthermore, the components needed to develop and build spatial applications are rather uniform, even though the applications are varied. A number of firms such as Large Insurance Company (LIC) and Norwich Union, cited data costs as being their highest. Both insurance firms purchased a lot of data from external sources, so those costs were high and also visible. Firms gave less emphasis to the cost of internal data. It is likely internal data costs are also high, but sometimes not broken out and not recognized in internal budgets or possibly the GIS use was incremental to existing uses of the data and not so significant.

No firm mentioned outsourcing as a cost item, pointing to its lesser presence for GIS versus its rampant role in more conventional systems. Its reduced extent may be due to: (1) GIS's specialized nature, (2) its importance in some firms as a core competency, obviating emphasis on outsourcing, and (3) shortages of spatially skilled people in the outsourcers. The topic is returned to in Chapter 10.

Benefits of GIS for the case firms, shown in Table 7.4, are quite varied, which corresponds to their less tangible nature, the broad variety of benefits already mentioned (see Table 7.2), and the wide differences expected for firms with different products, industries, customers, and strategies. Among benefits more prevalent for the case companies are improved facilities siting, quicker response, and better decision-making. These are fundamental benefits that managers should look for when implementing a GIS. Several companies pointed to the benefits derived from the value of certain spatial data, some so valuable it might be marketed as a separate product. One such firm, Norwich Union, will be discussed as a chapter case later. Four-fifths of the benefits cited are intangible, confirming *tangible costs,* but *intangible benefits.* However, it's important to keep in mind that "intangible" sometimes means that there are not the tools available nor the management commitment to divert sufficient company resources to measure it tangibly.

TABLE 7.3   Costs of GIS for Case Sample of Firms

Name or Description	Size	Uses C/B Formal Method	Method Used	Level of Net GIS Benefits	Strategic Level	Costs
Global Integrated Oil (description)	large	Yes	ROI and others for large projects	high	very high	people, data (largest cost), hardware, software
URS	large	Yes	Estimate simple tradeoffs.	high	medium	people, software, hardware
Large Credit Bank (description)	large	No		low	low	people, data, software, hardware
Rand McNally	large	No		high	high	people, data, software tools, opportunity costs
Southern Company	large	Yes	NPV for each cost category, aggregated Southern-wide and for each operating company.	high	high	hardware, software, IT support, other support, personnel
Sears Roebuck	large	Yes	NPV. Compute paybasck periods. For large scale projects, more detailed, rigorous financial models are used.	high	high	people, data, hardware, software development
Kaiser Permanente	large	No		medium	medium	people, hardware, software, outsourcing
Large Insurance Company (description)	large	Yes	ROI	high	high	salary and benefits of GIS team, hardware, software, large data cost for external data.

Company	Size				Description
Large Commercial Bank (description)	large	No	high	low	software, hardware (desktops and printer) salary and benefits, training, data.
Norwich Union	large	No	high	high	software, hardware, data (a lot external), personnel.
Baystate Health	medium	No	medium	low	undetermined
Lamar Advertising Company	medium	No	high	high	people, hardware, software, web services
Arizona Republic	medium	No	medium	high	people, hardware, software, data
Chico's	medium	No	medium	high	data (most expensive and from outside), software, people. Hardware is in IT budget.
Western Exterminator	medium	No	medium	medium	people, hardware, software
Sperry Van Ness	medium	No	high	high	personnel, hardware, software - Microsoft, training package
Prudential Preferred Realty	medium	No	medium	high	software, hardware, personnel. All is shared with IT and other functions.
Engineering Systems	small	No	high	low	people, hardware, software
MapGistics	small	No	high	high	training, hardware, software, financial costs
Motion-Based Technologies	small	No	high	very high	people, web services

ROI = return on investment. NPV = net present value.

TABLE 7.4   Benefits of GIS Case Sample of Firms

Name or description	Size	Benefits
Global Integrated Oil (description)	large	Know where assets located. Track assets over time.
URS	large	Better quality of output. Efficiency. The value of the data in the maps.
Large Credit Bank (description)	large	Analyze new branches and facilities.
Rand McNally	large	Better decisions on marketing Rand McNally products. Make high quality map products.
Southern Company	large	Consolidation benefits from GIS enterprise-wide. Identify substandard geographies for cost avoidance.
Sears Roebuck	large	Increased productivity for a huge workforce. Faster response. Stretch out periods of GIS capital investments.
Kaiser Permanente	large	Decision-making, better government submissions, presentations, identification of catchments areas.
Large Insurance Company (description)	large	Increase underwriter profit. Write better policies. Decision-making.
Large Commercial Bank (description)	large	Added revenue from making good branch location decisions. Support to sales campaigns that bring in customer dollars and business relationships.
Norwich Union	Large	Revenues from GIS for floods, better profits from customer base with GPS in cars. New data products.
Baystate Health	medium	Undetermined, since GIS projects are recent.
Lamar Advertising Company	medium	Closing contracts (maps are a key element in proposals to advertisers). Better control of marketing development expenses. Mapping available to sales team at 160 sites.
Arizona Republic	medium	Competitive edge.
Chico's	medium	Forecasting volume of merchandise and related sales and staffing. Accurate forecasting benefits suppliers. Improved marketing and response time to supply stores.
Western Exterminator	medium	Improved decision-making for marketing. Better siting of new centers. Better routing.
Sperry Van Ness	medium	Savings in employee time. Speed to market in making proposals to clients.
Prudential Preferred Realty	medium	Pleasing customers with new spatial web functions and tools leading to better customer retention. Better locational assessments by executive team of listings and agent performance
Engineering Systems	small	Revenues from clients for GIS projects that the firm completed.
MapGistics	small	Improved bed occupancy efficiency, speed of patient discharge, locating assets.
Motion-Based Technologies	small	Increase in proportion of web customers with paid subscriptions.

Based on the limited case sample, we can conclude that (1) GIS is beneficial, (2) informal "seat of the pants" methods are mostly used to measure the net benefits, except for very large firms, and (3) while costs are tangible, benefits are a mixture of tangible and intangible.

Benefits vary a lot by firm and industry circumstance. For example, since GIO as an exploration and production company needs to know where its huge base of assets is located over time, GIS provides its greatest benefits in asset tracking. The benefits are intangible. Kaiser Permanente has varied GIS applications, so its benefits are also diverse and mostly intangible. Large Insurance Company focuses its greatest use of GIS on underwriting and policies and that is where the mixed tangible-intangible benefits are. The tangible benefits for Sperry Van Ness are speed of response and better use of time for its national marketing managers. That's where its GIS is focused. In nearly all the cases, the benefits are specialized and keyed to the specific focus on the GIS applications, rather than generic ones. This reflects that GIS has not yet risen to become a tool in general use across enterprises.

Unit of Analysis

The difficulty in measuring the costs and benefits of GIS varies by the unit of analysis (King and Schrems, 1978; Obermeyer, 1999; Tomlinson, 2003). Among the units of analysis for GIS are the following:

Industry
Company
Department or division
Project
Individual

Considering the different units is useful to organizations performing C-B analysis, as well as to industry analysts and researchers studying trends and doing comparisons. C-B analysis is mostly commonly performed at the company level, and is easier to do where GIS is smaller but challenging if it's enterprise-wide for a larger firm. For budget analysts, it can be beneficial to disaggregate costs and benefits below the company level. Firms do not usually perform C-B analysis for GIS at the individual level as data are missing or it's too expensive, although it might apply for a small business.

Analyzing C-B at the project level offers a number of advantages. Firms need well-controlled project management procedures to track the project costs and benefits over time, with regular reporting intervals. This tracking can then be input to accomplish ROI and NPV calculations. Having the project detail helps a firm in its GIS planning, coordination, and auditing. For instance, benefits for GIS Project A are realized evenly for each of the five years after implementation, versus for GIS Project B, benefits are realized on a declining basis – 40 percent in the first year, 30 percent in year 2, 20 percent in year

3, 10 percent in year 4 and none in year 5. Having the project detail allows management to better plan its annual cash flows, and make adjustments to the projects if necessary.

Similar advantages of disaggregation apply by departments and divisions. The disadvantage to disaggregating is the higher data collection, monitoring and coordination costs of the C-B analysis. C-B analysis at the industry level is usually done by consultants or researchers.

For projects with small scope, such as a single-user desktop project, costs and benefits may be more readily estimated. For them, there is limited integration with other systems and technologies, intervening factors are reduced, and the external environment is not as influential. On the other hand, if the unit is a corporate-wide GIS system, it may be challenging to separate its costs and benefits from those of other systems inside the company, from inter-organizational systems, or from the outside environment. Furthermore, for enterprise-wide GIS, the attribute data are commonly shared with other company systems, such as marketing, or with the firm's enterprise resource planning (ERP) system. Inter-organizational GIS systems are even more challenging to assess. The shared aspect of the business data complicates the separation of GIS's costs and benefits. Since the trend in GIS is towards enterprise-wide web-based systems, the challenge of determining costs, benefits, and payoff is likely to grow.

THE SUBSTEPS IN COST-BENEFIT ANALYSIS FROM SYSTEMS DESIGN PERSPECTIVE

The last chapter examined the many dimensions of systems analysis and design for GIS. This section briefly considers the project steps in the C-B analysis, which is part of the feasibility stage in systems analysis. It is intended to encourage managers to plan the steps of C-B analysis carefully.

The following are the standard cost-benefit substeps for IT:

1. Develop an overall plan for the C-B analysis to be conducted over the system useful life.
2. Decide on the analyst or analyst team.
3. Consult with executive management and key user managers to identify which are the largest and most important categories of costs and benefits.
4. Determine the alternative C-B analyses to be performed . Decide on the unit of analysis, company, or by departments, or projects.
5. Determine all the material factors for costs and all the material factors for benefits.
6. For each tangible factor, decide how it will be measured.
7. Decide if intangible costs and benefits will be included. Decide on how they will be evaluated.

8. Measure the tangible costs and benefits. For benefits, the measurement methods include expert opinions, simulation modeling, and experimental comparisons.
9. If included, evaluate the intangible costs and benefits.
10. Compare the cost-benefit results over the entire time period of the study. Include financial summary measures such as break-even point, etc. and criteria to evaluate alternatives. If appropriate, conduct discounted cash flow analysis.
11. Perform a comparative analysis of the alternatives from step 4.
12. Decide on what recommendations to make to management, based on these results. Present the findings to management.

(Modified from King and Schrems, 1978; Ahituv and Neumann, 1990; Karikari and Stillwell, 2005; Maguire et al., 2007)

Before commencing C-B analysis, an analyst must be selected—a choice that is often critical for C-B's success or failure. There are a number of places to find the analyst (Ahituv and Neumann, 1990): (1) *Inside person.* This is someone within the organization who has the necessary financial management and technical skills, as well as experience and knowledge in GIS. (2) *Outside consultant.* Auditing, accounting, and GIS and IS consulting firms can provide such persons. (3) *Persons from other organization(s).* Someone from an affiliated organization may be loaned or made responsible to perform the C-B analysis. They may stem from government or corporate oversight, or through corporate alliances.

For GIS, the C-B substep steps differ in some respects. For Step 2 (develop an analyst team), GIS is influenced by its historical origin in the public sector, outside of the mainstream of business IT (Huxhold, 1991; Tomlinson, 2003). Thus, analysts from the public sector may be less well-trained in formal systems analysis and C-B techniques than those coming from careers in business or information systems. For Step 5 (determine the material factors for costs and benefits), the material benefits may be reduced or more difficult to measure, due to the presence of visualization. In Step 10 (comparative analysis), comparisons may be complicated by the problem discussed earlier of close coupling between GIS and other spatial systems and technologies.

How does GIS differ from non-spatial IS in relative importance of different categories of costs and benefits, given in Tables 7.1 and 7.2. For GIS, these categories are influenced by the relatively greater costs for acquiring spatial data (Huxhold and Levinsohn, 1995; Obermeyer, 1999; Tomlinson, 2003). The capital costs of data acquisition vary by whether the data and coverages come from the public or private domains. Since historically GISs were mainly in the public domain, large banks of public data and boundary files have been available for free or very low cost in the U.S. An example is the U.S. Census maps and associated data on population, housing, social characteristics, and the economy, distributed free over the internet (www.census.gov) (U.S.

Census Bureau, 2007). Other free geospatial data are available U.S. public portals such as GeoData.gov (www.geodata.gov), and NationalAtlas.gov (www.nationalatlas.gov). Internationally data are available from such portals as The Geography Network (www.thegeographynetwork.com), and Go-Geo! for the UK (www.gogeo.uc.uk).

The time spent organizing the data, entering it into databases such as Oracle, and checking it for quality, sometimes makes up for the "free availability" from governments. Another source of data is third-party service firms that make government and private sector data available in better organized form, but at cost. On the other hand, business proprietary data can be quite costly or unavailable for competitive reasons. In Europe and most of the world outside the U.S., the cost of government spatial data is often high, which adds to the data cost problem.

COMPARISON OF COSTS AND BENEFITS OVER TIME

As was seen in Figure 7.1, the concluding step in a cost-benefit analysis is to compare the costs against the benefits in order to determine whether or not the GIS investment has net benefit or not. Graphical and non-graphical methods are available to perform comparative analysis of cost-benefit results over time (King and Schrems, 1978; Kingma, 2001; Boardman, Greenberg, Vining, and Weimer, 2001; Karikari and Stillwell, 2005). Among the more prominent ones are the following.

- Break even point
  - The total investment cost is divided by the annual benefit of the GIS. This gives the number of years to break-even. However, this calculation may need to be adjusted for a multi-year investment due to changes in the time value of money.
- Formulae
  - Costs and benefits are directly compared through a formula.
- Baseline cost comparison charts
  - Use of a graph to compare the annual cost of running an enterprise without GIS and the cost of running the enterprise with GIS. The charts can show GIS costs savings annually or cumulatively, and can plot net present value on tangible benefits at different discount rate assumptions.
    A benefits yield curve indicates the percent of cumulative benefits realized from a GIS project or from GIS in the firm over a multi-year period (Maguire et al., 2007).
- Discounted cash flow
  - A common technique of cost-benefit analysis is to account for the discounted value of money over time. Both costs and benefits are discounted over time, assuming a regime of future discount rates for inflation. This is accomplished by the calculation of *net present value*.

THE METHOD OF DISCOUNTED CASH FLOW

The net present value (NPV) for a cost or benefit for a particular year in the future may be estimated by:

$$NPV = \sum_{t=0}^{n} \frac{x_t}{(1+d)^t}$$

where NPV is the present value, x_t is the cost or benefit value during time period t, and d is the discount rate. After choosing appropriate discount rate or rates, all the future costs and benefits can be estimated.

The present value of the costs and benefits can be summarized together in the equation:

$$NPV = \sum_{t=0}^{n} \frac{B_t - C_t}{(1+d)^t}$$

where B_t represents the benefit at time t and C_t represents the cost at time t.

There are fine points in calculating the net present value that are beyond the chapter's scope, but can be found in books on cost-benefit and financial accounting. They include at what point in a time period the inflation rate is calculated (beginning, middle, end); whether the inflation rate fluctuates (this equation assumes it remains steady); and whether costs are influenced differently by inflation than benefits (King and Schrems, 1978). The analyst needs to take into account that the precision of the cost and benefit figures will influence the accuracy of this calculation.

Since GIS projects tend to have long periods from start to break-even due to the higher investment in start-up and data acquisition (Tomlinson, 2003), the impact of net present value calculations may be large.

COMPARISON WITH A CRITERION

Usually the C-B analysis involves several alternatives having different values for costs and benefits. A criterion is used to compare them. Let's say that an analyst has prepared six alternatives under different cost-benefit assumptions. A *criterion* is used to select the most suitable one (King and Schrems, 1978). Among the criteria commonly used are:

- Maximize the present value of the benefits minus the present value of the costs.
- Maximize the ratio of benefits over costs.
- Assume a given level of costs for all alternatives and maximize benefits.
- Assume a given level of benefits for all alternatives and minimize costs.

Any of these criteria, or others, can be used. The choice depends on the particular problem and context of management decision-making.

A problem can occur if insufficient alternatives are examined for the problem at hand. For instance, for a small-scale GIS with a single data source, single boundary file, and clear uses, perhaps two or three alternatives would be appropriate. By contrast, for an enterprise-wide, web-based GIS involving millions of dollars in expenditure and tens of thousands of users, more alternatives are needed. Even for a large scale, complex GIS, however, it is not possible to include all the alternatives. Experience has shown that results may be improved, if the key interested parties are involved in determining which alternatives to include (King and Schrems, 1978; Maguire et al., 2007).

INTANGIBLE COSTS AND BENEFITS

Intangible costs and benefits are prevalent in GIS applications (Obermeyer, 1999; Tomlinson, 2003; Karikari and Stillwell, 2005). Some examples of intangible benefits are the following (Ahituv and Neumann, 1990; Tomlinson, 2003; Karikari and Stillwell, 2005):

- Image improvement of the organization
  ∘ Better planning
- Better decision-making
  ∘ Improved customer service
  ∘ Better understanding through visualization
- Enhanced employee morale
- Improved information to executives

After determining the intangible costs and benefits, the intangible costs and benefits can be prioritized by interviewing managers in user departments The intangible C-Bs are presented in summary form to management, along with the tangible ones (Ahituv and Neumann, 1990; Karikari and Stillwell, 2005). Some experts advise, in meeting with top management, to justify the net tangible benefits first, and then present the intangibles (Maguire et al., 2007). No matter how the C-Bs are presented, top management can ultimately decide how much to weigh the intangibles.

What is distinctive for GIS versus non-spatial IS concerning intangibles? First, the visualization capabilities of GIS may provide improved decision quality for certain classes of decisions (Mennecke et al., 2000; Swink and Speier, 2000), but the degree of improvement may be difficult to quantify. Visual responses tend to be difficult to measure. For example, if there are two GIS systems, where the first one produces low resolution maps and the second one yields maps with five-fold better resolution, how can the advantage of this intangible benefit on business effectiveness and decision-making be measured? A second feature of GIS that has stimulated more intangibles is the tendency of GIS to move up in the hierarchy of business applications to become more strategic once the benefits are realized. At the strategic/competitive level, the benefits are less tangible versus at the operational or middle management levels (Ahituv, 1989).

THE FEASIBILITY DECISION

Management must eventually weigh the results of a cost-benefit analysis and make a decision on one of the alternatives, including staying with the status quo (Ahituv and Neumann, 1990; Satzinger, Jackson, and Burd, 2002). Analysis of feasibility for IT systems is divided into three areas: (1) financial feasibility, (2) technical feasibility, and (3) institutional feasibility. Feasibility decisions are influenced by the total time period of commitment before the decision is revisited, for instance one year, five years, or ten years. If the feasibility decision needs to hold for ten years, then a much more in-depth study must be undertaken. No matter what depth, as the time frame extends out, it becomes increasingly difficult to accurately predict technological changes (Day and Schoemaker, 2000).

For financial feasibility, GIS is similar to a conventional IT application. It is based on the cost-benefit comparison described in the last section. Determination of technical feasibility for GIS follows standard methods detailed elsewhere (Satzinger et al., 2002), but may put more emphasis on the feasibility of linking GIS with associated technologies such as GPS, RRID, sensors, and mobile services. Institutional feasibility refers to the capability of the institution to support a GIS project. GIS requires specialized human workers, with sufficient knowledge to carry out a GIS project, either inside the institution or present in an outsourcer. Institutional feasibility is affected by GIS's distinctive features, especially visualization capability and presence of linked systems.

STAKEHOLDERS AND EXTERNALITIES

Cost-benefit outcomes vary depending on the vantage points of different stakeholders to an organization. For instance, GIS in an advertising firm will have different costs and benefits for the corporation itself, marketing and advertising people in client firms, investors, and the public who eventually view the advertisements. The effort of cost-benefit work is made more difficult and time-consuming by conducting separate C-B analysis for different stakeholder groups (Obermeyer, 1999). However, it may be worth the effort, if there is wide diversity in the stakeholder perspectives, and if stakeholders are critical elements in firm success. At the minimum, stakeholders should be mentioned in the cost-benefit analysis.

Positive and negative externalities of a GIS refer to the indirect impacts of system implementation. This can be seen by the analogy of environmental externalities of an industry process. A process intended for manufacturing a product may cause the indirect effects of pollution, noise, and human injuries. An example of a negative externality for GIS is the loss of the information security or competitive advantage in an environmental company, as its GIS system for environmental mitigation becomes more widely deployed. By contrast, positive externalities may arise from Google mashups that provide free GIS and mapping to the public, or from the GIS-driven website of a local government that provides GIS analysis and mapping to the public. There may be unintended benefits, for instance high school students visiting the mashup websites and learning about products and services might be converted as customers in a few years.

CASE STUDY OF GIS COSTS AND BENEFITS: SEARS ROEBUCK

The giant retailer has extensive enterprise spatial technologies in six areas: routing and deploying service technicians, routing/deploying home delivery drivers, warehouse optimization, demand forecasting in marketing, automated vehicle navigation, and capacity management of the technician workforce in the service territories (Jones, 2005). The scale is huge, for instance this set of tools, referred to as the Sears Smart Toolbox (SST) supports 10,000 technicians in all fifty states, and its GIS/GPS systems support eleven million in-home service orders yearly (Jones, 2005). The systems have been deployed carefully and cost-efficiently. There have been major gains in productivity of delivery and service maintenance that have enhanced the company's bottom line. As the leading firm using spatial technologies in its huge markets, there is strong competitive advantage.

The six coordinated home product repair and delivery system modules are shown in Figure 7.2. The in-vehicle navigation is shown at the lower right. The support systems for home deliveries are the three on the upper part of the diagram: Demand Forecasting in the upper left, Enhanced Home Delivery System to determine the optimal home delivery route in the upper center, and the Warehouse Optimization with GIS in the upper right. The latter system does spatial routing for forklifts in the warehouses to pick the merchandise for each truck loading. The CAMS and CARS systems (lower left and lower center) assess the capacity of service technicians in geographic areas (CAMS) and determine the optimal routing for service technicians (CARS). Mobile Mapping (lower right) supports naviagation of the truck drivers. All six systems in the Sears Smart Toolbox draw data from the same mainframe system, and the six systems communicate with each other through radio links and satellite.

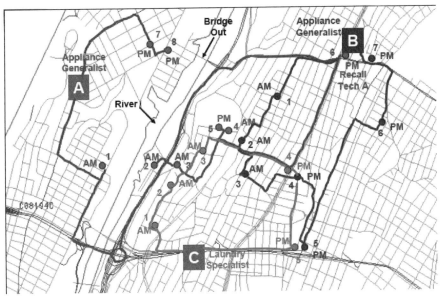

Figure 7.2   Sears Integrated GIS Systems for Product Repair Services and Home Delivery. Source: Jones, 2005

Sears has invested significantly in long-term and large-scale GIS systems. Fortunately, the payoff has been high (Kelley, 1999; Jones 2005). The costs include a twelve-person spatial team, annual data costs, high spatial development costs, hardware, and software. For instance, its investment of a few million dollars for SST, its latest automobile navigation system (lower right in Figure 7.2), resulted in GPS-referenced laptops being installed on 10,000 delivery trucks, which in turn improved delivery precision and efficiencies. The benefits are increased productivity multiplied across a large workforce, faster delivery response and optimized pathways, improved technician and delivery person productivity, reduced overtime, lower support costs, and capability to optimally re-arrange service territories. Sears uses traditional financial analysis with NPV, including computing payback periods. For very large million-dollar-plus spatial projects, more advanced financial modeling is done. Part of the challenge is to take into account integration of spatial systems with legacy mainframe systems. This legacy integration is common for GIS in large, data-rich companies. The company has measured huge productivity and performance gains. The firm-value gains are perceived to be there, but metrics do not yet break out the spatial contribution.

Prior to implementing GIS, the manual process at Sears was very time consuming and wasteful, with many hours each day spent by routing-center workers locating street addresses. In the early 1990s, an enterprise-wide GIS system was constructed by geocoding Sears' millions of customer addresses and setting up optimized delivery with the goal of 90 percent reliability in the promised delivery window (Kelley, 1999). The GIS calculates daily delivery routes, based on a model that includes "estimated travel times, in-home time, truck capacity, optimal stop sequence" (Kelley, 1999; Jones, 2005).

For tangible benefits, the system initially increased its efficiency by reducing the time for routing and addressing from an average of 5 hours daily to 20 minutes. The miles per delivery-truck stop were lowered by 0.6 mile, which allows four more stops per truck per day (Kelley, 1999). Subsequently, with further reduction in routing time, the system lowered the stops per truck per day by another one-half (Jones, 2005). All this has allowed reduction in the number of Sears national routing centers from forty-six to twelve (Jones, 2005). Delivery orders have expanded by 9 percent with the same-sized truck fleet. In all, equipment and facilities savings from the GIS-based networking enhancement are over $50 million per year (Kelley, 1999; Jones, 2005). All this was accomplished with only small additions to IT staff to support GIS (Jones, 2005).

The intangible benefits apply to Sears management and customers. Sears middle and top management are able to use the information in this system strategically to plan improved efficiency versus its competitors over long periods of time, a strategic efficiency approach resembling Wal-Mart's well-known inventory and just-in-time delivery systems. Service management improves, less customers are lost due to on-time deliveries; and competitive advantage is gained with better service quality. At the customer level, reducing the 20 percent of missed deliveries down to less than 5 percent has enhanced the image for Sears Delivery which has also helped in the marketing other company products.

The Sears Computer Aided Routing System (CARS) provides optimal routing for over 10,000 maintenance technicians servicing home appliances nationally. The system decides on which specialists are routed to which sequence of homes. Network algorithms group destinations into routes to minimize travel time. As seen in Figure 7.2, two appliance generalists and one laundry specialist each has a morning and afternoon route that has limited crisscrossing. The System is dynamic and can re-route if traffic blockages occur. This happened with Appliance Generalist A, who at the end of the simulated day was blocked by the upper bridge outage from getting from stop 6 to stop 7. Instead he was dynamically re-routed across the lower bridge, taking a much longer route, but getting to stops 7 and 8. It was a long day, but customers were served!

In summary, for this enterprise-wide spatial system deployed in a large corporation, the initial data acquisition was relatively expensive and time consuming, since over four million addresses had to be geocoded and then tediously corrected (Kelley, 2002). Another difference is the integration of GIS with GPS on the delivery trucks. Knowing the location of each truck in real-time allows more optimal management of the whole fleet. However, as we discussed, the necessity to couple GIS with other systems may increase the overall cost.

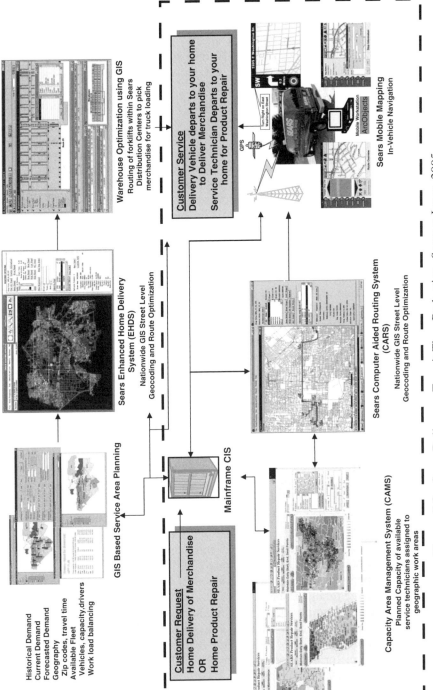

Figure 7.3 Sears Delivery—Transit Time Reduction. *Source:* Jones, 2005

THE PRODUCTIVITY PARADOX FOR GIS

In the information systems field, a special evaluation methodology has evolved, referred to as the "value of IT investment" approach. The method examines the level of IT investment and variety of returns on investment. It is sometimes referred to as "productivity paradox," i.e. the paradox that companies or larger economic units invest in IT but fail to realize appropriate productivity gains (Brynjolfsson, 1993).

This method is related to standard techniques of cost-benefit analysis. The difference is that it is especially sensitive to IT measurement problems in cost-benefit analysis. Hence, instead of the broad category of costs, it focuses on investment in IT, which implies monetary funds intentionally directed towards IT. Instead of encompassing the broad range of tangible and intangible benefits, it focuses on quantitative measures of value, productivity, and performance. Return on investment is regarded as best measured by multi-attributes, not by a single attribute (Ahituv, 1980, 1989). This approach has not solved the difficult problems of measuring benefits, since the difficulties remain in deciding which attributes to measure, how to measure them, and how to combine them in a multi-attribute function (Ahituv, 1989).

The relevance for GIS is that perceived value method is the most applicable, since GISs are increasingly utilized for managing and decision-making, rather than for low-level operations. *Perceived value of information* is valuation that is entirely a subjective rating of the user regarding information value. The two other types of valuation are *normative value of information*, i.e. a theoretical model producing a quantitative value, and *realistic value of information*, i.e. estimating differences in value by measuring before and after an information system has been put in place (Ahituv, 1989; Ragowsky et al., 2000). At the same time, the perceived value method has many more sources of error and should be utilized with caution. Permanent problems with perceived value are the following: (a) Individual respondents differ considerably in their subjective reactions. (b) It is hard to translate subjective rating scales into tangible dollar amounts.

In spite of these problems, the perceived-value approach can be applied to analyzing the value of past, present, and future GIS systems. Care should be taken to achieve a large enough sample, and to have a panel of questions that may be partly convertible to tangible values.

A final issue in this section for the value of IT investment approach is that of appropriate lag times for the value or productivity to be realized. Consider the case of investing some of your own funds to purchase a laptop GIS system for your individual use. How many months would be needed before you are at the peak of realizing the benefits of the investment? The same issue of lag time would occur for a large-scale enterprise GIS system. It may take many years after the firm's investment for such GIS payoffs to be realized (Devaraj and Kohli, 2002).

Overall, the value of IT investments methods offer many potential opportunities for persons responsible for assessing the benefits of GIS systems. Because of the expanding investments being made by organizations in GIS, these techniques should be seriously considered, to complement or replace standard techniques of cost-benefit methods.

CHAPTER SUMMARY

Chapter 7 has examined the methods and procedures of cost-benefit analysis for information technology, and sought to identify the distinguishing aspects for GIS, compared to non-spatial IS. One major difference is that GIS has high data-collection costs. This problem improved somewhat over time, as web-accessible digital libraries have become available, often at lower cost and improved quality.

Another area of relatively higher GIS costs is training and technical support, since training for new technologies may require extra expenditures—internally, by web-based training, or through outside training services. University training offerings, including in business schools, are currently limited.

The benefits for GIS may accrue somewhat later and be stretched out over a longer period than for the average IS. This is because (1) organizations often do not understand all the benefits where they are, and (2) benefits often are enterprise-wide, and less visible by themselves. One benefit that is frequently available is to sell GIS project results as a product. This needs to be factored into the cost-benefit analysis at the beginning, even if it is somewhat speculative.

This chapter leads to the following practical suggestions to GIS managers and users on how to improve the quality of a GIS cost-benefit analysis:

- Follow a careful plan utilizing all the conventional C-B methods and knowledge available for IS systems, as well as the more limited toolkit for GIS.
- Gather as much post-audit benchmarking information as possible from your organization.
- Give extra attention to estimating data acquisition costs. Examine what are the sources for spatial data and, if applicable, how they can be inexpensively converted to digital. How will the database be organized with its spatial and non-spatial components.
- Use a long enough cost-benefit timeframe that all the benefits can be realized.
- Consider the cost of training. Anticipate the delays in realizing benefits.
- Do a careful analysis of intangibles and include them in the report to management.

CASE STUDY: NORWICH UNION UNEXPECTED BENEFITS OF GIS

Norwich Union, one of the largest insurance firms in the UK, offers primary lines of life, property, automobile, and casualty, but also mortgage loans, and investment and health care products. Its GIS and GPS applications include modeling of floods and other terrain, weather mapping, distributions of pension risks, online geocoding, automatic flood risk assessment for homes in high flood-risk areas, and real-time spatial analysis of policyholders of auto insurance who have GPS-enabled cars. A four-person GIS team develops and implements spatial applications.

One of the two lead spatial products is Norwich's flood map for the UK, which is the country's leading source of flood insurance information, both for Norwich and other insurance companies that acquire the maps. The system has recently been upgraded so an individual home can be assessed very precisely online regarding the latest flood boundaries and an accurate rate can be given. Due to this individual-home precision, the extent of flood zones has been reduced.

The second lead spatial product, "Pay as You Drive" Insurance is a new one that Norwich launched for young drivers in 2005. A GPS device is installed in the car that estimates the customer's monthly insurance premium, based on when, where, and how often he/she drives. The data are transmitted from the car of the policyholder to Norwich, via satellite (Figure 7.4). Based on the real-time data and utilizing IBM software, Norwich adjusts the premium rates. This is different from traditional car insurance, which calculates premiums yearly based on actuarial tables. It's analogous to mobile phone use, where a person pays depending on usage. The young drivers have saved up to 25 percent on their premiums, versus traditional. The product was rolled out to customers in 2006. The benefit to Norwich is that the drivers with the devices tend to be more cautious, and thus lower Norwich's risk with this group of insured.

An unexpected plus is that the driving data for the driver population, with the identities of policyholders stripped off, are useful to Norwich Union internally for demographic and marketing studies. With appropriate legal sanction, the stripped data could also become a product marketed to other companies interested in driving and traffic patterns.

Norwich has a high level of net benefits, along with low costs, except for purchase of expensive external data. What is different from the other case studies is the collection of real-time spatial data on customer driving behavior, and proportionate reductions in auto premium costs. This is made up for by improvements in customer driving profiles through the ability of the customer to assess his/her driving and secondly by Norwich Union's potential to utilize population data with identities stripped off, in-house and possibly for sale on the outside. Along with the innovation associated with spatial technologies comes the possibility to realize new and sometimes unexpected cost savings and new areas of business. These savings and gains may be little known when the cost-benefits are first calculated, but can be added to subsequent C-B

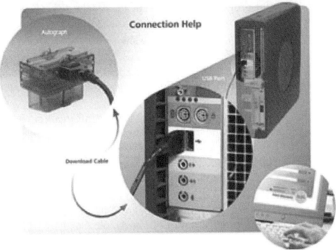

Figure 7.4   GPS Device for Norwich's "Pay as You Drive" Insurance. On top is the GPS unit being plugged into the vehicle. The data are automatically transmitted by satellite connection to Norwich Union. On the bottom, the driver can also plug the device into his/her pc and review his/her driving behavior. *Source:* Stevenson and Hunt, 2006

analyses in the later stages of product implementation once costs and benefits can be better determined.

ACKNOWLEDGMENTS

Parts of this chapter were modified with permission from a book chapter by James Pick in *Geographical Systems in Business* (James Pick, ed.), 2005, Hershey, PA, Idea Group Publishing.

REFERENCES

Ahituv, N. 1980. "A systematic approach toward assessing the value of an information system." *MIS Quarterly*, December, 61–75.

Ahituv, N. 1989. "Assessing the value of information: problems and approaches." Proceedings of the International Conference on Information Systems, 315–325.

Ahituv, N., and S. Neumann. 1990. *Principles of information systems for management*. Dubuque, IA: W.C. Brown.

Ahituv, N., S. Lipovetsky, and A. Tishler. 1999. "The relationship between firm's information systems policy and business performance: a multivariate analysis." In Mahmood, M.A., and E.J. Szewczak (Eds.), *Measuring information technology investment payoff: contemporary approaches*, Hershey, PA: Idea Group Publishing, 62–82.

Allaway, A., L. Murphy, and D. Berkowitz. 2004. "The geographical edge: spatial analysis of retail program adoption." In Pick, James B. (Ed.), *Geographic information systems in business*, Hershey, PA: Idea Group Publishing.

Aronoff, S. 1989. *Geographic information systems: a management perspective*. Ottawa: WDL Publications.

Baily, M., and A. Chakrabarti. 1988. "Electronics and white-collar productivity." In Baily, M., and A. Chakrabarti, *Innovation and the productivity crisis*, Washington: Brookings Institution.

Barua, A., C. Kriebel, and T. Mukhopadhyay. 1991. "Information technology and business value: an analytic and empirical investigation." Working Paper, Austin, TX: University of Texas, May.

Bertschek, I. (Ed.): 2003. "Information technology and productivity gains and cost savings in companies." In Bertschek, I., *New Economy Handbook*, Amsterdam: Elsevier, 213–249.

Boardman, A.E., D.H. Greenberg, A.R. Vining, and D.L. Weimer. 2001. *Cost-benefit analysis: concepts and practice*, 2nd Edition. Upper Saddle River, NJ: Prentice Hall.

Boyles, D. 2002. *GIS means business*. Volume 2. Redlands, CA: ESRI Press.

Breshahan, T.F., and S. Greenstein. 2001. "The economic contribution of information technology: towards comparative and user studies." *Journal of Evolutionary Economics*, 11: 95–118.

Brynjolfsson, E. 1993. "The productivity paradox of information technology." *Communications of the ACM*, 36(12): 67–77.

Brynjolfsson, E., and L. Hitt. 1993. "Is information systems spending productive?" In Degress, J., R. Bostrom, and D. Robey (Eds.), *Proceedings of the International Conference on Information Systems*, New York: Association for Computing Machinery, 47–64.

Chau, P.Y.K. 1995. "Factors used in the selection of packaged software in small businesses: views of owners and managers." *Information and Management*, 29: 71–78.

Clarke, K. 2003. *Getting started with geographic information systems*. Upper Saddle River, NJ: Prentice Hall.

Cron, W.L., and M.G. Sobol. 1983. "The Relationship between computerization and performance: a strategy for maximizing the economic benefits of computerization." *Journal of Information Management*, 6: 171–181.

Davila de Icaza, A., and J.B. Pick. 1998. "Quantitative model of size and complexity of prospective geographic information systems for regional governments in Mexico." Proceedings of Americas Conference on Information Systems, Atlanta, GA: Association for Information Systems, 396–398.

Day, G.S., and P.J.H. Schoemaker. 2000. "A different game." In Day, G.S., P.J.H. Schoemaker, and R.E. Gunther, (Eds.), *Wharton on managing emerging technologies*, New York: John Wiley and Sons, 1–23.

Devaraj, S., and R. Kohli. 2002. *The IT payoff: measuring the business value of information technology investments*. New York: Pearson Education.

Dickinson, H.J., and H.W. Calkins. 1988. "The economic evaluation of implementing a GIS." *International Journal of Geographical Information Systems*, 2: 307–237.

Dickinson, H.J., and H.W. Calkins. 1990. "Concerning the economic evaluation of implementing a GIS." *International Journal of Geographical Information Systems*, 4: 211–212.

Directions Magazine. 2003. "Daratech reports GIS revenues forecast to grow 8% to $1.75 billion in 2003; utilities and government increase spending." *Directions Magazine*, August 9. Available at http://www.directionsmagazine.com.

Doering, D.S., and R. Parayre. 2000. "Identification and assessment of emerging technologies." In Day, G.S., P.J.H. Schoemaker, and R.E. Gunther (Eds.), *Wharton on managing emerging technologies*, New York: John Wiley and Sons, 75–98.

ESRI Inc. 2003. Handheld product information available at www.esri.com.

Exler, R.D. 1988. "Integrated solutions for GIS/LIS data management." *GIS/LIS [']88 Proceedings*, Volume 2, ACSM, ASPRS, AAG, URISA, 814–824.

Gerlach, J., B. Neumann, E. Moldauer, M. Argo, and D. Firsby. 2002. "Determining the cost of it services." *Communications of the ACM*, 45(9): 61–67.

Greene, R.P., and J.C. Stager. 2004. "Techniques and methods of GIS for business." In Pick, J.B. (Ed.), *GIS in business*, Hershey, PA: Idea Group.

Grimshaw, D.J. 2000. *Bringing geographical information systems into business*, 2nd Edition. New York: John Wiley and Sons.

Harder, C. 1997. *ArcView GIS means business*. Redlands, CA: ESRI Press.

Harris, S.E., and J.L. Katz. 1989. "Predicting organizational performance using information technology managerial control ratios." In Proceedings of the Twenty-Second Hawaiian International Conference on System Science, Honolulu, HI.

Huxhold, W.E. 1991. *An introduction to urban geographic information systems*. New York: Oxford University Press.

Huxhold, W.E., and A.G. Levinsohn. 1995. *Managing geographic information system projects*. New York: Oxford University Press.

Jarupathirun, S., and F. Zahedi. 2001. "A theoretical framework for GIS-based spatial decision support systems: utilization and performance evaluation." Proceedings of the Seventh Americas Conference on Information Systems, Boston, August, 245–248.

Jarupathirun, S., and F. Zahedi. 2004. "GIS as spatial decision support systems." In Pick, J.B. (Ed.), *Geographic information systems in business*, Hershey, PA: Idea Group Publishing.

Jones, Steve. 2005. "Profiting from a Mobile Workforce GIS." Paper presented at ESRI Business GeoSummit, Chicago, April 19.

Karikari, Isaac, and John Stillwell. (2005). "Applying cost/benefit analysis to evaluate investment in GIS: the case of Ghana's Lands Commission Secretariat, Accra." *Transactions in GIS*, 9(4): 489–505.

Kauffman, R.J., and P. Weill. 1989. "An evaluative framework for research on the performance effects of information technology investment." Proceedings of the Tenth International Conference on Information Systems.

Kelley, T. 1999. "Put your business on the map." *Transport Technology Today*, April, pp. 20–23.

King, J.L., and E.L. Schrems. 1978. "Cost-benefit analysis in information systems development and operation." *ACM Computing Surveys*, 10(1): 19–34.

Kingma, B.R. 2001. *The economics of information: a guide to economic and cost-benefit analysis for information professionals*, 2nd Edition. Englewood, CO: Libraries Unlimited Inc.

Loveman, G.W. 1988. "An assessment of the productivity impact on information technologies." MIT Management in the 1990s Working Paper #88-054, July.

Lucas, H.C. 1999. *Information technology and the productivity paradox: assessing the value of investing in IT*. New York: Oxford University Press.

Maguire, David, Ross Smith, and Victoria Kouyoumjian. (2007). "Organizing for Success: Building an ROI-based GIS business case." Powerpoint slides from Workshop at ESRI Users Conference, San Diego, June 26.

McCune, J.C. 1998. "The productivity paradox." *American Management Association International*, March, pp. 38–40.

Meeks, W.L., and S. Dasgupta. 2003. "Geospatial information utility: an estimation of the relevance of geospatial information to users." *Journal of Decision Support Systems*, in press.

Meeks, W.L., and S. Dasgupta. 2004. "The value of using GIS and geospatial data to support organizational decision making." In Pick, J.B. (Ed.), *Geographic information systems in business*, Hershey, PA: Idea Group Publishing.

Mennecke, B.E., M.D. Crossland, and B.L. Killingsworth. 2000. "Is A Map More Than A Picture? The Role of SDSS Technology, Subject Characteristics, and Problem Complexity On Map Reading and Problem Solving." *MIS Quarterly*, 24: 4: 601–629.

Mitchell, A. 1999. *The ESRI guide to GIS analysis, Volume 1: Geographic patterns and relationships*. Redlands, CA: ESRI Press.

Mueller, B. 1997. "Measuring ROI: can it be done?" *AS/400 Systems Management*, November, 8–10.

Murphy, L.D. 1995. "Geographic information systems: are they decision support systems?" Proceedings of 28th Annual Hawaiian International Conference on Systems Sciences, Hawaii, 131–140.

Navarrete, C.J., and J.B. Pick. 2002. "Information technology expenditure and industry performance: the case of the Mexican banking industry." *Journal of Global Information Technology Management*, 5(2): 7–28.

Navarrete, C.J., and J.B. Pick. 2003. "Information technology spending association with organizational productivity and performance: a study of the Mexican banking industry, 1982–1992." In Shin, N. (Ed.), *Creating Business Value with Information Technology: Challenges and Solutions*, 89–124.

Navarrete, C.J., and J.B. Pick. 2003. "Information technology spending and the value of the firm: the case of Mexican banks." In Shin, N. (Ed.), *Creating Business Value with Information Technology: Challenges and Solutions*, 146–165.

Niederman, F. 1999. "Valuing the IT workforce as intellectual capital." Proceedings of the SIGCPR Conference, Association for Computing Machinery, 174–181.

Noyelle, T. (Ed.): 1990. *Skills, wages, and productivity in the service sector*. Boulder, CO: Westview Press.

Obermeyer, N.J., and J.K. Pinto. 1994. *Managing geographic information systems*. New York: The Guilford Press.

Obermeyer, N.J. 1999. "Measuring the benefits and costs of GIS." Chapter 42 in Longley, P.A., M.F. Goodchild, D.J. Maguire, and D.W. Rhind (Eds.), *Geographical information systems, Volume 2: Management issues and applications*, New York: John Wiley and Sons, 601–610.

Osterman, P. 1986. "The impact of computers on the employment of clerks and managers." *Industrial and Labor Relations Review*, 39: 175–186.

Phoenix, M. 2003. Personal communications based on ESRI Inc. Marketing Department.

Pick, J.B. 1996. "GIS-based economic and social cluster analysis applied to a giant city." Proceedings of Americas Conference on Information Systems. Atlanta, GA: Association for Information Systems, 515–517.

Pick, J.B., N. Viswanathan, and W.J. Hettrick. 2000a. "A dual census geographical information systems in the context of data warehousing." Proceedings of Americas Conference on Information Systems, Atlanta, GA: Association for Information Systems, 265–278.

Pick, J.B., W.J. Hettrick, N. Viswanathan, and E. Ellsworth. 2000b. "Intra-censal geographical information systems: application to binational border cities." Proceedings of European Conference on Information Systems, Vienna: Austria: ECIS, 1175–1181.

Pick, James B. 2005. "Costs and Benefits of GIS in Business." In Pick, James B. (Ed.), *Geographic Information Systems in Business*, pp. 56–79.

Pick, James B. 2006. "A Case-Study Analysis of Costs and Benefits of Geographic Information Systems: Relationships to Firm Size and Strategy." Proceedings of the Americas Conference on Information Systems, in press, Atlanta, GA: Association for Information Systems.

Ragowsky, A., N. Ahituv, and S. Neumann. 2000. "The benefits of using information systems." *Communications of the ACM*, 43(11): 303–311.

Reeve, D.E., and J.R. Petch. 1999. *GIS, organisations, and people: a socio-technical approach*. London: Taylor and Francis.

Roach, S.S. 1989. "America's white-collar productivity dilemma." *Manufacturing Engineering*, 104.

Sassone, P.G. 1988. "Cost benefit analysis of information systems: a survey of methodologies." Proceedings of Conference on Supporting Group Work, Association for Computing Machinery, 126–133.

Satzinger, J.W., R.B. Jackson, and S.D. Burd. 2002. *Systems analysis and design in a changing world*, Second Edition, Course Technology.

Smith, D.A., and R.F. Tomlinson. 1992. "Assessing the costs and benefits of geographical information systems: methodological and implementation issues." *International Journal of Geographical Information Systems*, 6: 247–256.

Sonnen, D., and H. Morris. 2005. "ESRI: Extending GIS to Enterprise Applications." White Paper, February, Framingham, MA: International Data Corporation.

Strassmann, P.A. 1997. "Computers have yet to make companies more productive." *Computerworld*, Sept. 15.

Strassmann, P.A. 1999. *Information productivity*. New Canaan, CT: Information Economics Press.

Strassmann, P.A. 1999. *Information productivity: assessing the information management costs of U.S. industrial corporations*. New Canaan, CT: The Information Economics Press.

Swink, J., and C. Speier. 2000. "Presenting Geographic Information: Effects of Data Aggregation, Dispersion, and Users' Spatial Orientation." *Decision Sciences*, 30(1): 169–195.

Tomlinson, R. 2003. *Thinking About GIS: geographic information system planning for managers*. Redlands, CA: ESRI Press.

U.S. Census Bureau (2007). U.S. Census Bureau Website. Washington, D.C.: U.S. Census Bureau. Available at www.census.gov.

Willcocks, L.P., and S. Lester. 1997. "In search of information technology productivity: assessment issues." *Journal of the Operational Research Society*, 48: 1082–1094.

Worrall, Les. (1994). "Justifying investment in GIS: a local government perspective." *International Journal of Geographical Information Systems*, 8(6): 545–565.

CHAPTER 8

MANAGING SPATIAL DATA

INTRODUCTION

The chapter concerns the design and uses of spatial databases and data warehouses. In the chapters on supporting business decisions and enterprise applications, databases and data warehouses were introduced as key constructs. This chapter digs in deeper to gain fundamental understanding of these concepts.

In the section on spatial data models, the relational, object-oriented, and object-relational models are explained and compared on their pluses and minuses. Situations appropriate for each are discussed. The case study of the centralized spatial data repository at Enmax, an electrical and gas utility firm owned by the City of Calgary, illustrates a success story in developing a modern, enterprise-wide spatial database in an inter-organizational context.

The section on data warehouses builds on the introductory coverage in Chapter 4 by discussing warehouse design, spatial functionality, and new directions including the SOLAP model. An auto insurance firm and the City of Portland illustrate alternatives in implementing spatial data warehouses. The chapter ends by considering spatial applications' data quality. This problem may seem dull, but is highlighted when things go wrong, such as in transportation emergencies, natural disasters, and insurance underwriting errors. Data managers need to continually scrutinize for multiple sources of error in spatial data.

Geo-Business: GIS in the Digital Organization, By James B. Pick
Copyright © 2007 John Wiley & Sons, Inc.

INTRODUCTION TO MANAGING SPATIAL DATA

Managing spatial data presents most of the issues of data management of non-spatial data (Hoffer et al., 2006), but GIS-specific issues as well. A summary of the key data management issues for MIS (see Table 8.1) shows that data must be gathered, organized, checked for quality, made available to the users, maintained, and updated.

A plan must be established to organize the data logically into a relational or object-oriented data model. The relational model is based on organizing data into a series of tables (Kroenke, 2005; Hoffer et al., 2006). For each table, the rows represent records, while the columns indicate attributes. For instance, XYZ Inc. has a relational table for its suppliers. Each row represents a supplier, while each column represents name, e-mail address, number of products sold to XYZ, total revenue of products sold per year to XYZ, and date the supplier relationship started. In its overall relational design, XYZ Inc. has tables for suppliers, parts, customers, employees, competitors, and sales. These tables are related to each other by *relational operators*, each of which causes logical operations on one or more of the relational tables such as to join and divide, and select and query data items (Hoffer et al., 2006).

In an object-oriented data model, the key unit is the *object*, which represents a real world "thing" having attributes and behaviors. It is able to relate to, and communicate with other objects by sending messages to them that activate their behaviors.

TABLE 8.1   Key Data Management Issues for MIS

- Organizational strategy for data management
- Data sources and gathering data
- Logical model for data
  - Relational data model
  - Object-oriented data model
  - Data warehousing data model
- Data cleaning and quality checks
- Physical model for data storage
  - Data-base management system
  - Data warehouse
- Architecture that data storage resides in:
  - Standalone
  - Client-server
  - Internet/web-based
- Data access versus data security
- User and customer training in data access
- Maintenance and updating of data
- Management, controls, evaluation

The objects can be organized into hierarchical classes, so that characteristics can be inherited from higher objects to lower ones. For instance, if the class is car, the highest object is "Car" which has attributes which apply for all cars. At the next level, the objects "Chevies," "Toyotas," "Mercedes," and "Volvos" inherit all the attributes for "Car," but may have additional specific attributes, for instance the "Volvo" adds the attribute, "ski compartment." The passing of attributes down the hierarchy is referred to as "inheritance." There are multiple other aspects of the object-oriented data model that are beyond the scope of this book (Hoffer et al., 2006). The object-oriented model is more suitable for models applied to rapidly changing environments having complex behaviors.

Data warehousing has a different data model. Chapter 4 introduced it, including how data enter and are processed in a data warehouse through the extract, transform, and load (ETL) process. Inside the data warehouse, data are logically organized into a central fact table that contains the most important attributes as well as keys to access other tables. The topic is expanded on in a major chapter section that emphasizes how data warehouses support spatial analysis and applications.

Another aspect of data management is how the data are incorporated into a network. They can be standalone, i.e. isolated from other systems, or in a client-server array in which databases reside on one or more servers that are connected to, and accessible by multiple client systems. Another arrangement is the enterprise web architecture discussed in Chapter 1 and 5, for which data located on web servers are accessible over the internet. There is frequently a middle layer, often called middleware, between the web server client software and the data-base or data warehouse. The middleware transfers processes and data between the top and bottom layers and provides logic to control the flows. This is often referred to as multi-tier, or n-tier architecture.

Other standard data management issues involve access and security, maintenance, customer training, and management (Hoffer et al., 2006; Dhillon, 2007; Laudon and Laudon, 2007). There is the tradeoff that tighter technical security implies reduced access (Dhillon, 2007). This tug-of-war can only be resolved by assessing the risks involved in security lapses versus those from reduction of information flow to users and customers. Data maintenance, training, data staffing, and training are other common operational practices for information management (Laudon and Laudon, 2007).

Spatial data management utilizes all of the key MIS issues from Table 8.1, but adds other ones specific to GIS and spatial. As seen in Table 8.2, GIS data management issues (in bold) supplement the MIS issues.

The spatial layers introduced in Chapter 2 are built from digital points, lines, and polygons. Combined together, the layers can produce a complex map. However, the spatial data in one layer needs to be synchronized with spatial data in the other layers in scale, coordinate system, and projection. Spatial data can be stored in a variety of data formats, but to produce a map they need to be converted to a common format.

TABLE 8.2   Key Data Management Issues for GIS (Issues in common between MIS and GIS are shown by lighter shading)

- Organizational strategy for data management
- Data sources and gathering data
  - **Data compatibility for spatial layers**
  - **Spatial data conversion**
- Logical model for data
  - Relational data model
  - Object-oriented data model
  - **Object-relational data model**
  - Data warehousing data model
    - **Accessing spatial attributes in the data warehousing model**
    - **SOLAP data model**
- Data cleaning and quality checks
- Physical model for data storage
  - Data-base management system
    - **Spatial data-base management systems such as Oracle Spatial**
  - Data warehouse
    - **Location of spatial data relative to the data warehouse**
- Architecture that data storage resides in:
  - Standalone
  - Client-server
  - Internet/web-based
    - **Standards and protocols for web-based access to spatial data**
- Data access versus data security
- User and customer training in data access
  - **User training to understand mapped and spatial displays of data**
- Maintenance and updating of data
- Management, controls, evaluation

The standard non-spatial data warehouse model can be spatially-enabled. This occurs in different steps in the ETL, inside the data warehouse, or in external models that access it.

Another distinguishing aspect of spatial data models involves commercial products that combine relational and object models. Leaders in the market include Oracle 10g and the Geodatabase of ESRI's ArcGIS.

The expanding area of spatial data management on the internet adds standards and protocols specific for web-based data. In the management realm, the biggest new spatial issue is managing security for the associated technologies of GPS, RFID, and sensors, and the enlarged issue of user training, since often business users are unfamiliar with web mapping concepts.

The growth in the spatial sector of the economy, covered in Chapter 1, as well as the greater internet and web-service delivery of spatial applications, has brought with it a growth in the amount and volume of spatial data available worldwide. It is not only a question of choosing the best data model and technical platform, but the explosion in information means that management of content is more challenging. This adds another spatial management challenge—managing the choice of data sources and also deciding how big to grow a spatial database i.e. how to include as much relevant and affordable information as possible without overloading it. The manager needs to know what data sources are available, their practical importance, what their metadata are, their level of quality, cost, and update cycles.

GIS, SPATIAL DATA, AND RELATIONAL DATABASES

The leading model for spatial databases is the *relational model*. As mentioned earlier, relational operators act on one or more relational tables to select, combine, enlarge, or reduce tables through a sequence of operations. The *Project* operator reduces a table to selected columns The *Select* operator selects particular records based on the value(s) of an attribute. The *Join* operator can combine two tables together based on common attributes. These operators are illustrated in a sequence of operations in Figure 8.1. An initial

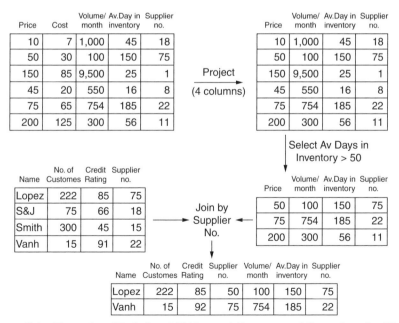

Figure 8.1 Example of Relational Tables and Sequence of Operations by Three Relational Operators on Supplier Data

table of supplier information is reduced from five attributes (columns) to four attributes (columns) by the Project operator. Next, only those suppliers whose products have average days in inventory greater than fifty days are chosen by the Select operator. Finally, that table is combined with a different supplier table containing three new attributes (name, number of customers, credit rating, and supplier number). The Join operator connects these tables based on supplier numbers that are common between the two tables, that is, Suppliers 75 and 22. The final table resulting from the Join consists of complete attribute information from the two prior tables, but for only two suppliers, Lopez and Vanh.

Other widely used operators are *Union*, which combines together the record of two tables that have the identical attributes into one table. *Difference* produces a third table that contains records present in the first table, but not in the second one. *Intersection* of two tables results in a third table containing the records that are common to both tables (Kroenke, 2005). Over twenty other relational operators are available.

Spatial Relational Data Model

Although simple in its treatment of the spatial data, the relational model is the most prevalent one for spatial data. It relates attribute data and spatial data through an ID number. As seen in Figure 8.2, an attribute table's ID values have a one-to-one correspondence with spatial features. For instance, for polygons at the top, polygon 3 corresponds to the ID value 3 in the table. The second table in the figure on the middle right links four ID-field values to four point locations, and the third table links five ID values to five line segments. Besides "ID," the tables contain other attributes. For instance, if the upper attribute table represents records for sales regions, Attribute A might be annual sales in the region, Attribute B number of stores in the region, and Attribute C area of the region. If the second table represents distribution centers, the attributes might be deliveries/day, floor area, number of employees, and number of conveyer belts.

The spatial relational data model usually has the constraint that each attribute table is associated with only one geometric form (point, line, or polygon). Through the overlay of multiple layers, the resultant map can combine the three geometric features as an end result, so any geometric form can be represented. Figure 8.3 repeats the example of the relational operators from Figure 8.1 but now shows the point maps. Each point represents a supplier. This clarifies how the relational data model can narrow down or expand the geometric representation, while also changing the associated attributes.

Think of this model applied to ten spatial layers with associated tables. A set of relational operators working on each table could alter the set of attributes and the features displayed for each map layer, leading to a complex

Spatial Data   *Attribute Data*

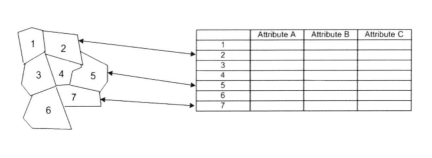

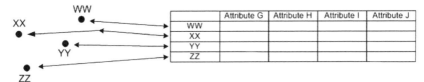

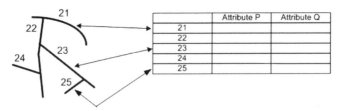

Figure 8.2   Relationship of Spatial Data and Attribute Data

map transformation. This small illustration demonstrates that this model can support sophisticated spatial transformations.

On the spatial side of the relational model, the coordinate systems, map projections, and scales of all the layers need to be adjusted to be the same, so they overlay exactly. The unit of measurement (feet, meters, kilometers) also needs to be identical for all layers. To keep track of projections and the other standards, the metadata for each layer is maintained and needs to be accurate and available.

The advantages and disadvantages of the spatial relational data model are given in Table 8.3 (Tomlinson, 2003). Pluses of this model are tables that are simple to understand and logical linkages between the tables and layers. The model nicely supports query sequences based on attributes. However, it is not as suitable for spatial analysis. As the leading spatial data model, it has extensive datasets available and a large pool of skilled GIS people who can utilize it.

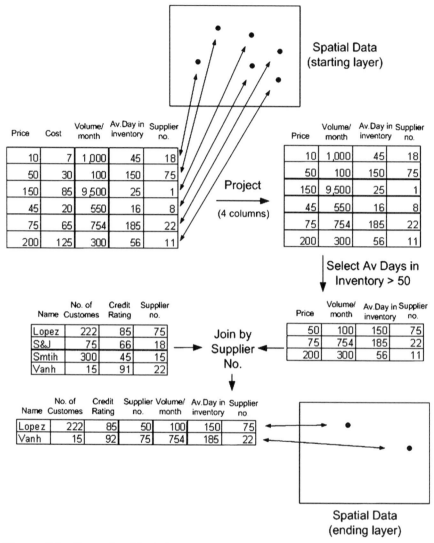

Figure 8.3 Example of Relational Tables and Sequence of Operations by Three Relational Operators on Supplier Data, with Spatial Layers Shown for Start and End

On the minus side, the layers of points, lines, and polygons are a vector representation of the real world, i.e. they don't support the raster-like detail. The model is not naturally suitable to spatial analysis involving more complex objects. Access speed is slower than for some other data models. Also, long and complex sequences of table operations are challenging to understand and program.

TABLE 8.3   **Relational Database Model—Advantages and Disadvantages**

Advantages
- Simple tables
- Linkage with spatial model simple
- User interface in software is simple and easy to read
- Tables, layers, and relational operators can be modified easily
- Data can be maintained independently of the application
- Well suited to query and analysis of spatial features
- Macros, tools, and wizards are fairly easy to program
- Is the worldwide standard, so extensive GIS datasets available
- Large group of skilled personnel to support development and use

Disadvantages
- Model provides limited representation of the real world
- Not naturally suitable for spatial analysis
- Slow query access, since data structures must be operated on each time there is access
- Complex data relationships (using relational algebra) are challenging to model

(Modified from Tomlinson, 2003)

Spatial Object-Oriented Data Model

The object-oriented data model is a very different approach to attribute and spatial data than for the relational one. As seen in the left on Figure 8.4, an *object* has a name, data attributes belonging to it, and the methods used to process the object (sometimes called behaviors). It can be thought of as more "active" than a relational table, since the methods perform calculations and analysis for an object. The right side of the figure illustrates the object for a fast food outlet. This outlet has non-spatial attributes (revenue, cost, etc.) as well as spatial features of city and state. The methods can perform several numerical calculations and merge spatial features.

The objects work together by relationships and communications. *Relationships* describe the way objects are associated with each other. Examples of the relationships of objects are *cardinality* and *class hierarchy,* as seen in Figure 8.5. The cardinality relationship indicates the ratios of number of instances of one object to another. For instance, in the figure, there are many customers for one fast food outlet, which is designated as M:1 cardinality. Cardinalities, which can be M:1, 1:1, 1:N, and M:N, were explained in Chapter 6 in the context of entity-relationship diagrams (see Figure 6.3). Cardinality relationships help to understand how objects are related to each other for access and retrieval of information. They also are useful in designing the optimal arrangement of the database.

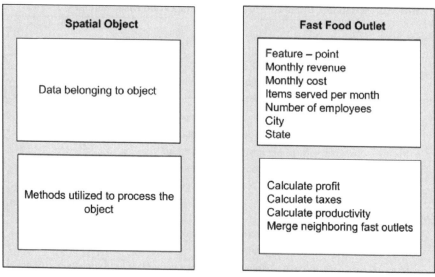

Figure 8.4 Spatial Object and Example

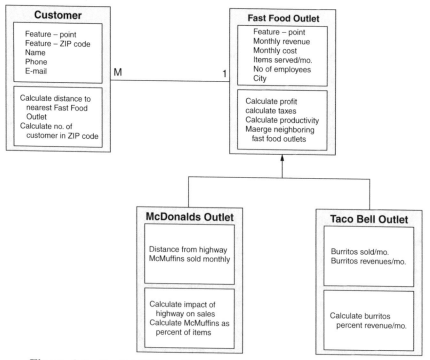

Figure 8.5 Spatial Objects Showing Multiplicity and Class Hierarchy

Communications are achieved by sending messages to other objects carrying the name of a method (behavior) that the object is capable of doing. A sophisticated object-oriented program has a sequence of messages flowing between objects.

Another type of object relationship illustrated in Figure 8.5 is *class hierarchy*. Classes represent different extents of generalization of objects. At the top of a class is a very general object such as, say "business." At the levels underneath are more specific objects, say "retail business" and "camera store business" at the next lower level. Each of those objects can be expanded into more specialized objects at the third level, and so on. An object at a lower level inherits the attributes from all the higher levels, plus it adds attributes and methods from its own level. In the figure, "McDonald's Outlet" inherits all attributes and methods from "Fast Food Outlet," such as "feature—point," etc. In addition, it adds two new attributes and two methods that are specific to McDonald's. Class hierarchy is helpful in organizing a group of objects and avoiding repeating information.

For spatial analysis, the object model organizes spatial attributes and methods hierarchically. This allows easy identification of what spatial attributes are generic and what are more specialized. For instance, if there are 200 fast food outlets, they all have the attributes and behaviors from the top level, but at lower levels, specialized additional spatial attributes can be added in an organized way. In this way, a large group of related objects can be given spatial properties. For instance, using the "Distance from Highway" attribute, a spatial operator can identify easily every MacDonald's within 1/8 mile of a major highway.

The spatial object-oriented data model is still being developed and may ultimately overtake the relational. Full coverage of the object model is beyond the scope of the book. Its importance is partly that some of its features can be combined in those of relational in an object-relational model, which is present for some commercial packages and is covered later.

The pluses and minuses of the object-oriented data model appear in Table 8.4. Advantages stress that the object can represent more complex things from the real world, that it's intuitive, and has behaviors. Also, it has multiple ways to organize objects, including cardinalities, classes, aggregation, and composition (Kroenke, 2005; Hoffer et al., 2006). Spatial attributes and behavior can be added to characterize individual and classes of objects.

Among the minuses are that spatial object-oriented (OO) models are difficult to design (Tomlinson, 2003). In the real world, the methods (behaviors) and communication sequences may be less well known. Since most databases are relational, there are conversion issues in importing and exporting data. Further, it is less likely that the GIS workforce knows OO models or is able to program in OO languages (Tomlinson, 2003).

TABLE 8.4   Object-Oriented Data Model—Advantages and Disadvantages

Advantages

- An object has attributes and behaviors that give it identity and make it accessible
- The real world can have complex representations through multiple objects
- OO has an intuitive sense, since the objects are simplified forms of real-world objects
- Multiplicities (same as cardinalities) can be expressed
- There can be a hierarchy of classes with greater or lesser generalization
- Objects can be associated through aggregation and composition
- Certain object-oriented (OO) simulation languages are based on objects
- The behavior rules for objects can be used to maintain data integrity
- On the average, less user-code needed in GIS software to conduct the same query or other user operation or series of operations

Disadvantages

- The complex OO models of the real-world are more difficult to design and build
- For the objects to mimic real world, the real world attributes, behavior, and communication need to be known. This not always the case, for instance in nature
- Some business applications are not suitable to OO approach, for instance financial models
- Large, complex OO models are difficult to execute
- Challenges of import and export with relational data-bases
- OO computer languages used to program the OO data model. There is less knowledge among GIS workforce of OO computer languages

(Modified from Tomlinson, 2003)

Spatial Object-Relational Data Model

In the *object-relational model*, object-oriented capabilities complement a relational database. Relational tables remain as the place for data storage, but the relational model can interact with some object-oriented functionality on top. This model is appearing in the commercial marketplace in varied products including Oracle Spatial 10g and ESRI's Geodatabase model of ArcGIS, which is mixed object-relational. There is a question of which data model is more suited for a specific business situation.

There are business situations where one or another of these major data models is appropriate, as seen in Table 8.5 (Tomlinson, 2003). For example, a utility firm has to store and model a large transmission network with numerous assets such as power lines, transformers, poles, and distribution stations. It needs to classify the relationships and inheritance of characteristics of these assets. This is easily done through an object-oriented or object-relational data model. In companies with flexibility and sufficient budget to choose between models, the developer needs to analyze the primary logical characteristics of the real-world attribute and spatial data, before selecting a data model.

TABLE 8.5   Appropriate Data Model for Certain Data Modeling Situations in Business

Data modeling situation	Logical data model characteristics	Recommended logical data model
Retail chain that has store locations, highways, and sales regions to do impact analysis of vehicle traffic on store sales	Simple relationships between features	Relational
Enterprise-wide application that connects data on a large company's sales with business-partner data-bases	Connection between large-scale relational data-bases	Relational
Small firm that needs to conduct side analysis with demographic and competitor data	Spatial analysis of data on demographics and competitors that currently is stored as a non-spatial relational model	Relational
Energy utility that needs to model energy tranmission network, including power lines, transformers, poles etc.	Complex relationships with inherticance of attributes and behaviors	Object-relational or object-oriented
Major petroleum firm must simultaneously updata multiple parts of its large pipeline data-base with hourly additions and repairs	Multiple simultaneous updating	Object-relational or object-oriented
An insurance firm has many legacy relational data-bases, legacy relational spatial data-base, and some object-oriented database	Links to varied types of relational and OO data-bases	Object-relational or object-oriented

(Modified from Tomlison, 2003)

Oracle Spatial 10g

Oracle Spatial 10g is a Spatial Relational Database that is a version of the Standard Oracle 10 Database product, which is among the leading databases for medium and large businesses. Besides advantages already discussed for relational databases, it also has accessing and language features that are keyed to the web and internet. Oracle Spatial 10g uses the open programming standards of SQL, XML, HTTP, HTML, Java, .NET, GML, OpenLS, ISO211, and SVG (Lopez, 2005). The Java language is object-oriented, so OO programmers and developers can use it for internet programming.

Within Oracle Spatial 10g, there are a number of Spatial Functions available (see Table 8.6). Among them is the *geodetic function* supporting the use of the

TABLE 8.6   Oracle Spatial 10g: Capabilities and Functioning of a Spatial RDBMS

STANDARD TYPES OF SPATIAL FUNCTIONS
SQL spatial type
R-tree index (a type of tree structure that can use coordinates)
Spatial operators (perform spatial analysis, leverage spatial indexes)
Spatial functions (perform spatial analysis, no leveraging of spatial indexes)
Geodetic support (Lat/Long)
Linear referencing
Spatial aggregates
Long transactions
Indexing, query, load
Partitioning

HIGHER LEVEL SPATIAL FUNCTIONS
GeoRaster Type
Network Data Model
Topology Data Model
Geocoding Engine
Routing Engine
Spatial Data Mining
Text Annotation Type
GML 2.0/SVG Support
Transportable Tablespaces

Reprinted with permission of the Geospatial Information & Technology Association, www.gita.org.

latitude/longitude coordinate system while other functions handle indexing, partitioning, and aggregation for spatial data. Relational spatial operators can change and transform spatial data.

The Spatial functions can determine the relationship of two spatial layers to each other. Figure 8.6 shows a pair of layers and several functions to manipulate them. *Original* refers to the starting layer, while *Difference* refers to the layer paired with "Original." *Union* includes both layers. *Intersect* is the overlapping portion of the two layers when they are put one on top of the other. XOR (exclusive OR) refers to the parts of the two layers that do not intersect. The spatial functions are direct and useful.

Oracle Spatial 10g's higher-level functions include the *GeoRaster Type* that accesses raster imagery, *network data model* for spatial features that are arranged in networks, *topology data model* for arranging spatial features in a topology, a *geocoding engine* that geocodes address, and *spatial data mining* that allows searching of spatial data. GML 2.0 is included that supports the new GIS standards of GML and SVG for display of vector data on the web. Overall the spatial analysis capability is moderate-level. However, for mainstream business processing, the moderate-level spatial capability is offset

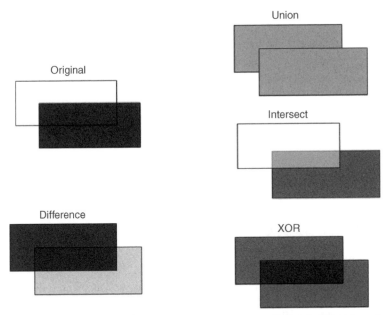

Figure 8.6   Spatial Functions in XML for a Spatial RDBMS. Modified from Lopez, 2006

by mainstream, highly efficient database processing capability for very large scale data storage and fast transactions.

In Oracle Spatial, SQL, a structured query language, creates, retrieves, updates, and deletes data. It is flexible for use on the internet. An example of SQL for a spatial retrieval (query) of information is shown in Figures 8.7 and 8.8 (modified from Lopez, 2005). The user is asking: "What FedEx offices are within 3 miles of my office?" Her office is located at 278 Corporate Avenue. The map portraying this query is seen in Figure 8.7. In the center is the user's office, with a 3-mile ring around it. The SQL code to answer this query is shown in Figure 8.8. This code asks to find all addresses from a list of Federal Express offices where the distance between 278 Corporate Avenue and a Federal Express office is within 3 miles. "MDSYS.SDO_WITHIN_DISTANCE," a spatial function in Oracle 10g, asks, given the office point and distance (radius), if the Fed Ex points are within that distance from the office point. The example illustrates how SQL spatial functions can be utilized to perform data retrieval.

The City of New York illustrates the full mainframe power of Oracle Spatial 10g. New York City standardized on this software, with the justification was that Oracle had for some time supported the non-spatial, heavy-duty database processing for the city (Lopez, 2005). The decision to centralize its spatial applications on Oracle Spatial 10g as the main repository leveraged on the

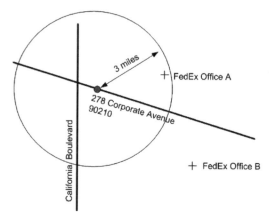

Figure 8.7   Locational Query for a Spatial DBMS. Modified from Lopez, 2005

city's existing Oracle knowledge and skill base, as well as offered the capacity to support a very large spatial processing demand. As seen in Figure 8.9, the data stored in Oracle Spatial 10g's central repository include the topography and cadastral information (i.e. land records), the physical assets of the city, and transportation. Major business applications, shown in the right in the figure, complement their own business data with spatially-enabled data from the repository. These are mainstay city applications that previously ran non-spatially under Oracle and are now spatially-enabled.

Another group of city departments, that includes environmental management, crime monitoring, and power/water services, which appear on the left in the figure, had previously run their own specialized GIS systems. They continue to run specialized GIS software packages, but now can access attribute and spatial data from the centralized Oracle 10g database. They use specialized GIS software for spatial analysis and processing, since their local

SQL Query to Find the post offices within 3km of my office.

```
SELECT P.Federal_Express_Name, P.Address
 FROM Federal_Expresses P,
Address_Master A
 WHERE
 A.St_Address = '278 Corporate Avenue'
  And A.City = 'Denver'
   AND MDSYS.SDO_WITHIN_DISTANCE
     (A.Location, P.Location,
      'distance=3') = 'TRUE';
```

Figure 8.8   Example of a Location Query in a Spatial RDBMS. Modified from Lopez, 2005

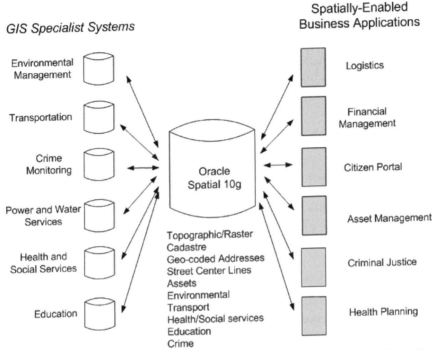

Figure 8.9 Oracle Spatial 10g Integrated Data Architecture for New York City. Reprinted with permission of the Geospatial Information & Technology Association, www.gita.org.

GIS needs exceed the spatial analysis functionality of Oracle Spatial 10g. This example demonstrates the huge mainframe scale possible for Oracle Spatial 10g, as well as the flexible range of spatial sophistication that can be provided to diverse city users.

The advantages of Oracle Spatial 10g (Lopez, 2005) are the potential for high-volume spatial applications in the enterprise environment, and potential in large IT shops to leverage the Oracle knowledge already present (see Table 8.7). A minus is that the GIS or IT department of a smaller enterprise may not have the knowledge or skills to support Oracle Spatial. Also, the spatial features are only moderate and the GIS interface may be less-friendly than for some other packages. Perhaps the greatest deterrent is the high cost of Oracle databases.

ESRI's Geodatabases

ESRI's Geodatabase in the ArcGIS software family is a way to query, store, and process spatial information. At the low level, the data are stored in a relational database (Rigaux et al., 2002), the logical design of which is seen

TABLE 8.7 Oracle Spatial 10g—Advantages and Disadvantages

Advantages

- The spatial and non-spatial information are stored in the same data-base which leads to improved efficiencies.
- Spatial data can be centrally stored and easily integrated with enterprise and other major business systems.
- Same SQL accessing method can be used for non-spatial and spatial data
- Utilities available for non-spatial are also available for spatial data including load, import, export, and backup
- Advanced security and processing features of non-spatial Oracle are available to Oracle Spatial, including security, replication, high availability, and parallel processing.
- For the internet platform, Oracle Spatial 10g uses open internet/web programming standards such as Java, SQL, SML, and .Net.
- Many IT departments in medium- to large-sized businesses have Oracle skills sets that can be leveraged for the Spatial version

Disadvantages

- The user interface for spatial features is more command-driven and less menu-driven than some other alternatives
- The merger of relational data model for the main data-base with object-oriented programming alternatives for the internet may add complexity for some developers
- GIS functionality within the spatial database is moderate and may not be suitable for complex spatial applications
- For smaller enterprises, the Oracle-database training and skill sets may not be available or affordable

(Modified from Lopez, 2005)

in Figure 8.10. Underpinning the Geodatabase are three key files, Relation, Index, and Geometry. The Relation file is a standard relational table. The Index file contains pointers, corresponding to the records in the Relation file, that point to the physical location in the Geometry file of the spatial record, which is variable-length. Relational operators can be used to join tables or query for values.

Spatial Objects are available for point, line, polygon, and multi-point (Rigaux et al., 2002). In additional to standard relational operators, the Geodatabase has structural elements that are summarized in Table 8.8. They include some object-oriented features such as the Relationship Class, that manages object classes. Feature Dataset collects together feature classes that share the same spatial properties. This is a strong way to alter all at once the spatial properties for a large group of geographic objects. Features are also available to manage network connectivity and terrain modeling, and to constrain the topology.

RELATION FILE

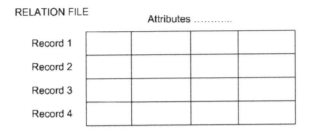

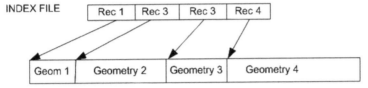

GEOMETRY FILE

Figure 8.10   File Design to Represent a Theme in ArcGIS. Modified from Rigaux et al., 2002

TABLE 8.8   Structural Elements of ESRI's Geodatabase

Dimension (lengths or distances on map)

Feature class (same geometry type) e.g. point, line, polygon. Like features are stored together, e.g. all ZIP code boundaries.

Feature dataset. A collection of feature classes stored together which share the same spatial reference."

Geometric network. A network where geometric coincidence implies feature connectivity.

Network dataset. The collection of all the network elements. These are elements for a generic network including edges, junctions, turns, and others

Raster catalog. Collection of all the raster datasets defined in a table.

Raster dataset. Raster format organization.

Relationship Class. Manages relationships between objects in one class and those in another class.

Schematic dataset. This dataset graphically represents network connectivity and sets of relationships.

Survey dataset. Integrated collection of specialized survey feature classes and the corresponding survey measurements.

Table. Relational table

Terrain. TIN-based dataset that uses feature classes to model using z-values. TIN (Triangulated Irregular Network) is an ESRI terrain modeling application.

Toolbox. Collection of processes for analysis, modeling, and data management.

Topology. Constraints "on how point, line, and polygon features share geometry within a geodatabase." Topology "defines and enforces data integrity rules, topological relationship queries and navigation, and sophisticated editing rules."

ESRI's Geodatabase offers a more elaborate and sophisticated spatial data model than the vendor's traditional shape file. It includes being able to apply spatial relationships and integrity rules on a layer-by-layer basis (Arctur and Zeiler, 2003). For instance, for a layer of "sales regions," integrity rules could be set so that no two sales regions can overlap. Another advantage is that a layout for finished output can be generalized across multiple applications. Geodatabase's metadata feature is more elaborate and conforms to leading standards such as ISO. Thus many organizations have a common way to understand spatial datasets (Arctur and Zeiler, 2003). Among disadvantages of Geodatabase is that it is more complex to understand and requires more training and skill to use.

In summary, the relational-object data model has been illustrated by two leading commercial products that utilize differently. The chapter completes its coverage of spatial databases with a case study of a city-owned utility company that developed and implemented a spatial database.

CASE STUDY OF ENMAX

Enmax is a private corporation wholly owned by the City of Calgary in Canada. It serves a territory around Calgary of 422 square miles and has over 360,000 customers. It distributes natural gas and electricity and has started an initiative in wind energy. Its huge physical asset base includes 3,720 miles of gas distribution, 65,000 utility poles, 70,000 steel flag poles, 42,000 transformers, and thirty-seven substations, one of which is pictured in Figure 8.11.

Before converting to enterprise-wide GIS, Enmax had cumbersome spatial and locational procedures. An example is One-Call locates. This service helps customers who need to know where Enmax-owned facilities are located underground. It is needed by builders and developers who must avoid cutting utility lines in construction projects. Enmax's records on the location of underground facilities were stored on microfilm and in paper map books.

Figure 8.11 Enmax Corporation Substation. *Source:* Enmax, 2007

Since storing and accessing this information was slow and cumbersome, One-Call was supported by twenty-five full-time staff.

The "hit rate," i.e. the frequency of a One-Call customer digging up the wrong location with its attendant hazards was a worrisome nine hits per 1,000 Locates. This and other problems led Enmax's management to proceed with a total overhaul of the spatial processing for the company. An enterprise-wide spatial GIS was implemented that not only serves Enmax, but through agreements serves other city and partnering agencies.

The Enmax configuration (see Figure 8.12) has the Oracle Spatial enterprise database at the center. As with New York City, the central repository serves several categories of users: (1) Enterprise applications. These formerly non-spatial business systems are being spatially-enabled where useful. (2) GIS-enabled applications. These departments previously had some form of GIS. Now most of their spatial and attribute data comes from the central repository, although local specialist GIS software is used. (3) Drafting design and maintenance applications. This unit operates with Autodesk GIS for drafting and construction, but that software is configured to access data in the central repository. (4) Other spatial applications. These are mostly partnerships between Enmax and other city agencies, regulatory agencies, and private utilities. For instance, JUMP (Joint Utility Mapping Project) is a formal collaborative agreement that sets the policies for spatial data sharing

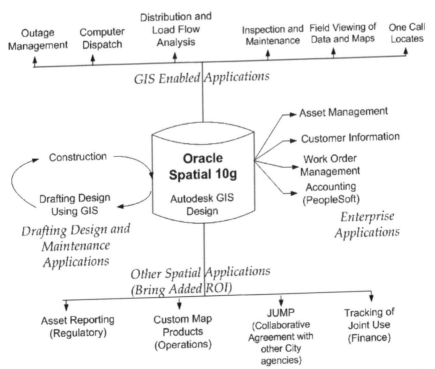

Figure 8.12 Enmax Database Configuration. Modified from Lawrence, 2005

among Calgary's water, sanitation, telephone, cable, and gas companies including Enmax (Lawrence, 2005). Maps and spatial analysis can be added to regulatory reporting documents. These applications increase the benefits of the investment in GIS, in the form of new internal capabilities that expand Enmax efficiencies and performance, and spatial deliverables for the partnership agreements and joint projects. For instance, outage management and load flow analysis were formerly two separate GIS applications but now access their data from the central repository. The cost savings from each is estimated at $250,000 in one-time data-entry costs and $75,000 per year in daily maintenance (Lawrence, 2005). In fact, benefits were realized across the range of spatial applications.

Returning to the One-Call application and looking at it subsequent to implementation of the enterprise spatial system, it is now supported by a specialized GIS application that accesses data in the centralized Oracle Spatial repository. Since One-Call Locates is part of the City of Calgary consortium, Enmax's underground GIS maps are shared with the other city utilities such as telephone and water that also have subsurface assets. Using Field View software, workers employ their laptops in the field daily to view the land, estimate the sub-surface situation and update the centralized repository daily. The improvements are large: One-Call Locates' staff lowered from twenty-five to five, while the error hit rate reduced from nine to one-quarter per thousand. Its operating cost yearly lowered from $1.8 million (Canadian) to $1.2 million. The better reliability and service times have resulted in much higher service demand (Lawrence, 2005). Because of the joint agreement, benefits are also realized by all the participating partners.

In summary, the Enmax case demonstrates how a bold move to a full enterprise spatial database transformed business efficiencies and performance at a mid-sized utility. It shows the benefits of locating corporate data in a centralized database, reducing redundancies, and encouraging cross flows of information internally as well as among cooperating partner organizations.

GIS AND DATA WAREHOUSES

Definition

The data warehouse, introduced in Chapter 4, is an alternative form of data storage that differs from the conventional relational database. It is oriented towards a subject-oriented view of data, rather than application-oriented. It receives data from one or multiple relational databases, stores large or massive amounts of data, and emphasizes permanent storage of data received over periods of time. Data warehouses can be spatially-enabled in several ways. The data in the warehouse can have spatial attributes, supporting mapping. Mapping functions are built into some data warehouse packages. OLAP "slicing and dicing" and what-if functions are performed on the data in the warehouse, and may include spatial characteristics. Furthermore, the data warehouse can be linked to GIS, data mining, and other software packages for more spatial and numerical analysis. Data warehouses and GIS used conjointly emphasize the advantages of each, namely the large size, time variance, and easy arrangement of data in the warehouse, along with the spatial visualization and analysis capabilities of GIS.

Historical Background

It was not until the 1980s that data warehouses began to appear for use (Gray, 2006). By 1990, the concepts of a data warehouse had developed enough that the first major data warehouse textbook appeared (Inmon, 1990). The analytical methods were a collection of methods drawn from statistics, neural networks, and other fields. The theory of the processing steps for data warehousing, OnLine Analytical Processing (OLAP), was formulated in 1995 by Codd (1995). The growth in the markets for data warehousing was driven by the expanding data storage and its analytical uses in organizations. During the past fifteen years, database companies such as Oracle and Sybase produced data warehousing products as well as computer vendors Microsoft and IBM, and ERP vendor SAP (Gray, 2006).

Fundamentals of the Data Warehouse

The principles of the data warehouse are covered first and then related to GIS. A data warehouse differs from a relational database in the following key characteristics: subject-oriented, time-variant, non-volatile, integrated, and oriented towards users who are decision-makers (Gray, 2006, Gray and Watson, 1997). Subject-oriented means that the user accesses information in the data warehouse through common business subjects, such as part, customer, competitor, order, and factory. This contrasts with relational databases that often show the user many detailed attributes to access, but ones not necessarily of high user importance. The traditional operational database focuses on the functional areas of the business, such as sales, finance, and manufacturing.

The data warehouse keeps its older data, which makes possible analysis of change tendencies over time. In other words, the warehouse data are nonvolatile, i.e. after being stored, they are fixed over time. This lends stability to the data in a data warehouse (Inmon, 1990). The data warehouse concept also favors the formation of summarized data, which are useful in decision-making and also become nonvolatile. Granularity distinguishes the individual data items from the summaries, i.e. the most granular refers to raw data, while less granular is summarized data (Gray, 2006). An example of summarized data is a summary of account totals for March, 2007, for a business department.

The data warehouse is *time variant*. For the data warehouse, data are extracted from multiple operational databases, made consistent, transformed, scrutinized for quality, and then written to the data warehouse, with no further updating allowed of those data, which is termed *non-volatile*. At the next desired time point, data are again written to the data warehouse and become non-volatile. Thus the data warehouse accumulates a time series of data by extracting them at multiple time points. Hence the data are "time variant," i.e. they are available over a time period.

Data are extracted for the data warehouse from multiple sources, some of which are legacy ones (Jukic, 2006), combined together, and written to the data warehouse. Thus the data warehouse transforms the diverse data sources into an integrated data set for permanent, long-term storage. Data are checked for accuracy; and errors corrected.

This transforming is referred to as integration (Gray, 2006). The resultant data, which are of high quality, diverse in sources, and extending over long periods, are particularly suitable to research analysts and decision makers, rather than operational transaction-based users.

In a large organization, data are gathered and transformed from a wide collection of operational databases. The whole process of input, extraction, error-checking, integration, and storing these data is known as ETL (extraction, transformation, and load) and was seen in Figure 4.9.

The data in the warehouse are organized by multiple dimensions and put into a structure of dimensional modeling (Gray, 2006; Jukic, 2006). Dimensional modeling consists of arrangements of data into fact tables and dimension tables. The fact table contains important numerical measures to the user, as well as the keys to the dimension tables, which in turn include numerical and descriptive attributes (Gray, 2006; Jukic, 2006). Spatial attributes can appear in the fact table if they are key numeric facts for users, but are more commonly put in dimension tables, where they can provide numeric and descriptive descriptions, including geographic ones.

Two well-known types of dimensional models are the star schema and snowflake schema (Gray and Watson, 1998). An example of a star schema, shown in Figure 8.13, gives information on fast food sales and locations. The fact table contains the keys to dimension tables and numeric attributes on total sales and total managers. The location dimension table gives, for each store, five geographic locations, ranging from county down to census block. They can be used for thematic mapping and spatial analysis. Exact point locations of stores (X-Y coordinates) could also be included, if deemed important enough. The other dimension tables provide information on store sales, products, and periodic reports.

GIS and spatial features can be present at several steps in the data warehouse, shown in Figure 8.14, that elaborates on Figure 4.9 by indicating the spatial features. The operational databases may be spatially-enabled. In that case, the geocoding of data took place prior to the ETL process. Location can be added as an attribute in the ETL step. Within the data warehouse, the fact tables or dimension tables may identify spatial units, such as ZIP code or county. The spatially-enabled tables may have address or X-Y coordinates.

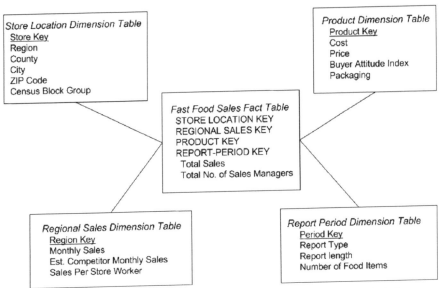

Figure 8.13 Data Warehouse Star Schema, with Location Included

Geographical attributes would be located in the fact versus dimension table(s) if location rose to high importance for the user. For example, in a data warehouse of marketing data for sales regions, the region-ID is in the fact table.

GIS functionality is often present in some of the analysis and modeling software packages shown on the right of Figure 8.14.

The most powerful functionality would be to process data from the data warehouse with a full-featured GIS software package such as ArcGIS or GeoMedia, which can perform a wide variety of GIS functions from overlays or distance measurement up to advanced features such as geostatistics, modeling, 3-D visualization, and multimedia. It can enrich the uses of data warehouse information for utilities infrastructure; energy exploration, production, and distribution; traffic accident analysis; large scale auto insurance risk analysis; management of fleets of vehicles; and business intelligence for decision-making (SQL Server Magazine, 2002; Reid, 2006). As seen in Chapter 4, GIS and data warehouses often serve as parts of an organization's enterprise architecture. They can function in a collaborative, coupled environment with the other enterprise applications. A challenge is to connect separate enterprise software packages together through robust and efficient plug-in and connector software.

OnLine Analytical Processing (OLAP) is a set of rules for accessing and processing multidimensional data in the data warehouse. Originally formulated by E.F. Codd (1995), OLAP rules are focused on simple business decision-making that directly accesses the dimensions of data in the warehouse rather than on complex models. Among the main types of analysis are:

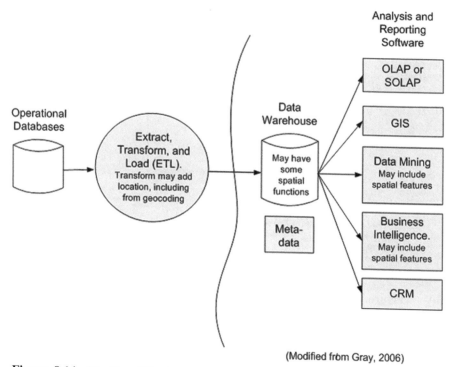

(Modified from Gray, 2006)

Figure 8.14 The Data Warehouse and Its Data Flows, Spatial Functions, and GIS Components. Modified from Gray, 2006

(1) slice and dice, i.e. to divide complex datasets into smaller dimensions; (2) drill down, to seek more detail in a report; (3) what-if changes for single or multiple dimensions; and (4) access to the static, time-slice stores in the data warehouse (Gray, 2006). OLAP is good at answering "why" and "what if" questions.

Specifically, OLAP (OnLine Analytical Processing) refers to the following characteristics of the information in the data warehouse (Codd, 1995): (1) viewable in multiple dimensions, (2) transparent to the user, (3) accessible, (4) consistent in its reporting, (5) based on client/server architecture, (6) generic in dimensionality, (7) handle dynamic sparse matrices, (8) concurrent support for multi-users, (9) has cross-dimensional operations, and (10) intuitive data manipulation, (11) flexible in reporting, and (12) aggregation is possible.

Spatial data can be integrated into the OLAP model, which is termed the SOLAP model (Bimonte et al., 2005; Malinowski and Zimanyi, 2003; Marchand et al., 2003). The aggregation features of OLAP are modified for SOLAP to handle geographic attributes. One approach is to modify the OLAP's multidimensional data model "to support complex objects as measures, inter-dependent attributes for measures and aggregation functions, use of ad-hoc aggregation functions and n-to-n relations between fact and dimension" (Bimonte et al., 2005).

SOLAP models are still under development, in particular to formulate improved SOLAP-based operators for spatial analysis, and more elaborate working prototypes (Bimonte et al., 2005). In the future, a standard accepted SOLAP model would allow OLAP's what-if efficiencies for quick and flexible access to multidimensional data in data warehouse to include the complexity of spatial objects such as points, lines, and polygons. For some applications, such a model might eliminate the need for standard GIS software packages.

Business intelligence. Business intelligence (BI) software packages often have spatial features, as seen in Chapter 3. BI consists of interactive models that are designed to assist decision-makers (Gray, 2006). In the context of data warehouses, BI can conduct modeling based on information from the data warehouse for forecasting, simulations, optimizations, and economic modeling. Spatial capabilities can be present that include location in the modeling and produce results as maps.

Data mining seeks to reveal useful and often novel patterns and relationships in the raw and summarized data in the warehouse in order to solve business problems. The answers are not pre-determined but often discovered through exploratory methods (Gray, 2006). The variety of data mining methods include intelligent agents, expert systems, fuzzy logic, neural networks, exploratory data analysis, and data visualization (Gray, 2006; Tan et al., 2005). The methods are able to intensively explore large amounts of data for patterns and relationships, and to identify potential answers to complex business problems. Some of the areas of application are risk analysis, quality control, and fraud detection.

There are several ways GIS and spatial techniques can be incorporated in data mining. Before the data mining occurs, the data warehouse can be spatially partitioned, so the data mining is selectively applied to certain geographies. During the data mining process, algorithms can be modified to incorporate spatial methods. For instance, correlations can be adjusted for spatial auto-correlation, and cluster analysis can add spatial indices (Viswanathan et al., 2005). After data mining, patterns and relationships identified in the data can be mapped with GIS software.

Physical Structure. Underneath the data warehouse's conceptual structure, data are physically stored either in multidimensional databases keyed to OLAP or in standard relational databases, which have slower performance. The biggest vendors for physical data warehouses are Oracle, IBM, and Microsoft. Some of their products have built-in spatial functionality, e.g. Oracle Spatial 10g.

Large data warehouses may store many terabytes of information, cost several million dollars, and take up to two or three years to implement (Gray, 2006). Their pluses include better decision-making capability, faster access, retention of data for longer time periods, and enhanced data quality (Oracle, 2006). Data quality is scrutinized and improved as part of the ETL process.

Spatially-Enabled Commercial Data Warehouses. Several major database and ERP vendors including Oracle, IBM, and SAP offer spatially-enabled database or data warehouse products. They are full-scale relational databases or data warehouses that have spatial functionality built into them, including spatial layers, geocoding, coordinate systems and projections, and spatial analysis techniques. Although the functionality is not as elaborate as the leading GIS software, it has gained in capability, to a level that satisfies many everyday business needs for maps and spatial processing.

This following discussion introduces essentials on commercial spatially-enabled data warehouses focusing on the Oracle Spatial 10g product. Earlier in the chapter, Oracle Spatial 10g was examined relative to large-scale spatial databases. However, Oracle Spatial 10g also supports the Oracle Data Warehouse. The data warehouse product has features that include a multi-dimensional OLAP engine and built-in ETL features. This emerging trend demonstrates how existing mainstream enterprise packages can be commercially modified for mid-level spatial applications, without the necessity of connecting to traditional GIS software.

Design and construction of applications can be done through Oracle Warehouse Builder, a graphical design tool having: (1) a graphical "design environment" to create the data warehouse based on metadata, and (2) a "run-time environment," to convert the design into the physical processes that run the data warehouse (Rittman, 2006). For viewing, Oracle Spatial 10g's low-level "Map Viewer" provides simple maps of the dimensional attributes and summary data in the data warehouse (Rittman, 2006). For higher-level spatial analysis, major GIS vendor software such as ESRI's ArcGIS or Integraph's GeoMedia can be applied.

Key Applications of Spatial Data Warehouses

Data warehouses and GIS are applied to large-scale datasets for analysis of complex spatial problems that can include time. Important temporal applications are for market segmentation, insurance analytics, complex urban transport, city traffic patterns and trends, patterns of credit results for regions or nations, international tourism consumer patterns, financial fraud, consumer loans (Gray, 2006; SQL Magazine, 2002; Reid, 2006). In this section, two examples are given of real-world temporal applications: (1) auto insurance applications (Bimonte et al., 2005) and (2) traffic patterns for the city area of Portland, Oregon, over a time span of almost two decades (SQL Magazine, 2002).

Example of an Auto Insurance Application. Spatial data warehouses can be built for large-scale analysis of auto insurance. In this example, the data warehouse resides in Oracle Spatial 10g. The business items in the data warehouse have location attributes that include census blocks, locations of policies, business sites, landmarks, elevation, and traffic characteristics. For data warehouses in auto risk insurance, maps can be produced that take spatial views from the usual ZIP-code geography down to hundreds of block groups, small areas within the ZIPs (Reid, 2006). This allows underwriters to set more refined policy pricing. The geoprocessing needs to be fast, many tens of millions of location data processed per day (Reid, 2006).

Example of a Local Government Application: City of Portland. The City of Portland illustrates use of a customized connector program to connect a data warehouse to a GIS. The data consist of city and regional traffic accidents from the Oregon Department of Transportation. The solution combined an SQL Server data warehouse with a customized program written in ArcObjects API (application programming interface) from ESRI Inc. There is a pre-defined schema of non-spatial and spatial attributes for transport of data between the data warehouse and the ArcObjects program.

The city's spatial data warehouse for city and regional traffic accidents has over fifteen years of data and fourteen dimensions, including time, streets, age and gender of participants, cause, surface, and weather. Following cleaning of data entering the data warehouse, location coordinates are added by the GIS team for each traffic accident. At the staging server, ETL extracts data weekly to two powerful clustered production servers. When updates are called for, the data warehouse repeats the ETL process, and outputs a new time slice of the data.

The volume of data is huge, so attention was given to mitigating performance bottlenecks (SQL Server Magazine, 2002). The solution included optimizing replication of a time-slice of data, and partitioning the data warehouse cube to speed up the average access time. Users of the city's system utilize interactive maps of all accident locations during the past decade and half, to supplement accident reports and give added insight for decisions (SQL Server Magazine, 2002). The data are stored in an SQL Server data warehouse.

The customized program allows the GIS software to utilize part or all of the data warehouse. The City of Portland assigned programmers from its Corporate Geographic Information System (CGIS) Group to program the ETL and access modules, based on ArcObjects API for ArcGIS from ESRI (SQL Server Magazine, 2002). Because of the scope of the programs, CGIS limited the types of questions users can ask to a pre-defined set. The accident outputs consist of tables and maps that are viewable on the web. Being able to both query tables and visualize maps is regarded as crucial for users.

The benefits of this data-warehouse/GIS approach included halving of replication time for a time slice of data, fast spatial queries, and response times shortened by twenty-fold or more (SQL Server Magazine, 2002).

Future Directions in Data Warehouses

GIS and spatial technologies to data warehouse applications by providing mapping and spatial analysis. Data warehouse applications can recognize locations of organizational entities such as customers, facilities, assets, facility sites, and transport vehicles. GIS provides visualization and exploration benefits to understand patterns and relationships of enterprise information in the data warehouse, and support better decisions. The challenges are to design spatially-enabled data warehouse architectures that provide added value to corporate users and customers, are flexible enough to change with the rapid technology advances in this field, and are efficient enough to achieve satisfactory throughput and response times.

Future advances are anticipated that make data-warehouses more efficient, improve integration of data warehouses with GIS, tune the analytic outputs to the typical data-warehouse users, and coordinate the spatial data warehouses with other enterprise software such as ERP, supply chain, and CRM. Since the large datasets for each time-slice are written permanently to the data warehouse, the location coordinates are often added in the ETL stage or earlier. Future software needs to have more efficient tools available during ETL such as geocoding, to minimize employee time spent.

There needs to be faster and more seamless connector software and interfaces between commercial data-warehouse and GIS software. Analytic software such as SAS and ArcGIS need to have analysis capabilities that coordinate better with the data warehouse. The future shows promise that SOLAP will become standardized as an extension of OLAP. Spatial data warehouses serve analytic users who are interested in patterns, associations, and longitudinal trends. In the future, the GIS and spatial functions will hopefully be better focused to serve these users.

MANAGING DATA QUALITY

A general challenge for spatial data management is the quality of the data. No matter how sophisticated the storage and access of data, for its ultimate use, the data are only as good as their quality. An example from the field of medicine is preventable deaths from medical errors, which was estimated as 44,000 to 98,000 Americans yearly (Institute of Medicine, cited in Pierce, 2003). Likewise with GIS, the impacts of poor data quality can sometimes be profound. What if a governmental spatial system tracking shipments of nuclear materials has errors so that it recommends the wrong nuclear shipment routes, compromising security. In business, what if an insurance underwriter receives erroneous data from a spatial database about a large customer commercial property and prices the property policy too low? What if a private health-care firm's ambulance routing software is inaccurate for section of a city, cutting crucial minutes from the transport of critically ill patients? Data quality is a crucial topic for the success of GIS. Management has the responsibility to exercise control and maintain data quality.

Spatial applications depend on attribute and spatial data. Some generic problems (Pierce, 2003) include: (1) multiple data sources i.e. there are inaccuracies if a dataset is not collected consistently, (2) subjective bias for qualitative data such as from questionnaires, (3) inconsistent data definitions and formats, (4) slow data access through too high data volume or too slow processors, (4) data accuracy problems, and (5) the conflict of security versus accessibility. As regards the latter, if security is made too high, then the data cannot be accessed which lowers the data quality. On the other hand, lax security lowers the quality since data can more easily be compromised or destroyed.

Data quality depends on the *context* of its use (Wang and Strong, 1996; Pierce, 2003). The nature of the problem being solved determines what is the appropriate data accuracy, speed of access, and completeness. For example, for the digital layer of street boundaries in the Phoenix metropolitan area, data quality criteria vary between a construction company that is re-building street curbs versus a fast-food company estimating numbers of car passengers passing by their outlets. The construction firm requires high ground accuracy with resolution in inches, while the fast-food company needs lower accuracy and resolution to assess traffic flows. A real estate company would see it differently. Another example is completeness of housing data. A marketing firm only needs a sample of the data, while city planning needs information on every house. Hence, there is no firm and fast data quality standard. The key questions are, who is the user? How does the user utilize spatial outputs? In specifying it, an organization needs to explain context as well.

Spatial data have some distinctive aspects of data quality (Kearney, 2003; Tomlinson, 2003). They include:

1. *Spatial completeness.* Are there sufficient types and numbers of spatial features for the problem at hand?
2. *Coverage.* Does the geographic extent of the data correspond to the extent of the problem at hand? Are the geographic features consistent in the procedures used to locate them across the whole coverage? For instance, a coverage having some points entered recently by GPS and others by scanning an old map is not consistent. The coverage concern is harder to address if the data provider didn't provide the metadata.
3. *Transforming spatial data.* When data are aggregated, joined, split apart, and queried in the data transformation inside databases and data ware-houses, errors can occur leading to erroneously transformed results.
4. *Accuracy.* This can be divided (Tomlinson, 2003) into referential (error in referring to a spatial feature), topological (error in the presenting of the topology, such as a broken line segment), relative (two features are not located correctly one to the other), and absolute (error in the map position relative to the true earth position).

For real-time spatial applications such as GPS-based trucking systems that are continually tracked, data quality is impacted by *fast response time*. Users expect to have the data within seconds. If it takes minutes to get answers about where the fleet is located, efficiency can be reduced and data quality lowered. Quality is also affected by *data conversion*. If data are transformed between departments or organizations, data quality may be reduced. As an example, a gas utility company converts geometric data from use in CAD (computer-aided design) to use in GIS for modeling network connectivity (Dangermond, 2006). For the firm, the conversion is expensive and lengthy, and many errors occur in the process.

Data quality is best planned as part of systems analysis and design from the start. It is a serious management oversight to not address it early but wait until users start complaining about mistakes based on faulty data produced by the system. Even if designed into a GIS, data quality is contextual so operating managers need to examine how the environment for the GIS is changing internally and externally, who are the current users, and what are its data-quality impacts.

CHAPTER SUMMARY

Data management is essential to GIS success. The chapter covered the fundamentals of spatial databases including its major types of relational, object-oriented, and object relational. Each data model type has pluses and minuses and is appropriate for certain problems. Two leading commercial data models from Oracle Spatial 10g and the Geodatabase of ArcGIS are both more complex than earlier models and more flexible for a variety of applications.

The Enmax case study demonstrates how a utility can be transformed through radical adoption of an enterprise-wide central data repository. The case had the additional aspect of showing benefits of inter-organizational sharing of a spatial database.

Data warehouses contrast with databases in being non-volatile and storing data historically. The data warehouse has a variety of possible places for spatial enablement. The examples of the City of Portland and an auto insurance firm demonstrate where the data warehouse may be preferred over databases.

The data quality issues permeate the chapter, since the use of data is compromised if quality is low. Data quality must not only be an early goal in GIS system development, but continue right on through for implemented systems.

ACKNOWLEDGEMENT

The section on GIS and Data Wavehouses was published in an ntry in Encyclopedia of Geographical Information Science "Data Wavehouses and GIS." by same B pich. It is used with the permission of Springer Verlag.

REFERENCES

Bimonte, S., A. Tchounikine, and M. Miquel. 2005. "Towards a spatial multidimensional model." In Proceedings of the 8th ACM International Workshop on Data Warehousing and OLAP, November 4–5, Bremen Germany, pp. 39–46.

Codd, E.F. 1995. "Twelve Rules for On-Line Analytic Processing." *Computerworld*, April 13.

Dangermond, Jack. 2006. "GIS Enterprise Architecture: Unifying the Utility." GITA 2006 Proceedings.

Dhillon, Gurpreet. 2007. *Principles of Information Systems Security.* New York: John Wiley and Sons.

Gray, Paul. 2006. *Manager's guide to making decisions about information systems.* New York: John Wiley and Sons.

Hoffer, J.A., M. Prescott, and F. McFadden. 2006. *Modern Database Management,* 8th Edition. Upper Saddle River, NJ: Prentice Hall.

Inmon, W.H. 1990. *Building the data warehouse.* New York: John Wiley and Sons.

Intergraph. 2003. "Toward a Spatial Information Repository Act." Madison, AL: *Intergraph Mapping and Geospatial Solutions.*

Jukic, N. 2006. "Modeling strategies and alternatives for data warehousing projects." *Communications of the ACM,* 49(4) 83–88.

Kearney, Pat. 2003. "Looking for Quality Geographic Data?" *GeoWorld,* **16**(9): 38–40.

Keenan, Peter B. 2006. "An Electronic Market for Spatial Data." Proceedings of the Americas Conference on Information Systems, Acapulco, Mexico, August 4–6. Atlanta, GA: Association for Information Systems. Available at http://home.aisnet.org.

Kramer, Gail, and Stuart Nisbet. 2006. "The Practical Union of OLAP Analysis and Geographic Mapping." *ArcUser,* 9(1): 34–37.

Kroenke, David. 2005. *Database Processing: Fundamentals, Design, and Implementation.* 10th edition. Upper Saddle River, NJ: Prentice Hall.

Laudon, Kenneth C., and Jane P. Laudon. 2007. *Essentials of Business Information Systems.* Upper Saddle River, NJ: Prentice Hall.

Lawrence, Brad. 2005. "Spatial Databases." Presentation at Geospatial Information and Technology Association Conference 28, Denver, CO, March 6. Aurora, CO: Geospatial Information and Technology Association. Available at www. gita.org.

Lopez, Xavier R. 2005. "Spatial Databases." Presentation at Geospatial Information and Technology Association Conference 28, Denver, CO, March 6. Aurora, CO: Geospatial Information and Technology Association. Available at www. gita.org.

Lopez, Xavier R. 2006. "Spatial Data Warehouse: Enabling Enterprise-wide Decision Support." Proceedings of the Geospatial Information and Technology Association, Conference 29, Aurora, CO: Geospatial Information and Technology Association. Available at www. gita.org.

Malinowski, E., and E. Zimanyi. 2003. "Representing spatiality in a conceptual multidimensional model." In Proceedings of the 12th annual ACM international workshop on geographic information systems. Washington, DC: ACM Press, pp. 12–22.

Marchand, P., A. Brisebois, Y. Bedard, and G. Edwards. 2003. "Implementation and evaluation of a hypercube-based method for spatio-temporal exploration and analysis." *Journal of the International Society of Photogrammetry and Remote Sensing,* 59:6–20.

Oracle. 2006. Oracle Data Warehousing. Available at www.oracle.com.

Pick, J.B., N. Viswanathan, and W.J. Hettrick. 2000. "A dual census geographical information system in the context of data warehousing." *Proceedings of the Americas Conference on Information Systems.* Association for Information Systems, Atlanta, GA, pp. 265–278.

Pierce, Elizabeth M. 2005. "Introduction." In Wang, Richard Y., Elizabeth M. Pierce, Stuart E. Madnick, and Craig W. Fisher (Eds.), *Information Quality*, Armonk, NY: M.E. Sharpe, pp. 3–17.

Reid, Hal. 2006. "Applying Oracle Spatial to a very large insurance problem." *Location Intelligence*, June 20. Available at www.locationintelligence.net.

Rittman, M. 2006. "An introduction to Oracle warehouse builder 10g." *DBAzine.com*, August 19. Available at www.dbazine.com.

Rittman, M. 2006. " GIS-enabling your Oracle data warehouse." *DBAzine.com*, April 18. Available at www.dbazine.com.

Sonnen, David, and Henry D. Morris. 2005. "Oracle 10g: Spatial Capabilities for Enterprise Solutions." IDC White Paper, February, Framingham, MA: International Data Corporation.

SQL Server Magazine. 2002. "City of Portland Tames Massive SQL Server Data Warehouse." *SQL Server Magazine*, June 27. Available at www.sqlmag.com.

Tan, P-N, M. Steinbach, and V. Kumar. 2005. *Introduction to data mining.* Upper Saddle River, NJ: Addison-Wesley.

Tomlinson, R. 2003. *Thinking About GIS: geographic information system planning for managers.* Redlands, CA: ESRI Press.

Viswanathan, Nanda. 2005. " GIS in Marketing," in Pick, James B. (Ed.), *Geographic Information Systems in Business*, Hershey, PA, Idea Group Publishing, 236–259.

Wang, Richard Y., and D.M. Strong. 1996. "Beyond Accuracy: What Data Quality Means to Data Consumers." *Journal of Management Information Systems*, 12(4): 5–33.

Wang, Richard Y., Elizabeth M. Pierce, Stuart E. Madnick, and Craig W. Fisher (Eds.). 2005. *Information Quality.* Armonk, NY: M.E. Sharpe.

Watson, Hugh, and Paul Gray. 1997. *Decision Support in the Data Warehouse.* Upper Saddle River, NJ: Prentice Hall.

CHAPTER 9

ORGANIZATIONAL AND INDUSTRY ASPECTS

GIS is implemented in businesses in a variety of organizational settings. For instance, a real estate firm is organized to have a very small GIS department, provide web-based access, and give responsibility for spatial use to highly paid sales agents nationwide. A large utility holding firm with many subsidiary companies has a corporate-wide department of twenty skilled GIS staff that plans strategically, implements enterprise-wide, and coordinates with small decentralized GIS departments in the subsidiaries. Industries differ in their organizational emphasis on spatial. While GIS is part of corporate culture in highly strategic industries such as transportation, typically it has a service-support function in health-care firms. In utilities, spatial technologies are transitioning from centralized and mainframe-based systems to field deployment by staff who are becoming empowered by spatial information and the ability to support spatial decisions in the field.

This chapter begins by examining GIS and the organization, drawing on results from the book's 20 research case studies and on published research studies to a limited extent. A general model of maturity stages of GIS by industry is presented that conforms to Nolan's six stages of IS growth from Chapter 3. From that classification, three of the most important industry sectors for GIS are discussed in this chapter and five others in Chapter 10, namely insurance, marketing/geodemographics, banking and finance, healthcare, and agriculture. It next turns to GIS in three spatially mature and leading industries of utilities, transportation, and retail. Due to space limitations, Chapters

Geo-Business: GIS in the Digital Organization, By James B. Pick
Copyright © 2007 John Wiley & Sons, Inc.

9 and 10 cannot cover the whole array of industry sectors, but some examples of the other sectors appear elsewhere in the book.

GIS AND THE ORGANIZATION

So far, relatively little research or business attention has been paid to the organizational aspects of GIS, while the differences between industry sectors are an important issue in business. Organizational structure is practically significant because GIS is an integrated function that needs to have organizational connections with IT, corporate planning, marketing, and customers. No matter if a company is small or large, outcomes depend on whether GIS staff and services are hierarchical or flat, centralized or decentralized, whether there is able leadership and/or good interpersonal communications, and how motivated are GIS developers, workers, users, and customers. To illustrate organizational factors, the Large Personal/Corporate Bank (LCPB) discussed in Chapter 3 has a decentralized approach to GIS. As part of a global bank headquartered in England, the U.S. division has a small GIS team that focuses on location and trade-area analysis for branch expansion. In the Mexican division, there is a much larger GIS group that is more technical and does more development and programming. Since the national units of the bank are distinctive, it makes sense that the GIS national goals are also distinctive.

People working in GIS are perhaps its most valuable resource, yet that side of geo-business has less known about it. Since GIS in business only gathered momentum within the last fifteen years, the workforce is heterogeneous and often multi-disciplinary (Marble, 2006). It is so young as a field that it has not yet reflected on or assessed the workforce and skills, although the U.S. Department of Labor has funded a project to do just that (Marble, 2006; Wachter, 2006). Since the spatial arena covers many different technologies, skills, and sciences, it's a challenge just to bound the set of skills involved, much less possess working knowledge of them (Marble, 2006).

Marble (2006) provides the following draft definition of the geospatial workforce:

"The geospatial industry engages, at a variety of spatial scales, in the acquisition, integration, analysis, visualization, management, and distribution of data having an explicit spatial and temporal context. A critical component of the industry involves the design, construction, and testing of both hardware and software tools to support these activities. Because of the highly technical nature of the industry, it is also essential to include in any definition those organizations and individuals in the higher education community who are engaged in relevant instructional activities."

This points to workers who have a mixture of IT, geography, management, and spatial analysis background and skills. The variety is also reflected in a

TABLE 9.1   Twelve Job Roles of GIS Professionals

Applications Development	Identify and develop tools and instruments to satisfy customer needs
Data Acquisition	Collect geospatial and related data
Coordination	Interorganizational facilitation and communication
Data Analysis and Interpretation	Process data and extract information to create products, drive conclusions, and inform decision-making reports
Data Management	Catalog, archive, retrieve, and distribute geospatial data
Management	Efficiently and effectively apply the company's mission using financial, technical, and intellectual skills and resources to optimize the end products
Marketing	Identify customer requirements and needs, and effectively communicate those needs and requirements to the organization, as well as promote geospatial solutions
Project Management	Effectively oversee activity requirements to produce the desired outcomes on time and within budget
Systems Analysis	Assess requirements to produce the desired outcomes on time and within budget
Systems Management	Integrate resources and develop additional resources to support spatial and temporal user requirements
Training	Analyze, design, and develop instructional and non-instructional interventions to provide transfer to knowledge
Visualization	Render data and information into visual geospatial representations

Source: Gaudet et al., 2001.

list of twelve job roles for geospatial professionals seen in Table 9.1 (Gaudet et al., 2001). The roles encompass data collection, management, marketing, systems, training, and visualization. Appropriate education pathways are diverse. Marble (2006) points to the critical roles that university education and commercial training will play in further developing an enlarged geospatial workforce. He emphasizes a need for universities to restructure and redesign their spatial programs and curricula.

The twenty research case studies included in this book reflect the organizational differences and variety of skills and background of the workforce involved. Regarding the organizational structure, the surveys yielded the following summary results.

- For large- and middle-sized enterprises, GIS tends to be located in its own corporate department separate from IT.
- Some middle-sized firms have GIS located in a marketing department.
- For large- and middle-sized enterprises, GIS does not have a staff representation at the corporation's executive level.

- Technical skills for spatial projects tend to be in the GIS group but are associated with IT skills in the IT group, or in some cases IT personnel loaned to GIS.
- Outsourcing of GIS workforce is not present in the twenty firms, although two firms (Engineering Systems and URS) provide consulting and partial outsourcing largely to government and somewhat to business. The outsourcing topic is returned to at the end of the next chapter.
- For most of the firms that had both GIS and IT groups, the amount of collaboration and teamwork between the two groups varies between extremes of strong to weak, and occasionally is contentious.
- For large- and medium-sized firms, GIS workforce tends to interact the most with people and customers in the key spatial application areas. For instance, at Lamar Advertising, GIS people interacted the most with the national sales department, which constitutes the most important user group.
- For small firms, GIS is a major part of the entire business. The key firm leaders were experienced and knowledgeable in it from management and/or technical aspects. Most of the workforce of these firms is spatially skilled. There are neither separate departments for GIS or IT nor is the distinction between GIS and IT evident organizationally or behaviorally.

Based on the interviews of twenty firms in the research case study sample, larger companies implementing GIS and spatial technologies tend to have specialized GIS departments. The departments are staffed by people with the wide variety of skills, education, and experience backgrounds that is typical of the geospatial workforce (Marble, 2006).

The organizational structure of GIS has been little researched, although one study of Indian regional governments implementing GIS pointed to the importance of organizational networks (Walsham and Sahay, 1999). Given the importance of having the right organizational structure and people, these areas hopefully will be studied more. The knowledge gained will be useful to business managers. It can also be included in GIS education and training. One goal of this book is to provide such practical knowledge.

GIS IN INDUSTRY AREAS

This chapter section examines GIS and spatial technologies in three leading industry sectors. Its objective is to gain general understanding of the spatial applications for particular industries and examine industry-specific versions of GIS applications. GIS plays significant roles for the lead industries, so a short summary appears at the beginning of each industry section of the factors that distinguish GIS for that industry. Some examples from these lead industries have been given in prior chapters and cases. The difference here is that industry features are the focus.

As pointed out in Chapter 3 for SDSS, GIS in business tends to be categorized in early stages of growth. SDSS is entering an expansion stage spurred by reduction in processing costs and the popularity of the web enterprise platform and consumer spatial web products. The level of spatial decision support in businesses tends to be at Nolan's Stage 1 (Initiation) or Stage 2 (Contagion).

In this chapter, spatial maturity stages are assessed by industry. In some industries spatial technologies have reached Stage 3 in which rapid growth is slowing down and management controls and accounting scrutiny are being applied. A few industries have progressed to Stage 4 by developing standard use of the spatial technologies and integration of them with other business systems and procedures. Based on the opinions of a group of four experts on sector maturity from the GIS industry, a classification of stage-of-growth maturity for twenty-five leading industries in the private sector is presented in Table 9.2. The experts gave subjective ratings of industry-sector classification based on what they considered the average GIS maturity level of firms in the sector.

The composition of industries is modified from a list by Hoovers Inc. (Hoovers, 2006). Four industries, Defense and Homeland Security, Energy and Utilities, Transportation, and Natural Resources and Environmental are classified in Stage 4 (Integration). They are some of the industry sectors that first utilized GIS and are among the largest today in spatial market size. The next group in Stage 3 (Control) includes Communications, Insurance, Marketing/Advertising, Oil and Gas, and Retail. They have become somewhat regularized with management controls in place, but are less integrated with other business systems and functions. Ten industries are categorized in Stage 2 (Contagion) which implies users are demanding much more use of them and they are in a growth phase. For instance, spatial applications are growing rapidly in parts of the banking industry, including for siting, CRM, and branch management, market analyses. Lastly, six industries, apparel, chemicals, electronics, food and beverages, manufacturing, and publishing, are categorized in the Stage 1 (Initiation). These industries offer instances of GIS and spatial uses, but they haven't yet taken off with rapid adoption and diffusion (Rogers, 1995). The industries tend to be more capital-intensive, which can hold back rapid technological advance due to capital budgets that are often tight, the cyclical nature of their business, and in some cases traditions and/or unions that resist new technologies.

Although the industries have been placed in these categories, individual firms vary within an industry. The real estate firm of Sperry Van Ness from Chapter 1 brought GIS into widespread and critical use, advancing it beyond the real-estate industry norm of Contagion Stage into the next stage of Control. Almost all industries in the classification are becoming more mature, so it is anticipated the chart entries will move to the right over time.

TABLE 9.2   Industries in the U.S. Classified Nolan's Stage of Growth for GIS/Spatial Technologies

Stage 1 Initiation	Stage 2 Contagion	Stage 3 Control	Stage 4 Integration	Stage 5 Data Administration	Stage 6 Maturity
			Defense and Homeland Security		
			Energy and Utilities		
			Transportation		
			Natural Resources and Environmental		
		Communications			
		Insurance			
		Marketing/Advertising			
		Oil and Gas			
		Retail			
	Agriculture				
	Banking and Finance				
	Construction				
	Education				
	Health Care				
	Leisure				
	Metals and Mining				
	Newspapers				
	Pest Management				
	Real Estate				
Apparel					
Chemicals					
Electronics					
Food and Beverages					
Manufacturing					
Publishing					

Note: Industry Classifications modified from Hoovers Inc., 2006.
Original Source for Stages of Growth: Nolan, 1979.

The eight industries selected for intensive coverage in Chapters 9 and 10 include two from Stage 4 (Utilities, Transportation), three from Stage 3 (Retail, Insurance, and Marketing/Geodemographics), and three from Stage 2 (Agriculture, Banking/Finance, and Health Care). Additional industries in Stages 3 and 4 are included in case studies throughout the book. The Stage 2 industries covered are rapidly growing and increasingly strategic. In this and the next chapter, industries will be covered starting from the spatially more mature ones in the upper right of Table 9.2 and working down and to the left. A detailed case study of the large utility, Southern Company, appears following the utility section. It sheds light on that industry and illustrates organizational issues and ways to solve them.

UTILITIES

Summary: The major spatial applications are:
Energy procurement and planning
Electric and gas transmission
Electric and gas distribution
Customer care
Demand studies and economic development
Asset management
Supply chain and logistics
Finance and accounting
Corporate services, regulatory compliance

The Utilities industry in the United States is an old one and heavily regulated. Its challenge is to fight bureaucracy and keep up with rapid changes on the outside. It is constrained from change by government regulations, the long cycle times for approvals and building of utility infrastructure, and by ingrained habits (Meehan, 2006). In spite of this, the industry often utilizes advanced engineering and technology for the production, transmission, and distribution of water, energy, and communications.

Among the shorter-term pressures and problems besetting utilities are air pollution controls (a good thing for the public), blackouts such as the Great Blackout of 2003, rise of consumer power to force changes, the Enron energy pricing scandal and subsequent regulations, and the additional security, regulation, and reporting in the outfall of 9/11 (Meehan, 2006). In response to the problems, utilities have often put their focus on core competencies, lowering costs, better customer service, more efficient operations, and use of technologies to achieve improvements.

Electric and gas utilities produce energy in a process cycle portrayed in Figure 9.1 (Meehan, 2006). Energy must be procured, transmitted, and

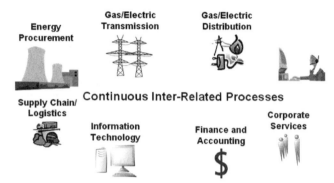

Figure 9.1   Business Model of Typical Electric or Gas Utility. Copyright © 2005 ESRI. All rights reserved. Used by permission

distributed. Corporate services, finance and accounting, and IT provide the information and money flows for the physical processes. The supply chain is essential for getting energy materials to the right places at the right time. Monitoring and maintaining a "just-in-time" inventory-based supply chain requires spatial technology since the inventory that is no longer in a warehouse but moving around the world at large can be referenced with geospatial coordinates. The business model for a communications utility looks similar to this one, except procurement, transmission, and distribution are replaced by sending, transmission, and receiving of communications.

GIS is a crucial technology at almost all points in the utility process cycle. In energy procurement and planning, GIS is utilized to design and construct energy plant sites and transmission networks. If the power grid is not adequately built, there are power losses or blackouts. An example is the design, construction, and continual monitoring of Great River Energy's Pleasant Valley turbine plant. GIS was utilized by engineers to visually analyze the plant design. Following the opening of the natural-gas-fired combustion plant in 2001, GIS has been used to monitor plant component reliability. For example, in Figure 9.2 the number of failures in tiles in the turbine is shown visually for years 2001 to 2006 (Cox–Drake, 2006). In other cases, GIS can show the impacts of power plant design alternatives on transmission lines, environment, surrounding neighborhoods and areas, and major customers. Outages in the utility grid can be tracked down through examining outage reports and looking for common grid elements, which is assisted by GIS. For instance, for an electric utility, all of the reported outages are on a given path and all have in common a particular feeder line and two transformers. This diagnostic can direct repair crews to the outage location more accurately. For electric utilities, the power is transmitted on the electric power grid, which is owned by utilities. The grid must be designed from a power engineering standpoint. GIS can produce schematic drawings that show all the major network components and simulate loads, which are visualized symbolically. In this way, load scenarios can be compared.

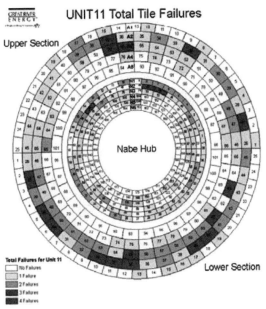

Figure 9.2 Total Tile Failures in Unit-11 of Great River Energy's Pleasant Valley Natural-Gas-Fired Combustion Turbine Plant, 2001–2006. *Source:* Great River Energy, 2007.

Other spatial concerns in transmission lines are to secure right-of-way, and meet state and local regulations, while for built lines, the aim is to remain free of vegetation intrusion or disaster damage. Many of these concerns are assisted by study of the corridors surrounding the transmission lines. Spatial analysis can place a buffer along the entire transmission grid, and phenomena within the buffer can be studied, including land topography, vegetation, landholdings, and security threats. Remote sensing can determine the type of vegetation and hence if its anticipated growth is sufficient to pose a threat to the lines. Satellite imagery and the grid can be overlaid, along with a buffer, as seen in Figure 9.3, for a 400 kV line in rural areas of Great River Energy's grid in Minnesota, in order to evaluate and resolve the exposures and problems within the buffer.

GIS is used to evaluate the encroachment of vegetation onto high-voltage power lines. The vegetation threat to these lines becomes critical under certain conditions. In the New York Blackout that commenced on August 14, 2003 and affected more than fifty million people in the U.S. and Canada, the primary cause was intrusion of trees onto transmission lines in Ohio (Wingfield and Garnett, 2006). GIS is an excellent tool to assess the growth and impingement of vegetation (Wingfield and Garnett, 2006). For example, the New York Power Authority (NYPA) runs a vegetation management program that checks on encroachment for 16,000 acres of rights-of-way

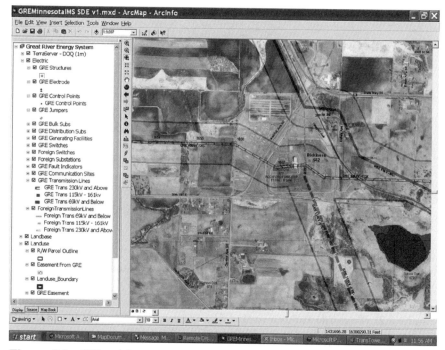

Figure 9.3 GIS and Satellite Overlay of 400 kV Transmission Line of Great River Energy in Minnesota. *Source:* Great River Energy, 2007.

(ROW). The GIS application is linked to other systems that manage environmental, land management, and equipment maintenance data. The GIS-ROW application evaluates current vegetation and estimates the potential effectiveness of vegetation control projects (Wingfield and Garnett, 2006). At NYPA, GIS is set up as a portal, to provide diverse users with the work status of vegetation containment, as well as other operational and weather information.

GIS can be coordinated with utilities' SCADA systems. SCADA (Supervisory Control and Data Acquisition) senses, monitors, and controls the chemical or physical processes of utility flows. For instance, SCADA for natural gas monitors regularly-spaced flow sensors that indicate the volume of natural gas in the pipeline. Managers receive flow data for the whole network. Spatial displays allow them to visualize and remedy problems occurring in large-scale, complex networks. Some SCADA responses can be programmed to automatically occur. Regional transmission lines can be monitored over large geographies, even an entire nation. For example, a map of above normal voltage readings for high-voltage regional transmission lines across the Mid-Atlantic region, in Figure 9.4, can be studied to diagnose causes of problems network-wide and alert local utilities to undertake maintenance or repairs.

Besides SCADA, GIS for utility distribution assists in outage management, asset management, leak assessment, and "One Call." Outages may be

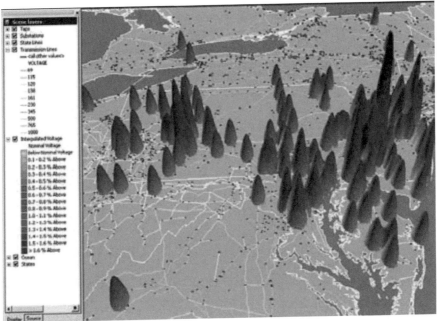

Figure 9.4 Regional Transmission Lines in Mid-Atlantic United States (115–1000kV) Showing SCADA Above Normal Voltage Readings. *Source:* PJM Interconnection.

due to equipment failures, high demand, aged or malfunctioning equipment, or disasters. In an outage, utility customers face work stoppage, financial loss, inconveniences, and safety risks. Using SCADA and other data, maps can be produced of outage locations, both for internal response teams and external community-based information. When Hurricane Isabel happened in September of 2003 causing severe power losses in eastern Pennsylvania in its aftermath (see Figure 9.5), GIS analysis revealed detailed patterns of outages, which were useful to utility customer support, repair crews, and public safety (PPL Utilities, 2007).

A common safety threat to a utility distribution network is that a building contractor will accidentally cut a subterranean utility line, causing environmental damage, economic loss, or injury (MapInfo, 2006). Most states require a "One Call" system (sometimes known as "Call Before You Dig"), that consists of an 800 number or website to inform a builder whether the subsurface of a site is safe to go ahead with. Maps can pinpoint the underground utility lines and store historical and descriptive attribute information. Figure 9.6 shows a "Call Before You Dig" GIS display screen for a water utility showing housing parcels, subsurface water lines, and an incident record.

The field aspect of utilities concerns the operation, inspection, inventory, maintenance, and replacement of the tens of thousands of physical facilities,

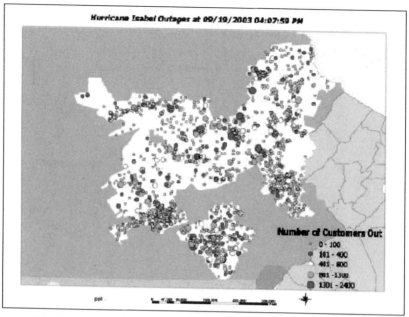

Figure 9.5   Outages in Eastern Pennsylvania from Hurricane Isabel. *Source:* PPL Utilities.

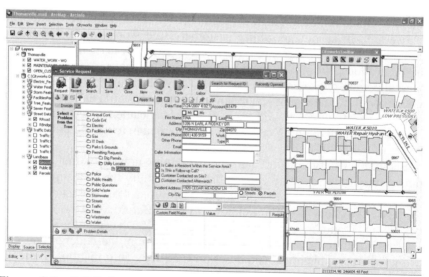

Figure 9.6   Call Before You Dig Management for Water Utility. *Source:* Azteca Systems. Copyright Azteca Systems, 2007.

TABLE 9.3   The Leading GIS Applications for Electric and Gas Utility Firms, 2004

Leading GIS Applications for Electric Utility Firms
1. Trouble Call and Outage Analysis
2. Engineering Work Order Design
3. Field Automation and Workforce Automation
4. Work Management
5. Data Maintenance
6. Engineering Analysis
7. Customer Information System (CIS) Integration
8. Distribution Automation/SCADA Interface
9. Conversion and Data Capture
10. Executive Information Support System

The Leading GIS Applications for Gas Utility Firms
1. Mobile Collection, Viewing, and Access to Data
2. Work Management and Process Automation
3. CIS Integration with GIS and Facilities Management
4. Facility Maintenance
5. Management of Leak Detection
6. Asset Management and Plant Maintenance
7. Gas Outage Management System
8. Corrosion Protection
9. Replacement Maintenance
10. Marketing and Business Geographics

Reprinted with permission of the Geospatial Information & Technology Association, www.gita.org.

equipment, and devices. The significance of this aspect for GIS is seen in Table 9.3 that lists leading GIS applications for electric and gas utility firms in 2004 (GITA, 2005). Ones with major field components are mobile data collection, managing work orders, leak detection, and outage management. (GITA, 2005).

In the field, assets can be monitored and maintained through mobile, GPS-based devices. Mobile spatial architectures, discussed in Chapter 5, are becoming more important. A utility's web services can be extended to mobile devices in the field (Figure 9.7). Although the screen size in the field is often small as seen in the top of the figure, cartographic adjustments can be made to simplify the symbol sets in the field, but keep them consistent with the desktop (Rude, 2006). Map labeling may need to be done later, since crews in the field are more keyed to their immediate surroundings than office workers at desks, i.e. they're more interested in plugging a pipeline leak than, documenting what they are doing. However, redlining changes can be performed in the field by working on a tablet PC as seen in the bottom of Figure 9.7 (City of Burbank, 2007).

Figure 9.7 Mobile Field Display of Neighborhood Utility Network. *Sources:* Meehan, 2006; City of Burbank, 2007.

There are numerous benefits for a utility to make the transition to mobile GIS for its field force. For instance, at Xcel Energy, Rude (2006) pointed to benefits of greater efficiency, knowledge, and reduced travel (see Table 9.4). The change to mobile can be challenging for field workers (Rude, 2006), who are often loath to give up the daily paper maps they have used for years. However, at Xcel Energy, crew members were optionally allowed to retain paper maps in the transition, yet they all soon moved to a mobile GPS device, as they perceived its greater knowledge base, functionality, and accuracy.

Utilities can provide better customer care by using GIS. Most utilities such as electricity, gas, and water are metered. Meter reading has traditionally been conducted by meter readers in trucks. Mapping displays in GPS-enabled vehicles assist meter readers to locate customers. Managers plan and monitor

TABLE 9.4   Benefits of Mobile Mapping, Based on Lessons Learned at Xcel Energy

1. Electronic gathering of large quantities of information in the field.
2. Graphic (map) display in field.
3. Drill down on field maps to detailed engineering data.
4. Variety of information in the field can be expanded, for instance gas leaks, reporting of damaged facilities, and scouting of storm impacts.
5. Immediacy of input and ability to immediately notify crew mates.
6. Whole field team updated daily.
7. Crews can track distribution lines and pipes in much more detail. They can more quickly and accurately locate values, switches, etc.
8. Reduced printing costs.
9. Broader variety of data accepted by field workers.
10. Reduced travel time and productivity improvements from mapping of work orders, for best routing.
11. Use of GPS to identify assets in the field, to know where the field worker is, check on driving directions, and communicate among the crew on locations.

Source: Rude, 2006. Reprinted with permission of the Geospatial Information & Technology Association, www.gita.org.

locations of a whole force of meter readers. Some utilities have automated meter reading. As the truck gets within Bluetooth-communications-range of a house, the updated meter information is automatically transmitted to the truck by Bluetooth, and then forwarded by wireless to a central database. Other electrical utilities such as Southern California Edison with IntelliGrid, offer more advanced two-way meters that send and receive information on an hourly basis, monitoring home electrical devices and providing richer usage data to the utility, as well as allowing the homeowner to better manage use of utility devices (SCE, 2006). The utility has richer data to spatially model household consumption and behavioral patterns.

Utilities can service customer inquiries through call centers and web centers that offer outage data, billing information, home energy management tips, and service order tracking. GIS visualization assists service personnel where location is pertinent such as for outage zones. In the case of emergencies, utilities can expand call-center and web-based information flow to customers. In normal situations, utilities conduct target marketing to bring in new customers and retain existing ones.

At the regional level, utilities need to understand and forecast demand. This involves detailed demographic and consumption modeling that includes location. For instance, in the first decade of the twenty-first century, greater Los Angeles metropolitan population is expanding rapidly to the east in San Bernardino and Riverside counties. Utilities need to model population growth, types of new businesses, and locations using demographic and GIS software. Along with modeling, utilities support governments and businesses in economic development, especially in fast-growing regions, such as the aforementioned ones. For instance they participate in regional growth planning and contribute information and knowledge regarding the location of present and future populations.

Finance and accounting were discussed in Chapter 4 in the context of ERP. Since the location and proximities of utility assets are crucial to their valuation and taxation, GIS systems track utilities' extensive property and asset holdings. This detailed finance and accounting information is also required for certain regulatory filings such as for the Federal Energy Regulatory Commission (FERC). It also becomes essential if the firms undergo merger or acquisition.

Utility companies must comply with many government regulations, directives, and federal and state laws. One example is FERC's Vegetation Management Reporting Order that requires regular reports from power transmission operators, controllers, and owners on current vegetation conditions (ESRI, 2004). Report information can be more efficiently collected by field crews with GPS-enabled mobile devices, who can check compliance status on the spot and take actions in the field to comply. The central database for reporting can be updated in real-time as the field work gets completed.

A crucial gas-utility regulation is the management of pipeline integrity in High Consequence Areas (HCAs). They are portions of the pipeline where the flows and surroundings pose grave risks of damage and injury if an incident occurred. Regulations require inspections, repairs, and mitigation steps. HCAs are examined through modeling of pipeline scenarios. This is supported by GIS software with modeling extensions to assess the HCA risks, perform spatial analysis of HCAs, and conduct associated hydraulic simulations. In the field, a GPS-enabled mobile force can perform these tasks more efficiently. To recap, the vegetation and HCA examples illustrate the multiple spatial applications that respond to government regulations.

Utilities are a prime concern for homeland security. The pulse beat of modern economies depends on reliable water, energy, and communications. As seen in Table 9.5, threats specific to utilities include direct ones to facilities and transmission lines, indirect targets that cause associated damages and injuries while reducing the ability to respond and recover, and other associated facilities and events that may be impacted by loss of energy and communications (Kirk, 2006). In 9/11, electricity was cut off in parts of Manhattan. Restoration and repairs were hampered by indirect target losses such as transportation closings and hazardous fumes. The three-year-old New York City Emergency Operations Center containing integrated GIS for the city located in one of the twin towers was destroyed in the attacks. Within a day or two, a new GIS center had to be rapidly set up and replacement data quickly gathered from multiple sources that enabled mapping and analysis of outages and utility lines (ESRI, 2002). Among the most important mapping contributions

TABLE 9.5 GIS and Homeland Security: Threats to Utilities

Direct targets
Electric generation plants (nuclear, coal, gas, hydro)
Gas storage facilities
Water treatment plants
Oil refineries
Gas pipelines and pump stations
Electric transmission grid
Telecommunications central offices, switching stations, and substations
Utilities offices and other facilities

Indirect targets
Road closings and gas station losses
Other public transportation closings
Fires/explosions of non-utility assets nearby to damaged utility assets
Hazardous chemical releases
Disease outbreaks that lower workforce
Employee residential locations

Other associated facilities/events that could be targeted
Hospitals, universities, public buildings (indirect effect on utilities)
Transportation centers (indirect effect on utilities)
Historical sites
High-profile events (parades, rallies, elections, sporting or cultural events)

Source: Kirk, 2006. Reprinted with permission from the GITA 2006 Conference Proceedings, a publication of the Geospatial Information & Technology Association, www.gita.org.

in the aftermath was to locate the oil fuel tanks and Freon tanks underneath the World Trade Center site so that threat of explosion was averted.

Utilities can ready themselves for homeland security threats by target identification, risk assessment, preparedness planning (pre-disaster), response and recovery plans (post-disaster), and mitigation planning (post-recovery). The steps can be consolidated into a comprehensive business continuity plan. Geography is important. For instance, natural gas supply and transmission can be protected ahead of time from major disruptions by mapping and analysis of production facilities, networks, and storage units to highlight security weaknesses and exposures, which can lead in turn to prevention by expanded security surveillance and staffing (Kirk, 2006).

For any type of potential disaster, there is a need to share spatial information beforehand with government agencies and industry partners (Kirk, 2006). Shared information helps the partnered governments and businesses to prepare together. Consequently, in a catastrophe the governments, utilities, and other enterprises can more quickly assess the damage and injury impacts and know the status of each others' intact capabilities. Although utilities may resist the cost of data sharing, the potential long-term benefits are reduced damages and losses.

Enterprise utility applications are large-scale and can involve tens of thousands of facilities and millions of customers. They may extend over multi-state regions or entire nations. In Chapter 4, enterprise GIS was seen to be designed to work together with other major functional systems such as marketing, supply chain, and finance/accounting. The Pidpa and Nesa case studies highlight how enterprise integration can be achieved for a water and electrical utility. Building a utility enterprise architecture involves workflow and process models, data models, databases, output design, underlying physical infrastructure, integration with other corporate systems and with those of other organizations. (Dangermond, 2006). An example is the Enmax case in Chapter 8. Another example of a successful initiative to develop an enterprise utility system is this chapter's case of Southern Company. The practical implication is that management needs to spend extra time considering the best enterprise design incorporating utility processes and the underlying physical architecture, while integrating the business and utility enterprise modules with a GIS.

CASE STUDY OF SOUTHERN COMPANY

Southern Company is one of the nation's largest utility holding companies. Through its five operating companies, Georgia Power, Alabama Power, Mississippi Power, Gulf Power, and Savannah Electric, the combined Southern Company serves 4.2 million customers in four states covering 120,000 square miles (Adams and Johnson, 2006). Prior to 2003, Southern had different GIS implementations in each of the five operating companies and operated them independently, with little inter-organizational coordination or data sharing (ESRI, 2006). GIS applications included asset management, marketing, SCADA, economic development support particularly by Georgia Power, real estate especially at Alabama Power, and a limited mobile GIS-GPS system for field workers.

In 2003, Southern Company's management set up an Enterprise GIS Project with the goal to consolidate investment in GIS into common architecture, structure, and data across all operating units. Southern formed a GIS Core Strategy team that reported to Southern's IT steering committee. It consisted of a technology management representative from each of the five operating companies. In 2003 the team developed a strategic vision for spatial technologies across all companies and formalized an enterprise vendor alliance with ESRI. A GIS management consultant was called in to formulate an approach to implementing the enterprise plan. The architecture was client server with a spatial database (ArcSDE) and specialized utility add-on software (ArcFM from Miner&Miner).

The operating companies moved at different speeds to develop their migration to the enterprise standards. Alabama Power quickly implemented it within a year so its results constituted a model for the others. By 2006, Gulf

Power, Mississippi Power, and Savannah Power had migrated to the common architecture.

Georgia Power (GP) took a slower route and needed to call back the outside GIS consultant to more deeply develop its plan to migrate from AutoCAD to the new standard of ArcGIS/ArcSDE (ESRI, 2006). The Georgia Power implementation project was finally approved in June 2005, with implementation in 2007. Why was Georgia Power delayed? GP's prior CAD system known internally as Automated Mapping and Construction (AMC) was a very high quality system that had good reviews from its over 300 users (Powers and Johnson, 2006). It had taken considerable effort and investment to implement. However, Southern's needs trumped the local preference to keep AMC as is. Yet the conversion of such a large existing system and user base would take more time.

A GP project transition team was set up to do the conversion. It included business and field utility employees, experienced systems analysts, ESRI experts, and a consultant. The project team had to go slow as it worked through the often contrasting opinions of strong-willed members (Powers and Johnson, 2006). The team did not yield to "group think," but went in the opposite direction, often reviewing and reconsidering prior decisions, which took more time (Powers and Johnson, 2006). The project was delayed but in the end there was buy-off by the whole team of a conversion plan that was approved and is now in implementation.

Overall, Southern considers that the biggest benefit of its enterprise GIS is economic. Purchase in bulk lowers costs, and data and expertise can be shared more efficiently among the units. A useful web-based application TransView was developed in-house during the project to allow a common interface for query and work design among the GIS teams in the operating companies. (ESRI, 2006). Overall, the costs were high in terms of dollars spent, people's time especially at Georgia Power, and some intangible losses of morale (hopefully temporary). Nevertheless, the change was strategic and Southern expects to stay its course with this application for ten years or more which provides ample time for payback. The Enterprise GIS Project correlates with corporate strategy and was intentionally positioned high up to report to the Corporate IT steering committee.

This case provides lessons regarding the organizational structure and leadership of GIS for a large company. The project represented disruptive change. Outside consulting was necessary to develop the unprecedented five-company transitioning path. Expertise and motivation to make the change were more available at some operating units than others. Georgia Power, the slowest to transition, encountered some inertia and even resistance that reflected the large success of its prior CAD implementation. Working through it organizationally required extended team discussions, but finally it gained consensus and approval. The case highlights the importance for GIS success of leadership, carefully planned change, consensus building, and overcoming resistance. It also demonstrates the benefits of outside, uninterested expertise to gain clarity during a period of organizational change.

TRANSPORTATION

Summary: The major spatial applications are:
Routing and scheduling
Vehicle tracking and dispatch
Emergency vehicle tracking
Fleet management
Aviation, airports, and maritime
Railroads

Spatial technologies are used extensively by businesses to plan, manage, route, and maintain transport, and respond to emergencies. A key aspect is the potential for real-time locational information exchange through combinations of GIS, GPS, wireless, and satellite communications. For instance, Apex Office Supply in Vinton, Iowa, is a small, twenty-year-old office supply firm with 1,500 customers in a 50-mile surrounding region. Trucks are loaded in the morning to deliver to retail outlets in the region. The daily loads need to be balanced between drivers. The delivery person's territory has been decided beforehand through spatial modeling that balances territories throughout the city for the delivery team. Balance refers to evenness among drivers in daily time, workload, and costs.

GIS and optimization models can determine drivers' routes for the day. An on-board mobile computer provides route maps; database information on load, customers, and schedule; real-time navigation; audio directions while driving; the ability to re-route that day or the next if obstacles occur; and capability to key in new locations and customers while in the field (ESRI, 2006).

Information is accumulated daily for the whole fleet and made available to managers to model longer-term trends, and assess routing performance. Another benefit is that the bar codes of items being loaded on a truck in the morning can be checked against the driver's manifest, and discrepancies corrected. The driver has load sheets both in paper and on-line that list and describe exactly the items for each stop. Although there was some driver resistance, it was quelled by inviting drivers to attempt to "best the software" with their own routing, but no driver was able to do this, and so the benefits became more evident as a result (ESRI, 2006).

GIS routing and scheduling software is available from major software vendors and specialists for industries. Vehicle tracking can be applied to entire fleets of vehicles. For instance, a national trucking fleet utilizes GPS-based

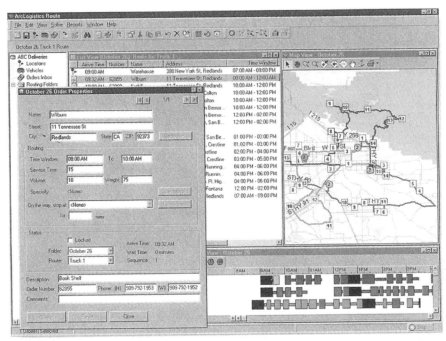

Figure 9.8   Business Fleet Routing and Scheduling (ArcLogistcis Route from ESRI). Copyright © 2006 ESRI. All rights reserved. Used by permission.

vehicle tracking to manage and monitor hundreds of large trucks nationwide. This is referred to as *automatic vehicle location* (AVL), which is the capability to determine the exact location of a vehicle and transmit the information in real time to a centralized location for management use. Although locations are usually registered by a GPS receiver on-board, inertial navigation or RFID can also be used. AVL-managed fleets are present in trucking, construction, business deliveries, police and fire, and public transport. AVL can be combined with project and task management. For instance, as seen in Figure 9.8, a three-truck fleet is being routed. At the lower right, a pert chart displays the day's time allocations for different color-coded tasks by each of the drivers. The route for Truck 1 is shown on the screen. The driver has requested information on the customer from the first stop of the day at 9:32 am arrival (ESRI, 2006). The "order properties" window on the left provides information from the work order for first stop, including service duration, items delivered, and the time-delivery window, which was realized. Besides use to the driver, accumulated daily information from such a system can be analyzed by the manager for decision support on long-term fleet routing.

Sears, a case study examined in Chapter 7, uses AVL systems to support its home service technicians who make fourteen million service calls yearly. Delivery trucks, such as the one in Figure 9.9, have on board an AVL system

Figure 9.9   Sears Delivery Truck and Driver. *Source:* ESRI, 2006

that includes GPS, GIS, satellite and terrestrial communications, audio links, and ruggedized laptops with touch screens (ESRI, 2006). Each truck has a Mobile Base Station communications device on top that communicates information every four seconds via wireless to the Sears Command Center. The driver can view current location, his/her route, and route stops on the laptop screen that is shown in Figure 9.10. The display functionality is simplified to allow messaging, marketing information, an activity list, and other basic features. If the driver's route changes, a new one can be added by dynamic updating that day. Each truck has the nationwide TeleAtlas street data on-board (ESRI, 2006).

Emergency vehicle tracking follows a similar routing and AVL framework, but has more need to optimize the fleet actions. For instance, a police department has vehicle routing and AVL in a city. For a police emergency, the dispatcher can see where the entire police fleet is located, which patrol cars are nearest to the incident and what staff and equipment resources among them are appropriate to deploy. Ultimately the dispatcher decides on which vehicle(s) to send. Subsequently, the driver dispatched can monitor his/her distance from the incident and other resources in case they are needed for back-up. The difference for emergencies is the time urgency, the incident coordination, and enhanced capability to optimize the fleet.

Aviation, airlines, and airports depend on GIS. Airline firms and air traffic controllers plan routes in airspace through GIS. Map layers of satellite and digital aerial photos are registered with those airport and flight-path features to allow aircraft to be positioned exactly relative to other aircraft and ground features. This can be useful for flight control, security considerations, noise studies, and even planning of noise-impacted real estate developments. The

Figure 9.10   Sears Smart Toolbox Routing Feature. *Source:* ESRI, 2006

GIS imagery has become available in 3-D which especially helps assess airspace availability as it gets more crowded (ESRI, 2006). A map of Las Vegas International Airport and the surrounding city area overlaid with the runway noise plumes, shown in Figure 9.11, allows business, government, and community stakeholders to evaluate noise versus current and future building developments in this rapidly growing city.

Another example of GIS for airports (Figure 9.12) is a mobile device for monitoring terminal concessions relative to the airport layout. Within the terminal, concessioned and unconcessioned spaces are colored differently to allow tenants and airport management to understand the flows of customers over time and space.

GIS is used extensively to assess security threats of airports and aircraft. It "provides a powerful analytic capability for understanding vulnerability in existing facilities as well as in pinpointing trends in incidents and past security breaches" (ESRI, 2006). Another use that applies to airports, railway stations, or other transport terminals is to display engineering design plans relative to layers of transport, parking, hotels, commuter access, and neighborhood proximities.

Railroads likewise are concerned about the geographic layout of their facilities and networks. They need to know about and map terminal design, environmental impacts, security, and the detailed locations of present or prospective maintenance problems. When tracks are out-of-use in maintenance,

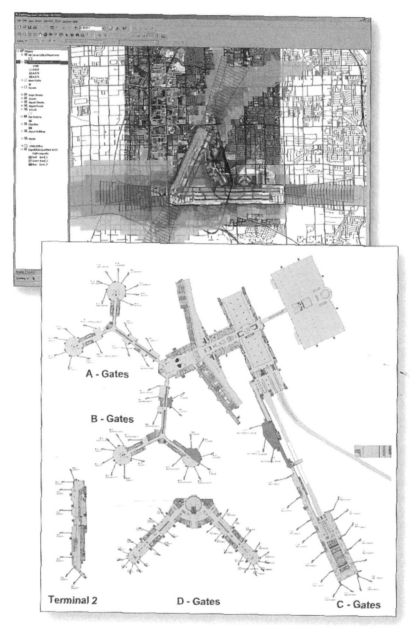

Figure 9.11 Airport Runways with Noise Plumes. *Source:* McCarran International Airport, 2007.

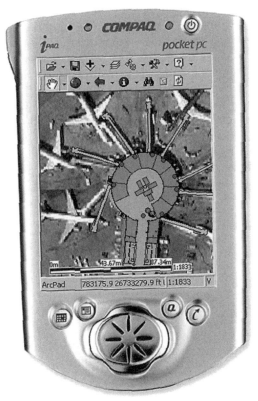

Figure 9.12 Mobile Device for Airport Inspection and Maintenance. *Source:* ESRI, 2006

"slow-order maps" are displayed that indicate locations of current track repairs, when they will be finished, and the consequent slowing down of train flows on the network. Some train companies such as Conrail have on-board, real-time monitoring of engine performance (Lang, 2000). That information can be viewed spatially for the entire locomotive fleet in a control center, with color coding showing the severity of maintenance issues. This allows certain Conrail engines to be diverted for maintenance, using spatial algorithms to lower the cost to the nearest repair center (Lang, 2000).

The popular NavStar and OnStar devices in cars highlight the use of spatial technologies for personal transport. These systems display road maps that are complete for continental areas, and provide visual and audio directions to find locations. The base maps are provided by companies such as TeleAtlas that collect detailed and exact road-network information worldwide. Data are available for the U.S., Canada, Europe, and increasingly in developing parts of the world.

For advanced transportation problems, the modeling occurs at the level of an SDSS or Spatial Business Intelligence. Algorithms from vehicle routing models are combined with the spatial qualities of GIS (Keenan, 1998). For instance, customized multi-vehicle, multi-depot routing models have been studied by researchers for decades. The traditional operations research models used simplistic representations of spatial relationships. The use of GIS offers more sophisticated modeling of spatial relationships in routing. It also allows interaction with other models and information in the GIS (Keenan, 1998).

Transportation is critical in logistics and supply chain applications, which were discussed in Chapter 4. In summary, GIS and GPS have become essential for modern transportation management whether by large transport firms, smaller companies, or security and regulatory departments in business and government.

RETAIL

Summary: The major spatial applications are:
Site location
Merchandising
Geodemographics, customer segmentation
Sales and marketing
Trade areas
Store renovation, cannibalization closure

The retail industry utilizes GIS with a focus on the customer who is key to its sales and profits. Of particular interest are where the suitable customers are located relative to the retail outlets, competitor outlets, transportation, and other attractions and amenities. For larger retail chains, the balance of national and regional products and markets is evaluated spatially. As seen in Chapter 4, Customer Relationship Management Systems (CRMs) allow retail firms to gather information on customers with emphasis on cultivating and developing the best ones. The Chico's case study illustrated how CRM and GIS could form a strong pair of enterprise applications that succeeded in enhancing Chico's goal of achieving valued customer relationships. Chico's also used GIS for locating stores, direct mailings, and business intelligence. This sub-section builds on that background.

Retail GIS accesses large variety and quantity of retail attribute data, mostly governmental, some of which is presented in Table 9.6 (Roussel-Dupre, 2002; ESRI, 2006). For spatial analysis, digital map layers of census geography, business territories, and shopping center locations that correspond to the attribute data are gathered and input into the GIS.

Site location is critical for any retail company. GIS allows mapping of the sites of the firms' retail outlets, that can be overlaid with sites of competing

TABLE 9.6   Retail Attribute Data Used for Spatial Applications in the Retail Industry

Demographic data
Decennial census data
One-year and five-year forecasts of census data
American Community Survey

Segmentation
Descriptions of the neighborhood profiles in the U.S. Example: Community Tapestry from ESRI and PSYTE from MapInfo. Consists of 50–100 segments by using demographic and socioeconomic composition.

Consumer expenditure
Consumer Expenditure Surveys from Bureau of Labor Statistics

Market potential
"Data on goods, services, attitudes, activities"
Projections of number of consumers. Gives indices for market potential.

Retail marketplace
Businesses can study retail supply and demand

Businesses
List of tens of millions of businesses giving "name, location, franchise code, industrial classification code, number of employees, sales"

Shopping centers
Major databases on shopping malls. National Research Bureau and Directory of Major Malls. Tens of thousands of shopping centers.

Traffic counts
U.S. national data on vehicular traffic

Modified from Roussel-Dupre, 2002, and ESRI, 2006

retail firms, as well as demographic, traffic, and neighborhood segmentation (i.e. geodemographic) layers. Chico's did this to locate new sites for its rapidly growing branch network, to analyze cannibalization among its own stores, and evaluate the locations of traffic and other access barriers. Cannibalization refers reduction in revenues in old stores when a new one arrives.

Another example is Marco's Pizza, a rapidly expanding chain founded in Toledo, Ohio in 1978 (MapInfo, 2006). In 2005, Marco's had 148 stores and was Number 1 for growth among U.S. pizza chains. Marco's performed site location analysis by overlaying layers of its other and competitor locations, sales estimates, and the size of trade areas (see Figure 9.13). A modeling software package calculated the prioritized best locations based on the size and proximity to trade areas, buffer distances between sites and other Marco's/competitors' locations, and distance from markets. As part of this analysis, it used MapInfo's PSYTE segmentation software to analyze the neighborhood profiles of proposed locations and obtain forecasts of demand (MapInfo, 2006). For a new site to be eligible, it had to have restaurant sales potential of $550,000 or more yearly. The model showed the quantity, location,

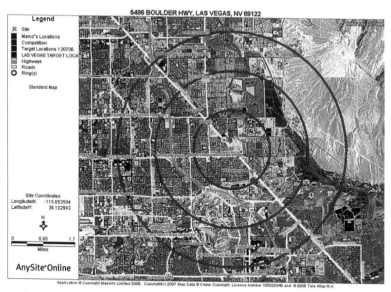

Figure 9.13 Target Site for Marco's Pizza in Las Vegas, with Marco's and Competitors' Locations and Buffer Rings. *Source:* Marco's Pizza, 2007

and priority of potential sites as well as each site's index of trade-area sales potential (MapInfo, 2006). Marco's has used this spatial siting approach successfully. Top management indicates it provides a "strategic blueprint for expansion" (MapInfo, 2006).

Analysis of trade areas is important for deciding on locational sales approaches. A retail trade area is the geographic area from which the majority of a store's customers and/or sales originate. Mapping of trade areas is useful because it reveals to a business what the competitive landscape is (Thrall and Fandre, 2003). A number of models can be used to estimate it. The simplest is a *point map*, i.e. one that shows where customers reside. A crude trade area can be created around the points (Thrall and Fandre, 2003). A slightly more sophisticated approach is *radial analysis* (also referred to as "ring analysis"), which assumes that a trade area is circular. Different diameters of rings in the model account for certain percentages of a retailer's customers. Levi Strauss North America manufactures and markets clothing products, the most famous of which are jeans. The firm and its distributors sought to analyze for a hypothetical new retailer location what customers, existing authorized retailers, and potential retailers were located in a trade area. A model of rings around the potential location was created using the web-based ESRI Business Analyst Online with 1-, 3-, and 5-mile radii. This was useful for decision support on the new locations (ESRI, 2006). An example is seen in Figure 9.14 of such circles emanating from a hypothesized Levi Strauss location in San Francisco.

More sophisticated trade area analysis can be done by the *Huff Trade Area Model* (Dramowicz, 2005). This model formulated by David Huff (1963)

Figure 9.14   Web-Based Ring Analysis for Prospective Retailers.

maps a probability surface for customers that is the ratio of a measure of attractiveness of a particular store (or shopping center) divided by a distance measure, to the sum of attractiveness of all stores (or shopping centers) divided by a distance measure. Hence this trade area measure not only takes into account distance, but also the attractiveness of stores and the influence of competitors.

The Huff trade-area model is formally represented as follows:

$$P_{ij} = \frac{A_j^{\alpha} D_{ij}^{-\beta}}{\sum\limits_{j=1}^{n} A_j^{\alpha} D_{ij}^{-\beta}}$$

Where A_j is a measure of attractiveness of store j, such as square footage,
   D_{ij} is the distance from i to j,
   α is the attractiveness parameter estimated from empirical observations,
   β is the distance decay parameter estimated from empirical observations,
   n is the number of stores including store j.

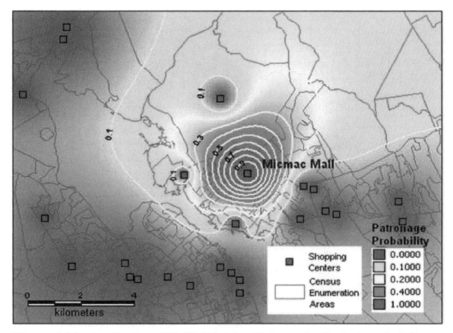

Figure 9.15 Application of Huff's Model to Estimate the Trade Area for Micmac Mall, Dartmouth, Nova Scotia. Note: attractiveness of a shopping mall was determined by a single variable, Gross Leasable Area. *Source:* Dramowicz, 2005

The term $A_j^\alpha D_{ij}^{-\beta}$ is called the perceived utility of store j by a consumer located at i.

The α parameter is the exponent to which store attractiveness is raised. It allows a nonlinear attractiveness.

The β parameter simulates the decay rate of the drawing power of the store depending on customer's distance from it. If β is higher, there would be less influence of the store on more distant customers.

The model is illustrated in Figure 9.15 for the Micmac Mall in Dartmouth, Nova Scotia, where the store attractiveness is Gross Leasable Area (Dramowicz, 2005). It's evident that Micmac Mall's trade area forms an oblong shape that is circular towards the competitors but bulges out in the northeast direction, away from the competitors. This information can be useful in understanding locational market draw. It informs marketing campaigns tailored to different zones of the trade area. A weakness of Huff's model is that data on attractiveness and the locations of all the competing stores must be gathered and updated.

Another retail use of spatial analysis is to assess spatial aspects of national marketing initiatives. For large retail firms, products and marketing programs are brought forward on a national basis. However, the local customers, competitors, tastes, markets, and environments differ around the country. Spatial analysis can be applied to make comparisons, model geodemographic influences, assess consumer tastes, and look more broadly at geographic strategies to engage nationally against competitors, locate different sizes of stores optimally, avoid cannibalization, perform well-reasoned closures and relocations, assess demand, and take into account regional population and economic growth. These efforts require sophisticated models and lots of data, resources, and oftentimes consulting expertise. The benefits, however, are to sharpen the national thrust of marketing, rising above local specific issues.

Jo-Ann Stores provides an example of such broader retail marketing. The firm, founded in 1943, is the leading fabric retailer in the United States. Particularly for families or individuals engaged in hobbies and crafts, the firm is dominant, capturing about three-quarters of the household market. The products consist of crafts, framing and floral products, fabrics for home decorating, seasonal home items, and varied home accessories. In 2005, Jo-Ann Stores had 915 traditional stores in forty-nine states and seventy superstores in sixteen states. Superstores first appeared in 1995. The map of Jo-Ann Stores in New York and surrounding states in Figure 9.16 reveals nine superstores and thirty-three traditional ones for New York state (Jo-Ann Stores, 2006).

Five years after the superstores were rolled out, the marketing problem confronting Jo-Ann was to develop a future plan for the superstores, particularly what mix of superstores to have, whether superstores would attract a different demographic profile than traditional ones, and where to locate new superstores (MapInfo, 2006). Jo-Ann first used its three-million record customer base to compare the customer demographics of the two store types, and it found to its surprise that they were the same regardless of what region around the country. The analysis implied that a group of traditional stores could be relocated and combined into a superstore without losing customers while achieving economic efficiencies. Subsequently, new superstores were added without worrying about losing prior customers from the traditional ones facing closure (MapInfo, 2006).

Retail companies are heavy users of GIS for marketing, site locations, CRM, and in-store merchandising. They are able to gain enhanced understanding of the geographies of customers, competitors, products, store types, and geodemographics leading to better performance and market appeal. GIS often leads to improved integration across corporate databases (Roussel-Dupre, 2002). As seen for the Chico's case, some of the spatial techniques are sophisticated and the databases can be large, but firms such as Chico's, Marco's, Levi Strauss, and Jo-Ann have planned the technology carefully and understood the necessary investment and training, leading to competitive gains.

Click on the map to find the Jo-Ann stores nearest that point. You may also select another state or enter a specific location, or browse the complete list of 42 locations in New York.

Figure 9.16   Jo-Ann Stores' Web-Based Customer Application to Access Retail Outlet Information. *Source:* Jo-Ann Stores, 2006

CHAPTER SUMMARY

Spatial technologies are implemented in organizations. Spatial technologies can alter the organization and vice versa. GIS tends to be the responsibility of individuals in small businesses and specialized GIS departments in middle and larger ones. Since IT is usually a separate and larger unit, a compatible organizational relationship between GIS and IT is important for success. The Southern Company case illustrates organizational change accompanying the roll-out of spatial enterprise GIS, consolidating five prior GIS applications for separate units. Some organizational resistance was encountered but worked through.

The chapter applies Nolan stage theory to categorize twenty-five industries by their spatial maturity. There is a range from initiation through integration stages. This chapter discusses three of the most mature and important industries for GIS, Utilities, Transportation, and Retail. The next chapter examines five industries in the contagion and control stages for GIS. The goal of presenting the industry applications is to emphasize that GIS has significant applications specific to users and customers in particular industries. The business person in GIS needs to be aware of these distinctions and know the most important ones. The Utilities industry is naturally spatial and has urgent real-time applications including service for the customers and field-work by the company, which is becoming mobile-GPS enabled. Transportation has been revolutionized by locational technologies that allow improved navigation of the vehicles while giving management better tools for routing, maintenance, and security. Retail can strengthen its marketing and customer relationships by combining GIS with CRM, siting analysis, geogdemographics, and with marketing methods such as direct mailing. Singly or in combination, these methods sharpen locational decision-making in retail and increase competitiveness and customer awareness, care, and services.

REFERENCES

Clarke, Ian, and Jennifer Rowley. 1995. "A Case for Spatial Decision-Support Systems in Retail Location Planning." *International Journal of Retail and Distribution Management*, 23 (3): 4–10.

Dangermond, Jack. 2006. "GIS Enterprise Architecture: Unifying the Utility." GITA 2006 Proceedings.

Daratech. 2004. *Geographic Information Systems Markets and Opportunities*. Cambridge, MA: Daratech.

Directions Magazine. 2002. "Navigation Technologies Unveils Real-Time Traffic Solution." *Directions Magazine*, October 14. Available at www.directionsmag.com.

Directions Magazine. 2004. "NAVTEQ Announces TrafficData Solution for North America." *Directions Magazine*, April 8. Available at www.directionsmag.com.

Dramowicz, Ela. 2005. "Retail Trade Area Analysis Using the Huff Model." *Directions Magazine*, October 19.

ESRI 2002. "New York City—Creating a Disaster Management GIS on the Fly." *ArcNews*, Winter. Available at www.esri.com.

ESRI 2004. "GIS Solutions for Regulatory Compliance." *Energy Currents*, Fall, Redlands, CA: ESRI Inc., pp. 1–6.

ESRI 2006. "GIS Solutions for Retail." Redlands, CA: ESRI Inc.

Fritz, Oliver, and Petter Skerfving. 2005. "Monitoring and Analysis of Power Line Failures: An Example of the Role of GIS." In Pick, James B., *Geographic Information Systems in Business*, Hershey, PA: Idea Group Publishing, pp. 301–323.

Gaudet, Cyndi, Helen Annulis, and John Carr. 2001. "Workforce Development Models for Geospatial Technology." GeoSpatial Workforce Development Center, The University of Southern Mississippi, Hattiesburg, MS. Available at www.geowdc.com/research/research.htm.

Geotab. "Welcome to the Geotab Checkmate Features Section." Available at www.geotab.com.

GeoWorld. 2005. "Industry Outlook 2005." *GeoWorld*, December, pp. 24–31.

GITA. 2005. "Geospatial Technology Survey." Aurora, CO: Geospatial Information and Technology Association.

GPS World. 2004. "NAVTEQ.XM satellite hit the road." *GPS World*, May. Available at http://www.findarticles.com.

Kirk, Kevin. 2006. "The Need for Geographic Information, Analysis, and Sharing for Homeland Security in the Utilities Industry." Proceedings of 2006 GITA Conference.

MapInfo Inc. 2006. "PCOS: Web-enabled 'Call Before You Dig' Application Cuts Operating Costs for Utilities and Provides Greater Public Safety." Troy, NY: MapInfo Corporation. Available at www.mapinfo.com, September 1.

Marble, Duane F. 2006. "Who are We? Defining the Geospatial Workforce." *Geospatial Solutions*, May, pp. 14–21.

Meehan, William J. 2006. "Enterprise GIS: If You Build It, It Will Fund." *GeoWorld*, March.

Pun-Cheng, Lillian S.C., and Alice W.C. Chu. 2005. "GIS in Business—Routing Analysis of Plaza Shoppers." Proceedings of Map Asia 2004, Beijing, China, August 26–29.

Ray, Julian J. 2005. "A Web-based Spatial Decision Support System Optimizes Routes for Oversize/overweight Vehicles in Delaware." *Decision Support Systems*, in press.

Rogers, E.M. 1995. *Diffusion of Innovations*, 4th Edition. New York: Free Press.

Roussel-Dupre, Stephanie. 2002. "What Are Your Customers Telling You?" *Integrated Solutions for Retailers*. Available at www.ismretail.com.

Rude, Tony. 2006. "Moving GIS from the Office to the Field." GITA 2006 Conference Proceedings.

SCE. 2006. "Designing the Future: A Smart Grid Newsletter Case Study." Rosemead, CA: Southern California Edison, November, 11 pp.

Segal, Donald B. 1998. "Retail Trade Area Analysis: Concepts and New Approaches." *Directions Magazine*, November 18. Available at www.directionsmag.com.

CHAPTER 10

INDUSTRIES AND OUTSOURCING

INTRODUCTION

In this chapter, the applications of GIS in industries are explored further. The chapter follows the industry maturity-stage framework introduced in Chapter 9. The objective is to explain specialized spatial applications in important GIS sectors. The emphasis is on the distinctive aspects of these sectoral applications, rather than on commonalities which have been the focus of earlier chapters. Five key industries in GIS maturity stages 2 (Contagion) and 3 (Control) are examined, insurance, marketing/geodemographics, banking and finance, agriculture, and health care. The chapter provides breadth of insight into the benefits, costs, and challenges of these particular industries, illustrated by case studies. The chapter concludes with a discussion of GIS outsourcing.

The chapter begins by discussing with two industries classified in Table 9.2 in Stage 3 (Control), namely Insurance and Marketing/Geodemographics. Insurance utilizes GIS both externally with customers and internally to run complex insurance operations, while Marketing/Geodemographics, uses GIS for geo-segmentation, target marketing, CRM, direct mailing, and global marketing. Three industries classified in Stage 2 (Contagion) are discussed: Banking and Finance, Agriculture, and Health Care. In the former, GIS is applied to site location, branch networks, trade area analysis, marketing, and portfolio analysis. The reinsurance firm SwissRe has vast spatial capabilities especially for disasters. The Agriculture industry has changed rapidly due to precision agriculture i.e. applying agricultural cultivation and treatments to tiny micro-plots, based on a combination of GPS, environmental sensors, GIS,

Geo-Business: GIS in the Digital Organization, By James B. Pick
Copyright © 2007 John Wiley & Sons, Inc.

and mobile technology. The spatial information can be stored and analyzed to aid farming decisions and strategies. Health Care has diverse uses of GIS, that range from epidemiological study to locational analysis of patients, physicians, and facilities; emergency dispatch of ambulances; mapping of hospital beds; and target marketing of drugs to physicians.

Further insight is provided by case studies. In banking, a Large Credit Bank is challenged in breaking out of its traditional "legacy" orientation by demands for use of new technologies including GIS in the branch networks of acquired banks. For agriculture, Cargill's Palm Oil operations shows how GIS can help to plan plantations. In Health Care, a small firm, MapGistics, provides spatial analysis of bed occupancies in hospitals, while the larger Kaiser Permanente has multiple GIS uses in site locations, patient and member travel, and much more.

The final section of the chapter considers the growing trend towards GIS outsourcing, which can be local, regional, or global. In IT, outsourcing has become prevalent and continues to grow. It has tended to start with outsourcing of low-level IT functions such as data entry and move to higher ones such as systems planning and designing database architecture. Another trend has been the growing proportion of global outsourcing, i.e. to outsourcers in another country such as India. GIS outsourcing resembles IT outsourcing in most respects but has some differences. The case of Southern California Edison's GIS contract with Patni illustrates the benefits and challenges of global outsourcing.

INSURANCE

Summary: The major spatial applications are:
Risk analysis
Catastrophe management
Business continuity planning
Claims
Customer analytics
Support for agents
Marketing

Insurance companies inherently are concerned with risk. Specifically, underwriting is the process of calculating the rates and pricing for insurance premiums incorporating risk analysis. GIS helps develop the process by measuring proximities to risk. For casualty and property insurance, GIS can overlay risk exposures to natural hazards such as hurricanes and earthquakes with man-made ones such as oil spills and terrorism events. GIS helps improve the statistical confidence in risk estimates, by taking into account location.

It was seen in Chapter 7 that Norwich Union, the leading British insurance firm, produced a detailed flood map of the UK as an early and successful step into GIS. Presently, its GIS for floods includes the analysis of elevations of individual residential and commercial properties throughout the UK to evaluate risk. Another example, RVOS Insurance, a small property insurance firm in Texas, uses GIS to map risk concentrations (MapInfo, 2006). The firm checks for extent of locational diversification of risk, and make changes over time to diversify risk more.

In Chapter 3, a prototype spatial decision support system for assessing the risk of typhoons in China was examined. It utilizes expert systems, spatial statistics, and graphical displays to analyze historical data on typhoons in order to model the pricing of premiums.

Besides identifying risk zones and mapping estimated premiums, there is further spatial modeling and analysis that can be done. These include: (1) developing models to diversify geographically the exposures for high-risk policies, (2) developing region-specific models to determine risk and pricing, and (3) projecting the types of claims that are likely for a region (ESRI, 2006). The model outputs lead to preventative steps for insurers so policy holders can reduce risk and obtain a lower rate (ESRI, 2006).

Since inevitably catastrophes will occur, including hurricanes, tsunamis, or terrorism, insurance firms must provide support and assistance to policyholders who are impacted with losses. They need to be able to spatially forecast unfolding events and consolidate a total picture of losses. The Large Insurance Company case study in Chapter 3 concerned catastrophe analysis and management. It demonstrated the use of GIS to avoid massing too many policies in the same location.

Another service that insurance firms provide to clients is Business Continuity Planning (BCP). BCP consists of the policies and procedures to keep a firm's key systems running in the event of a disaster. A well-thought-out BCP makes it easier for an insurance company to respond to and offer help in a catastrophe. Among the contributions of GIS to BCP are the following (ESRI, 2006):

- Reinforces the capability for emergency response
- Helps a firm in a disaster make necessary notifications
- Helps manage the gathering of field data in a disaster
- Helps manage and account for corporate assets
- Improves the preventative sharing of data between the insured and government agencies
- Adds maps to the BCP itself to understand the spatial dimensions of business continuity processes

An insurance claimant is often distressed and seeks quick, even immediate service. The provision of service to the client is however complex, involving multiple locations, such as those of the incident, claimant, claims adjuster, and insurance claim offices. The company must decide how to allocate the adjusters. An SDSS that considers the workload and capability of adjusters and their driving distances from the incident or claimant can optimize the allocation of claims adjusters.

SDSS is also used to analyze service areas, assess historical adjuster coverage, and make what-if assumptions on adjuster numbers, territories, specialties, and schedules. This feature is available in Oracle's Siebel Systems Insurance Module, which can be connected to MapInfo software to check on the proximities of policyholders, commercial clients, dealers, agents, and sales and service territories (MapInfo, 2005).

GIS helps in monitoring compliance with federal insurance regulations and ratings. An example is the Florida Farm Bureau Insurance Companies (FFB). FFB provides auto, farm, homeowners, dwelling-fire, and business-owner insurance to members of the Florida Farm Bureau Federation. In 2004, FFB insured $23 billion in property. GIS supports regulatory applications at FFB through GeoVerify, a customized integration of data on regulations, rating territories, and policyholder locations (MapInfo, 2006). The maps were overlaid, so discrepancies between policyholders' regulation ratings and those actually applied in the customers records could be compared, and corrected in the records at the next renewal time. FFB's ROI for GeoVerify in the first year was 1000 percent (MapInfo, 2006). Generally, any regulatory requirement that has locational differences is opportune for GIS. A related application is to check policy premiums by location in tax jurisdictions and make record corrections whenever a customer's record shows incorrect property taxes. Property taxes serve as one indicator of property value and attendant risk (Bedell, 2006).

Insurance firms compete to acquire customers and then the firms must continue to provide care and services to retain them. To accomplish this, marketing strategy includes spatial methods such as tailoring the locations of marketing campaigns to particular customer profiles, focusing the sites for direct mailings, and enabling call centers to map caller locations. GIS can contribute to target marketing, geodemographics, CRM, customer service, and marketing campaigns. Several variables specific to insurance customers that are important to map in marketing studies are the premium rate structures by region and customers by categories of insurance risk.

Insurance agents also benefit by GIS. Maps of sales territories by type of policy can be used to determine workload balance among agent teams. GIS can help the human resources department in mapping recruitment pools of agents (ESRI, 2006).

SWISS REINSURANCE COMPANY

Swiss Reinsurance Company (SwissRe) is a 145-year-old reinsurance company headquartered in Zurich (Figure 10.1). Reinsurance refers to insurance

Figure 10.1   SwissRe Headquarters Building in Zurich, Switzerland. *Source:* SwissRe, 2006

that shares risk beyond what direct insurance firms can carry by themselves. SwissRe is the world's largest reinsurance company with 2005 sales of $26.6 billion (Hoovers, 2006). It offers health, property, life, auto, and liability reinsurance mostly to small- and medium-sized insurers that cannot afford the full risk of certain coverages.

At the core of its business is the GEOdatabase (see Figure 10.2), a vast compilation of business data from private insurance data firms such as GFK Macon, map data provider Europa Technologies, U.S. Census for urban sprawls, ESRI for topographic datasets, CRESTA for insurance industry zones, and environmental data providers. GEOdatabase is connected to other systems such as Radio Data System (RDS) for navigation and location-based solutions, data of International Hydropower Association (IHA), SICS/nt (reinsurance administration software), the Incremental Update File (IUF) which receives datasets and updates GEOdatabase on a time-critical basis, and CatNet, the

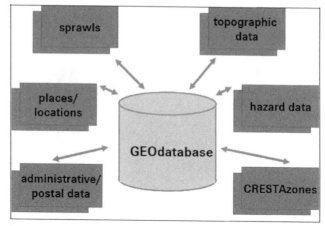

Figure 10.2   Available Data in SwissRe's GEOdatabase. *Source:* Bayerl, 2006

firm's own global natural hazards information and mapping system (Bayerl, 2006).

This case focuses on CatNet (Catastrophe Network) which has been available to SwissRe and its direct insurers since 2000. It is a web services application, based on ESRI's ArcIMS server and ArcSDE data for management, and the Oracle database. The web design is Java based (J2EE and Java objects), with the XML data exchange standard. The architecture is a form of the web-based spatial applications covered in Chapter 5. Web services have been slower to catch on in insurance so CatNet stands out as an early and sophisticated example.

CatNet provides a detailed multi-layer view of major natural perils for almost any location worldwide. In fact a user can search for 650,000 locations, request estimated risk rates, show all potential natural hazards for a location, and see chronological tracking of past catastrophic sequences (SwissRe, 2006; Bayerl, 2006). An example of an application is mapping historical disaster events and intensities for "earthquakes and tropical cyclones worldwide, floods in selected countries, windstorms in Europe and tornadoes in the U.S." (SwissRe, 2006). The number of natural hazards stored is considerable, including 2,500 cyclones for the twentieth century, and events on 1,500 volcanoes. Within minutes, a user can accurately visualize hazards and estimate risks for any place on earth (Schmidt, 2002).

In the tracking of historical hurricane paths in the U.S. CatNet can access data from the GEOdatabase on urban sprawl, places/locations, administrative boundaries, topographic data, hazard data, and CRESTA zones for insurance risk exposures. Figure 10.3 is an example of a user request that shows the paths of devastating hurricanes Wilma, Katrina, and Rita overlaid on layers showing cities, urban areas, capitals, roads, rivers/canals, and water bodies.

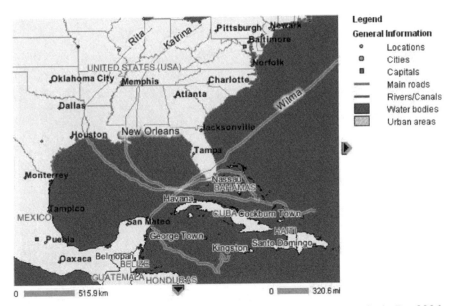

Figure 10.3 CatNet—Tracking of U.S. Hurricane Paths. *Source:* SwissRe, 2006

Although not all of this appears in the figure, users can drill down to get more specific information and map greater detail. In the case of Hurricane Katrina, SwissRe and some its direct insurers were responsible for claims stemming from damages in six states (Table 10.1) such as structural damage (Figure 10.4). CatNet supported rapid, interactive access to information on Katrina to the SwissRe and direct insurers during and after the event. It now has available the historical information and maps on Katrina and other hurricanes to help insurers and insured plan for risks and exposures in the Gulf of Mexico region.

TABLE 10.1   Losses and Insurance Claims from Hurricane Katrina, by state

State	Losses ($millions)	No. of Claims
Louisiana	22,600	900,000
Mississippi	9,800	490,000
Alabama	1,300	123,000
Florida	458	110,000
Tennessee	46	8,400
Georgia	22	3,300
TOTAL	34,226	1,634,700

(Source: preliminary estimates by ISO's Property Claim Services Unit, 10/2005)

Figure 10.4 Structural Damage to Superdome in New Orleans from Hurricane Katrina. *Source:* FEMA, 2005

MARKETING/GEODEMOGRAPHICS

Summary: The major spatial applications are:

Target marketing

CRM

Geodemographics

Spatial adoption/diffusion

The goals of Marketing and Geodemographics are to analyze the markets for products and services and achieve success in marketing to potential and existing customers. Marketing and geodemographics exist not only as a separate industry, but also exist within firms across a spectrum of industries. For the retail industry covered in Chapter 9 and the insurance industry in this chapter, most companies have internal departments that perform marketing and geodemographics.

The role of GIS in marketing is to track and analyze the map layers of locations of customers, employees, products, and stores, overlaid with layers of transportation networks, topography, geodemographic profiles, and other layers such as financial, economic, and behavioral. This section goes over the main marketing/geodemographic spatial applications including target marketing, market segmentation, customer relationship management, and analysis of diffusion. A case study is presented that applies spatial adoption/diffusion methods to the roll out of a loyalty adoption program for a large retailer in a major metropolitan area (Allaway et al., 2003, 2005).

Target marketing is the process of searching for, identifying, acquiring, and retaining customers. Simple target marketing examines potential customers based on a single attribute to identify those with greater potential (Bourgault, 2005). Spatial analysis can display customer density and dispersion relative to siting of customer facilities (Bourgault, 2005). For instance, a national fast-food chain can map for a region the density of customers' residences relative to three fast-food outlets of one brand in the area and five competitor outlets. A further analysis leads to maps of the travel distances for customers to each of the outlet locations. Regional management can better decide how to add additional outlets and whether to close or re-locate existing locations.

Several techniques that can include GIS are helpful in target marketing and other types of marketing. Statistical analysis can project attributes or groups of customers or outlets based on particular characteristics, and the results can be mapped. Regressions forecast one dependent attribute, say store spending, based on historical data on other attributes which are considered to be associated with it. Spatial regression is also available that adjusts for spatial differences in forecasting the dependent variable. For instance, based on averages for a ZIP code, over a thirty-year period, customers' store spending on mufflers (dependent attribute) is associated through regression with percent of car ownership, income, and average commuting time. After estimating the next five years of values for the three independent variables, store spending on mufflers can be projected for five years. The forecast can be done for all the ZIP codes in a metropolitan area, and a map created of the projected values for muffler spending. The map is helpful in target marketing for muffler buyers.

In addition to regression techniques, CHAID (Chi-Square Automatic Interaction Detector) can also be used for forecasting. CHAID is an exploratory method for forecasting where a qualitative or quantitative dependent variable can be projected by a complex model that chooses the predictor variables and specifies interactions among them in order to optimally predict the dependent variable. The predictor variable could be a target marketing variable of interest to a business. CHAID can be run for a group of areas, such as the ZIP codes in a county or the cities in a large metropolitan area, and the estimated dependent variable can be mapped.

CRM (Customer Relationship Management), covered in Chapter 4, is a business application or strategy that is intended to enhance customer satisfaction and expand revenues and profits. For larger firms, CRM may be implemented as an enterprise system that follows customers intensively for long periods of time and provides personalized services to help develop long term relationships between customer and marketer. GIS can be connected to CRM so customers' locations are taken into account in providing the services. The Chico's case study illustrated how CRM and GIS complement each other so the rich information from a CRM can be strengthened through knowledge of location, and vice versa.

Geodemographics is a segment of the Marketing Industry defined as analysis of people by the locations in which they live (Sleight, 1997). Geodemographics helps identify market segments and consequently enables the appropriate targeting of markets. If you live in an area, geodemographics assumes you are likely to have the characteristics and behaviors associated with that zone. For instance, if you live in a neighborhood profiled as "Prosperous Empty Nesters," geodemographics assumes you are likely to resemble that profile. Of course, there are errors built into the assumptions, e.g. you might be of the profile "Aspiring Young Family" living in an "Empty Nester" neighborhood. However, geodemographics is willing to tolerate some errors, as long as the neighborhood is correctly assigned for most of the residents.

Geodemographics is significant in size: one study estimated its revenues for 2000 at $300 million (Weiss, 2000). Geodemographics applications in marketing, in addition to segmentation, include survey design, retail planning, direct marketing, advertising, and marketing media analysis (Harris et al., 2004). The advantage of geodemographics is that once the small areas of a region have been characterized into segments, then a person living in a particular small area can be ascribed a set of characteristics without having to tediously research that person's actual characteristics. Some functions of GIS for geodemographics are the following (Harris et al., 2004): (1) connect survey results to general-purpose characteristics of the geographical zones of the region, (2) group the data based on geodemographic zones, (3) perform statistical studies for a larger set of identical geodemographic zones, and (4) visualize the results of geodemographic analysis in maps, charts, and graphs. For instance, for (1), a marketing survey is conducted over a zone of twenty-five ZIP codes to determine the extent of appeal of Magazine X. The appeal can then be compared to the segmentation profiles for the twenty-five zones.

Community Tapestry, a commercial geodemographics product for the United States, has fifty-five segmentation categories (ESRI, 2006). They are grouped into the twelve LifeMode Summary Groups and shown in Table 10.2. Figure 10.5 gives the income ranges for the twelve groups. The income ranges are useful in identifying potential buyers for a product or service. The national distribution of LifeMode categories for the U.S. is mapped in Figure 10.6.

There are dramatic differences between regions. For instance, the High Society LifeMode covers seven categories and is defined as follows: "affluent, well-educated, married-couple homeowners" (ESRI, 2006). It clusters in affluent metropolitan counties nationwide, including ones on the West Coast of San Diego, Santa Barbara, San Francisco and the Silicon Valley, Marin County, Portland, and Seattle. The Coastal Northeast falls into this category, stretching from northern Delaware though Philadelphia, New Jersey, New York City and into Connecticut, Rhode Island up to the Boston Area, as do the major metropolitan areas in the Midwest. Another way to divide up the fifty-five categories is into a dozen Urbanization Summary Groups (ESRI, 2006). The groups fall along an urban-rural range that includes such categories

TABLE 10.2   Community Tapestry Categories, Arranged by LifeMode Groups

High Society
Top Rung
Suburban Splendor
Connoisseurs
Boomburgs
Wealthy Seaboard Suburbs
Sophisticated Squires
Exurbanites

Upscale Avenues
Urban Chic
Pleasant-Ville
Pacific Heights
In Style
Enterprising Professionals
Green Acres

Metropolis
City Lights
Metropolitans
City Strivers
Metro City Edge
Urban Rows
Modest Income Homes

Solo Acts
Laptops and Lattes
Trendsetters
Metro Renters
Old and Newcomers
Young and Restless

Senior Styles
Prosperous Empty Nesters
Silver and Gold
Rustbelt Retirees
Retirement Communities
The Elders

Senior Sun Seekers
Heartland Communities

Scholars and Patriots
Military Proximity
College Towns
Dorms to Diplomas

High Hopes
Aspiring Young Families
Great Expectations

Global Roots
International Marketplace
Industrious Urban Fringe
Urban Melting Pot

Family Portrait
Up and Coming Families
Milk and Cookies
Urban Villages

Traditional Living
Main Street USA
Rustbelt Transitions
Midlife Junction
Family Foundations

Factories and Farms
Salt of the Earth
Prairie Living
Southern Satellites
Home Town
Rural Bypasses

American Quilt
Midland Crowd
Rural Resort Dwellers
Crossroads
Rooted Rural

as principal urban centers, urban outskirts, and small towns. Other companies offer different geodemographic segmentations, such as the seventy-two categories in MapInfo's PSYTE, which are available for 208,000 neighborhoods in the U.S., as well as for Canada (MapInfo, 2006). The PSYTE categories were constructed from block-group level census data through a combination of principal components analysis and cluster analysis (MapInfo, 2006).

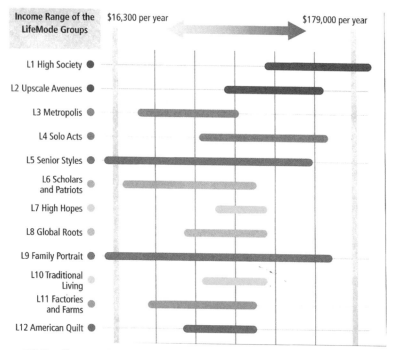

Figure 10.5 Community Tapestry Income Range for LifeMode Groups. Copyright © 2006 ESRI. All rights reserved. Used by permission

A spatial example of applying PSYTE is Ekornes USA, the U.S. subsidiary of furniture manufacturer Ekornes, headquartered in Norway. Ekornes USA had problems in evaluating the performance of its U.S. dealers, since it didn't know the locations of its best potential customers. Using PSTYE, it identified a priority target market segment as follows: "Couples between the ages of 45–65 whose children no longer live at home and who have a median family income of $75,000 and above. They lead an active, affluent lifestyle and vacation often, especially abroad. They go to the theatre and read more than the average person. As an age group, they tend to act and feel as through they are 10 years younger than they are." (MapInfo, 2006). The goal of gaining more prominence with this segment has influenced Ekorne's marketing, advertising, and distribution of resources. Several other geodemographic segmentation products are PRIZM from Claritas and ACORN from CACI.

Geodemographic segmentation can be applied in spatial analysis, including as follows (Harris et al., 2004):

1. Map the most prevalent segment for geographic units such as block groups.
2. Compare the proportions of segments from a small area (say a ZIP code) to the proportions of segments for a larger area (e.g. metropolitan area).

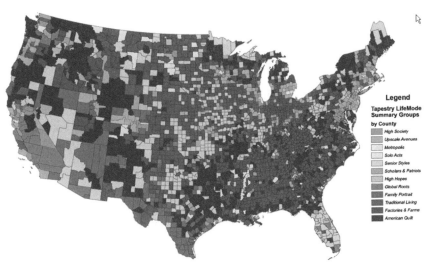

Figure 10.6 Community Tapestry LifeMode Summary Groups by U.S. County. Copyright © 2006 ESRI. All rights reserved. Used by permission

3. Map indices of geodemographic features. For instance, the ratio of a geodemographic feature to the national average can be mapped by county.
4. Correlate a non-segmentation attribute with the proportion in a certain segment group for geographic units. For instance, cell phone calls by census track can be correlated with percent of respondents in the Tapestry category "Upscale Avenues."
5. Statistically analyze a sample of zones that have common geodemographic features.

Geodemographic analysis is a powerful method based on enormous databases and extensive pre-processing to determine the segmentation. However, it needs to be used cautiously, since it's only as accurate and timely as the underlying data used to create it.

A further weakness is that a segmentation is a generalization of a neighborhood population which has considerable variation within it (Harris et al., 2004). There also is the problem in geodemographics of the "ecological fallacy." This refers to analyzing a problem at one geographical level, say census tract, and applying the results and explanations to another geographical level, say county. Geodemographic segments are initially determined for small areas, commonly block groups in the U.S. If the results are applied for larger areas, the ecological fallacy cautions against interpreting and explaining results for them. In spite of these critiques and weaknesses, geodemographics constitutes a large industry subsector and is used extensively by mid- to large-sized companies for target and other marketing decisions.

While target marketing provides improved product adoption for a product or service at a certain time and place, adoption and diffusion theory tracks the adoption and diffusion of a product or service over both time and space. Originally developed by Rogers (1995), this theory postulates that initial adoptions will be slow, then gain momentum quickly as the product diffuses and more and more potential adopters learn and adopt it. Eventually the diffusion will be over and the rate of new adoptions will approach zero. Figure 10.7 plots new adoptions based on an adoption/diffusion process divided into three stages, Stage 1 (lift-off), Stage 2 (rapid increase), and Stage 3 (leveling off). The boxes give the cumulative percentage of adoptions. This process also takes place over space, starting with the location(s) where the product is introduced, and spreading out. Consider a new car model that appears simultaneously at 500 dealerships nationwide. Its adoption/diffusion process can be compared to the Rogers theory (Figure 10.7) and its spatial process studied. Initial buyers are located nearer to the dealerships. As more and more potential buyers hear about the model, more distant buyers will come to the dealerships and some will purchase. Eventually the market will become saturated and the process will level off. This illustrates the process of spatial adoption/diffusion.

To research spatial adoption/diffusion, extensive data must be gathered on the adopters, the elapsed time from product introduction to adoption, and the residential locations for adopters. Data need to be collected at regular intervals, best collected daily or weekly for maximum insight. For example, daily or weekly data is necessary if adoption diffusion takes place over a one-year period. Data for the entire adoption/diffusion process can be analyzed by geocoding the location of the central store and of all potential customers (adopters and non-adopters) in the surrounding areas. Other topographic features can be added as needed such as freeways or rivers, highways, billboard locations, and competing stores.

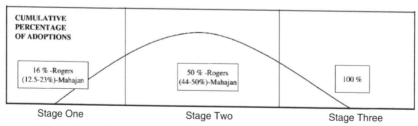

Figure 10.7 Stages in Adoption-Diffusion Theory, Measured by Cumulative Percentage Adoptions. *Source:* This article was published in Journal of Retailing, Vol 79, A.W.Allaway, David Berkowitz, and Giles D'Souza, Spatial Diffusion of a New Loyalty Program through a Retail Market, Pages 137–151, Copyright Elsevier 2003

The information is not easy to collect, as customers may not readily volunteer it, much less over a one year period. However, a firm is able to overcome this by offering premiums or bonuses to customers in exchange for gathering the data.

An example of this is adoption of loyalty cards by a very large retailer in a major U.S. city, which was studied by Allaway et al. (2003, 2005). The retailer made available to the academic researchers a database on nearly 18,000 adopters of loyalty cards, spanning a one-year period following the loyalty card introduction. The researchers expanded the database with further attributes that they calculated, including distances, locations of billboards, and the extent of presence of early adopters in surrounding areas to see their influence on spatial patterns and velocity of adoption (Allaway et al., 2003). Very small geographic units were used, even smaller than the census block group, namely the Neighborhood Information Field (NIF). This is defined as "the geographic area within which a person has a relatively high probability of contacts on a regular basis with other persons living around him or her." The area has a radius of 0.06 mile, and involves only thirteen to seventy-five households (Allaway et al., 2003).

The three adoption stages assumed for the project are the following. Stage 1 is early adoption by a random group of consumers mostly near the center. Stage 2 reflects the spread of adoptions away from the center and the presence of the "neighborhood effect," i.e. groups of new adopters that surround early adopters (Allaway et al., 2003). Stage 3 is called the "saturation stage," and involves the filling in of gaps in the spatial pattern until the diffusion is finished (Allaway et al., 2003). One month after introduction, the spatial diffusion is summarized in Figure 10.8.

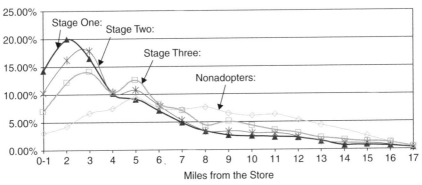

Figure 10.8 Retail Study of Loyalty Card Program—Percentage Distribution of Adopter Groups by Distance from the Central Store. *Source:* This article was published in Journal of Retailing, Vol 79, A.W.Allaway, David Berkowitz, and Giles D'Souza, Spatial Diffusion of a New Loyalty Program through a Retail Market, Pages 137–151, Copyright Elsevier 2003

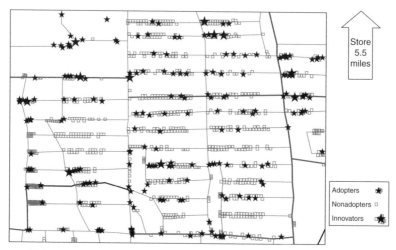

Figure 10.9   Retail Study of Loyalty Card Program—Pattern of Adoption Activity 5.5 Miles from the Central Store. *Source:* This article was published in Journal of Retailing, Vol 79, A.W.Allaway, David Berkowitz, and Giles D'Souza, Spatial Diffusion of a New Loyalty Program through a Retail Market, Pages 137–151, Copyright Elsevier 2003

It's clear that there was considerable range in the distribution of all the adopter groups, with successive stages distributed farther from the center. The non-adopters were the most spread out from the center of all the adopter groups, with 5 percent still present 12 miles away from the center.

Using maps based on this model, it was possible to study the effect of billboards, positioned at 2.6, 2.8, and 2.9 miles from the center. A positive "billboard effect" was present based on differences between adopters and non-adopters in the vicinity of the billboards (Allaway et al., 2003, 2005). Given the small size of the NIFs, it was possible to study the spatial patterns of adoption within NIFs, and clusters of adoption were apparent around the earliest adopters, called Innovators. "At every distance from the store, a much higher percentage of Stage 2 and 3 adopters had Stage 1 adopters within their NIFs than for non-adopters" (Allaway et al., 2003). Figure 10.9 is an example of the spatial pattern of adoption activity 5.5 miles from the central store. It is evident that the Innovators (Stage 1 adopters) tend to have a grouping of Stage 2 and 3 adopters closely surrounding them.

In short, this retail example of spatial adoption/diffusion shows how cumulative daily customer data on a new product can be modeled in space based on stages of adoption/diffusion. The model provides insight into spatial diffusion in different adoption stages, the influence of the earliest Innovators, and the importance of modeling physical advertising, in the form of billboards. The approach requires a lot of data and a sophisticated model, but pays off in the deep insights into micro changes in adopter and advertising roles in spatial diffusion.

The Marketing/Geodemographics industry sector has a powerful range of tools available for spatial marketing analyses. The approach taken depends on the availability of data and the constraints on the amount of time and resources that can be spent in developing models. Another challenge is to educate executives about how to interpret the sometimes complex outputs.

In the U.S. there is wide availability of demographic data at no cost for geodemographics and other marketing techniques that incorporate GIS. The U.S. Census collects large amounts of data through the decennial census held every 10 years. Hundreds of demographic, social, and economic attributes are available for individuals and households. The data are available for many geographical units including counties, metropolitan areas, cities, tracts, and block groups, i.e. small areas of about 1,500 people.

Updated socio-demographic data are now also available on an annual basis from the Census's American Community Survey, a large three-year, rolling national survey, and those data in 2010 will be available down to the census tract level. All these data and much more including specialized surveys are available for free and largely web-accessible from the Census website (www.census.gov). The website even provides web mapping for selected characteristics. Few other nations have this quantity and ease of access, but many other countries provide substantial demographic data, especially at census times, although often with costs. In all, marketers in countries with modern censuses and policies of open access can usually find the data they need for the variety of GIS-based marketing applications discussed.

BANKING AND FINANCE

Summary: The major spatial applications are:
Site selection and market planning
Facility property management
Branch and ATM network planning
Regulatory compliance

Geography matters for the Banking and Finance Industry in tracking and locating customers, facilities, and financial assets. Even in the era of the web and mobile technologies, physical sites remain crucial in developing the personal relationships that have characterized success in this industry. The case study example of the Large Personal/Corporate Bank (LPCB) in Chapter 3 illustrated how a rapidly expanding bank in the Northeast of the U.S. utilized GIS for decision support in planning new branch locations. Banking and finance also have to meet regulatory requirements with locational provisions, for example regulation of lending to poorer and minority customers.

In site selection, GIS can model the often complex branch account structures and the distribution of branch services (ESRI, 2006). GIS can identify areas that are underperforming in sales, or missing potentially high-value customers. Spatial models can include transport times and distances, obstacles such as rivers or mountains, competitor locations, and proximity to urban amenities that attract customers. Markets surrounding branch or ATM sites can be assessed and modeled using trade-area techniques. The relationship of multi-channeling and the branch network can be spatially studied.

An example is the Altura Credit Union, a small but fast-growing credit union in Riverside, California, with 106,000 members and $750 million in assets. Credit unions are open to certain allowable members, in this case to a person who lives, works, attends school, or worships in Riverside and San Diego Counties and parts of two others (Khan and Lackow,). The bank partnered with an outside banking consultant to build a GIS to analyze the potential of prospective sites. In a branch study in 2005, the spatial analysis pointed to three prospective sites for new branches, two in Temecula and one in Murietta Hot Springs in southwestern Riverside County (Khan and Lackow, 2006). An initial mapping of existing sites was achieved by mapping a combination of population and geodemographic data available in ESRI's Business Analyst Online. Competitor information was then added using commercially available branch information on competitors' branches (Khan and Lackow,).

Next, maps and reports were produced on the three prospective sites. For instance, the map seen in Figure 10.10 shows estimated market potential levels for the three potential branches with thematic shadings ranging from white (very low) to black (very high). It is overlaid with the competitor locations shown as circles, with radii proportional to the amount of deposits. Squares showing competing credit union locations are all of the same size, since deposit information was not available. This map was one of several that Altura used to narrow the potential new sites to three: Murieta Hot Springs, Temecula/79, and Temecula/Ynez.

Although the GIS analysis indicated one of the Temecula sites was the most favorable based on marketing-potential level, Altura ended up deciding to locate the new branch at the Murieta location due to short-term real estate considerations. However, at the same time, management planned to open the GIS-favored Temecula/79 site a year later (Khan and Lackow,). This case of a small credit union demonstrates how GIS can assist in site decision making through market and competitor analysis, even though in this particular instance the final choice was based on managers' gut experience and the existing real estate opportunities on the ground.

CASE STUDY OF LARGE CREDIT BANK

Large Credit Bank (LCB) is one of the largest credit card banks in the U.S., with over $50 billion in deposits. It has not had branches until recently when

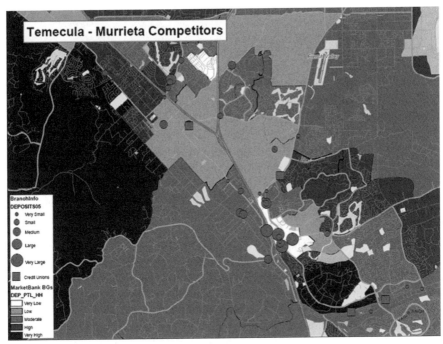

Figure 10.10   Altura Credit Union—Market Potential and Competitor Analysis for Three Prospective Branch Sites in Temecula and Murrieta Hot Springs, California. *Source:* Khan and Lachow,

it acquired two consumer banks in the South that utilize GIS for their branch networks. LCB has depended for its IT on legacy mainframe systems. LCB's GIS is outsourced to a small outside GIS consulting firm. The bank's primary use of GIS is to map internal data for existing bank sites including customer and competitor locations. Although demographic data are available, they are not included in the siting maps. Locational mapping falls very short of its potential to integrate internal and geodemographic data to study existing and future sites relative to trade areas, competition, topography, and transportation.

The firm's IT group is not accepting of GIS, making it even more difficult to implement. A glimmer of hope comes from the newly acquired banks, which already have GIS and are pushing for more of the technology. Due to resistance to change, GIS is not regarded as strategic, but rather is relegated to minor and simple locational studies. This case highlights organizational resistance to technological change. It also illustrates how acquisition by a larger bank of more technologically advanced consumer banks can potentially stimulate openness to contemporary spatial approaches.

AGRICULTURE

Summary: The major spatial applications are:
Precision agriculture
Planning and management of crops on farms
Monitoring of livestock
Epidemiological analysis

Spatial systems are utilized in Agriculture for management, planning, precision treatment of fields, livestock monitoring, and epidemiological analysis. They improve agricultural efficiency and productivity, allow better controls, and track disease. The technologies impact stakeholders, including farmers, agribusiness managers, government agencies, and regulatory authorities, and investors.

Precision agriculture is the use of agricultural methods, treatments, and information to farm micro sections of fields. The concept is to provide specialized treatments to areas in the range of several meters square. This is possible by sampling information for the tiny areas through sensors, yield monitors, and remote sensing, utilizing large-scale digitized federal soil maps and recording the precise locations through GPS. The model for precision agriculture seen in Figure 10.11 starts with the input data from these sources, which are stored in a GIS. The GIS processes them to plan out the management zones. In other words, the micro-plot information allows the farmer to divide the field into smaller sections based on differences in soil, plantings, and micro-climate in order to apply the optimal micro-treatments. The GIS also provides decision support regarding daily field treatments, and longer-term field management. GIS can help optimize the farmer's daily tractor routes that provide the micro-treatments and can model monthly or yearly yield trends for micro sections of the field. Mobile devices such as the ruggedized, in-cab computer for a tractor or sprayer seen in Figure 10.12 provides the graphical display, mapping, application coverage logging, and record keeping for an automated steering system used for precision agriculture.

More specifically, field-oriented steps and tools that can be applied for spatially-enabled farming include:

- *Equipment guidance.* A farmer can utilize NavStar-like equipment to support accurate routing in fields. This equipment is referenced by GPS and/or an inertial guidance system (Ping et al., 2004), and has guidance software that allows it to minimize fuel, labor, and maintenance costs (Adrian et al., 2005). For instance, in treating a field, the equipment can reduce criss-crossing the same area or avert not covering a zone. Further, it can lower environmental damages from pesticides and herbicides.
- *Auto-steer system.* It is a combination of a computer in the vehicle with GIS software, a device that gives direction indication to the driver known

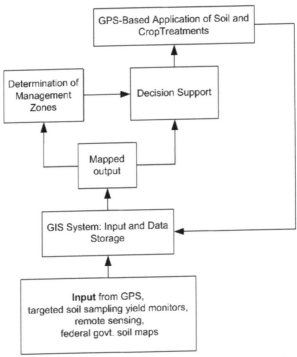

Figure 10.11   Model of GIS in Precision Agriculture. *Source:* Adrian et al. (2005). Copyright 2005, IGI Global, www.igi-pub.com, reprinted by permission of the publisher

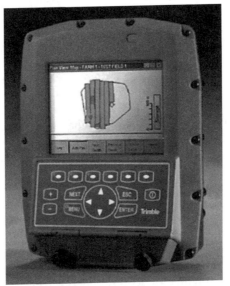

Figure 10.12   Agricultural Computer for Field Operations and Decision-Making (Trimble Ruggedized AgGPS 170). *Source:* Trimble, 2006

as a lightbar, and ground-referenced GPS that allows centimeter accuracy. The auto-steering gives guidance accuracy to within two inches of a location for planting and irrigation, lowering cost.

- *Yield monitor.* A yield monitor on a harvester or crop picker indicates the volume of crops harvested, keyed to GPS readings and to sensor readings on elevation and climate (Adrian, 2005).
- *Soil sampling.* The soil conditions on a micro basis profoundly influence agricultural productivity. Soil samples can be taken meter by meter. Sometimes soil sampling divides the field by square grids or by zones based on federal soil maps (Adrian et al., 2005). Based on soil and other factors, precision agriculture is able to apply water and fertilizer with meter accuracy (Ping et al., 2004).
- *Remote sensing.* Remote sensing by satellite or airborne sensors provides information on soil moisture content, organic matter, and an estimate of plant health (Adrian et al., 2005). Although the method is expensive, can be deterred by clouds, and requires careful overlaying at meter accuracy, it can cover large areas and is amenable to longitudinal comparison (Adrian et al., 2005). The remote-sensed images are sometimes useful to recognize areas with plant disease and insect damage (Ping, 2004). As remote sensing is a relatively new approach, training is essential.

The planning and management of fields and crops are helped by consolidation of the rich database collected. Using decision support systems and expert systems, a longer-term production plan can be developed. For example, a year of production data at micro-level accuracy can be used to plan the next year's production (Ping, 2004).

An example is Cargill's Palm Oil operations in Hawaii, formerly Pacific Rim Palm Oil Ltd. (MapInfo, 2005; Cargill, 2006). The unit uses an integrated agronomy management information system, to analyze agricultural data on the plantations over time and space, covering "yield, leaf analysis, soil analysis, environment, climate, pest and disease, and palm census" (MapInfo, 2005). Map displays show the results of models that track crop production and other performance indicators. Satellite images are overlaid on attribute maps to provide highly accurate physical features. The managers consider the spatial application user-friendly. The benefits are higher palm oil production, better management of crops, and mitigation of environmental damages (MapInfo, 2005).

A different kind of spatial application involves livestock. Diseases in livestock can be monitored through use of RFID equipment (Stewart, 2005). This is important in controlling the spread of livestock-carried illnesses. Obstacles include inaccurate reading of RFID sensors attached to very large livestock such as cattle, and fragility of RFID readers in the context of cattle and other livestock handling. The coordination of disease outbreaks, done jointly between private companies and the government, is advanced by the detailed inventory and GIS tracking that RFID makes possible.

In sum, spatial technologies are useful in agriculture as they monitor and treat agricultural events on the ground, assist in managing and planning farm production, and track and mitigate disease.

HEALTH CARE

Summary: The major spatial applications are:

Siting, access, catchments

Facilities management, bed control

Epidemiology and disease management

Health emergency services

Marketing

Forecasting

The Health Care industry has many locational applications. Health Care is a large economic sector that comprises a mixture of intertwined public, private, and nonprofit organizations. The industry can be viewed as a value chain that starts with manufacturing, including pharmaceutical, hospital supply, and hospital construction; progresses to intermediaries such as equipment distributors and pharmaceutical warehouses; and ends up with service providers such as hospital chains, pharmacy chains, managed care facilities, and elder care communities. Many general services are provided to the value chain, such as market consultants and lending institutions. Baystate Health, covered in Chapter 2, is a for-profit health-care network that applies GIS to emergency planning, epidemiology, routing, marketing, facilities planning, emergency services, and surgery. Baystate's GIS champion, a surgeon, gave emphasis to its medical and health benefits. Other health-care enterprises have spatial applications more weighted towards the operational and business aspects, as in the Kaiser Permanente case.

A common spatial application in health care is to determine siting, access, and catchment areas. GIS analyzes the siting of hospitals, clinics, physicians, patients, equipment, and members of networks. This can be performed based on methods to identify trade areas, including the Huff model covered in Chapter 9. Analysis can show the best locations with respect to accessibility, demographics, and avoidance of cannibalization (Thrall, 2000).

For instance, Jewish Hospital and St. Mary's HealthCare Services (JHSMHS) is the service wing of a regional health-care network of 70 health care facilities and 1,900 patient beds in Kentucky and Southern Indiana

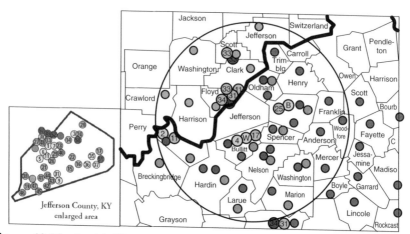

Figure 10.13   Jewish Hospital and St. Mary's HealthCare Locations. The map shows county names and an inset for Jefferson County that includes Louisville, Kentucky. *Source:* JHSMHS Website, 2006

(JHSMHS, 2006). JHSMHS serves the health-care locations with 24-hour treatment services for specialized rehabilitation and preventative health-care programs such as employee alcohol and drug screenings. The spatial challenge for JHSMHS was to analyze where patients and employers were located relative to JHSMHS facilities. Maps were developed to show the health centers, service catchment areas, and patient locations. Figure 10.13 shows JHSMHS facilities including the major hospitals at Louisville along the Ohio River in northwest Jefferson County and others in a fifty mile circle around Jefferson County encompassing 40 other Kentucky and Indiana counties. The numbered symbols represent hospitals, medical centers, rehab facilities, and clinics, while the unnumbered ones are home care facilities and service areas. Location analysts can use the GIS system to recommend new locations that have a sufficient patient base and yet do not cannibalize the patient base of existing sites (Lang, 2006). Examining the number and location of employers in that service area is also useful for understanding the typical type of injuries.

GIS helps in managing facilities. The layout of hospitals and medical centers can be visualized and modeled. In hospital bed tracking, since beds are often difficult to locate and also expensive, costs can be reduced through a GIS that can model the bed occupancy over time to identify more efficient bed locations and groupings for certain patients. For example, MapGistics is a small company that provides bed management consulting. Its "Enterprise Bed Management System" product mimics the whiteboards that nurses use on floor stations to designate patient locations. Using GIS it is able to provide maps of hospital floor plans showing bed occupancies A benefit of more accurate bed management is that discharge times are more accurately known, and their sub-steps can be better planned. As a result, discharge takes about half the time it did prior to automating bed management.

In epidemiology, maps are utilized to track and monitor disease spread, and better understand the causes of diseases. Point maps show the locations of patients with particular illnesses. The amount of clustering or separation of ill patients helps to diagnose cause and determine where treatments are working. Since certain illnesses are more likely in susceptible environments GIS can map those locations (Thrall, 2000). For certain infectious diseases, crowded and high-density urban places stimulate communicability. Maps can indicate areas of high risk (Thrall, 2000).

When health emergencies occur involving transportation, spatial technologies are significant in real-time tracking, communications, and planning. The reader is referred to the Transportation section of Chapter 9, on spatial tools in emergency transportation. In emergency health care transport speed and accuracy of routing are essential and even a matter of life and death. Optimized route management software complement real-time databases indicating the patient's condition and the availability of medical services at different destination locations.

Marketing permeates many health-care organizations. Spatially-enabled marketing tools described earlier in the chapter under Marketing/Geodemographics can provide more effective marketing to targeted markets. For instance, a managed care company can market its membership benefits by targeting its advertising to small areas dominated by certain geodemographic segments.

An example of GIS-enabled marketing is Health Products Research Inc., a division of Ventiv Health Inc. (Lang, 2000). The firm offers a model that predicts how many physician visits are necessary by a field representative, in order to achieve cost-efficiency. It is based on data on all prescriptions written by U.S. physicians in the last two years. This model of sales potential for physician prescription writing on a national basis is used by drug company sales reps. The maps guide sales campaigns and show geographical areas in the U.S. with deficits in detailed prescription-writing and opportunities on a cost-benefit basis (Lang, 2000).

SPATIAL TECHNOLOGIES AND OUTSOURCING

Outsourcing of information technology is a major factor in business today (Willcocks and Lacity, 1998; Lacity and Willcocks, 2001). There has been enormous growth in IT outsourcing worldwide. The total size of IT outsourcing in 2007 is estimated by Gartner Inc. at $236 billion with a compound growth rate from 2002 to 2007 of 7.8 percent (Caldwell et al., 2004). By dollar value, the segments of outsourcing in 2007 are data center (39 percent), network (28 percent), enterprise applications (21 percent), and desktop (12 percent) (Caldwell et al., 2004). GIS outsourcing is a growing part of IT outsourcing (Daratech, 2005). Its growth is changing the way companies organize, staff, and conduct spatial projects. This section looks at key factors in IT outsourcing that also apply to GIS outsourcing, and presents a short case study of outsourcing for a U.S. utility firm to an offshore outsourcing provider.

Outsourcing is defined for GIS as the provision to an outside party of the management of GIS activities, resources, and assets, in order to achieve a result required by the requesting firm. A similar definition applies for IT outsourcing by substituting "IT" for "GIS" (Willcocks and Lacity, 1998). Outsourcing involves the contracting of the GIS responsibility, either on a project-by-project basis or in a long-term relationship as a preferred contractor. Outsourcing is different than hiring temporary personnel or having a regular firm that provides contract programmers on call. Contracting firms provide contract employees that work in-house and report to in-house managers, but the contracting firms do not take outside responsibility for managing projects and functions (Willcocks and Lacity, 1998). Instead the firm that hires the contract employees maintains the management responsibility.

Why do organizations undertake outsourcing? One study indicates four underlying reasons: (1) cost reduction and containment, (2) organizational restructuring, (3) management desire to rid the firm of direct management of a "troublesome" and unprofitable part of the business, and (4) conformity to industry trends i.e. do what others are doing (Willcocks and Lacity, 1998; Earl and Feeny, 1994).

IT outsourcing varies along two dimensions: local versus global, total versus selective. Local outsourcing is a service in the local area. Since there is potential for closer physical interactions, it often suits the needs of smaller firms. Global outsourcing applies to larger firms. One study of large organizations indicated that the proportion of outsourcing transactions for local, regional, and global was 60, 15, and 25 percent respectively, while by average outsourcing transaction size was biggest for regional ($378 million), followed by global ($210 million) and local ($136 million) (Everest Research Institute, 2004). Thus the proportion of transactions locally would be much higher for small firms that outsource some of their work

A firm can contract their outsourcing totally to a provider, in which case they only retain management oversight. Alternatively a firm can contract selectively with the provider, retaining some aspects internally. Selective outsourcing has been shown to be the most common approach for IT (Lacity, Willcocks, and Feeny, 1995). Another study found that short-term selective outsourcing is a very successful approach, and is preferred to long-term arrangements (Lacity, Willcocks, and Feeny, 1995). Multi-sourcing, i.e. selective outsourcing to multiple providers that work together (Cross, 1995), has become somewhat common for large companies. It involves a trade-off between the risk of escalating prices relying on a single provider versus the expanded coordination cost of utilizing multiple providers (Cross, 1995).

Multi-sourcing sometimes involves outsourcing IT to one vendor and GIS to another. In sum, IT outsourcing is large and growing in business. It can be done through varied arrangements, time periods, and proximities of the provider. A key issue is the cost and sometimes the bother of having IT in-house versus the coordination costs and loss of control of having it outside.

In GIS, there are many outsourcing services, of varied types. Some offshore providers in GIS offer the lowest cost. However, given the complexity of GIS, client companies often will not opt for the lowest cost but seek the data quality, accuracy, experience, and capabilities to handle complex projects (Daratech, 2005). Utilities have tended to outsource non-core GIS applications (GeoWorld, 2004). The arrangements vary from total to selective outsourcing of non-core GIS, with most core GIS work done in-house. Some utilities allow the outsourcer to perform some of the IT processing and upload the results into special web portals for the utility's asset management and work management systems (GeoWorld, 2004).

As discussed in Chapter 6, LCB and Kaisen among the book's cases outsourced GIS significantly but not completely, while Sears & GIO had limited selective outsourcing. The case experiences with it were generally positive.

Another example of GIS outsourcing is Southern California Edison (SCE). The provider Patni is based in India and has over 15,000 employees (Dighe, 2005). Patni has 300 people on its GIS team in India, who support the leading GIS software packages. These employees receive GIS training from ESRI India or in-house. SCE uses ESRI software and a utility-specific commercial package.

Although usually Patni has allocated far more of its GIS people in India than in the U.S., the SCE contract specified that there would be a dozen Patni people assigned to SCE facilities in the U.S. and only five in India. The Patni people at SCE have the identical GIS software, interfaces, and data as the Patni staff in India, so groups can communicate better during projects. Also, Patni in California can work in the middle of the day, while Patni in India is asleep, so work occurs at all hours. Patni had to learn about some business practices culturally different from India such as who participates and speaks up at meetings and where authority rests. Lower-level projects such as data conversion and GIS software maintenance can take advantage of a much larger and less expensive pool of GIS talent in India, while SCE employees can focus on planning and high-level design. In sum, GIS outsourcing at SCE is working. Patni communicates well with SCE and responds to cultural differences.

KAISER PERMANENTE

Kaiser Permanente is a non-profit and one of the largest health-care organizations in the U.S. Founded in 1945, it has approximately 12,000 physicians, 431 medical offices, and thirty medical centers. Its 8.4 million members who enroll voluntarily are mostly located in California, but some are in eight other states. It emphasizes cost-effective integrated health care.

GIS is utilized in travel-time analysis, site selection, long-term forecasts, regulatory information, in-house reference maps, spatial websites to serve members, support for an ambulance service, sales and marketing, and finance/accounting.

Most Kaiser members live in urban areas with potentially high levels of traffic congestion. To gauge access to medical services, members need to know the travel times to Kaiser offices and centers. The travel-time spatial application computes rush-hour travel times for specific types of services in urban areas. For instance, the estimated travel time to access end-stage renal disease treatment sites are available for parts of San Francisco's East Bay (Figure 10.14). ESRD (End State Renal Disease) sites are shown, as well as MOB (Medical Office Buildings) and hospitals. Although most of this area is well covered, some hilly areas in the middle of this figure have 30+-minute drive times, which can present problems for patients with kidney failure.

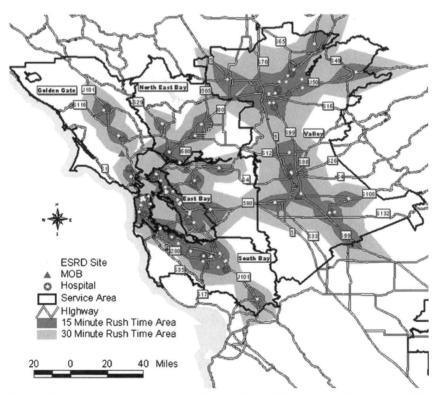

Figure 10.14   Kaiser Permanente Estimated Travel Times to End Stage Renal Disease Treatment Sites, 2005. *Source:* Schoenhaut, 2005

This travel-time application was developed over many years through a combination of in-house design and outside consultants. In other words, some of its development was outsourced. For instance, GIS consultants in Oakland, California, Hammond, Jenson, and Wallen, developed a minimum-travel-time matrix. Another outside group from Cal Trans drove the routes to determine travel times. Recently consultants from the Berkeley Institute of Transportation Studies have focused on design of a network of detectors to measure vehicle speeds. Based on the data purchased from TeleAtlas, the travel-time applications give travel speeds for the morning and afternoon rush hours. The approach was selective outsourcing, combining some tasks better done in-house with others better outsourced.

Site selection is analysis of areas to arrive at the best locations for services. The goal is to maximize the number of members with access. For instance, in northern California Kaiser conducted a Radiation Therapy study using location-allocation modeling that identified the fifteen best radiation therapy sites from over forty potential sites (Schonhaut, 2005).

Fifteen-year forecasts are performed for medical services and membership at the ZIP-code level. For instance, the map of Kaiser Permanente's forecasted member densities can be overlaid on the Kaiser facilities and current service areas (Figure 10.15). These studies help middle managers and executives strategize future growth.

Kaiser's spatial web applications consist of an intranet-based library of several hundred reference maps that are widely accessible by employees across the Kaiser system. The GIS team has developed limited web services for members, including access maps. Mapping is done of ambulance pick-ups for all of the Kaiser emergency cases in San Francisco that are sent to non-Kaiser hospitals. In San Francisco, regulatory restrictions on Kaiser force members to seek services out-of-network. As some patients visit non-Kaiser emergency rooms this system allows patients to be tracked and their records be retained in the Kaiser database.

CHAPTER SUMMARY

This chapter continued the previous chapter's focus on industry differences and organizational aspects, presented five additional industries which are classified as less mature in GIS than those covered in Chapter 9, and discussed GIS outsourcing. Each industry has critical specialty areas—for example, climate/disaster management for insurance, segmentation for marketing/demographics, branch and facilities locations for banking, precision agriculture, and travel time analysis for health-care companies. Banking is illustrated with the LCB Case Study, while health care services is exemplified by the Kaiser Permanente case. While GIS outsourcing provides the benefits

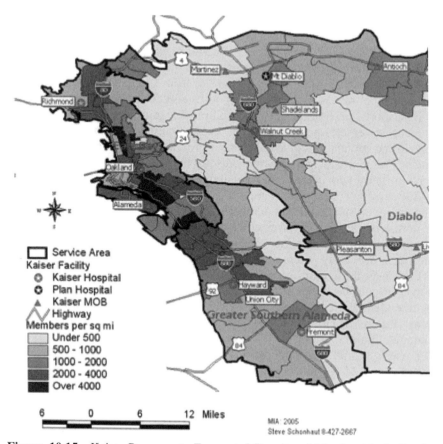

Figure 10.15 Kaiser Permanente Forecasted Density of Membership in Service Areas of East Bay, Greater Southern Alameda, and Part of Diablo, 2005. *Source:* Schoenhaut, 2005

of lower cost and larger pools of specialized talent, there are weaknesses in increased coordination costs, communication problems, and loss of control.

REFERENCES

Adrian, Anne Mims, Chris Dillard, and Paul Mask. 2005. "GIS in Agriculture." In Pick, James B. (Ed.), *Geographic Information Systems in Business*, pp. 324–342.

Allaway, Arthur W., David Berkowitz, and Giles D'Souza. 2003. "Spatial Diffusion of a New Loyalty Program through a Retail Market." *Journal of Retailing*, 79: 137–151.

Allaway, Arthur W., Lisa D. Murphy, and David K. Berkowitz. 2005. "The Geographical Edge: Spatial Analysis of Retail Loyalty Program Adoption." In Pick,

James B. (Ed.), *Geographic Information Systems in Business*, Hershey, PA: Idea Group Publishing, pp. 260–277.

Anselin, Luc, Raymond JGM Florax, and Sergio J. Ray (Eds.). 2004. *Advances in Spatial Econometrics: Methodology, Tools, and Applications*. New York: Springer.

Bedell, Craig. 2006. "Location Technology Directs Insurers To Greater Efficiency, Higher Profitability." *National Underwriter Property and Casualty*, January 20.

Bourgault, Steve. 2005. "Target Marketing and the Spatial Advantage." *MapInfo Magazine*, 9(1): 18–30.

Cross, J. 1995. "It Outsourcing: BP's Competitive Approach." *Harvard Business Review*, 73(3): 94–104.

Earl, M., and D. Feeny. 1996. "Is Your CIO Adding Value?" *Sloan Management Review*, 37(3): 26–32.

ESRI. 2006. "Insurance Overview." Redlands, CA: ESRI Inc.

Foust, Brady. 2006. "Integrated Enterprise Geo-Spatial Technology—Insurance Risk Examples." *Directions Magazine*, January 27. Available at www.directionsmag .com.

Harris, Richard, Peter Sleight, and Richard Webber. 2005. *Geodemographics, GIS, and Neighborhood Targeting*. Hoboken, NJ: John Wiley and Sons.

Khan, Adam, and Steve Lackow. 2006. "Case Study: Developing Market Intelligence in Very High Growth Areas." Proceedings of ESRI User Conference, Redlands, CA: ESRI Inc.

Lacity, Mary C., and Leslie P. Willcocks. 2001. *Global Information Technology Outsourcing: In Search of Business Advantage*. Chicester, England: John Wiley and Sons.

Lang, Laura. 2000. *GIS for Health Organizations*. Redlands, CA: ESRI Press.

MapInfo Magazine. 2006. "Alliance Story: Siebel Systems and MapInfo Combine to Offer Insurance Solution." *MapInfo Magazine*, pp. 9–12.

MapInfo Magazine. 2006. "Florida Farm Insurance Case Study." Troy, NY: MapInfo Corporation. Available at www.mapinfo.com, September 1.

MapInfo Magazine. 2006. "RVOS Insurance Case Study." Troy, NY: MapInfo Corporation. Available at www.mapinfo.com, September 1.

Morton, Kimberly. 2002. "Insurance: Leveraging Location is Core to Managing Risk." *MapInfo Magazine*, **7**(2): 3–11.

Ping, Wang, Xiang-nan Liu, and Fang Huang. 2004. "Research on Mobile Mapping System and Its Application in Precision Agriculture." Map Asia 2004 Conference Proceedings, Beijing, China: GISdevelopment.net.

Rogers, E.M. 1995. *Diffusion of Innovations*. 4th Edition. New York: Free Press.

Sleight, Peter. 2004. "Targeting Customers: How to Use Geodemographic and Lifestyle Data in Your Business." Henley-on-Thames, UK: World Advertising Research.

Steward, May Ann. " Tracking Cattle in the Heartland." *Geospatial Solutions*, 15(9): 20–25.

Swinton, S.M., and J. Lowenberg-DeBoer. 1998. "Evaluating the Profitability of Site-specific Farming." *Journal of Production Agriculture*, 11(4): 439–446.

Thompson, Paul. 2005. "Closing the Loop Between Real Estate and Marketing." *MapInfo Magazine*, 9(1).

Thrall, Grant Ian. 2000. "The Future of GIS in Public Health Management and Practice." *Geospatial Solutions*, September, pp. 2–7.

Villalon, Maria. 1999. "GIS and the Internet: Tools that Add Value to Your Health Plan." *Health Management Technology*, 20(9): 16–8.

Weiss, M. 2000. *The Clustered World*. New York: Little Brown.

Willcocks, Leslie P., and Mary C. Lacity. 1998. *Strategic Sourcing of Information Systems*. Chicester, England: John Wiley and Sons.

CHAPTER 11

ETHICAL, LEGAL, AND SECURITY ISSUES OF SPATIAL TECHNOLOGIES

INTRODUCTION

GIS and spatial technologies have provided remarkable monetary and other benefits to organizations in the case studies in this book. At the same time, GIS has sometimes failed from a financial standpoint to the detriment of businesses, investors, and customers. This chapter reaches beyond business benefits and costs, and considers ethical and legal questions involving these technologies. Consider for example geodemographics from Chapter 10. The technique provides information profiles about small neighborhoods and areas. In doing so, it averages the information into a common profile. There may be people living in a neighborhood who are different from the profile of say "Connoisseurs" or "The Elders," to use categories from ESRI's Community Tapestry segments, and they may be at times misrepresented by being merged into a profile. There is an ethical issue in how far geodemographics should be pushed by companies in marketing, telemarketing, advertising, credit, and financing. After a brief general background on GIS ethics, the first section considers examples of ethical dilemmas. The goal is not to prescribe behavior or business policy, but to raise awareness of ethical issues.

Privacy is the right to be left alone, in the absence of reasonable grounds for interference. Such grounds might be illegal activity or instances where a normal person would not expect privacy. One of the best examples is one's home, which in some countries including the U.S. is constitutionally assured of

Geo-Business: GIS in the Digital Organization, By James B. Pick
Copyright © 2007 John Wiley & Sons, Inc.

privacy rights. Since GIS and spatial technologies pinpoint locations, sense the environment, and record movement of people and objects, they can challenge individual privacy. In a broader context, major changes in spatial technologies have changed the entire notion of privacy, eventually leading to altered legal interpretations of it. The privacy section begins with a short background and proceeds to spatial examples, where privacy is threatened.

The law has long recognized concepts of place and space, way prior to the advent of commercial GIS in the 1960s. Today, traditional legal concepts are challenged by GPS, RFID, sensors, satellite imagery, and GIS. This is analogous to the changes in criminal law that resulted from widespread laboratory capability to analyze DNA in legal evidence. After presenting a short background on law, the section proceeds to examine some examples with particular emphasis on legal and ethical controversies involving geosurveillance, i.e. satellite or airborne imagery, and how some of them have been resolved. Law for GIS and spatial technologies is evolving, and many more legal issues will appear as these technologies become more prevalent.

The chapter case study examines a well-known legal case of geosurveillance, Kyllo v. United States 533 U.S. 27 (2001). It involved an illicit small business where the legal basis of geosurveillance detection was challenged in a series of court decisions.

The last part of the chapter considers security issues of spatial technologies. How can organizations assess their GIS and spatial security problems and set up means to reduce security threats? This chapter raises issues, many of them important to businesses with spatial systems and products, but is usually not able to definitively answer them. The goal of the chapter is to encourage awareness of these issues among concerned people in businesses and organizations, and the stakeholder community.

ETHICAL ISSUES

Ethical concepts and theories are useful as background to the practical examples to follow. Only three categories of theories are briefly mentioned here: (1) ethical relativism, (2) utilitarianism, and (3) deontological theories. Other ethical theories and theoretical background (Johnson, 2001) are beyond the scope of this book.

Ethical relativism is based on the assumption that ethics is relative. In one's society, there are no universal rights and wrongs, nor are there universal moral norms. Thus two people may differ in their ethical views, and both views can be considered valid. Although open to diversity of viewpoints, ethnical relativism has a number of problems including that the theory has limited logical arguments to justify it. Another problem with this theory is that there cannot be prescriptive claims, i.e. "you ought to do this." Since cultures simulate relativistic differences it is hard to apply it across cultures.

Relativism relates to GIS and spatial technologies by supporting differences of opinions, but leaving the differences unresolved. For the fast-moving spatial technologies, relativism may be applicable, since settling on fixed ethical rules may not be durable if the environments are turned upside down by new innovations. On the other hand, the fixed rules might be interpreted or applied differently in a new technological context.

Utilitarianism determines right and wrong depending on the consequences (Johnson, 2001). Behavior and actions are good, if they imply that happiness dominates in the consequences. This can apply to the choices that have been often made, for example, between paper mapping and GIS. Utilitarianism can justify choice of GIS over mapping, arguing that GIS leads to greater happiness. Since spatial technologies often have many stakeholders (users, managers, investors, vendors, customers), it may be a complex challenge, in a spatial decision, to determine what leads to greater happiness and for whom. Utilitarianism results in more consistent rules than relativism, and holds together better across cultures.

Deontological theories emphasize the inherent character of an act. A person who adheres to these theories has a sense of "duty." By contrast to relativism and utilitarianism, these theories support that some actions are always right or always wrong, even if the cost/benefit ratio is not favorable to an individual, business, organization, or society. An important tenet of deontological theories is that humans have the rational capacity to think and decide, in weighing ethical choices. Although there may be decision-making that identifies a phenomenon as a means to an end, that's not the sole basis of the decision, but other rational thinking must go into it.

Deontologists would indicate that happiness is not the highest good for people. Rather the highest good relates to rules, moral principles, and laws (Johnson, 2001). Deontological theories give value and respect to other humans, who are trying to rationally decide on ethical problems.

This class of theories also applies to ethical issues of spatial technologies. An example would be for a delivery firm to not just base the decision to adopt GPS devices for its entire fleet on the means to the ends of greater efficiency and more profits, but to consider the rational moral principles. Is it morally right for a driver's location every minute during his work career to be recorded? GIS codes of ethics that have been brought forward in the GIS profession based on deontological theories are discussed later.

The final ethical concept to introduce is that of *dialectic*. An ethical dialectic is the process of moving back and forth between theory and practice. The process is a slow one, that may involve slight changes, but cumulatively it leads to better ethical justifications. An example from the GIS field is the ethical issue of the piracy of GIS software. The initial concept (deontological) might say it's never morally right. However, what about in an earthquake or disaster, when more copies may need to be made very quickly to save lives. The dialectic would allow the change in practice of copying to move back to theory for possible modification.

A wide range of ethical dilemmas and issues regarding GIS and spatial technology apply to businesses and their stakeholders. In this section some will be mentioned, followed by deeper discussion of RFID devices. Among the issues are the following:

(1) The ethical question of what map accuracy is best for the customer. This has been a controversy between surveyors and GIS professionals. Some sub-industries and professions demand high positional accuracy, including commercial real estate, architecture, land development, and civil engineering. Both surveyors and GIS analysts have certain competencies in map accuracy, but they compose and produce maps through quite different procedures (Butler, 2005). Map accuracy in fact involves three concepts: (a) accuracy, i.e. how close a mapped observation is to true position, (b) precision, i.e. can the locational measurement be repeated, and (c) resolution, i.e. how close together do two observations need to be before they merge as one (Butler, 2001). Both surveyors and GIS professional strive for all three, but they use different methods. There is the ethical question of whether professional "territory" is more important or providing the highest type of accuracy to solve the customer's problem.

The ethical issue is whether to fully disclose these different professional claims and the full aspects of accuracy to clients or customers. The issue is further complicated by legal requirements in certain states to have one or the other type of professional assigned for certain mapping tasks (Butler, 2001).

(2) Internet map services such as Google Earth and Yahoo Maps show maps and satellite imagery for a large portion of the globe at a resolution that reveals building structures and even large vehicles. It allows scrutiny of land surface areas that some governments are averse to having as public knowledge, as well as other types of secure areas. This leads to an ethical issue of full freedom of information and service to customers versus respecting the security concerns of certain countries. This issue may appear settled on the side of the service providers and customers, but will become a larger issue for the private citizen if the resolution of map imagery improves even more for the public. It may become a domestic issue for the private citizen if more detailed features of homes and other private places become public knowledge. Such imaging may challenge the "reasonable expectation" of privacy that an individual has, say in his or her fenced backyard.

(3) Geodemographics characterize neighborhoods and small areas, so everyone in a small area might be consolidated together to have one profile. This becomes an ethical issue if the representation of the individual affects eligibility for economic and social benefits such as credit.

(4) Issues in GIS map design, in particular visualization that exaggerates the dimension of particular features to make them more prominent. An example is an environmental map from an activist group that emphasized the noise impact from freeways by increasing ten-fold the width of freeways on the map relative to other features. Although it makes the point better for clients, it raises ethical questions of responsible and fair display of information.

These four examples suffice as an introduction to the variety of spatial ethical issues. The issues surrounding RFID are considered more deeply.

The uses of RFID are raising many contemporary ethical dilemmas. As seen earlier in the book, RFID tags can be affixed to business high-value items, inventory items, vehicles, animals, and people. Some common applications are U.S. military inventory, business inventories such as Wal-Mart, vehicles moving past toll booths on freeways, taking school attendance, monitoring medical patients, checking and counting livestock, reading drivers' licenses in some states, and since 2006 reading U.S. passports. Ethical issues occur when businesses consider when to dispose of the RFID tags in the supply chain. A decision to leave tags on for-sale or sold merchandise raises ethical issues of full disclosure and potential for privacy invasion. For instance, a retail merchant might leave tags on durable items sold, without telling the customer, in order to have information on the customer and transaction available to the merchant (or anyone else with a portable RFID reader) in the future.

Regarding RFID tags for people, there are even more worrisome emerging ethical issues. People can carry or wear RFID devices, but an RFID tag also can be injected by a syringe under a person's skin (Havenstein, 2005), where it is durable for up to 100 years (see Figure 11.1). The procedure cost only about $200 in 2005 (Bradley, 2005). As discussed in Chapters 1 and 5, the chip in an RFID tag contains a lengthy and unique ID number. That number is the key to accessing a computer-based record that can be of unlimited length. For inventory, the ID number commonly identifies the pallet and lot, but a longer ID also identifies the individual item. For a person, the ID tag is a key that uniquely identifies a computerized record for the individual.

In health care, the implanted RFID chip can be scanned at locations in a hospital or other health facility, providing access to the patient's medical record. For example, the patient's record can be scanned on check-in to a waiting room, increasing efficiency. If the patient receives a test in a hospital area, his/her full record can be available on arrival of the patient in order to administer the test under correct protocols. At the same time, at each RFID read point, the patient's spatial location is recorded. Consolidating the information from multiple patients, the mapping and spatial analysis of the patient population and its movements in the hospital can be performed.

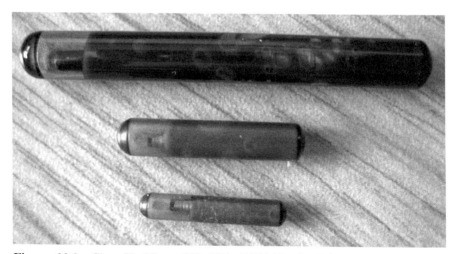

Figure 11.1   Close-Up View of VeriChip RFID Tag for Injection under Patient's Skin. *Source:* Graafstra, Amal; RFID Toys: Cool Projects for Home, Office, and Entertainment; John Wiley & Sons, 2006, reprinted by permission

The FDA approved the uses of the implanted RFID tags for patients in October of 2004. There are several constraints to their use. One is the patient's fear of being injected with an unfamiliar device that appears to intrude on privacy. A second problem is the paucity of RFID readers at hospitals and clinics. Presently, a person injected with an RFID chip has spotty availability of RFID readers. John Halamka (see Figure 11.2), Chief Information Officer of both Harvard Medical School and Beth Israel Deaconess Medical Center and emergency room physician, is an example of an early adopter, having received his VeriChip implant in late 2004 (see Figure 11.3). Dr. Halamka sought to get familiar with the device for his roles in medical IT planning and his own patients. He also has a personal reason, since he is an avid mountain climber, so the device might be life-saving, assuming that the doctors who might care for him have access to an RFID reader and can link through the internet to his record at Beth Israel Deaconess Medical Center (Havenstein, 2005).

As the world's population ages, the elderly will become more prevalent, many of whom are debilitated and have problems with simple daily tasks. RFID tags can be placed at key locations in the living areas of the elderly, and the elderly person can be outfitted with a small, portable RFID reader on a glove or necklace. As seen in Figure 11.4, a home or health-care facility can have tags placed on key items such as a toothbrush, doorway, toilet seat, and tea cup. As the person moves around in his/her daily activities, the wearable RFID reader activates tags in the environment, showing the daily individual's daily movements and indicates activities, as well as any glitches or problems that occur. For hospital patients who have an implanted tag, RFID readers record their whereabouts, so patients throughout

Figure 11.2   John Halamka M.D., CIO of Harvard Medical School. He was implanted in 2004 with a VeriChip RFID Chip. *Source:* John D. Halamka

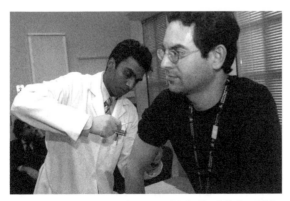

Figure 11.3   John Halamka M.D. of Harvard Medical School Viewing His RFID Implant in 2004. *Source:* John Halamka, 2007

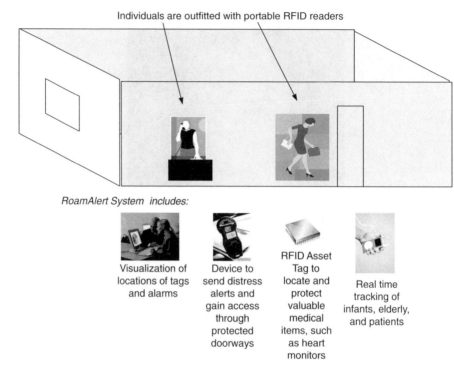

RFID tags are located at key ambulatory points in the building and room environment.

Individuals are outfitted with portable RFID readers

RoamAlert System includes:

Visualization of locations of tags and alarms

Device to send distress alerts and gain access through protected doorways

RFID Asset Tag to locate and protect valuable medical items, such as heart monitors

Real time tracking of infants, elderly, and patients

Figure 11.4 VeriChip Roam Alert System. *Source:* Modified from VeriChip Corporation, 2007

a hospital can be located. For patients and the elderly, RFID offers quick and effortless recording of personal information and location.

However, ethical issues have been raised by implantation of tags in patients and use by the elderly. Implantation is opposed by groups both on the basis of ethical issues of privacy and religious concerns. For instance, the medical history of the patient is automatically known to any RFID reader able to read it, which would be restricted to hospitals and medical facilities, but is exposed to being read by unauthorized persons. The spatial locations of patients could potentially be tracked, without the patient's knowledge. For the elderly, their movements and activities are tracked and stored, which some say compromises their privacy. One way that these ethical issues for patients or the elderly could be mitigated would be regulatory or policy changes requiring informed consent. There are some religious groups that are adamantly opposed to implantation of RFID devices. Several Christian groups claim it conflicts with the book of Revelation, which they indicate states that Satan will force people to have a mark placed on their foreheads or hands in order to engage in buying or selling.

Another RFID example is the Speedpass tag at Exxon-Mobil, which was made available starting in 2004 to 10,000 ExxonMobil gas stations and over seven million customers. Speedpass is an electronic-security-key device with an RFID ID that links to the customer's credit-card record. At the gas pump, the customer places the RFID tag in front of a special reader, which automatically deducts charges from the user's credit-card account (Scheeres, 2003). Although the tag's ID was encrypted, the encryption algorithm is vulnerable. It was broken by a Johns Hopkins professor and students from its Information Security Institute. As an exercise, they were able to copy the Speedpass tag and use it to buy gas. Speedpass has responded by taking increased security precautions including asking customers for ZIP codes at time of purchase.

Like Speedpass, Paypass is an RFID tag, in this case embedded in certain MasterCards. It allows a customer to make purchases by wanding the bar codes of purchase items and waving the RFID-enabled credit card near a reader, resulting in a purchase that is deducted from the card account (MasterCard Canada, 2007). Paypass has been successful and is being expanded.

Paypass and Speedpass raise potential ethical spatial issues. For instance, Paypass insiders at MasterCard could make copies of certain customer records including their ID codes, and provide the information to outsiders who could use it for identity theft or covert tracking. RFID technology serves as an enabling of ethical issues, rather than being the inherent issues. ExxonMobil, MasterCard Canada, and others providing these services face the ethical issue of how much to expose customers to such risks, versus pushing the marketing appeal of an innovation in customer convenience. As tags and readers become more prevalent, the issue might grow.

An example of high-profile adoption of implanted RFID tags has involved Mexico's Office of the Attorney General in Mexico City (Weissert, 2004). In 2004, the then attorney general of Mexico, Rafael Macedo de La Concha, along with 160 others in his office, had an implant of an RFID tag from VeriChip (Applied Digital Solutions, 2007) that enabled him to gain access to the secure areas of the headquarters office, including the Federal Anti-Crime Information Center (Weissert, 2004). During the implantation procedure, a sixteen-digit ID code is scanned by a portable reader (Weissert, 2004). The intent of the implant policy was to overcome alleged corruption of some officials. For an RFID-implanted attorney, the reader devices in the headquarters can store information on when, where, and by whom confidential information was accessible. Since kidnapping is a critical problem in Mexico City and the surrounding area, there is a perception that the implants could serve as a way for police to track the location of victims, but implanted passive RFID tags can presently only be read at distances of 100 feet or so, so the employees would benefit very little. Ironically, the suspected presence of a tag might expose an implanted employee to greater bodily risk, if kidnapped.

Having the very-visible Mexican Attorney General's Office implanted raises ethical and privacy issues. For instance, employees would be exposed to the risk of readers being illicitly located outside of the headquarters' office. The ethical issue for the attorney general and other leaders is how much to inform the employees about risks, without compromising the program. From an ethical theory standpoint, this raises the question of utilitarianism ("ends justifies the means").

In summary, following a brief foundation in ethical theory, the section covered some examples of spatial ethical issues involving business and government. Because of the growth in GIS and spatial technologies, related ethical questions are likely to expand and take new forms.

PRIVACY

Privacy is defined as the capability of an individual to determine and decide "when, how, and to what extent information about him/her is communicated to others" (Westin, 1967, cited in Cho, 2001). The U.S. Supreme Court has held the right to privacy is provided in the First, Fourth, Fifth, and Ninth Amendments to the Constitution (Griswold v. Connecticut, 381 U.S. 679 (1965)). At the same time, some states have legislated privacy-protection rights.

A number of U.S. federal laws (see Table 11.1) determine privacy rights, in some instances covering locational aspects. The Privacy Act of 1974 provides the foundation in the U.S. of privacy protection of government data. Counterbalancing this act are the Freedom of Information Act of 1966 and subsequent updates, which authorize access to many types of public information. For the private sector, a series of acts, starting with the Fair Credit Reporting Act of 1970, regulate certain industries by giving consumers access to, and awareness of their credit information.

Two acts specifically give privacy protections for locational information. The Location Privacy Protection Act of 2001 provides that a company that has spatial information must notify customers and obtain their permission to use it. Consent is required to sell the data. The Act does not cover public spatial information, which is governed by the Privacy Protection Act of 1974 and others. The Wireless Privacy Protection Act of 2003 requires customers' consent for ISPs or other firms to provide location information from GPS-enabled wireless devices such as cell phones. The two locational acts are forward-looking. While they put strong restrictions on what businesses can do with spatial data of customers without consent, they may be hard to enforce. They rely a lot on the integrity and ethical propriety of managers and leaders in business.

The state of privacy regulation today has evolved in major ways from the nineteenth century view that privacy involved defining a geographic area in which a person or people can be left alone (Curry, 1999). In a notable Harvard

TABLE 11.1   U.S. Federal Privacy Legislation Significant for GIS

Privacy Act of 1974
Limited protection given on privacy for government databases.

Privacy Protection Act of 1980
Protections regarding privacy for communications and public materials. The materials cannot be seized, unless there is a criminal offense involved.

Data-Matching Legislation of 1988.
Prevents large dossiers on individuals through record-matching of databases.

Privacy of Financial Information (Fair Credit Reporting Act of 1970; Fair Debt Collection Practices Act of 1977; Right to Financial Privacy Act of 1978)
Provide regulation of data in credit bureaus. Keep debt organizations from sharing consumer debt information with 3rd parties. Regulation of access to data in financial institutions.

Transactional Information Privacy (Telecommunications Act of 1996; Cable Communications Policy Act of 1984). Require cable firms to let customers know what information they collect and what the uses of it are.
Protect transactional information regarding telephone calls

Children, Video, Health, and Education Privacy Legislation (a group of privacy statutes 1974 to 2002)
Regulation of information and records on identifying children on-line, videotape rentals, health information, student records, and driver's license info.

Location Privacy Protection Act of 2001
Firms must notify customers about the presence of location specific collecting of data, and obtain permission to use the data. The information cannot be sold or used without consent. Implied is a right to privacy for locational information.

Wireless Privacy Protection Act of 2003. It amends the Communications Act of 1934 "to require customer consent to the provision of wireless call location information."

Freedom of Information Act of 1966; (Electronic Freedom of Information Act Amendments of 1996).
Protects privacy for individuals who "utilize internet-connectable devices that can pinpoint a person's location."

Source: Cho, 2004

Law Review article in 1890 co-authored by future U.S. Supreme Court Justice Louis Brandeis, the individual's formal privacy right was defined centering on the home and its close surroundings as the locus for private activities. This article was a watershed, after which privacy could be defined legally instead of solely as an ethical concept.

A particular problem of spatial privacy concerns the perception that GIS and maps will remain accurate as the user drills down further and further to larger scales (Curry, 1999). In fact, this drill-down mostly leads to diminished accuracy, which ironically reduces the need for privacy rights. However, spatial resolutions are continuing to increase and become available to wider publics, as manifest in 2005 by the arrival of Google Earth, Microsoft Virtual

Earth, and other web-based, high-resolution map viewers. As everyone gains access to high-resolution imagery, the very concept of privacy will change, and privacy legislation might have to be weakened (Curry, 1999).

Public pressure may build up not to release spatial data of the ultimate resolution. For instance, seeing the behaviors of individuals in their fenced backyard may raise public outcry. An analogy is what happened in 1996 when Lexis-Nexis was rumored to shortly introduce its "P-Trak System," that had a record on nearly every person in the U.S., including the mother's maiden name and the individual's social security number. Facing a public uproar, Lexis-Nexis decided to release the product without social security numbers. Google has felt analogous resistance of some foreign governments and others to its high-resolution map images, and this may portend a growing spatial-privacy debate. The nature of spatial-privacy has changed, so more is acceptable to be revealed today about the details of a person's home or yard (e.g. from satellite imagery) than occurred in the nineteenth century. However, there are limits on how far the spatial-privacy concept can be taken to offer protection, an issue that is central to this chapter's case study.

Another source of privacy controversy is geodemographics, introduced in Chapter 10. Geodemographics tends to characterize an entire small area with one profile, reducing the individual to what is called a "digital individual" (Agre, 1994) or "digital personae" (Clarke, 1995). In other words, the real person may be lost, and replaced by a generic digital profile. The individual might lose control of the virtual self created for him or her (Curry, 1999). If John lives in the "Trendsetters" small-area but is old-fashioned, for many purposes affecting him, John is misrepresented. However, he has no control over it. It may boil down to cutting off at the geocoding stage much of the geodemographic information. Some point to the need that may arise to restrict geocoding through law or regulation (Curry, 1999), in order to restrain what some consider excessive geocoding that might not only threaten the individual's privacy but also misrepresent it, if it is presented in a geodemographic form without caveats. Excessive geocoding might for instance enable categorizing buildings or a few households in such detail that unsolicited target marketing or government micro regulations (e.g. zoning) would be burdensome.

In short, privacy is an old concept, which has become formalized by legislation. However, the nature of privacy itself is changing. For instance, the old concept of total privacy of the home is no longer possible through spatial and other technologies. The challenge is to see today what are the limits on how far the privacy concept can be reduced. It is an ongoing controversy in the courts, Congress, and the public arena.

GIS Codes of Ethics recommend ethical approaches for GIS practitioners. They have been brought forward by non-profit organizations, including by the Urban and Regional Information Systems Association (URISA) and the American Society for Photogrammetry and Remote Sensing (ASPRS). URISA's Code of Ethics, adopted in 2003 and seen in Table 11.2, emphasizes the GIS professional's obligations to society, to employers and funders, to colleagues and the profession, and to individuals in society. Provisions are included that avert or reduce some of the ethical and privacy problems covered in this chapter. The URISA Code includes practicing integrity, providing clear and accurate information, trying to do what is right (not just legal), protecting individual privacy especially as regards sensitive information, encouraging the autonomy of the individual, striving for quality work, and being honest and professional. For practitioners, the provisions balance the business goals of efficiency and profit-maximization, with concern that the individual is respected, privacy preserved, and the quality of work and integrity emphasized. The inclusion of this Code is not meant to imply it is better than other codes or appropriate for all business situations, but to only offer it as one an example of a code.

LEGAL ISSUES

Law is "the body of enacted or customary rules recognized by a community as binding" (Cho, 2005). In contrast to ethics, law tries to be clear-cut on regulating the actions and behavior of citizens. In the U.S., common law prevails. It is a widely accepted and general body of law that has evolved over a long period of time prior to the legislation on it. New laws are added by (a) legislation and (b) court decisions. Common law in the U.S. has the major characteristics of "individual rights, equality before the law, and the universality of the law" (Cho, 2005).

There are many categories of common law that apply to GIS and examples of spatial problems. They include:

Civil law. Law that regulates the conduct between individuals. Contracts define relationships between parties in society. Example: determining whether the contract between a company and a GIS outsourcing firm has been breached for poor performance. Torts such as defamation, trespass, liabilities, negligence, result in litigation to determine court actions. Examples: Determining if a GIS data provider should pay a fine for errors in its commercial data files. Evaluating liability for supply-chain errors due to a large lot of malfunctioning RFID tags.

Criminal law. Law that governs charges of crimes of individuals and resulting in decisions on punishment. Example: To determine if executives of a satellite company authorized providing data to a Mafia organization, which used it to locate targets for destructive attacks.

Procedural law. The law regulating the procedures of the court system. Technical legal rules that might determine the outcome of the appeal process of a GIS legal case, such as occurs in this chapter's case study.

TABLE 11.2   GIS Code of Ethics. Urban and Regional Information Systems Association. Adopted 4/9/2003

I. Obligations to Society

The GIS professional recognizes the impact of his or her work on society as a whole, on subgroups of society including geographic or demographic minorities, on future generations, and inclusive of social, economic, environmental, or technical fields of endeavor. Obligations to society shall be paramount when there is conflict with other obligations. Therefore, the GIS professional will:

1. *Do the Best Work Possible*
   Be objective, use due care, and make full use of education and skills.
   Practice integrity and not be unduly swayed by the demands of others.
   Provide full, clear, and accurate information.
   Be aware of consequences, good and bad.
   Strive to do what is right, not just what is legal.
2. *Contribute to the Community to the Extent Possible, Feasible, and Advisable*
   Make data and findings widely available.
   Strive for broad citizen involvement in problem definition, data identification, analysis, and decision-making.
   Donate services to the community.
3. *Speak Out About Issues*
   Call attention to emerging public issues and identify appropriate responses based on personal expertise.
   Call attention to the unprofessional work of others. First take concerns to those persons; if satisfaction is not gained and the problems warrant, then additional people and organizations should be notified.
   Admit when a mistake has been made and make corrections where possible.

II. Obligations to Employers and Funders

The GIS professional recognizes that he or she has been hired to deliver needed products and services. The employer (or funder) expects quality work and professional conduct. Therefore the GIS professional will:

1. *Deliver Quality Work**
2. *Have a Professional Relationship**
3. *Be Honest in Representations (4 subcategories not shown)*
   Be forthcoming about any limitations of data, software, assumptions, models, methods, and analysis.

III. Obligations to Colleagues and the Profession

The GIS professional recognizes the value of being part of a community of other professionals. Together, we support each other and add to the stature of the field. Therefore, the GIS professional will:

1. *Respect the Work of Others**.
2. *Contribute to the Discipline to the Extent Possible**

(continued)

TABLE 11.2 (*continued*)

IV. Obligations to Individuals in Society

The GIS professional recognizes the impact of his or her work on individual people and will strive to avoid harm to them. Therefore, the GIS professional will:

1. *Respect Privacy*

   Protect individual privacy, especially about sensitive information.

   Be especially careful with new information discovered about an individual through GIS-based manipulations (such as geocoding) or the combination of two or more databases.

2. *Respect Individuals*

   Encourage individual autonomy. For example, allow individuals to withhold consent from being added to a database, correct information about themselves in a database, and remove themselves from a database.

   Avoid undue intrusions into the lives of individuals.

   Be truthful when disclosing information about an individual.

   Treat all individuals equally, without regard to race, gender, or other personal characteristic not related to the task at hand.

---

*Subcategories not shown
Sources: URISA, GIS Certification Institute (GISCI).

Although this chapter mainly concerns legal matters in the U.S., other countries' legal systems also determine GIS cases. International law regulates the conduct by independent states among themselves (Cho, 2005). It is very complex with two or more jurisdictions competing, and beyond the chapter's scope. However, since spatial technologies apply globally, international law is relevant for international geobusiness.

Six major areas of GIS and the law are the following (Onsrud, 2001):

1. intellectual property conflicts
2. conflicts that involve personal information privacy
3. liability issues due to damages and losses from GIS and spatial data and technology
4. conflicts involving competing access to spatial information from government, private sector firms, nonprofits, and individuals
5. conflicts regarding the commodity status of information in spatial libraries
6. problems and conflicts from the sale of tax-funded spatial data by some governments, and the restrictions sometimes placed on the use of the data

In this section, the first four areas are given the most attention. For the first, the major areas of copyright, trade secret, and patenting are reviewed and examples given with respect to GIS and spatial phenomena. For the second, issues of geosurveillance are highlighted.

The third area of liability issues is mostly resolved by contract and warranty law (Onsrud, 1999). However, if the harm is alleged to have been done to the general public, then it is governed by tort law. An example of such an issue involved charter boat captains offshore Alabama (Cho, 2005). Using GPS, the captains take passengers to "private reefs" that are natural and untouched, appealing to the typical nature-loving passenger. The legal issue arises when a charter captain tries to prevent a fisherman from bringing a GPS unit on board the charter boat. The legal issue to determine is whom the GPS technology is damaging—the captain or the fisherman.

Issues 4 to 6 revolve around access to spatial information. Can particular parties benefit or not from the sale of the data; and what restrictions might parties place on the data? Many of these issues are similar to non-spatial information legal conflicts and often follow the same precedents in contract law. However these spatial data issues vary considerably between countries. Some such as the U.S. favor free provision of government data and others such as the UK have in the past provided considerable government fees for data access.

The full set of legal problems on this list and more are reviewed in other sources (Cho, 2001; Cho, 2005).

Returning to the first legal focus topic of intellectual property law and GIS, *intellectual property* is defined as "the property of the mind or intellect [which is] any intangible thing that gives one an operational and functional advantage over others." (Cho, 2005). The law of intellectual property protects the intellectual property of creative people for limited periods of time. It includes copyright, trade secrets, and patents. In the GIS world, there are many creative people and organizations that produce a large volume of intellectual property every month. Some of this property is protected by the developers through legal means. Later, when the intellectual property gets into widespread use, disputes can arise about the protection and whether it is sufficient to stop similar property brought forward by others.

Copyright is a form of protection for creative works. There are two requirements for the works: (1) they are original, and (2) they are fixed in a durable medium. For instance, new GIS software that is original and in a lasting storage form can be copyrighted which prevents others from copying the software without permission of the owner (Johnson, 2001). The copyrighted software is prohibited from being reproduced, distributed in the form of copies, or shown publicly, without obtaining permission from its author or authors (Johnson, 2001). The present term of copyright coverage is the author's lifespan plus seventy years. If a user legally obtains copyrighted material, the statutory exception of fair use may apply, meaning the user can make copies for personal use, but is prohibited from distributing the material. A subtle aspect of copyright is that facts, ideas, and data cannot be copyrighted, but the expression of them can—a legal concept called the "merger doctrine" (Cho, 2005). Hence, the population of a place on a map cannot be copyrighted, but the map that portrays the population size can.

Several examples of legal cases illustrate the issues with copyright for GIS and spatial technologies. In *Kern River Gas Transmission Co. v. Coastal Corp* (1990), a plaintiff created a map from topographic features of USGS topographic maps, but added a gas transmission pipeline and data that the company collected. The court's ruling was that the company did not have copyright protection, since the gas elements shown on the map, even though "new," were pictorial and hence ideas. The "merger doctrine" applied so the map could not be copyrighted (Cho, 2005). This points to the need for spatial companies to go beyond simple pictorial elements on maps and do more complicated map expression to achieve copyright.

A second example underscores that converting a paper map to digital form, without changes, does not circumvent the copyright of the paper map. In *Albert R. Sparaco v. Lawler, Matusky, Sekklly Engineers*, a surveyor had created the original plan in the form of a paper map (Cho, 2005). A new team came in of owner, architect, developer, and a new surveyor, and copied the original surveyor's map into digital form. The court ruled that the original surveyor had the copyright, and his copyright had been infringed, so license fees would need to be paid. An implication of this case for the spatial industry is that digitizing is considered a form of copying, so the rights of the designer of the original source map are preserved. With rampant scanning and digitizing in place in business and society in general, this case cautions that copyright is held by the originator. There are other cases and precedents on copyright of GIS and spatial materials that cover databases, creativity in maps, software, and other aspects (Cho, 2001, 2005; Moon, 2005) that provide a basis for businesses to evaluate copyright situations and make decisions on the strength of protection.

Trade secret provides protection to a company from losing a competitive advantage involving a key information item (Johnson, 2001). Certain types of information can be kept secret, that vary between jurisdictions. The following steps are all required for a trade secret to hold up in court: (1) novelty; (2) constitutes an economic investment for the holder; (3) involved significant effort to develop; and (4) the company exerted effort in keeping it secret (Johnson, 2001). Trade secrecy laws are jurisdictional and vary in their tests of whether a trade secret is maintained over time. For GIS and spatial technologies, novelties keep occurring that might benefit by trade secret protection, so it would appeal. However, in many cases GIS firms, which tend to be small, fast-moving, and changing, may not be able to spare the time and tenacity to achieve and maintain a trade secret.

A *patent* involves a formal series of steps carried out with the U.S. government to protect an original invention. If a patent is granted, the inventor is given protection against others from using, making, or selling the property, while also giving the inventor the ability to license others to use the patented property (Johnson, 2001). An issue for the prospective patent proposal is that a lengthy and costly search must be made to determine whether the invention has already been patented. If parts of it have, then licenses need to be obtained for those parts. The patent term in the U.S. is either seventeen years after the date of issue or twenty years from the earliest date of claimed filing, the latter applying for patents issued since 1995. In 2004, the U.S. Patent and Trademark Office had registered 104 GIS patents, mostly in "image processing, GPS navigation and routing, vector- and raster-based geographic data, map-based directory systems, 3-D interactive image and terrain modeling systems, and methods for mapping and conveying product location" (Cho, 2005). If there is a patent infringement, then the patent holder can file a lawsuit suit against the infringer, which must prove that the infringer violated the patent, often a complex undertaking.

A well-known but controversial patent example is U.S. Patent No. 6,240,360, granted to Sean Phelan of Multimap Inc., a London-based company, on May 29, 2001, and listed as a computer system to identify local resources (Reed, 2003; Cho, 2005). It is also covered by European Patent EP0845124B and patents in other countries. Hence Multimap Inc. can claim royalties on it. The patent covers a fairly broad class of arrangements for map serving over the internet (see Figure 11.5). The arrangement involves a request for a map by a client computer. The request goes to two servers: (a) an information server that retrieves and responds with data on at least one place of interest, and (b) a map server that responds to the map request with a map. The information on the place or places of interest is overlaid on the requested map, giving the full display to the client. For a patent infringement to occur, all the steps shown in the figure must be involved.

To successfully challenge this patent, the challenge must be based on evidence that the patent is either obvious or not new, with "new" referring to before the date of the U.S. patent application of August 16, 1995. The patent has been upheld so far and is in effect until 2016. The Multimap patent dominates in internet mapping, although it doesn't cover all types of system arrangements. Some critics (Radcliffe, 2003; Reed, 2005) question the validity of this patent, not considering it to be "new" at the time of its granting in 1995.

In summary, patents require a lot of effort to achieve and often are outmoded by fast-moving technology. However, some in the spatial industry such as Multimap have created a durable and competitive patenting.

The discussion now turns to the second legal highlighted topic of *geosurveillance*, which exemplifies issues in information privacy law. Geosurveillance refers to using spatial technologies (often satellites, sensors, GPS, or RFID, combined with GIS) to monitor the activities of individuals. This was already illustrated in the privacy section with respect to monitoring of the very small but growing number of persons implanted with RFID devices. A less intrusive form is to provide wearable RFID tags or GPS monitors

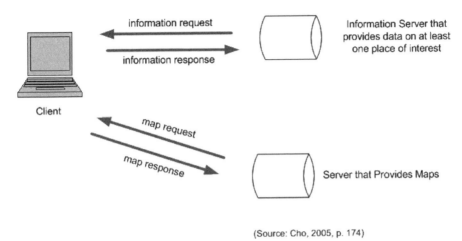

(Source: Cho, 2005, p. 174)

Figure 11.5 Design Covered by U.S. Patent No. 6,240,360, "A Computer System to Identify Local Resources". *Source:* Cho, 2005

for classes of persons, such as children in school, offenders on parole, or soldiers in combat. For instance, in Iowa, some criminal offenders are outfitted with a wearable device, iSecureTrac, that is GPS-enabled and transmits the offender's location to a map server, which allows parole officers to monitor movements of the parolee (Chabrow, 2002). The map can be configured for a specific parolee and show obstacles that must be avoided, e.g. a paroled sex offender must avoid a school playground. Such monitoring devices have become more common with children as well, so parents or day-care workers can see at all times where children are located and avert any dangers.

Another type of geosurveillance is satellite mapping (Monmonier, 2002), introduced earlier in the book. It can be used by businesses, law enforcement, and intelligence services to monitor changes to the earth, including land features, built structures, transportation, agriculture, and military movements. For instance, in attempts by law enforcement units to destroy marijuana crops, investigators used a GIS assisted by an expert system to interpolate and combine information, enabling it to achieve an accuracy of 87 percent for ninety sites (Monmonier, 2002). However, since police were now able to locate nearly all the sites, the illegal growers responded by bringing the marijuana plants indoors and using hydroponic methods. Such a sequence of events points to the legal issues of conflicts involving privacy versus geosurveillance. The chapter case study will pick up on the legal issues involved in satellite sensing of alleged criminal activity.

In summary, geosurveillance, whether by RFID, GPS, satellite, or other technology, has benefits and costs to the parties involved. Not only are there ethical issues, but legal disputes as well. As new technologies appear and more cases come forward, the laws of privacy related to geosurveillance would be refined.

CASE STUDY OF LEGAL ASPECTS OF SURVEILLANCE: KYLLO V. UNITED STATES

Before examining the Kyllo case, it is necessary to set a backdrop on rulings regarding remote imaging and sensing of property. In a key case, *Dow Chemical Company v. United States* in 1986 (Monmonier, 2002), the Environmental Protection Agency (EPA) contracted with an airborne photogrammetry firm to take overflight photos of Dow Chemical's huge plant in Midland, Michigan, which revealed illegal activities taking place. The photos not only revealed buildings, but exposed equipment, conduits, and fittings between the buildings. Dow in mounting its defense argued that the interior areas between buildings were equivalent to the private courtyard and walled areas of homes, referred to as curtilage. The Court of Appeals ruled in favor of Dow, but it was overruled in favor of the EPA by the U.S. Supreme Court—that the open field areas between plant buildings have much less privacy than the curtilage of homes, and thus the concept of private home was not allowed (Cho, 2005; Bruzzese, 2006) This resulted in a concept of "intimate details," i.e. that a home's curtilage could reveal intimate details of private personal life, but not so for outdoor areas of the industrial plant.

With this as backdrop, the 1998 case of *United States v. Kyllo* involved the legality of police obtaining a search warrant for the home of Danny Lee Kyllo (Woessner and Sims, 2003; Bruzzese, 2006). Police suspected that Danny was growing marijuana in his triplex home. They used ground-based FLIR imaging to show unusual thermal activity from the home. *Forward looking infrared technology* (FLIR), sometimes called *thermal imaging*, is a sensor technology that can detect heat being emitted from distant objects. The police used this as evidence to obtain a search warrant, and indeed discovered a marijuana growing operation taking place in the heated environment inside. The lower court ruled in favor of Mr. Kyllo, reasoning that "intimate details" such as baths, showers, and dryers, could be revealed by thermal sensing in homes throughout the country (Monmonier, 2005). However, a year later the U.S. 9th Circuit Court of Appeals overruled the argument that the thermal technology did not reveal much about the inside of homes. The Supreme Court in 2001 reversed this decision in Mr. Kyllo's favor. The justices argued that without a search warrant, surveillance use of a technology not in common use violated the normal expectation of home privacy (Bruzzese, 2006). Although there was a division with the minority doubting that thermal imaging revealed anything intimate, most agreed it did. However, they left the door open for a change of interpretation if thermal imaging technology were to become commonplace. The implication is if it were commonplace, the concept of privacy would change to expect this surveillance as an ordinary police activity.

Today, as surveillance technologies of different types become both more prevalent and commonplace, the Kyllo case is a key ruling that touches on the fundamentals of what is privacy and how far can technology go in invading and reducing it. Spatial technologies particularly sensing and imaging have the potential to reduce privacy, in the home, workplace, or elsewhere. Kyllo is not the last word on these surveillance and privacy issues, but encourages awareness of the issues and risks.

CRIME AND SECURITY

GIS and spatial technologies are a valuable asset for businesses and need to be protected through security procedures. If they are abused, damaged, or intruded into, the results can be injurious to businesses and organizations. Some of the spatial crime and security issues considered in this section are shared in common with information systems. Consider that many key functions of the book's case-study businesses would be interrupted, stopped, or rendered inaccurate by security breaches. For firms such as Rand McNally and Sears that have real-time dependencies of spatial technologies from hour-to-hour, protracted damage could be devastating. Another aspect of this section is that spatial technologies can be employed to help criminals.

Consider that financial theft can occur when hackers break into databases, which may include spatial information. This can be extended further to identity theft. For instance, the databases of Equifax Canada, a branch of the huge credit information firm, were broken into, and over 1,400 personal records stolen, with financial, credit, and personal data including addresses, which could be geocoded for spatial analysis. The criminals who were later apprehended reported their interest in the spatial attributes (Cho, 2005).

It is well-known that drug smugglers and illegal distributors use GPS technologies to pinpoint transit routes and drop-off points. This parallels the U.S. military uses of GPS and GIS for supply chain in Chapter 4.

Perhaps the most notorious criminal use of spatial technologies was the likely use of portable GPS equipment by the 9/11 terrorists. Although this cannot be definitively proven, much circumstantial evidence points to it. One of the 9/11 terrorists had tried to purchase four GPS units at a shop for pilots in Miami three weeks before the attack—he ended up purchasing one (National Commission on Terrorist Attacks, 2004). Zacarias Moussaoui, the alleged twentieth hijacker, tried to purchase a GPS unit, according to U.S. prosecutors (Smith, 2002). Some reports have indicated that Mohamed Atta, leader of the attacks, visited the observation deck of the Twin Towers on September 10 in order to confirm the spatial coordinates of the towers and enter them into the GPS units used the next day on the two flights bound for the Twin Towers (Smith, 2002; CNN, 2002; Cooperative Research History Commons, 2007). It's likely that the terrorist pilots did not know how to operate the sophisticated planes' guidance systems, so relied instead on these handheld GPS devices.

Regardless of exactly what happened, this example emphasizes that spatial technologies have a potentially evil and sordid side, involving major crimes and even terrorism. It underscores the need for GIS security.

GIS security involves steps that are commonly utilized in IT security. This includes physical security, passwords, audit trails, encryption, software maintenance, training of users, and scrutiny in hiring practices for GIS and IT professionals (Oliva, 2005; Dhillon, 2007). As pointed out by Dhillon (2007) often the greatest vulnerability of security systems are at the very core—involving the trusted people in the GIS and IT departments. At the higher levels of these departments and the firm as a whole, the potential security threat becomes that much greater, since the higher-ups have access to most, or all of the firm's information (Oliva, 2004).

Dhillon (2007) considers the security layers to be like layers in an onion The *technical system* is the core of an organization's security, surrounded by the *formal system* of security controls, which in turn is surrounded by the *informal system* of security controls. The technical system applied to GIS and spatial technologies shown in Table 11.3 consists of supportive controls, preventative

TABLE 11.3   Technical Security Controls for GIS and Spatial Technologies

Supportive controls.

User identification. Achieved by required and options access control through passwords and other means.

Cryptography. Encryption of messages and information.

Technical security administration. Covers IS and GIS areas.

System protections. Software and system design that reveals security threats or breaches, such as modular programming, separation of business processes, and reuse of objects in software.

Preventive controls

Authentication. Smart cards, tokens.

Authorization. Authorizing users, IS and GIS employees, and others.

Access control enforcement. Access control lists, user profiles, clear roles.

Protected communication. Virtual private network, packet sniffing, wiretapping.

Transaction privacy.

Detection and recovery

Audit. Needs to extend to full set of GIS and spatial technologies.

Detection of intrusions *and containment* of problems, damages, and outbreaks.

Restoration to secure state.

Virus detection.

Source: Modified from Dhillon, 2007

TABLE 11.4 Formal and Informal Security Controls for GIS and Spatial Technologies

Formal Controls	Informal Controls
Preventative	
Security-responsibility allocation	Security awareness program
Personnel controls – separation of responsibilities and duties	Security training including technical and organizational issues
Clarity of security roles between IS and GIS Departments	Development of security subculture throughout the organization
Detection	
Personnel background checks	Encourage informal feedback
Clearances, rotation of duties	Reward structures for reporting breaches
Management audits	
Continual risk management	
Recovery	
Disaster and business continuity plans	Provision of ownership of activities
Incident-response capability	Encouraging sense of stewardship for recovery

Source: Dhillon, 2007.

controls, and detection and recovery (Oliva, 2005; Dhillon, 2007). Since GIS and spatial technologies often have coupled technologies that work together, such as GIS and GPS, the *technical security controls* need to encompass the full array of spatial technologies, even if they reside in different departments.

Formal controls are those formal rules in the organizational system that support the technical structure of security. They mitigate the misunderstanding of rules and assist in determining clear roles and responsibilities. As seen in Table 11.4, formal security controls emphasize allocation of responsibility for security and separation of duties of security personnel. Many of the case-study businesses in this book have separate IS and GIS departments. Formal controls need to be set up to formalize what are the security responsibilities between the two. The GIS department may be less versed in such controls, since its people tend to be trained in geography, environmental, and other areas outside business and IS. *Informal controls*, which also are organizational, help in stimulating awareness of security as an issue through training, education, and informal user support and encouragement. Informal controls (Dhillon, 2007) are shown in Table 11.4. They involve in general creating an atmosphere that recognizes organization-wide security awareness, training, and employee "ownership" of GIS and information security. Many tenets of the GIS Code of Ethics in Table 11.2 encourage employees to take due care in implementing security to forestall forseeable misuses of spatial technologies.

GIS security needs to involve people who have had training and education in it. This includes broad-based awareness training across the organization. The users and employees need to understand what are the underlying reasons it is important and what are the broad strategies to achieve it. At the level of departments that interact with GIS and spatial technologies, training needs to focus on specific security threats and preventions. For example, if an operations department manages a corporate supply chain that is RFID enabled, those employees need to be aware of the potential for counterfeit tags, improper tagging, and intrusion into the storage files connected to supply chain items. For security and networking managers and staff who deal with GIS and spatial technologies, they need continual, in-depth, and up-to-date training in order to fulfill their challenging roles related to management and effecting the controls in Tables 11.3 and 11.4, as well as to keep up with the emerging technologies that have characterized this field.

GIS and spatial security may further need to meet the provisions of federal laws on information such as the Sarbanes-Oxley Act of 2002, HIPAA (Health Insurance Portability and Accountability Act of 1996), and Gramm-Leach-Bliley Act of 1999. The Sarbanes-Oxley Act has strict provisions that guard the integrity and correctness of internal financial information in businesses. It requires internal controls on financial data that include information systems security. It applies to the spatial data on finance for example in the book's banking and insurance case-study firms. HIPAA mandates rules and procedures to maintaining security and privacy of health-care information, for simplifying health-care accounting, and for the secure exchange of information among health-care firms. It would apply for health-care firms such as Kaiser Permanente and Baystate. The Gramm-Leach-Bliley Act has provisions to assure secure, accurate, and confidential customer information. It limits the use of customer information in spatial applications that are available publicly.

In summary, achieving GIS and spatial security is a daunting task that every spatially based business and organization needs to set as a goal. It is a continuing and never-ending battle of security readiness and capability, versus new emerging threats (Oliva, 2005; Dhillon, 2007). The GIS security can have great technical barriers and controls in place, but in the end it is no better than its "trusted" agents. Some of the worst security breaches have occurred from trusted security professionals on the inside. This section has stressed the various levels of security controls that are not only technical but managerial and organizational.

CHAPTER SUMMARY

Spatial technologies have developed extensively in business and serve important functions. As their capabilities have improved, the benefits that are sought can sometimes be misdirected or usurped causing harm and damages. Ethical questions arise regarding how much businesses should push their profit-enhancing potential versus fairness and respect for stakeholder individuals. At its worst, abuse can take the form of malicious activities, crime, invasion of privacy, financial harm, and information sharing. The legal system is coping with defining the limitations and boundaries of proper conduct regarding GIS, geographic information, and spatial technologies. Businesses can strengthen the threat of misuse, intrusions, and crime by adopting GIS security plans and putting in place a skilled and honest team to effect controls and preventatives. Achieving and maintaining such security requires continual effort, education, and quick adaptation to new technologies.

REFERENCES

Agre, P.E. 1994. "Understanding the Digital Individual." *The Information Society*, 10: 73–76.

Ahearn, Sean C. 2004. "Case Study 3: GIS at the World Trade Center After September 11, 2001." Pp. 241–252 in Clarke, Keith, *Getting Started with Geographic Information Systems*, Upper Saddle River, NJ: Prentice Hall.

Barr, Robert. 1997. "Nowhere to Hide." *The Geographical Magazine*, 69: 30–31.

Biever, Celeste. 2004. "RFID Chips Watch Grandma Brush Teeth." *NewScientist.com*, March 17.

Bouchoux, Deborah E. 2005. *Intellectual Property: The Law of Trademarks, Copyright, Patents, and Trade Secrets*, 2nd Edition. New York: Thompson.

Bradley, Theresa. 2005. "You've Been Chipped: Microchips Tag People Under the Skin." *Columbia News Service*, April 19. Available at http://jscms.jrn.columbia.edu.

Bruzzese Jr., Joseph. 2006. "Legal Aspects of Forward-Looking Infrared Technology: Understanding Probable Cause." *Air Beat Magazine: Journal of the Airborne Law Enforcement Association*, October. Available at www.alea.org.

Butler, Al. 2005. "Map Scale: A Guide to Practicing Ethical GIS." *Geoplace.com*, March 1. Available at www.geoplace.com.

Candiotti, Susan. 2002. "Records Suggest Atta in NY on Sept. 10." *CNN.com*, May 22.

Chabrow, E. 2002. "Every Move You Make, Every Breath You Talk." *Information Week*, August 30. (Monitoring of offenders.)

Cho, George. 2001. *Geographic Information Systems and the Law*. Chichester, England: John Wiley and Sons.

Cho, George. 2005. *Geographic Information Science: Mastering the Legal Issues*. Hoboken, NJ: John Wiley and Sons.

Clarke, Keith. 2004. *Getting Started with Geographic Information Systems*. Upper Saddle River, NJ: Prentice Hall.

Clarke, R. 1994. "The Digital Persona and Its Application to Data Surveillance." *The Information Society*, 10: 77–94.

Coleman, Kevin. 2003. "Technology and Homeland Security." *Directions Magazine*, March 6. www.directionsmag.com.

Crampton, Jeremy W. 2003. "Cartographic Rationality and the Politics of Geosurveillance and Security." *Cartography and Geographic Information Science*, 30(2): 135–148.

Cranor, Lorrie F. 2001. "The Role of Privacy Enhancing Technologies." Available at http://www.cdt.org/privacy/ccp/roleoftechnology1.shtml.

Curry, M.R. 1998. *Digital Places. Living with Geographic Information Technologies.* London: Routledge.

Curry, M.R. 1999. "On the Possibility of Democracy in a Geocoded World." *Social Science Computer Review*, 17: 10–15.

Curry, M.R. 1999. "Rethinking Privacy in a Geocoded World." In Longley, Paul A., Michael F. Goodchild, David J. Maguire, and David W. Rhind, *Geographical Information Systems*, New York: John Wiley and Sons, 757–785.

Curry, M.R. 1997. "The Digital Individual and the Private Realm." *Annals of the American Association of Geographers*, 87: 681–699.

Cutter, Susan L., Douglas B. Richardson, and Thomas J. Wilbanks (Eds.). 2003. *The Geographical Dimensions of Terrorism*. New York: Routledge.

Dhillon, Gurpreet. 2007. *Principles of Information Systems Security*. New York: John Wiley and Sons.

Dobson, Jerome E. 2004. "The GIS Revolution in Science and Society." In Brunn, Stanley D., Susan L. Cutter, and J.W. Harrington Jr., *Geography and Technology*, Dordrecht, The Netherlands, Kluwer Academic Publishers, 573–587.

Durocher, J.M. 2002. "Webrasks CEO Proposes 'Laws of LBS.'" http://www.mtravel.com/20614.shtml.

Edson, Curtis, B. Garcia, J. Hantman, N. Hartz, H. Jensen, J. Leale, K. Lewelling, J. Marks, J. Maxted, B. Moore, B.V. Rivera, and A. Weitzel. 2001. "Code of Ethics for GIS Professionals." Madison: Environmental Monitoring Program, Institute for Environmental Studies, University of Wisconsin Madison. May 8.

EPIC. "EPIC Online Guide to Practical Privacy Tools." Electronic Privacy Information Centre. Available at http://www.epic.org/privacy/tools.html.

Federal Reserve Bank of New York. 2004. "Stored Value Cards: An Alternative for the Unbanked?" July. New York: Federal Reserve Bank of New York. Available at 7/2005 http://www.ny.frb.org/regional/stored_value_cards.html.

Goss, Jon. 1995. "We Know Who You Are and We Know Where You Live: The Instrumental Rationality of Geodemographic Systems." *Economic Geography*, 71(2): 171–198.

Haque, Akhlaque. 2003. "Information Technology, GIS, and Democratic Values: Ethical Implications for IT Professionals in Public Service." *Ethics and Information Technology Dordrecht*, 5(1): 39. Available on Proquest.

Havenstein, Heather. 2005. "Med School CIO Tests RFID for Patients." *Computerworld*, February 11.

Johnson, Deborah G. 2001. *Computer Ethics*, 3rd Edition. Upper Saddle River, NJ: Prentice Hall.

Kwan, Mei-Po. 1999. "Gender and Individual Access to Urban Opportunities: A Study Using Space-Time Measures." *The Professional Geographer*, 51(2): 210–227.

Kwan, Mei-Po. 2002. "Introduction: Feminist Geography and GIS." *Gender, Place, and Culture*, 9(3): 261–262.

Kwan, Mei-Po. 2002. "Is GIS for Women? Reflections on the Critical Discourse in the 1990s." *Gender, Place, and Culture*, 9(3): 271–279.

Kwan, Mei-Po. 2002. "Feminist Visualization: Re-envisioning GIS as a Method in Feminist Geographic Research." *Annals of the American Association of Geographers*, 92(4): 645–661.

Monmonier, Mark. 2002. *Spying with Maps*. Chicago: University of Chicago Press.

Moon, George. 2005. "Software Patents Cause Mixed Emotions in GIS." *Geoplace.com*, February 8. Available at www.geoplace.com.

Murphy, Clare. 2003. "Tracking Down Your Child." *BBC News*, October 28.

National Commission on Terrorist Attacks. 2004. "The 9/11 Commission Report: Final Report of the National Commission on Terrorist Attacks Upon the United States." Washington, D.C.: National Commission on Terrorist Attacks, United States Government.

Oliva, Lawrence. 2004. *Information Technology Security*. Hershey, PA: CyberTech Publishing.

Onsrud, H.J. 1999. "Liability in the Use of GIS and Geographical Datasets." In Longley, Paul A., Michael F. Goodchild, David J. Maguire, and David W. Rhind, *Geographical Information Systems*, New York: John Wiley and Sons, 643–652.

Pickles, J. 1999. "Arguments, Debates, and Dialogues: the GIS-Social Theory Debate and the Concern for Alternatives." In Longley, Paul A., Michael F. Goodchild, David J. Maguire, and David W. Rhind, *Geographical Information Systems*, New York: John Wiley and Sons, 49–60.

Radcliffe, J. 2003. "Death of Copyright—Long Live Patents." Cambridge Conference 2005, Ordnance Survey. UK Paper 4D.2B. Southampton, England.

Reed, Carl. 2003. "Intellectual Property, Patents, and Web Mapping." *ISPRS Journal of Photogrammetry and Remote Sensing*, 8(3): 33–35.

Scheeres, Julia. 2003. "When Cash is Only Skin Deep." *Wired News*. Available at www.wired.com.

Smith, Greg B. 2002. "Hijacker in City Sept. 10 Used Navigation Tool to Pinpoint WTC Site." *New York Daily News*, May 22.

Smith, N. 1992. "Real Wars, Theory Wars." *Progress in Human Geography*, 16(2): 257–271.

Spinello, Richard A. 2003. *Case Studies in Information Technology Ethics*, 2nd Edition. Upper Saddle River, NJ: Prentice Hall.

Sui, Daniel. 2004. "Are Robotics Laws Applicable to Location-Based Services." *Geoplace.com*.

The Economist. 2003. "The Revenge of Geography." *The Economist*, March 15, 366(8315): 19–22.

Timander, Linda M., and Sara McLafferty. 1998. "Breast Cancer in West Islip, NY:

A Spatial Clustering Analysis with Covariates." *Social Science and Medicine*, 46(12): 1623–1635.

Valentine, Gill. 2004. "Geography and Ethics: Questions of Considerability and Activism in Environmental Ethics." *Progress in Human Geography*, 28:2: 258–263.

Warren, S., and L.D. Brandeis. 1890. "The Right of Privacy." *Harvard Law Review*, 4: 190–230.

Weiner, Daniel, Trevor M. Harris, and William J. Craig. 2002. "Community Participation and Geographic Information Systems." In Craig, William J., Trevor M. Harris, and Daniel Weiner, *Community Participation and Geographic Information Systems*, London: Taylor and Francis.

Weissert, Will. 2004. "Microchips Implanted in Mexican Officials." *MSNBC.com*, July 14.

Westin, Alan. 1967. *Privacy and Freedom*. New York: Athenaeum.

Woessner, Matthew C., and Barbara Sims. 2003. "Technological Innovation and the Appplication of the Fourth Amendment." *Journal of Contemporary Criminal Justice*, 19(2): 224–238.

CHAPTER 12

GIS AND BUSINESS STRATEGY

GIS is one of the many tools and technologies that can be used competitively by business. This chapter evaluates the strategic and competitive role of GIS. Factors that predispose GIS to rise up in a firm competitively, among so many other components in business, are considered. Strategy theories are examined from the marketing and IS fields, including Michael Porter's theory of internet strategies and the IT strategic alignment model. GIS practitioners (Huxhold and Levinsohn, 1995) have added useful insights and frameworks.

The case study of Norwich Union, which was highlighted in Chapter 7 from the standpoint of cost-benefit analysis, is viewed in this chapter from the different perspective of GIS's influence on competitiveness and barriers the firm has encountered in incorporating GIS into its strategy.

Based on the strategy findings for the twenty research case studies in the book, the chapter develops an evolutionary model of GIS strategy. It incorporates the dimensions of extent the firm's GIS is customer-facing versus internal-facing, extent that geography is important to business revenues and profits, and degree that a firm has adopted the web-integration enterprise platform for its GIS, versus the more traditional GIS approaches such as client server or desktop. Based on the case sample, the latter two dimensions influence the GIS strategic importance. This model is not quantitative, but may be useful to managers in making a first assessment of how strategic GIS can be for an organization.

The chapter next turns to the Rand McNally case, which demonstrates how the famous map company achieved a high strategic level for GIS. It asks what are some of the secrets of its success. The chapter recommends practical steps for managers to clarify, align, and strengthen GIS strategy. The chapter finishes by considering future trends influencing spatial strategies and a chapter summary.

STRATEGIC VISION FOR GIS AND ESTABLISHING A STRATEGIC PLAN

For business success stories of GIS such as Sears Roebuck and Rand Mc-Nally, having all the right technologies, skilled people, and a budget to invest were not enough. Attaining industry leadership with spatial technologies also requires the *vision* to foresee years into the future to a spatially-enabled business with GIS and associated technologies providing sustained efficiency and productivity that add value. This points to leaders in these firms who fostered or developed the vision, gained commitment of stakeholders, and led in making it happen through implementation of the strategies over many years. The intangible leadership factors are crucial, and a part of this chapter.

At some point for most firms, the vision needs to be formalized into the strategic planning process. Mid-size and large firms are more likely to have formal corporate strategic plans than smaller ones. The corporate strategic plan includes the firm's mission, guiding objectives, mid-term milestones to reach the objectives, sub-plan for development of employees, and section on how stakeholders have been involved in establishing the strategic plan (Tomlinson, 2003; Applegate et al., 2007). The firm needs to have leaders in GIS who will take the initiative to formulate strategies and gather the support of company top leadership to include GIS in its business strategies. The GIS plan needs to be in synchrony with the corporate strategic plan.

It is a breakthrough point at which top leadership understands that GIS is strategic for the organization (Tomlinson, 2003). Once in the corporate plan, there needs to be continual effort to monitor progress and keep the planning components moving forward. The chapter will include case studies of strategic planning at Norwich Union and Rand McNally that tell contrasting stories. For Norwich, although GIS has made valuable contributions and provided some tactical benefits, there hasn't been the critical mass to establish GIS as part of Norwich's overall strategy. On the other hand, for Rand McNally, there has been strategic vision for GIS and it is not only in the firm's strategic plan but GIS is viewed throughout the company as strategic.

THEORIES OF IT ALIGNMENT, INTERNET STRATEGY AND SITUATIONAL ANALYSIS

This section reviews theories of business strategy that are useful in evaluating the strategic level of GIS and spatial technologies for firms and industries.

Most of the theories were developed for information technology, rather than GIS. The reason is that information technology has had major presence in business for much longer than GIS, and has much larger and higher profile than GIS in most firms.

After a brief review from Chapter 1 of strategic grid theory and its relevance as well as limitations, the theories of IT alignment, internet strategy, and situational analysis are presented. The relevance of each theory to spatial technologies is brought out. This section provides the background for the book's strategic theory for GIS which is covered later on.

In Chapter 1, the strategic grid was presented (see Figure 1.15) (McFarlan, 1984; Applegate, 2007). The grid considers roles of IT based on four quadrants consisting of high and low values of two variables, (1) impact of IT on business operations and (2) impact of IT on strategy. As seen in Figure 1.15, there are four quadrants based on high and low values for the two variables. In applying it to GIS, GIS can be substituted for IT in the grid, which leads to the following four quadrants: (1) *support*, i.e. GIS has low impact on business operations and business strategy, (2) *factory*, i.e. GIS has high impact on business operations and low on strategy, (3) *turnaround*, i.e. GIS has high impact on business strategy and low on operations, and (4) *strategic*, i.e. GIS has high impact on operations and strategy.

The strategic grid theory is helpful in gauging how operational GIS is, and in trying to determine when its impacts rise above the level of operations. For Sears, GIS is clearly operationally important, but has also been identified as a strategic factor. It falls into the "strategic" quadrant. At the other extreme the Large Credit Bank has not put GIS to use operationally, except for inheriting some operational uses in an acquired bank; nor has it recognized any business strategic value. It falls into the "support" quadrant. Each of the book's research case studies could be classified in the GIS strategic grid. However, the usefulness of this theory is limited because it does not recognize the key factor today in spatial technologies of the internet and doesn't have a way that the interactions of GIS and IT can be considered.

IT Alignment

In considering GIS strategies, it is useful to look at models of strategic IS alignment (Henderson and Venkatraman, 1992; Papp, 2001; Applegate et al., 2007; Cegielski, 2005), competitive forces (Porter, 2001), strategy and the internet/web (Porter, 2001; Hagel and Brown, 2001), and situational analysis (Huxhold and Levinsohn, 1995).

The IT strategic alignment model (Henderson and Venkatraman, 1992; Papp, 1995; Papp, 2001; Applegate et al., 2007) divides strategy into four quadrants—business strategy, IT strategy, organizational infrastructure, and IT infrastructure (see Figure 12.1). Relationships between these quadrants determine the extent to which business and IT strategies and infrastructure operate in synergy. The model postulates the closer the alignment that

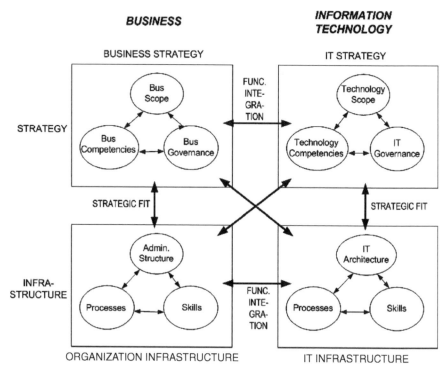

Figure 12.1   Business-IT Strategic Alignment Model. Copyright 2001, IGI Global, www.igi-pub.com, reprinted by permission of the publisher.

exists between the quadrants, the greater the synergy. In aligning business and IT capabilities, for example the business administrative structure and IT infrastructure need to be consistent (Papp, 2001). Likewise the strategies and infrastructures need to be consistent, for instance IT strategy may call for a spatially-enabled supply chain but the IT infrastructure (people, expertise, networks, RFID equipment) may not be sufficient to support it. A firm's strengths and weaknesses in the quadrants can help determine where investment needs to be prioritized and what results can be expected (Henderson and Venkatraman, 1992; Papp, 2001).

The IT alignment model can be extended to include GIS Strategy and GIS Infrastructure (Figure 12.2). Now the alignment needs to exist between six cells, which requires more time and resources in planning, coordination, and communication. If the IT and GIS functions and organizational units are combined together, then the functional integration becomes simpler, again with only four quadrants, and similar to Figure 12.1. However, based on the cases in the book, the GIS and IT functions are more likely to be separate, with loose connections. Regardless of the arrangement, this theory stresses

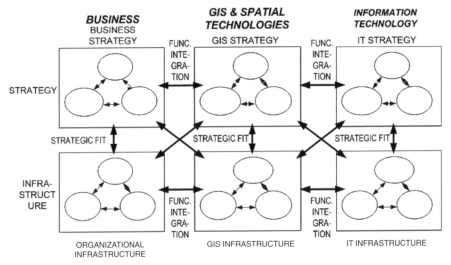

Figure 12.2   Business-GIS-IT Strategic Alignment Model. *Source:* Modified from Papp, 2001

that GIS strategy can succeed only if effort is made to align it with business and IT strategies, as well as have a fit between GIS strategy and infrastructure.

A version of the IT alignment model was tested for emerging information technologies (EITs) in an interview study of senior IT executives (Cegielski et al., 2005). Both business alignment issues and technical alignment issues were important for successful and timely IT strategy. Adhering to IT alignment strategies to implement EITs has the advantage to a firm of being aligned early on the technology adoption curve, so strategies can last longer (Cegielski et al., 2005; Luftman, 2001). For an emerging spatial technology, this study supports early effort to align the new technology with the business strategy, so as to reap longer and more profitable benefits. Early alignment involves risk-taking (Luftman, 2001). A book case example of early alignment paying off is the Motion-Based case, where GPS-enabled devices for runners were aligned early with the business strategy of athletic performance monitoring. The early alignment continued to work well in growing its market, leading to buyout by a larger firm.

Internet Strategy

The internet has profoundly influenced business strategy (Porter, 2001). At the industry level, the internet has tended to increase competitive challenge because of more openness of business activities, reduced bargaining power of suppliers and buyers, lowered barriers to entry, and expanded geographic range. The internet can strengthen a firm's strategic positioning by building on and complementing the firm's basic business strengths, rather than being set up as an isolated corporate unit restricted to web services or e-business (Porter, 2001). This also implies that "old economy" firms can have the strongest internet strategies by complementing already major or dominant strengths. Effective internet strategies for firms don't take advantage of "giveaways" of goods to temporarily bolster revenues and unstable cost reductions but complement and strengthen existing strategies (Porter, 2001). This theory implies that the best strategy for spatial internet and map web services is to complement existing business strengths, rather than placing them in an isolated unit. A good case-study example is Sperry Van Ness, which complemented the existing marketing strength of its regional sales managers with user-friendly and corporate-based spatial web services on-the-spot in the regions, rather than placing those services in an isolated unit.

The adoption of the web-services architecture yields many benefits and increases strategic competitiveness (Hagel and Brown, 2001). Since it requires standard web protocols and open architecture, a business system can be quickly and flexibly re-configured by combining internal and external web services. It encourages firms to move away from secretive, proprietary IT that depends only on internal staffs toward combining the "best of breed" of web services which are publicly available. This approach might evolve as far as a "service grid" or "grid computing," for example groups of firms that share parts of their web services (Hagel and Brown, 2001).

This strategy is consistent with the trend for spatial technologies in business to grow beyond traditional GIS systems to enterprise-wide systems that run on web-based architectures (Sonnen and Morris 2005; Guerrero, 2005). Although it has powerful functionality, traditional client-server GIS requires considerable geographic and GIS expertise to develop. Often traditional systems have a limited and specialized set of clients who are knowledgeable in geography and GIS. The enterprise-wide web-service systems run more flexibly, with a broader user base, and in an interconnected manner discussed in Chapter 5.

Situational Analysis

Another strategic method available for GIS strategic practitioners is situational analysis (Huxhold and Levinsohn, 1995), which is defined as "an understanding of the organization: its purpose, how it operates, its culture, and the management style" (Huxhold and Levinsohn, 1995). The elements to be included in a situation analysis for GIS include the following (Huxhold and Levinsohn, 1995):

- Fundamentals of the organization
- Management philosophy and style

- The culture or cultures of the organization
- Driving force for GIS. (Who is pushing for GIS? Impacts of different driving forces on the project.)
- Technological maturity
- Available resources
- Complexity of the business functions of the organization
- Assessment of implementation success risk/uncertainty. In particular will there be adequate ROI that does not imply large structural changes.

The situation analysis adds to the "softer" parts of the background information for the strategic plan. Questions need to be asked about the relationship between the organization and GIS, including what kind of GIS would work best, what is the human and technological readiness for GIS, how quickly can the organization learn about GIS, who is its champion, and what is an appropriate and manageable rate of implementation (Huxhold and Levinsohn, 2003). In addition to the situation analysis, solid information is added such as GIS hard costs, productivity estimates, and description of existing organizational structure before developing the strategic plan. These authors see GIS strategy not as a separate planning process, but integrated with corporate strategic planning. They even envisage GIS inter-organizational strategic planning, which they term "multiparticipant" (Huxhold and Levinsohn, 1995). Several partner organizations would share their strategic planning for GIS. This was seen in the Enmax case, in which a city-owned utility shared and cooperated on GIS strategic planning with other local government agencies and utilities. Their practitioner recommendations support a chapter theme of the necessity for alignment or even integration of corporate and GIS strategic planning. Their interest in situational analysis of the softer side of GIS strategy links with many of the case-study findings.

In sum, several leading models of business-IT alignment and internet strategy, and situational analysis extend the theoretical foundation to understand and formulate GIS strategy. They form a basis also for understanding and interpreting the chapter's case studies, evolutionary model, and its practical recommendations.

CASE STUDY: NORWICH UNION

As seen in Chapter 7, the Norwich Union has implemented major uses of GIS in flood insurance and innovated with GPS installed in cars to give special lower rates for auto insurance. Norwich has benefited from spatial technologies. Thus it would be expected that the company and its top management would recognize GIS and position the firm strategically to take advantage of it to a greater extent. This continuation of the case study addresses

Figure 12.3   Norwich's GIS-Based Flood Map for the Flood Plain in Eastern Shrewsbury, England. *Source:* Pt.Exsa, 2007

why GIS, although recognized as yielding competitive benefits, has not been incorporated into Norwich's strategic plan. It draws on alignment theory and on parts of situational analysis.

Norwich leads the UK in flood maps and in turn its flood insurance leads the country. The flood map's competitive position is underscored by the demand from competing insurers, reinsurers, and the property market to purchase it (see Figure 12.3). Norwich has given a "nuanced" response to this demand. It will sell some of its flood data, but not all. Because Norwich sells three of its seven flood coverages, the customer is able to discriminate flood risk at only three levels, versus the ten levels the firm has available internally. In this way, Norwich has capitalized on a lead product, while retaining some competitive advantage. Its strong position in flood data also stems from the high prices and bureaucracy in obtaining government flood data in the UK.

Norwich's GPS-based "Pay as You Drive" product (see Chapter 7) is not only a leader competitively and saves money for customers, but the firm has also gained a favorable public image, since the new product and its traffic database improve driving and public safety, while relieving congestion.

Norwich is competitive and profitable from its GIS and spatial products, and respected for them by the UK insurance industry and government. Thus, it is surprising that GIS is not included in the company's strategic plan. The problem is in large part due to an organizational barrier between the GIS and IT departments. Norwich's IT department is responsible for huge databases located on mainframes, many of them aging systems, and it processes massive amounts of claims while at the same time it is growing capacity to handle new business. It has a problem in integrating the massive data across multiple storage "silos" which restrains company-wide access to some data. This narrow and legacy-based IT focus has lowered the IT department's interest in GIS and diverted attention away from it.

The GIS department has its own strategic plan, but the obstacle is to obtain the requisite money and support. It depends on IT for storage of its data and maintenance of its GIS software. However, the problems in communications between IT and GIS have hobbled the GIS department with insufficient computer support and resources. It cannot plan big for the future, even though it perceives the benefits of spatially-enabling extensive data and developing new applications. Beyond IT, the upper-middle management at the company has not understood the GIS benefits. As one GIS employee stated, [Norwich's upper middle managers] "don't get it, they don't understand, and they don't have any vision. The are not educated about spatial." Curiously, some of the company's highest executives have visited the GIS department and are aware of its activities.

Norwich's situation can be explained using the IT strategic alignment model. The model advocates corporate and IT strategy alignment (Figure 12.1) and was extended to corporate and GIS alignment. Norwich's problem is that, although IT is aligned to a part of corporate strategy and GIS is aligned to a different part, IT and GIS are dysfunctional with each other. Since the scale of the GIS systems is much smaller than for IT and because of the attitudes mentioned, GIS is being overshadowed by IT. Hence, GIS is viewed from above as part of the overall IT strategy which is somewhat misaligned with corporate strategy. Although GIS's lead applications are competitive and well-known externally, it has low internal visibility and thus it is not surprising that GIS has not made it into the strategic plan or vision of Norwich.

What can be done to remedy this situation? A strong-willed top corporate management could (a) force integration of IT's data resources into a corporate data warehouse, (b) require spatial enablement of many parts of this data warehouse, and (c) task the GIS department to provide beneficial and innovative applications based on the data warehouse, which will be included in the corporate strategic plan. It would be critical as part of this process for IT and GIS to start working together.

AN EVOLUTIONARY FRAMEWORK FOR STRATEGIC GIS

This part of the chapter presents an evolutionary framework for GIS Strategy that takes into account three key dimensions: (1) extent that spatial applications are customer-facing, (2) extent that geography is part of the industry or business, and (3) extent that the industry or business utilizes a spatially-enabled enterprise-wide integration platform.

The evolutionary model was developed by consultation with industry experts, scrutiny of industry literature (Harder, 1997; Tomlinson, 2003; Barnes, 2005; Guerrero, 2005; Maguire, 2005; Reed, 2005; Sonnen and Morris, 2005), GIS academic sources (Grimshaw, 2000; Francica, 2005; Longley and Clarke, 2005; Lopez, 2005), and IT strategic literature (Robson, 1994; Huxhold and Levinsohn, 1995; Papp and Luftman, 1995; Papp, 2001; Hagel and Brown, 2001; Porter, 2001; Brown and Hagel, 2003; Galliers and Leidner, 2003; Cegielski et al., 2005; Lai and Wong, 2005; Applegate et al., 2007).

The first dimension of the framework consists of the extent that spatial applications in the industry or company are directed towards a user base that is predominantly customers (i.e. customer-facing) versus spatial applications that are directed towards internal users. Internal users include executives, managers, marketing specialists, middle-level analysts, operations personnel, sales force, and field workers.

The second dimension, extent of geography as part of the business, refers to whether the major business products and processes relate closely to geography. An example of an industry linked to geography is transportation, for which the key function of moving goods, inventory, and people is inherently tied to geography; another example is the utility industry, for which the products of energy, purified water, and essential materials are provided through geographic networks of transmission lines, pipelines, and specialized transport vehicles. Real estate, another obvious example, has land as its central element. On the other hand, the legal services industry has slight linkage with geography for its essential products and processes. In semiconductors, the vital products and services are usually weakly linked to geography. In between in extent of geography are industries such as health care, banking, metals manufacturing, and pharmaceuticals.

The extent that an industry or business utilizes a spatially-enabled web integration platform refers to whether it is based on "traditional" desktop or client-server spatial applications versus those based on the web-based enterprise architecture consisting of web servers, content servers, the internet, thin and thick clients (Guerrero, 2005; Lopez, 2005; Sonnen and Morris, 2005). The architecture was discussed in Chapter 5 and is shown in Figure 5.1(d). Sometimes this web architecture is extended to include GPS-enabled

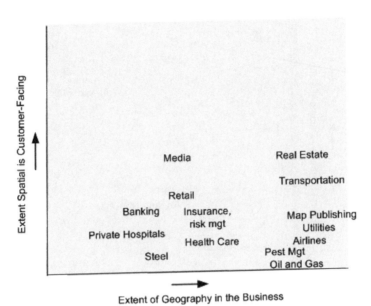

Figure 12.4 Evolutionary Framework of Industry Categories by Two Spatial Dimensions, 1995

portable mobile devices connected through a wireless network. That mobile-web architecture was also examined in Chapter 5 and is shown in Figure 5.1(e). In between are mixed architectures, in which industries or companies depend on a mixture of the traditional technical GIS platform and the emerging web- and location-based integration platform.

Changes in the evolutionary framework over time are shown circa 1995 in Figure 12.4, and in 2006 in Figure 12.5. The 1995 arrangement of industries was based on industry books written in the mid 1990s (Longley and Clarke, 2005; Harder, 1997; Grimshaw, 2000) and by interviews of three GIS industry experts knowledgeable of the industry in the mid 1990s. The 2006 company arrangement is drawn from the results of the book's twenty research case studies. Figure 12.4 only shows two dimensions since the spatially-enabled web integration platform was not present, but only the traditional desktop or client-server. Geography-oriented industries such as transportation and utilities are shown with higher values on the x axis while ones with much less spatial linkage such as steel and private hospitals have low values. On the y axis, industries that are not customer-facing in spatial technologies include pest management and oil and gas, while industries such as real estate were moderately customer-facing in GIS, but no industries in the mid 1990s are highly spatially customer-facing. The deficit of high customer-facing is because map delivery was still cumbersome, bandwidths were not high enough for effective interactive mapping, and businesses mostly had not yet recognized the benefits of providing maps and spatial analysis to customers.

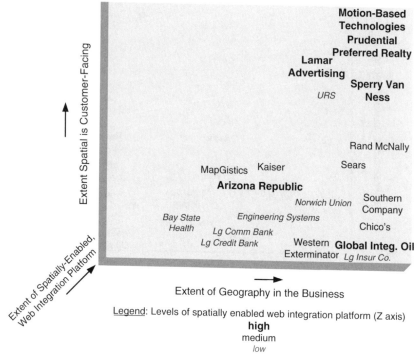

Figure 12.5 Evolutionary Framework of Firm. *Source:* Cases, 2006

In 2006, the complexion of industry distributions changed. The web integration platform appeared, and is added to the framework as the z dimension. Compared to 1995, there are only moderate changes in some industries with respect to extent of geography in the business. These changes arose because some industries recognized and utilized geographic phenomena more. An example is health care. Many health care providers expanded into networks encompassing larger geographies. On the y-axis of extent GIS is customer-facing, there were substantial changes in some industries due to fast, web-based delivery of enhanced map products in real-time. An example is real estate, where increasing use of multimedia and map enhancements occurred. At the low end of the customer-facing scale, some industries remain at 1995 level such as pest management and oil and gas, for which consumers are not demanding GIS services and the firms are not emphasizing to provide them. Other industries such as real estate and advertising have become more customer-facing in certain spatial functions such as automated vehicle navigation (AVN) and GIS in marketing.

In the z-axis dimension of extent spatially-enabled web integration platform, industries such as oil, newspapers, and real estate lead the way, with continual, powerful, and appealing delivery of maps and spatial analysis to users and customers. Industries that have mostly not adopted the web-based platforms include banks, health care, and insurance. These regulated industries did see sufficient benefits in spatial applications to justify the high costs of upgrading from desktop/client-server to web-based enterprise platforms. They are also held back somewhat by legacy mainframe systems which are more challenging to connect to the web-enterprise platform. For the research cases, such obstacles occurred with the Large Credit Bank and somewhat with Norwich Union.

This evolutionary framework can be expected to change further, since spatial technologies are rapidly advancing in business due to reduced costs and realization of the competitive importance of the benefits (Sonnen and Morris, 2005; Francica, 2005). The framework can be useful to managers who conduct mid- to long-range planning of their spatial architecture and applications.

FINDINGS OF CASE STUDY ANALYSIS

This section looks at the book's full set of twenty research case studies to examine how strategic each one is in GIS and why. For many of the firms, it discusses whether GIS strategy is aligned with corporate strategy. The cases are grouped by strategic level of GIS and spatial technologies.

CASE FINDINGS FOR HIGH STRATEGIC FIRMS

Global Integrated Oil

For GIO, the global integrated oil giant discussed in Chapter 1, spatial technologies are applied enterprise-wide, including in exploration, transportation and storage, refining, environment, marketing, supply chain, and strategic planning. The company is pushing the technology limits in areas such as sub-surface mapping, web-based applications, 3-D maps, data warehousing, and advanced analytic tools. Overall, the sum of all these applications, some of which have common data-bases, results in highly-strategic GIS. The GIS manager pointed out that GIS is an important tool in making long-term strategic decisions lease/sale decisions and in realizing the competitive advantage of geophysical data. Spatial data are used at the top executive strategy level. GIS and IS work together organizationally and are technically integrated. Thus GIS and IS strategies are aligned and in synchrony with corporate strategy.

MotionBased Technologies

This very small Bay-area firm, which was purchased by a middle-sized technology company, serves performance athletes worldwide, by receiving and analyzing athletic performance training data uploaded from the athletes' GPS-enabled devices. The data are input into a database server and are combined with topographic and routing data from commercial web services. The MotionBased proprietary spatial analysis software computes customer profiles which allow these performance athletes to evaluate and compare their route performance. MotionBased programmers wrote the web applications and configured the customer-facing web platform. Thus these spatial technologies constitute the company's product and are inherently competitive and strategic. The general manager pointed out that it is the combination of internet, aggregated data, and spatial technologies that creates competitive advantage. The key is the web services architecture. Also, GIS, IS, and company strategies are inherently aligned.

Rand McNally

At this large private firm, the world leader in map publishing, GIS is highly strategic and is discussed as a full case study later in the chapter.

Sears Roebuck

The giant retailer covered in Chapter 7 has extensive spatial technologies in six areas: routing and deploying service technicians, delivery, warehouse optimization, marketing, Sears Smart Toolbox automated vehicle navigation, and capacity management of workforce in service territories. Significant gains in productivity of delivery and service maintenance have enhanced the company's bottom line. As the leading competitor in spatial technologies in its huge markets, there is strong competitive advantage. The GIS manager in routing considers that Sears is stronger competitively in spatial technologies than any competitors, including GE and many smaller-sized ones. GIS is included in Sears' written strategic plan and there is also a GIS strategic plan. The competitiveness is achieved through greater productivity, lowered cost for service calls, and reduced staffing costs for a large delivery workforce.

Southern Company

This large parent utility company dominates electrical production and distribution in many parts of the southeastern U.S. As seen in Chapter 9, it moved from distributed management of spatial technologies that differ among the operating companies, to an integrated and centralized enterprise-wide GIS, encompassing all its companies. At the level of the parent holding company, this led to closer GIS alignment with IT and corporate strategies. The GIS is internally directed and is planned to maximize enterprise returns on investment. There is total dependence on GIS for asset management Southern-wide. Southern's electrical production is regulated, but the transmission side of the business is increasingly competitive and open. The strategic approach is to partner with leading generic and utility-specific GIS vendors and to seek enterprise deployment of the technology.

The former head of enterprise GIS points out that strategic benefits are obtained by lowered costs and improved customer satisfaction. GIS improves strategic competitiveness in the transmission part of Southern, since it's unregulated, but not in the regulated production part of the company. The GIS enterprise initiative had executive sponsorship indicating top management support, even though it's not yet included in Southern's corporate plan. As part of the enterprise project, strong alignment of GIS and IT was emphasized and achieved.

Arizona Republic

The mid-sized newspaper focuses its spatial technologies on targeted advertising, as seen in Chapter 2. To accomplish this, it has spatially-enabled its mailing capabilities to allow for refined addressing as well as market saturation. The platform combines technical desktop GIS to support object-oriented programming and web development in-house, with an enterprise, web-services platform for inside and outside users. The newspaper's GIS has become an enterprise, strategic system, although the functional areas of application are limited. The GIS competitive advantage stems from being able to pick geographical areas that are suited to a particular advertiser. This competitive element is included in the newspaper's corporate strategic plan. Many other aspects of GIS are more operational i.e. GIS can help in getting the product out.

Chico's

This rapidly growing women's apparel chain has utilized GIS primarily in real estate location, customer relationship management (CRM), direct mailing, and business intelligence (see Chapter 4). For site location, GIS can predict the extent of cannibalization of one store from another, leading to adjustments in store-performance targets. GIS tracks the sequences and patterns of shopping locations for high-end customers, personalizing service. GIS is written into the firm's strategic plan and aligned with corporate strategy which is based on customer service and loyalty, and seeking to create new markets. Competitive advantage has been achieved by better understanding store operations, better planning for new stores, and the servicing better the existing customer base through CRM methods. There is good alignment and collaboration between GIS and IT, which relates in part to the strong customer-centric mission.

Lamar Advertising Company

Lamar's biggest spatial application is to supply maps to its 900-person sales force that provides them in turn to customers to enable them to decide among alternative outdoor billboard placements. Other applications are routing of its maintenance workforce and support for real estate acquisitions. Lamar utilizes an integrated, web-based platform that accesses mostly commercial data, albeit with limited spatial-analysis functionality. Since Lamar is unique among its competitors in having a spatially-enabled national billboard base, it draws strategic advantage especially in selling. GIS and IT are combined functionally and organizationally. The corporate and GIS/IT strategies are aligned, and GIS is included in Lamar's corporate strategic plan. There is focus on a long-range vision for GIS and the GIS and marketing people are working together to consider new spatially driven technologies for billboards.

Prudential Preferred Realty

This Chicago-area residential real-estate brokerage firm applies GIS internally for demographic analysis and for agent performance profiling by area while externally customers and consumers have been attracted by the competitive web portal that allows them to search and view properties with convenient tools and imagery of the city areas, amenities, and properties. The spatial applications are entirely based on an enterprise web architecture. Strategically it allows the firm to "stay ahead of the pack" by creating customer loyalty through robust, repeatable spatial services. The competitive importance of spatial systems is not formalized in a written plan but the firm by habit does little written planning. The firm emphasizes in its corporate strategy having the technologies available that appeal to customers and retain their loyalty and repeatability. Geospatial services are regarded as an important current technology that is a complementary technology piece in appealing to customers. There is alignment of IT and GIS, since Prudential seeks to be fast-moving and integrated in presenting technologies to its customers.

MapGistics

This small health-care consulting firm provides geographic mapping applications to several hospitals with a focus on one in southern California (see Chapter 10). The most important use of spatial analysis is bed management, with lesser use in mapping emergency response and a prototype application of spatial tracking of certain RFID-tagged patients. GIS is inherent in the firms' products and is strategic. The ceo pointed out that GIS is strategic at MapGistics and the bed management product is also in the organizational strategic plans for certain of its customers. The vision for GIS is to emphasize environmental scanning to locate hospital chains and independents that are more modern in outlook and receptive to its spatial product.

CASE FINDINGS FOR MEDIUM STRATEGIC FIRMS

Kaiser Permanente

Kaiser Permanente, the national hospital chain centered in California, applies GIS in web map services, travel time analyses, travel accessibility studies, site selection, and some marketing and medical uses (see Chapter 10). GIS is significant to meet regulatory requirements that dictate classification of areas as in-service versus out-of-service, understand where clients are located, determine what disease profiles a region has, and spatially analyze Kaiser health-care resources including physicians, MRI equipment, and clinics. GIS is considered strategic for predicting member travel times, locational analysis, and facilities siting, but less so in the other areas. GIS's strategic role is dwarfed by some other overriding health-care issues. Although not in Kaiser's strategic plan, GIS undergoes periodic reviews by top management that tend to align it more with corporate goals.

Large Insurance Company

This large casualty and property insurance firm utilizes GIS mostly for underwriting, catastrophe planning and management, and capacity planning, as examined in Chapter 3. The spatial applications are client-server based, with active planning to move to web-based. GIS is essential to firm underwriters throughout the country to assess risk and price policies. GIS has become crucial for the catastrophe unit to spatially allocate risk and manage disaster response. Corporate IT is largely legacy-based, which has held back its alignment with GIS. The executive level is aware of GIS and includes it in the strategic plan, but it has not seen it as highly strategic and competitive.

URS

URS, the very large integrated engineering design services company with a global reach, depends on client-server based GIS internally rather than spatial web services. However, it does develop spatial web services for some of its clients. GIS and spatial technologies have been of moderate corporate strategic importance. They are not included explicitly in URS's strategic plan, but are implicit in the categories of overall automation and best practices. In the Dot Com era, they were explicitly included. URS does appear to be getting "back on track" in giving more support for development of spatial technologies. One reason is the rapid growth of GIS. Past vision for spatial technologies has not always been correct such as mapping of underground utilities, but other spatial vision items such as compliance and regulatory uses have been realized.

Sperry Van Ness

Sperry Van Ness, the rapidly growing national commercial real estate brokerage firm discussed in the first chapter, utilizes GIS for sales presentations, property websites, brochures, and internal searching and viewing of properties. It is entirely based on an enterprise web-service platform. The firm's leadership emphasizes the importance of the sales advisors, and generally plans everything in the short- and mid-term, rather than long-term strategically. To the extent GIS helps the sales advisors be more productive, it's important. GIS is of moderate strategic significance and not currently in the vision of the firm.

Western Exterminator

This middle-sized private firm provides pest control management to residential and business customers in California, Nevada, and Arizona. The leading use of GIS is to map the complete customer base for use by the sales force. GIS is applied to re-align routing and to determine locations for new service centers. The firm utilizes predominantly commercial web services. There are only a handful of internal users for the GIS. The moderate-level strategic advantages of GIS are to target homeowners, locate service centers, and recognize underserved areas. GIS is not included in the firm's corporate strategic plan. However, it is aligned with the corporate strategy that emphasizes marketing and customer service.

CASE FINDINGS FOR LOW STRATEGIC FIRMS

Large Personal/Corporate Bank

As seen in Chapter 3, the case study of this large international bank concerns its U.S. division. GIS is used for siting and relocation for its rapidly growing network, trade area analysis, market share study, and ad-hoc thematic mapping. The GIS group is very small and utilizes a traditional, client-server set-up. GIS is not regarded as strategic. It's not in the bank's strategic plan and the executives are not focused on it. The small GIS group is aware of its potential but has not yet been able to convince bank strategists of its importance. GIS is regarded as creating competitive advantage by providing branch-related customer data to decision makers in an understandable way and to support service of current customers and attact new ones.

Large Credit Bank

This very large bank, as seen in Chapter 10, has had a monoline product line in the credit card area. Several years ago, it acquired several medium-sized regional consumer banks. Although GIS had been only tangential previously, the acquired banks raised the need to adopt spatial technologies. The initial spatial applications are site location, real estate evaluation, and marketing for the acquisitions, plus planning of the corporate campus. Since the acquired consumer banks are in competitive markets, the siting of their existing branch locations needs to be evaluated, new sites explored, and geodemographics performed. The large credit bank, which has been resistant to GIS and held back by its legacy IT systems, is beginning to apply it in the acquired banks, but continues to give GIS little recognition so it's low in strategic level. GIS, IS, and corporate goals are not aligned.

Norwich Union

Norwich, one of the largest general insurance firms in the UK, was discussed in Chapter 7. GIS is low in strategic importance as discussed as a full case study at the beginning of this chapter.

Baystate Health

Baystate Health is a large New England health-care system with three member hospitals in western Massachusetts (see Chapter 2). Its eight-year-old GIS program provides GIS for medical and health applications, environment, spatial statistics, spatial epidemiology, hospital facilities, routing, marketing, and emergency and disaster planning and response. Since its big applications were implemented recently, GIS has not yet attained a strategic level in the organization. It is not in the firm's strategic plan, nor does it have its own plan. Baystate as a whole does not yet have a long-range vision for spatial. The small GIS department has a long-range vision for GIS, but hasn't yet been able to convince others to do so. This may change, however, since the GIS director and champion of GIS, who is the chair of the surgery department, has his own vision for GIS to become enterprise-wide and is communicating that to Baystate's vice presidents,who are attuned to it.

Engineering Systems

ES is a small consulting firm that provides GIS services to local governments as well as to utility and transport firms. Its in-house GIS is traditional client-server. Its own systems serve only in-house users, although systems ES has installed in client firms serve varied external users. Some employees are assigned to client sites for extended periods, a form of outsourcing. The firm's GIS systems products are very tied to geography. Its in-house GIS systems are not strategic, relative to its consulting competitors, many of which have more advanced spatial analysis and/or web-based platforms to reach out to clients. ES's GIS and IT are aligned, since they are managed together in this small firm.

SUMMARY OF FINDINGS

The book's case companies vary on the three dimensions of the evolutionary framework as shown in Figure 12.5. The results are categorized in Table 12.1.

Size of firm has no consistent association with strategic level in the framework. Some small firms such as MapGistics and MotionBased Technologies have centered their business on spatial products and services from their founding, so spatial is immediately strategic. Larger firms are older; many were founded decades before GIS was invented. Their adoption of spatial technologies has progressed more slowly over time through stages of growth, as outlined by Nolan's stage theory in Chapter 3. Medium-sized firms are in between these, and tended to have adopted and elevated the importance of GIS and spatial in shorter time spans than the large firms, for instance Chico's and Lamar Advertising.

Strategic level is not related to extent that GIS is customer-facing. This may reflect that many GIS and strategic spatial applications for the case firms tend to be more intensive internally than externally. Examples of internally-focused cases are Global Integrated Oil, and Rand McNally. However, extent that GIS is customer-facing does relate to type of industry. Consumer services, billboard advertising, newspapers, and retail are industries that often serve their customers directly with GIS. By contrast, the oil and utilities industries are more proprietary about retaining geographic information for inside use. Furthermore, post 9/11, those industries have been restricted by government policy from making most types of spatial information publicly available, such as detailed maps of their network configurations and loads. The giant Credit Bank is in the very early process of shifting from centralized service of customers with credit needs that are not spatially-based to serving emerging retail customers who often need spatial displays, but overall the bank maintains traditional, legacy habits that are not spatially oriented. Regarding Western Exterminator, the pest industry has not yet offered spatial information to its customers who don't seem ready to accept it.

Spatial strategic level is positively related to extent of geography in the business. Seven out of ten of highly strategic firms have a high extent of geography in the business, while those with low strategic levels are all medium to low in extent of geography in the business. The medium-strategy firms are in between. Extent of geography in the business is also keyed to industry characteristics. For the twenty research cases, those with the largest geographical component come from oil and gas, utilities, real estate, insurance, retail, and consumer services, while geography is less important for banking and consulting.

In comparing the extent the twenty firms are highly strategic in GIS to the adoption of spatially-enabled enterprise-wide web integration platforms, the two attributes are highly associated for this sample. Five of the six firms that adopted web-based, enterprise-wide platforms have high strategic levels for spatial technologies, whereas five out of seven firms in the traditional

TABLE 12.1 Strategic Levels and Model Dimensional Attributes for Case Study Sample

Name or description	Size	Customer-Facing	Platform	Extent Geography in Business	Strategic Spatial Level
Global Integrated Oil	large	low	Web-based, Enterprise-wide	high	high
Motion-Based Technologies	small	high	Web-based, Enterprise-wide	high	high
Rand McNally	large	medium	Intermediate. Client-server, Enterprise-wide, moving to web	high	high
Sears Roebuck	large	medium	Intermediate. Client-server, Enterprise-wide, moving to web	high	high
Southern Company	large	very low	Intermediate. Client-server, Enterprise-wide, moving to web	high	high
Arizona Republic	medium	medium	Web-based, Enterprise-wide, limited to circulation and advertising	medium	high
Chico's	medium	low	Intermediate. Is moving towards more web-based.	high	high
Lamar Advertising Co.	medium	high	Web-based, Enterprise-wide, moving to more functionality	med-high	high
Prudential Preferred Realty	medium	high	Web-based, Enterprise-wide	high	high
MapGistics	small	low	Intermediate. Is partly web-based enterprise-wide	medium	high
Kaiser Permanente	large	medium	Intermediate. Mostly traditional, client-server	medium	medium
Large Insurance Co.	large	low	Traditional Client-server	high	medium
URS	large	medium	Traditional, Client-server	med-high	medium
Sperry Van Ness	medium	high	Web-based, Enterprise-wide	high	medium
Western Exterminator	medium	low	Intermediate. Commercial web services	med-high	medium
Large Commercial Bank	large	low	Traditional Client-server	medium	low
Large Credit Bank	large	low	Traditional Client-server	medium	low
Norwich Union	large	high	Traditional Client-server	med-high	low
Bay State Health	medium	low	Traditional Client-server	low	low
Engineering Systems	small	low	Traditional Client-sever	medium	low

client-server mode have low strategic levels for their spatial technologies. The seven firms in the intermediate level of spatially-enabled enterprise-wide web integration platform have medium to high strategic levels (three medium, four high) for spatial. This strong tie confirms a premise of the book that the spatially-enabled, enterprise-wide web integration platform is the direction that spatial technologies are moving to achieve competitive results. This finding is explained by Porter's theory that justifies the advantages of the internet to successful corporate strategy (Porter, 2001). For companies that are moving in their business overall corporate strategy towards the internet and e-business, for instance Prudential Preferred Realty and MotionBased Technologies, IT strategic alignment theory reinforces that the spatial-web-integration platform corresponds to a corporate strategy of e-business (Porter, 2001; Hagel and Brown, 2001).

Spatial technologies have grown in the business world. Uses are evolving, supported by newer technology platforms, in particular the spatially-enabled, enterprise-wide web integration platform. As costs decreased, more profitable uses were discovered. The extent of customer-facing spatial applications has steadily expanded over time. This is due both to the convenience and user-friendliness of the new technologies as well as to broadened user bases. Porter (2001) concluded that the web services platform encourages greater direct contact, without intermediaries, between the customer and the product or service. This trend is also consistent with findings that web-services platforms are beneficial (Hagel and Brown, 2001). Porter's reasons for the competitiveness of the web-services platform, namely reducing costs, increasing openness, and lowering barriers to entry, all apply to the spatial realm. Consistent with his reasoning, GIS can emerge from its departmental niche and serve broad internal users and/or outside customers. GIS can be included as part of a broader IT strategy of implementing the web services platform, as long as the IT and GIS capabilities are present to support it (Henderson and Venkatraman, 1992; Papp, 2001; Cegielski et al., 2005; Applegate et al., 2007).

The extent GIS is customer-facing is not associated with the level of GIS strategy. This result reflects the differences on GIS's internal or external impacts, across a range of firms and industries. For some, such as GIO, the GIS impacts are highly significant and realized by internal efficiencies and productivity. At the other end, Sperry Van Ness's successful GIS strategy principally benefits the customer. The bottom line is that spatially strategic firms can be at either extreme or in between.

The extent of geography in businesses overall has grown slowly but steadily, as the structure of industries altered or new industries emerged. An example is the web-portal industry sector, which emerged in the last ten years and in 2005 took a giant step towards the wide public consumption of GIS with such geographic-based offerings as Google Earth, Yahoo Maps, and Microsoft Virtual Earth. Porter (2001) observed that a firm with a web services platform would tend to have a broader reach of geography. For established industries such as banking, the trend towards mergers and acquisitions can broaden the geography of the firm and make spatial applications more important for it. Drawing on the IT alignment literature, the business strategy for some companies might be naturally keyed to geography, for example Rand McNally's business is to produce maps and for Sperry Van Ness's to map and visualize commercial properties. Alignment theory would thus point to the benefit for a corporate strategy tied to geography to be aligned with a GIS strategy (Papp, 2001; Cegielski, 2005; Applegate et al., 2007).

PRACTICAL ADVICE TO MANAGERS ON STRATEGIES FOR GIS AND SPATIAL TECHNOLOGIES

The implication from the book's research case studies is that a company should evaluate its industry to determine how suitable it is to spatial technologies, as well as to gauge how much competitive advantage these technologies offer the firms in the industry (Hagel and Brown, 2001). A firm should consider deploying spatial applications on web-services platforms, as long as it can rationalize the investment from a cost-benefit standpoint and support it technologically. A manager should assess how naturally geographical his/her business is, to help in determining the strategic potential of GIS for the company. Once underway with GIS, corporate management should consider evolving the applications to an enterprise-wide web-based platform. Some firms such as MotionBased have been able to leap-frog directly to full web-based, enterprise spatial platforms and take the lead in market niches. Of course, the springboard approach increases risk and requires a robust business plan, technological capacity, and understanding of customer markets.

Matching the GIS Strategic Plan with the Corporate Strategic Plan and the Corporate IT Plan

Another practical implication of the cases for managers is that the alignment of GIS strategy with corporate strategy is recommended, but with a difference. GIS applications need to be aligned with corporate strategy and also with IT strategy. For a company in which IT and GIS are combined together organizationally such as Sperry Van Ness, IT and GIS strategies can easily be integrated. However, IT and GIS are organizationally combined for only a quarter of the book's cases, which tend to be smaller ones.

For most firms, GIS and IT are separated, so coordination of their strategic planning might be problematic. Norwich best represents this problem. It has had limited coordination and communication between GIS and IT. On the other hand, for firms such as Sears and Rand McNally, GIS and IT work together well including in coordinating strategies.

The alignment of strategies for GIS, IT, and the corporation is a challenge that GIS managers must address. Based on the experiences in the book's case

TABLE 12.2 Practical Steps for GIS Managers to Better Align GIS Strategy

1. Meet and communicate with managers who are responsible for the corporate strategic plan.
2. If GIS and IT are separate, maintain regular communications with the leadership of the IT department
3. Consider the extent the company has already emphasized e-business. If the extent is high, consider incorporating web-based enterprise GIS in the GIS strategic plan if not present already.
4. Coordinate for future planning of web-based enterprise GIS with the corporate strategic plan and the IT strategic plan. Coordinate the web and internet emphasis with the other plans.
5. Consider the infrastructure of GIS, IT, and the business. Are the infrastructures in sufficient synchrony so all three aspects work together.

studies, steps are recommended for the manager or executive in charge of GIS, as seen in Table 12.2.

CASE STUDY: RAND MCNALLY

Rand McNally is the famous map company founded in 1856 that has a premier brand name. It produces maps, atlases, and electronic map products for consumer, business, transportation, and education markets. Its products are available in 55,000 stores worldwide. GIS is used integrally throughout the company to create and update its map and electronic products, support direct store delivery (DSD), i.e. locating and stocking retail outlines that carry its products, manage inventory and supply chain, provide specialized maps to its marketing and planning departments, sell exact maps to the trucking industry, and support mapping for cell phones and handheld GPS devices. Most of the map users are internal, centering on the Geographic Information Services Department, but also include people in marketing, sales, supply chain, and other areas. GIS is recognized throughout the company workforce, from operations people up to executives. GIS is integral to the firm's competitive strategy.

Some users are external, including data providers and licensers, supplies, industry users of electronic products, users of the company's web services, consumers who utilize cell-phone map products, and customers of the Rand McNally GPS Navigator. The firm is the nation's dominant supplier of truck routing maps, so much so that Rand McNally is the de facto standard in that aspect of trucking. Intelli Route Online, shown in Figure 12.6, offers truckers a web service that provides routes, maps, cost estimating, and HazMat information.

Rand McNally has integrated its data into large data warehouses accessible through data mining. The data extracted can be entered into GISs for conversion into maps or electronic products. The data warehouse approach allows massive amounts of data to be stored and re-used for different applications.

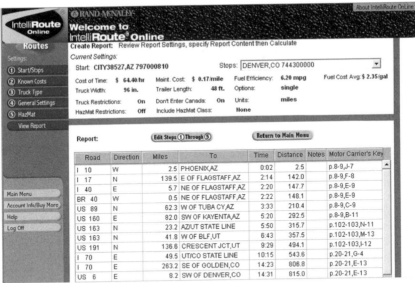

Figure 12.6 Rand McNally's Intelli Route Online showing Phoenix to Denver Route. *Source:* Rand McNally, 2007

One of the firm's biggest GIS functions is in direct store delivery (DSD). DSD predictive models combined with GIS are able to estimate stocking requirements for 55,000 retail outlets and deliver target amounts of maps on a daily basis. It even can estimate by Plan-o-grams the shelf-space layouts and map placements in the retail stores.

The company is involved in leading mobile and web services applications. It provides small-sized maps for mobile phones, but not for PDAs. As seen in Figure 12.7, Rand McNally Traffic transmits metropolitan traffic conditions and accident reports to cell phone users. Its web services appear as products on its highly rated website, RandMcNally.com, including a wide variety of maps and driving directions. Customers can enter online, customized requests for high-quality, large maps that are mailed.

There is excellent cooperation between the GIS and IS groups. The company doesn't underestimate that GIS is very challenging to implement and "not for the faint-hearted," so it invests in people and resources for GIS. It perceives that although the web simplifies access to maps, the user tools remain often challenging, and the often complex outputs may need to be explained to even sophisticated users.

GIS is regarded as highly strategic and competitive. For instance, in its central function of producing a map, largely automated tools allow the selections of a medley of the best of the data from multiple data sources. There are huge efficiencies in being able to access data warehouses again and again. The same data can be re-used extensively for a broad range of products from large, custom-finished wall maps to 1.5 inch cell phone displays.

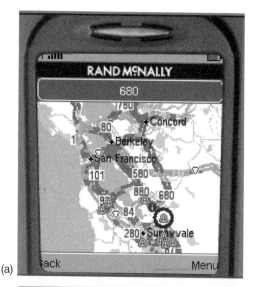

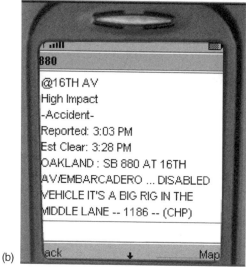

Figure 12.7 Rand McNally Traffic for Mobile Phones. *Source:* Rand McNally, 2007

Both the company and the GIS department have instituted strategic plans. They are closely aligned in contrast to the Norwich case. For emerging spatial technologies, Rand McNally emphasizes being out in front of the vendors, sometimes building applications in-house ahead of major GIS software vendors such as ESRI. It has focused on improvements in the "basics," i.e. on high-quality data from the best data sources that is processed and delivered by paper and the latest electronics, phones, web services, and other technologies.

The firm has reached a mature integration stage for GIS. It is not surprising that the company dominates its market niche. GIS contributes by enabling best practices for producing paper maps, electronic maps and services, and by attaining efficiency and precision in store deliveries. There is close alignment between GIS, IS, and corporate strategies. The firm emphasizes emerging technologies and R&D, and demonstrates vision in GIS.

THE FUTURE AND SPATIAL STRATEGIES IN ENTERPRISES

As seen throughout the book, implementing spatial solutions has required risk taking, modifying business processes, overcoming resistance, and sometimes organizational change. At Lamar Advertising, the sales manager's business processes were changed by being able to quickly show prospective customers visual representations of advertising alternatives. At Chico's, new locational strategies became available for locating stores through visual display of store cannibalization, traffic patterns, and sites of the competitors. This has stimulated cross-organizational flows of information.

For the future, new and unexpected inroads of GIS and spatial technologies can be expected for companies and industries already heavily into GIS as well as ones with little of it currently. By taking risks and applying spatial applications to unforeseen business problems, future impacts can be expected on business processes, employees, and organizations. Several factors discussed in the book that may influence where GIS and spatial technologies are heading in the future are shown in Table 12.3.

Because changes in spatial technology are expected, management in organizations needs to include in strategic planning the assessment of technological change. Two-thirds of the GIS managers interviewed from the cases in the book responded that they did not do this as part of their strategic planning. In spite of the proximate large time demands of developing and operating the company's spatial functions, GIS managers must carve out time and allocate resources to explore and assess long-range technological change.

CHAPTER SUMMARY

The capacity of a company to implement geobusiness depends on excellence in technology, appropriate spatial applications, an IT base, and skilled personnel. However, these alone will not lead to durable and lasting success. Companies having enduring spatial competitive advantage such as Sears made GIS and spatial technologies a corporate priority. GIS is written into these companies' strategic plans. There is knowledge and interest in GIS at the executive level. Such firms continue to invest in GIS and to research the best ways to do deploy it in the future.

TABLE 12.3   Trend Factors Likely to Influence Geo-Business in Future Years

Factors in data, architecture, software, technology
- Transition to a more web-centric environment for GIS
- Integration and interoperability of GIS software with enterprise systems. More enterprise software with built-in spatial functionality
- Geocoding and digitizing of growing amounts of business information
- Expanded public data sets of spatial information worldwide.
- Private, proprietary spatial data sets for a wider reach of business functions, linked to broader and enterprise-wide attribute data.
- GIS incorporated extensively into mobile devices
- Enhanced enablement of spatial data-bases and data warehouses
- Personal, consumer use of GIS and spatial technologies globally
- A world of increasingly RFID-tagged objects, with greater spatial analysis of RFID-based data.
- GIS applications available across the entire enterprise in simple formats
- Sophisticated systems to support spatial decision-making and business intelligence

Factors in GIS industry, workforce, management, organizations
- More manufactured products that are GPS-enabled
- Expanded spatial service products, both consulting and web-based.
- Larger and better-trained GIS workforce
- Business education that includes GIS and spatial technologies in standard curricula
- Improved integration even up to merger in organizations of the GIS and IS functions and departments.
- Expanded selective or complete outsourcing of the GIS and spatial functions
- Stronger security measures in organizations for GIS and spatial applications.
- Broader laws and court precedents that businesses and society can recognize and plan for.
- Continuing importance of ethical awareness in spatial decision making.

The chapter offers theoretical background, case-study experiences, an evolutionary model, and practical recommendations on how the best strategic results have been achieved by some, while other firms implement GIS at low to moderate strategic levels. A key aspect is vision—the leader's ability to picture the benefits and advances from spatial systems. The leader cannot make things happen by himself or herself, but must gain commitment of others in key roles in the organization.

Theories are helpful in understanding how GIS strategies can be put in place. Since the book has emphasized the trend towards the internet and web-services architecture, Michael Porter's framework helps to explain the rise of map web services. The open architecture, quick development times, and flexibility to change rapidly justify this approach.

IT Alignment theory is a mainstay for understanding strategic IS. Since GIS and IS functions are usually separate organizationally, a variation of this theory is that GIS planning also needs to be aligned with the corporate strategic plan and the IS strategic plan.

An evolutionary framework for strategic GIS is given. The dimensions examined are extent to which GIS is customer-facing, extent of geography in the business, and extent of a spatially-enabled, enterprise-wide web intergration platform. The latter two factors are associated positively with a high level of strategic GIS. Another factor not associated with strategic level is size of firm. New, small companies such as MotionBased can jumpstart GIS and spatial technologies as their core strategy, while mature ones such as Sears can evolve more slowly to achieve more importance for GIS and spatial technologics.

Practical steps are recommended for leaders and managers of firms seeking a strategic approach to GIS. Will and tenacity are necessary to raise a firm's strategic competitiveness in spatial technologies, as they are new and may be disruptive to traditional approaches. Assessing future spatial technological change needs to be a part of the GIS manager's agenda.

Geo-Business: GIS in the Digital Firm has approached GIS from the perspective of business and industry. While government has historically been the major economic sector for spatial technologies, GIS in the private sector is on the ascent. The book has organized its contents according to the context of the business manager or GIS specialist. Relative to many book approaches, geography and spatial science have been covered less, and the frameworks and empirical experiences of businesses with GIS and spatial technologies emphasized more. A core foundation has been provided in GIS technical principles, mapping, spatial databases, architecture, and spatial technologies. Although future changes in the technologies will be fast and likely dramatic at times, one goal of the book is to cover the "softer" spatial areas as well of decision-making, marketing, management, systems development, intangible benefits, organizational change, industry differences, outsourcing, ethics, law, managing security, and strategy. Compared to technology, the content of these areas will likely prove more durable over time, but also subject to the continual need to learn and update. In the end, it is hoped that managers and practitioners of Geo-Business will understand the knowledge and experiences of this field, set lofty goals, and move their enterprises forward to provide benefits to their stakeholders and to society.

REFERENCES

Applegate, L.M. 2007. *Corporate Information Strategy and Management*, 7th Edition. Boston: McGraw-Hill.

Barnes, S. 2005. "Beyond the niche." *Geospatial Solutions*, May 1.

Brail, R.K., and R.E. Klosterman (Eds.). 2001. *Planning Support Systems*. Redlands, CA: ESRI Press.

Cegielski, C.G., B.J. Reithel, and C.M. Rebman. 2005. "Emerging information technologies: Developing a timely IT strategy." *Communications of the ACM*, 48(8), 113–117.

Daratech. 2004. *Geographic Information Systems Markets and Opportunities*. Cambridge, MA: Daratech Inc.

Dun and Bradstreet. 2005. *Dun and Bradstreet Small Business Solutions*. New York: Dun and Bradstreet.

ESRI Inc. 2004. "Law Enforcement and the GIS Enterprise." Available at www.esri.com.

Francica, J.L. 2005. "GIS and the Future in Business IT." In Pick, J. (Ed.), *Geographic Information Systems in Business*, Hershey, PA: Idea Group Publishing, pp. 358–372.

Galliers, R.D., and D.E. Leidner (Eds.). 2003. *Strategic Information Management*. Oxford, England: Butterworth/Heinemann.

Ghosal, S. 1987. "Global Strategy: An Organizing Framework." *Strategic Management Journal*, 8, 425–440.

Guerrero, I. 2005. "Emerging technologies in the geospatial industry." In Proceedings of the Annual Conference of the Geospatial Information and Technology Association, GITA: Aurora, CO.

Hackbarth, G., and B. Mennecke. 2005. "Strategic positioning of location applications for Geo-Business." In Pick, J. (Ed.), *Geographic Information Systems in Business*, Hershey, PA: Idea Group Publishing, pp. 198–235.

Hagel III, J., and J.S. Brown. 2001. "Your next IT strategy." *Harvard Business Review*, October, 105–113.

Hendriks, Paul H.J. 1998. "Information Strategies for Geographical Information Systems." *International Journal of Geographical Information Science*, 12(6): 621–639.

Hoover's. 2005. *Hoover's Online*. Hoover's Inc., Austin, TX.

Huxhold, W.E., and A.G. Levinsohn. 1995. *Managing Geographic Information System Projects*. New York: Oxford University Press.

Jarupathirun, S., and F. Zahedi. 2007. "Exploring the influence of perceptual factors in the success of web-based spatial DSS." *Decision Support Systems*. Article in press and available in proofs at www.sciencedirect.com.

Lai, V.S., and B.K. Wong. 2005. "Business types, e-strategies, and performance." *Communications of the ACM*, 48(5), 80–85.

Laudon, Kenneth C. 2005. *Management Information Systems*, 9th Edition. New York: Prentice Hall.

Longley, P.A., M.F. Goodchild, D.J. Maguire, and D.W. Rhind. 2005. *Geographic Information Systems and Science*. New York: John Wiley and Sons.

Lopez, X.R. 2005. "Location-based services." In Hassan, K., and A. Hammad (Eds.), *Telegeoinformatics: Location-Based Computing and Services*, Chapter 6, Boca Raton, FL: CRC Press.

Luftman, J.N. 2001. "Assessing Business-IT Alignment Maturity." In Papp, R. (Ed.), *Strategic Information Technology: Opportunities for Competitive Alignment*, Chapter 1, Hershey, PA: Idea Group Publishing, pp. 105–134.

Maguire, D.J. 2005. "Enterprise geographic information servers: a new information system architecture." In Proceedings of the Annual Conference of the Geospatial Information and Technology Association (GITA), GITA: Aurora, CO.

McFarlan, E.F. 1984. "Information technology changes the way you compete." *Harvard Business Review*, 62(3), 98–103.

Murphy, L.D. 1996. "Competing in space: the strategic roles of geographic information systems." In Proceedings of the Association for Information Systems, AIS, Atlanta, GA.

Nolan, Richard, and F. Warren McFarlan. 2005. "Information Technology and the Board of Directors." *Harvard Business Review*, October, 1–10.

Papp, R. 1995. "Determinants of Strategically Aligned Organizations: A Multi-industry, Multi-perspective Analysis." Ph.D. Dissertation. Hoboken, NJ: Stevens Institute of Technology.

Papp, R. and J. Luftman. 1995. "Business and I/T Strategic Alignment: New Perspectives and Assessments," *Proceedings of the Association for Information Systems*, Atlanta, GA: Association for Information Systems. Available at home.aisnet.com.

Papp, R. 2001. "Introduction to Strategic Alignment." In Papp, R. (Ed.), *Strategic Information Technology: Opportunities for Competitive Alignment*, Chapter 1, Hershey, PA: Idea Group Publishing, pp. 1–24.

Porter, M.E. 2001. "Strategy and the internet." *Harvard Business Review*, 79(3), 63–78.

Reed, C. 2005. "The spatial web." White paper, available at www.opengis.org, Open Geospatial Consortium, Wayland, MA.

Sonnen, D., and H. Morris. 2005. "ESRI: extending GIS to enterprise applications." White paper, February, International Data Corporation, Framingham, MA.

Standard and Poors. 2005. Stock Reports. Short Hills, Standard&Poors, McGraw-Hill, New York.

Tomlinson, R. 2003. *Thinking About GIS: Geographic Information System Planning for Managers*. Redlands, CA: ESRI Press.

INDEX